Java EE 7 Performance Tuning and Optimization

Boost the efficiency of your enterprise applications by performance tuning and optimization with Java

Osama Oransa

BIRMINGHAM - MUMBAI

Java EE 7 Performance Tuning and Optimization

First published: June 2014

Production reference: 1160614

Published by Packt Publishing Ltd.
Livery Place
35 Livery Street
Birmingham B3 2PB, UK.

ISBN 978-1-78217-642-8

www.packtpub.com

Cover image by Sean FitzGerald (sfitzgerald@sfitzgerald.com)

Credits

Author
Osama Oransa

Reviewers
E.P. Ramakrishnan

Chirag Sangani

Deepak Vohra

Jeff Zhang

Commissioning Editor
Mary Jasmine Nadar

Acquisition Editor
Nikhil Karkal

Content Development Editor
Dayan Hyames

Technical Editors
Novina Kewalramani

Humera Shaikh

Copy Editors
Alisha Aranha

Roshni Banerjee

Adithi Shetty

Project Coordinator
Priyanka Goel

Proofreaders
Simran Bhogal

Maria Gould

Ameesha Green

Paul Hindle

Indexers
Mehreen Deshmukh

Rekha Nair

Tejal Soni

Priya Subramani

Graphics
Sheetal Aute

Ronak Dhruv

Disha Haria

Abhinash Sahu

Production Coordinator
Manu Joseph

Cover Work
Manu Joseph

About the Author

Osama Oransa is an IT solution architect with more than 12 years of solid technical experience in Java EE. He is a certified Java enterprise architect and an SME in web services technology. He has worked for most of the key players in the IT industry, such as IBM, Oracle, and Hewlett Packard. He previously worked as a performance consultant at DevFactory, and he is currently working with the Vodafone Group as a solution architect. He has also participated in establishing Pulse Corp as a medical software services company in Egypt.

He has a diploma in IT from the Information Technology Institute (ITI) and a diploma in CS from the Arab Academy for Science, Technology and Maritime Transport (AASTM). He is currently working towards a Master's degree in CS. Being from Cairo, he is a frequent speaker at the Java Developer Conference (JDC) in Cairo.

In 2010, one of his projects in Pulse Corp, "Health Intact", won Oracle Duke's Choice Award. He is the founder of more than 12 open source projects hosted on SourceForge. He has also been selected by Oracle for the future of the Java campaign for his valuable contribution to the industry.

He is a volunteer Java technology evangelist who gives technical sessions at different companies, conferences, and on blogs. His technical blog can be found at http://osama-oransa.blogspot.com/.

Acknowledgments

After more than 17 years since my first IT book on the Assembly language, I got the chance to write my second book. It was really a nice experience to deal with the wonderful people at Packt Publishing. After thanking my God, I would like to thank my parents and my wife for their full support while writing this book.

Special thanks to Reshma Raman, the Author Acquisition Executive who contacted me to write this book.

I would like to thank Priyanka Goel, the Project Coordinator who helped me to deliver the book following the agreed timeline and who gave me her full support.

I would like to thank Nikhil Karkal, the Acquisition Editor, for his support in the early, critical phases of the book and his continuous efforts in providing me with the proper guidelines.

I would like to thank Dayan Hyames, the Lead Technical Editor, for his efforts in reviewing the content of this book and guiding me to provide the best outcome.

I would like to thank the technical reviewers E.P. Ramakrishnan, Chirag Sangani, Deepak Vohra, and Jeff Zhang, who caught my errors and provided me with very constructive and valuable comments to enhance the content of this book.

I would like to thank the technical editors Novina Kewalramani and Humera Shaikh for their tremendous efforts in the book.

Finally, thanks goes to all the people who participated in this book who I don't know by name—without you, this book wouldn't see the light. Thank you!

About the Reviewers

E.P. Ramakrishnan is an enthusiastic developer and a technical writer. He earned his postgraduate degree in Computer Science and Engineering from Anna University, Tamil Nadu, India. He has a steady industry exposure of 6 years. His areas of expertise include Java Server Faces (JSF), the Java Persistence API, CDI, RESTful Services, Swings, Tomcat Clustering, and load balancing. Also, his areas of interest are Linux, Android, and systems security. Besides development, his major interest lies in writing technical blogs which simplify the latest technologies for beginners. You are welcome to visit his blog at `http://www.ramkitech.com` and give your feedback. He can be reached at `ramkicse@gmail.com`.

Chirag Sangani is a computer scientist living in the Seattle area. He holds an MS degree in Computer Science from Stanford University and a B.Tech degree in Computer Science and Engineering from the Indian Institute of Technology, Kanpur.

An exposure to computers since his early childhood has allowed Chirag to explore his varied interests while witnessing the birth of the Internet. He has dedicated the last 10 years to perfecting his skills while simultaneously diving deep into computer science theory.

He has had varied interests and experiences — from computer architecture to networking, distributed systems to machine learning and data mining, complexity theory to cryptography, and mobile and web development to 3D game design. He has found that merging different fields of computer science allows for a holistic approach towards solving any problem. He currently works for Microsoft.

Deepak Vohra is a consultant and a principal member of the NuBean.com software company. He is a Sun certified Java programmer and web component developer, and he has worked in the fields of XML, Java programming, and Java EE for over 5 years. Deepak is the co-author of the Apress book *Pro XML Development with Java Technology,* and he is the technical reviewer for the O'Reilly book *WebLogic: The Definitive Guide.* He is also the technical reviewer for the Course Technology PTR book *Ruby Programming for the Absolute Beginner.* He is also the author of the Packt Publishing books *JDBC 4.0 and Oracle JDeveloper for J2EE Development, Processing XML Documents with Oracle JDeveloper 11g, EJB 3.0 Database Persistence with Oracle Fusion Middleware 11g,* and *Java EE Development with Eclipse IDE.*

Jeff Zhang started working with middleware software in 2002. He joined IONA and worked on Corba and web service products. In 2008, Jeff entered Redhat and became core developer of the JBossAS team.

After more than 10 years of working on middleware, Jeff has learned a lot about application servers, PAAS, containers, and services. He believes that mobile technology and the Internet will change people's lives.

I would like to thank the author who has written a great book. Thanks goes to Priyanka Goel and Aurita D'souza for their help in the reviewing stage.

Thanks also goes to my wife and my son—your support is most important.

www.PacktPub.com

Support files, eBooks, discount offers, and more

You might want to visit www.PacktPub.com for support files and downloads related to your book.

Did you know that Packt offers eBook versions of every book published, with PDF and ePub files available? You can upgrade to the eBook version at www.PacktPub.com and as a print book customer, you are entitled to a discount on the eBook copy. Get in touch with us at service@packtpub.com for more details.

At www.PacktPub.com, you can also read a collection of free technical articles, sign up for a range of free newsletters and receive exclusive discounts and offers on Packt books and eBooks.

http://PacktLib.PacktPub.com

Do you need instant solutions to your IT questions? PacktLib is Packt's online digital book library. Here, you can access, read and search across Packt's entire library of books.

Why subscribe?

- Fully searchable across every book published by Packt
- Copy and paste, print and bookmark content
- On demand and accessible via web browser

Free access for Packt account holders

If you have an account with Packt at www.PacktPub.com, you can use this to access PacktLib today and view nine entirely free books. Simply use your login credentials for immediate access.

To my dear parents, the owners of all my life achievements.

To my lovely wife, Rasha, the angel of my life.

To my diamond daughters – the best gifts in my life – Judy and Kenzy.

–Osama Oransa

Table of Contents

Preface	**1**
Chapter 1: Getting Started with Performance Tuning	**9**
Understanding the art of performance tuning	**10**
Understanding performance issues	**12**
Classifying performance issues by the discovery phase	13
Requirement phase and design-time issues	14
Development-time issues	15
Testing-time issues	16
Production-time issues	16
Classifying performance issues by the root phase	17
Requirement phase issues	18
Design/architecture phase issues	18
Development phase issues	18
Testing phase issues	18
Operational and environmental-specific issues	19
Performance-handling tactics	19
Proactive measures (preventive)	19
Reactive measures (curative)	21
Understanding the different layers of an enterprise application	21
The three pillars required for performance tuning	22
The cycle of learning	24
Tuning yourself before tuning the application	26
Be a true leader	26
Use your power	26
Be responsible	26
Trust your team	27
Keep it simple	27
Respect roles and responsibilities	27
Understand the application domain and context	27
Protect your reputation	28

Standalone applications versus web applications   29
  The standalone application   29
  Thick client application – client-server model   30
  Thin client application – web-based model   30
Dealing with web applications' performance tuning   31
  The two dimensions of web applications' performance tuning   32
    Horizontal dimension (node-to-node)   32
    Vertical dimension (intranode)   32
  Exploring vertical dimension nodes in horizontal dimension nodes   33
    Client side   33
    Network components   33
    HTTP servers (web servers)   34
    Application servers   34
    Database servers   34
    Middleware integration servers   35
    Operating system and hardware   36
    CPU utilization   36
    Network traffic   36
    Memory usage   37
    Storage I/O performance   37
Summary   37
Chapter 2: Understanding Java Fundamentals   39
Discussing the new Java EE 7 features   40
  Bean Validation 1.1 (JSR 349)   40
  Java API for JSON processing – JSON-P 1.0 (JSR 353)   41
  Java API for RESTful web services – JAX-RS 2.0 (JSR 339)   42
  Java Servlet 3.1 (JSR 340)   42
  Context and Dependency Injection – CDI 1.1 (JSR 346)   43
  Interceptors 1.2 (JSR 318)   44
  Enterprise JavaBeans – EJB 3.2 (JSR 345)   44
  Java Message Service – JMS 2.0 (JSR 343)   45
  Concurrency Utilities 1.0 (JSR 236)   46
  Batch Applications 1.0 (JSR 352)   46
  Java Persistence APIs – JPA 2.1 (JSR 338)   47
  JavaServer Faces – JSF 2.2 (JSR 344)   47
  Expression language 3.0 (JSR 341)   48
  Java Transaction APIs – JTA 1.2 (JSR 907)   48
  Java API for WebSocket 1.0 (JSR 356)   49
Understanding memory structure in the JVM   50
  The JVM specifications   51
    Heap area   52
    Method area and runtime constant pool   52
    JVM stack   52

Native method stacks (C stacks)   53
PC registers   53
Memory structure in the Java HotSpot virtual machine   53
Generational memory structure   53
The Java HotSpot virtual machine generations   54
Understanding the Java garbage collection policies   **56**
Different GC options   56
Concurrent versus stop-the-world   56
Serial versus parallel collector   57
Compacting versus non-compacting   59
The Garbage-first collector – G1   60
Different application scopes   **62**
Understanding concurrency in Java   **63**
Process versus thread   64
Exploring an object monitor   65
Using the Java concurrency utilities   **66**
Creating a thread pool   67
Using explicit locking with the Lock interface   68
Concurrent resources and utilities   71
The ManagedExecutorService class   71
The ManagedScheduledExecutorService class   72
The ManagedThreadFactory class   72
The important Java EE concurrency features   **73**
The SingleThreadModel interface   73
Asynchronous servlet and filter   74
The new Java EE non-blocking I/O APIs   74
Session beans asynchronous method invocation   75
A singleton session bean   76
Sending asynchronous JMS messages   77
More information about Java EE 7   **78**
Summary   **79**
Chapter 3: Getting Familiar with Performance Testing   **81**
Dissecting performance testing   **81**
Exploring performance testing aspects   82
Selecting the performance test environment   83
Project milestones and performance   84
Defining different rules and responsibilities   84
Performance testing types   85
Performance testing components   85
Performance testing tools   88
Performance benchmarking and baseline   89
Isolation testing   89
Performance fixing cycle   90
When to stop tuning?   90

Performance testing terminologies	**91**
Performance testing in a cloud environment	**92**
Starting with Apache JMeter	**94**
Different components of the JMeter test plan	95
The execution order of components	97
Testing with JMeter	**97**
Using JMeter to test web services	98
Creating a thread group	102
Creating the SOAP sampler	102
Creating listeners	103
Using JMeter to test a web application	107
Recording our testing scenarios	108
Using JMeter to test database scripts	114
Configuring the JDBC connection	114
Adding a JDBC request sampler	115
Adding a CSV dataset configuration	115
Adding listeners to capture test results	115
Summary	**116**
Chapter 4: Monitoring Java Applications	**117**
Exploring the Java monitoring tools	**117**
The operating system monitoring tools	118
The Microsoft Windows tools	118
The Unix/Linux tools	122
The Java monitoring tools	126
The JDK monitoring tools	126
The monitoring tools for application servers	126
The IDE monitoring tools	127
The standalone monitoring tools	127
The multifunction monitoring tools	127
Understanding the profiling tools	**127**
Profilers modes	128
JVM TI	128
Profiler agent	129
The command-line options	129
Agent start-up	129
Different profiling patterns	129
What we need to know from this section	130
Understanding the different JDK tools	**130**
The monitoring tool for Java virtual machine statistics	131
The JVM memory map tool	133
The Java heap analysis tool	135
The Java monitoring and management console tool	137
Java VisualVM	138

Oracle Java Mission Control   140
Starting with the NetBeans profiler   **141**
The NetBeans profiler calibration   142
Using the NetBeans profiler   143
The Eclipse tools/plugins   **147**
The JVM monitor   147
The Test and Performance Tools Platform   148
Advanced profiler – JProfiler   **151**
Using the offline profiling mode   **156**
Building our script using JProfiler triggers   156
Further reading   161
Summary   **161**
Chapter 5: Recognizing Common Performance Issues   **163**
Going through a slow response time umbrella   **164**
Isolating the issue   164
Client side   165
HTTP server side (web servers)   165
Application server issue   165
Database server issue   166
Integrated systems   166
Networking components   166
Code and script analysis   166
Profiling the application   166
Common performance issues   167
Threading performance issues   167
Memory performance issues   167
Algorithmic performance issues   168
Work as designed performance issues   168
Interfacing performance issues   168
Miscellaneous performance issues   169
Fake performance issues   169
Threading performance issues   **169**
Blocking threads   170
Performance symptoms   170
An example of thread blocking   170
Thread deadlock   172
Memory performance issues   **173**
Memory leakage   173
Performance symptoms   173
An example of memory leakage   174
Improper data caching   177
Improper caching issue types   177
Performance symptoms   179
An example of improper caching techniques   179

Work as designed performance issues   **181**
Synchronous where asynchronous is required   181
    Performance symptoms   181
    An example of improper synchronous code   181
Neglecting remoteness   182
    Performance symptoms   182
    An example of using remote calls as local calls   182
Excessive serialization performance impact   182
    Performance symptoms   183
    An example of excessive serialization   183
Selected performance issues   **185**
Unnecessary application logic   185
Excessive application logging   186
Database performance issues   187
Missing proactive tuning   189
Client-side performance issues   **189**
Chrome developer tools   190
    Network analysis   190
    JavaScript profiling   192
    Speed Tracer   193
Internet Explorer developer tools   194
Firefox developer tools   196
Navigating time specifications   196
Summary   **197**

Chapter 6: CPU Time Profiling   **199**
When to use CPU profiling   **199**
Different CPU profiling options   **200**
Using a NetBeans profiler   200
    Profiling a Java application   201
    Profiling a web application   203
Using Java Mission Control (JMC)   206
Using JProfiler   208
Reading and interpreting CPU profiling results   **210**
The call tree view   211
The HotSpots view   211
Analyzing the method time versus the method invocation count   **213**
The HotSpot method types   214
    Methods with high self-time   214
    Methods with high invocation events   214
    Methods with high self-time and invocation events   215
Identifying a HotSpot type   215
Identifying potential performance issues   **218**
Algorithmic/logic issues   219

Caching issues	220
Resourcing issues	221
Threading issues	221
Fixing algorithmic/logic performance	**221**
Simple algorithmic evaluation	222
Evaluating an algorithm's complexity	224
Our first performance fixing strategy	**228**
Fixing the application logic/algorithm	229
Adding support for caching	230
Optimizing the performance of resources	231
Implementing concurrency or multithreading	231
Using asynchronous methods	231
Summary	**232**
Chapter 7: Thread Profiling	**233**
Determining when to use thread profiling	**233**
Exploring the different thread profiling options	**234**
Thread monitoring using NetBeans	234
Thread monitoring using JProfiler	238
Thread monitoring using Java Mission Control	241
Reading the thread profiling results	**244**
Dealing with thread dumps	**247**
Taking a thread dump using the operating system commands	248
Using the keyboard shortcut Ctrl + Pause Break	248
Sending SIGQUIT to the Java process	250
Taking a thread dump using the JDK tools	251
Thread dump using jstack	251
Thread dump using the Java VisualVM	251
Taking thread dumps using an application's server admin console/tools	252
Taking a thread dump using profiler tools	253
Reading and analyzing the thread dumps	**254**
Understanding the thread dump structure	255
Analyzing the thread dumps	256
Using Thread Dump Analyzer	257
Exploring potential threading issues	**259**
Threading performance issues	259
Threading deadlock	259
Blocked/starving/stuck threads	259
Low/over threading	260
Threading memory issues	260
Using unmanaged threads	261
Detecting the root cause of a hung application	262
Detecting the hang location using thread dumps	262

Detecting the hang location using profilers	262
Enhancing our fixing strategy	**263**
Fixing thread deadlocks and thread blocking	265
Summary	**265**
Chapter 8: Memory Profiling	**267**
When to use memory profiling?	**268**
Different memory profiling options	**268**
Memory profiling using NetBeans	269
Memory profiling using JProfiler	275
Analyzing memory profiling results	**279**
Analyzing memory space graphs	280
Analyzing detailed object statistics	281
Analyzing garbage collection activity logs (HotSpot JVM)	282
Reading garbage collection activity logs (HotSpot VM)	282
Visualizing the garbage collection activity	285
Dealing with memory heap dumps	**287**
Taking heap dumps on the occurrence of JVM OutOfMemoryError	287
Taking heap dumps using the JDK tools	288
Taking heaps dump using jmap	288
Taking heap dumps using Java VisualVM	289
Taking heap dumps using the JRockit command utility	291
Taking heap dumps using the profiler tools	291
Taking heap dumps using the NetBeans profiler	291
Taking heap dumps using Eclipse Memory Analyzer Tool (MAT)	292
Taking heap dumps using JProfiler	293
Analyzing the heap dump	**294**
Navigating inside a heap dump using visual tools	294
Query heap dumps using OQL	296
Using simple OQL queries	297
Using OQL built-in objects and functions	298
Potential memory performance issues	**299**
Application memory leakage (session leakage versus global leakage)	301
Improper caching implementation	301
Memory issues of objects that contain the finalize() method	302
Invalid contract for the equals() and hashCode() methods	302
Different reasons for OOME	303
Adding memory performance issues to our fixing strategy	**304**
Fixing memory leakage issues	306
Summary	**307**
Chapter 9: Tuning an Application's Environment	**309**
Understanding environment tuning	**310**
Tuning the JVM	**311**

Tuning the Java HotSpot virtual machine   312
    Understanding the different types of the JVM parameters   312
    Selecting the HotSpot JVM type   313
    Tuning memory size   314
    Tuning garbage collection   316
Tuning the JRockit virtual machine   317
    Tuning JRockit memory size   318
    Tuning JRockit garbage collection   318
Tuning application servers   **320**
    Tuning the Oracle GlassFish application server   320
        Deployment tuning options   320
        Web container tuning options   321
        EJB container tuning options   321
        Thread pool tuning options   322
        JDBC connection pool tuning options   322
        Tuning file cache components   323
        Tuning DNS caching   323
        Tuning logging information   323
    Tuning the Oracle Weblogic application server   324
        Tuning the internal applications' deployment   324
        Tuning network components   324
        Tuning stuck thread configuration   325
Tuning web servers (HTTP servers)   **325**
    Tuning the Apache web server (Apache HTTP server)   326
    Tuning the Oracle web server (Oracle HTTP server)   329
Tuning the operating system and hardware   **331**
    Optimizing capacity planning and hardware   331
    Optimizing operating system configurations   332
Summary   **333**

**Chapter 10: Designing High-performance
Enterprise Applications**   **335**
    Potential performance impact of different design decisions **335**
        Potential performance impact of the application layer's decisions   336
        Potential performance impact of a component's selection decisions   338
        Potential performance impact of integration decisions   339
        Potential performance impact of security decisions   341
        Potential performance impact of framework and UI decisions   343
        Potential performance impact of application interaction decisions   343
        Potential performance impact of regulatory decisions   344
        Potential performance impact of some miscellaneous decisions   344
    Avoiding performance anti-patterns   **345**
    Performance aspects of Service Oriented Architecture (SOA) **347**
    Performance aspects of Resource Oriented Architecture (ROA) **351**

Dissecting performance aspects of data caching	**357**
Data caching versus no caching	357
Caching concurrency and performance	358
Different levels of application data caching	358
Caching an invalidation/expiration algorithm	360
Caching data store interaction	361
Caching replacement policies	363
Data caching performance evaluation	364
Performance considerations in cloud deployment	**365**
Summary	**368**
Chapter 11: Performance Tuning Tips	**369**
Performance and development processes	**370**
Agile and performance	370
Performance and test-driven development (TDD)	371
Manual and automated code review	372
Java EE performance tuning tips	**375**
Web service (WS) performance tuning tips	376
EJB performance tuning tips	376
Servlets and JSP performance tuning tips	377
JSF performance tuning tips	378
JPA performance tuning tips	379
Java performance tuning tips	**381**
String manipulation performance tuning tips	381
String creation tips	381
String concatenation tips	382
The JVM String tuning parameters	383
Java collections and performance	384
Using synchronized blocks	385
The I/O operations and performance	386
Exception handling and performance	386
Application logging and performance	388
Using the javap tool to understand micro-optimizations	**391**
Database performance tuning tips	**394**
Client-side optimization	**398**
Summary	**400**
Chapter 12: Tuning a Sample Application	**401**
Reaching our final destination	**401**
Setting up the ExcellentSurvey application	**402**
Functional overview of the ExcellentSurvey application	**404**
ExcellentSurvey performance assessment	**407**

Performance investigation plan   **410**
Profiling our ExcellentSurvey application   **411**
  Getting CPU profiling results   412
  Getting memory and thread profiling results   414
  Getting database CPU profiling results   414
Profiling performance findings   **416**
  Detected HotSpot methods   416
  Detected HotSpot database statements   416
  Potential wrong logic issues   416
ExcellentSurvey issues and possible resolutions   **417**
  Fixing the EmailSender.sendEmail() HotSpot method   417
  Fixing the DAOHelper.createNewSurvey() HotSpot method   419
  Fixing the LoginFilter.log() HotSpot method   421
  Fixing the HotSpot autogen table update statement   421
  Fixing HotSpot statements to insert questions and survey questions   422
  Fixing HotSpot queries that get the notification templates/question
  rating types   422
  Fixing the HotSpot query that counts user surveys   423
Performance code review   **424**
Testing the application after our fixes   **426**
Result and conclusion   **427**
Summary   **429**
Index   **431**

Preface

Performance tuning is one of the biggest challenges in dealing with the Java Enterprise applications, where each delay in response to the customer might cause the enterprise to lose valuable customers. In particular, during marketing campaigns, such as launching a new product, the load over the application jumps to a peak. It is common to see some enterprise applications that do not respond to customers! If such a thing happens and the application cannot withstand such load, it will not only lead to a loss of the expected sales, but also destroy the reputation of the enterprise.

During years of working in many large companies with different enterprise applications, which are usually composed of many integrated applications that are provided by different vendors, many challenges have contributed to the performance tuning of these applications, such as how to design a high performing application, how to minimize the occurrences of performance issues, how to build a performance team, how to test the application performance efficiently, how to create an investigation plan, and many other questions that need to be answered correctly. We tried to address these questions and others in this book, aiming to help establish a clear, organized, and smooth way of dealing with performance tuning of enterprise applications.

We have focused, in particular, on simplicity and clarity to remove any mystery around the art of performance tuning. This book is designed in a progressive pattern where each chapter represents a step forward towards completing the complete process of handling the performance issues from end-to-end in any enterprise application, starting from the requirement phase to the production support phase.

Performance tuning activities happen usually in the most stressful times in the enterprise application's life! When I started my work in performance tuning, it was the task that I needed to accomplish as soon as possible. This led to an unnecessary increase in stress and tension. Later, I learned the best way to deal with performance tuning; dealing with it as an art and enjoying the work in performance tasks (just like painting a picture or completing a puzzle). It is an art that we need to respect and enjoy. In this book, we will try to cover all the required details to understand performance tuning and the best way to deal with this art.

Dealing with performance tuning as an art and organizing our thoughts are the most important concepts here, and are also the most helpful factors (other than the person's luck!). Spending months to write this book and organizing its different sections was a very challenging procedure, in particular, to establish a well-defined, organized way of dealing with performance tuning—starting from the knowledge, which is considered as our solid foundation here, up to the strategic thinking. While dealing with these issues, establishing and finding this thinking strategy is much more important than having a look-up book that describes each problem and the possible resolution. This thinking strategy along with the required skills and mastery of different tools will provide the best way to guarantee the resolution of any new performance issues whenever this strategy is strictly followed.

In addition to that, Java Enterprise Edition 7 (Java EE 7) platform introduced a lot of new features and improvements that enterprise applications can benefit from performance perspective. This is a part of our essential knowledge to work in performance tuning of Java EE 7 applications.

Because of all of this, I encourage you to go through this book chapter by chapter, be patient and read the book to the end, download the required tools, and practice all the examples to gain the maximum value from this book.

What this book covers

Chapter 1, *Getting Started with Performance Tuning*, takes you through the art of performance tuning with its different components and shows you how to think when we face any performance issue. It focuses on preparing you to deal with the world of performance tuning and defining the handling tactics.

Chapter 2, *Understanding Java Fundamentals*, lays the foundation of required knowledge of the new features in Java Enterprise Edition 7 and different important Java concepts, including the JVM memory structure and Java concurrency. It also focuses on the different Java Enterprise Edition concurrency capabilities.

Chapter 3, *Getting Familiar with Performance Testing*, discusses performance testing with its different components, defines useful terminologies that you need to be aware of, and then gives hands-on information about using Apache JMeter to create your performance test plans for different components and get the results.

Chapter 4, *Monitoring Java Applications*, dissects the different monitoring tools that will be used in performance tuning, starting from the operating system tools, different IDE tools, JDK tools, and standalone tools. It covers JProfiler as an advanced profiling tool with its offline profiling capabilities.

Chapter 5, Recognizing Common Performance Issues, discusses the most common performance issues, classifies them, describes the symptoms, and analyzes the possible root causes.

Chapter 6, CPU Time Profiling, focuses on the details of getting the CPU and time profiling results, ways to interpret the results, and ways to handle such issues. It discusses the application logic performance and ways to evaluate different application logics. It provides the initial performance fixing strategy.

Chapter 7, Thread Profiling, discusses thread profiling with details on how to read and interpret thread profiling results and how to handle threading issues. It also highlights the ways to get, use, and read the thread dumps.

Chapter 8, Memory Profiling, discusses how to perform memory profiling, how to read and interpret the results, and how to identify and handle possible issues. It also shows how to read and query memory heap dumps and analyze the different out of memory root causes. The chapter finishes your draft performance fixing strategy.

Chapter 9, Tuning an Application's Environment, focuses on tuning the application environment, starting from the JVM and passing through other elements such as the application servers, web servers, and OS. We will focus on selected examples for each layer and discuss the best practices for tuning them.

Chapter 10, Designing High-performance Enterprise Applications, discusses design and architecture decisions and the performance impact. This includes SOA, REST, cloud, and data caching. It also discusses the performance anti-patterns.

Chapter 11, Performance Tuning Tips, highlights the performance considerations when using the Agile or Test-driven Development methodologies. This chapter also discusses some performance tuning tips that are essential during the designing and development stages of the Java EE applications, including database interaction, logging, exception handling, dealing with Java collections, and others. The chapter also discusses the `javap` tool that will help you to understand the compiled code in a better way.

Chapter 12, Tuning a Sample Application, includes hands-on, step-by-step tuning of a sample application that has some performance issues. We will measure the application performance and tune the application issues, and re-evaluate the application performance.

What you need for this book

The following tools should be downloaded and installed on your machine, as we will be using them throughout the book. You can have the mentioned versions or later versions. Some additional tools will also be required in some chapters:

- Java JDK jdk1.7.0_45 (or later)
- NetBeans 7.4 (or later)
- Glassfish Version 4.0 (packaged with NetBeans 7.4)

  You can download the JDK, NetBeans, and GlassFish from the following URL:
  `http://www.oracle.com/technetwork/java/javase/downloads/jdk-7-netbeans-download-432126.html`

- MySQL Server 5.5 (or later)

  You can download this from the following URL:
  `http://dev.mysql.com/downloads/mysql/`

- Eclipse bundled with TPTP

  You can download this from the following URL:
  `http://www.eclipse.org/tptp/home/downloads/`

- Apache JMeter 2.10

  You can download this from the following URL:
  `http://jmeter.apache.org/download_jmeter.cgi`

- JProfiler 8.x

  You can download this from the following URL:
  `http://www.ej-technologies.com/download/jprofiler/files`

  If you do not have a license, you can get a trial evaluation license from the following URL:
  `http://www.ej-technologies.com/download/jprofiler/trial`

Who this book is for

This book is for experienced Java developers, architects, team leaders, consultants, support engineers, and all people working in the performance tuning in the Java applications, and particularly in Java Enterprise applications.

This book represents a strong entry point for the persons without any performance tuning experience and who want to work in the performance tuning in the Java applications.

Conventions

In this book, you will find a number of styles of text that distinguish between different kinds of information. Here are some examples of these styles, and an explanation of their meaning.

Code words in text, database table names, folder names, filenames, file extensions, pathnames, dummy URLs, user input, and Twitter handles are shown as follows: "The code example will select data from the Employees table."

A block of code is set as follows:

```
@NotNull
@Size(min=1, max=12)
private String name;
@ValidEmail
public String getEmailAddress() {
  return emailAddress;
}
```

Any command-line input or output is written as follows:

```
apache-jmeter-2.10\bin\jmeter.bat (for windows)
Or jmeter.sh (for non-windows)
```

New terms and **important words** are shown in bold. Words that you see on the screen, in menus or dialog boxes, for example, appear in the text like this: "By adding it at the **Thread Group** level, we ensure that all HTTP requests share the same cookies/session."

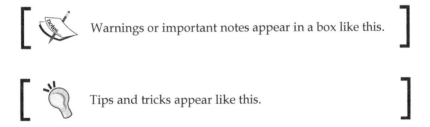

Warnings or important notes appear in a box like this.

Tips and tricks appear like this.

Reader feedback

Feedback from our readers is always welcome. Let us know what you think about this book—what you liked or may have disliked. Reader feedback is important for us to develop titles that you really get the most out of.

To send us general feedback, simply send an e-mail to feedback@packtpub.com, and mention the book title via the subject of your message.

If there is a topic that you have expertise in and you are interested in either writing or contributing to a book, see our author guide on www.packtpub.com/authors.

Customer support

Now that you are the proud owner of a Packt book, we have a number of things to help you to get the most from your purchase.

Downloading the example code

You can download the example code files for all Packt books you have purchased from your account at http://www.packtpub.com. If you purchased this book elsewhere, you can visit http://www.packtpub.com/support and register to have the files e-mailed directly to you.

Downloading the color images of this book

We also provide you a PDF file that has color images of the screenshots used in this book. You can download this file from https://www.packtpub.com/sites/default/files/downloads/6428EN_ColorGraphics.pdf.

Errata

Although we have taken every care to ensure the accuracy of our content, mistakes do happen. If you find a mistake in one of our books—maybe a mistake in the text or the code—we would be grateful if you would report this to us. By doing so, you can save other readers from frustration and help us improve subsequent versions of this book. If you find any errata, please report them by visiting http://www.packtpub.com/submit-errata, selecting your book, clicking on the **errata submission form** link, and entering the details of your errata. Once your errata are verified, your submission will be accepted and the errata will be uploaded on our website, or added to any list of existing errata, under the Errata section of that title. Any existing errata can be viewed by selecting your title from http://www.packtpub.com/support.

Piracy

Piracy of copyright material on the Internet is an ongoing problem across all media. At Packt, we take the protection of our copyright and licenses very seriously. If you come across any illegal copies of our works, in any form, on the Internet, please provide us with the location address or website name immediately so that we can pursue a remedy.

Please contact us at `copyright@packtpub.com` with a link to the suspected pirated material.

We appreciate your help in protecting our authors, and our ability to bring you valuable content.

Questions

You can contact us at `questions@packtpub.com` if you are having a problem with any aspect of the book, and we will do our best to address it.

1
Getting Started with Performance Tuning

Before we start digging in our book to discuss performance tuning in Java enterprise applications, we need to first understand the art of performance tuning: what is this art? Can we learn it? If yes, how?

In this chapter, we will try to answer these questions by introducing you to this art and guiding you through what you need to learn to be able to master this art and handle performance issues efficiently.

We will try to focus more on how to prepare yourself to deal with performance tuning, so we will discuss how to build your way of thinking before and after facing performance issues, how to organize your thoughts, and how to lead your team successfully to build an investigation plan.

In this chapter, we will cover the following topics:

- Understanding the art of performance tuning
- Understanding performance issues and possible root causes from a software engineering perspective
- Tactics to follow when dealing with performance issues
- The difference between handling standalone and web applications from a performance perspective
- How to troubleshoot web application performance issues

Understanding the art of performance tuning

Performance tuning is an art. Yes, a real art, and fortunately we can learn this art because it is based on science, knowledge, and experience. Like any artist who masters the art of drawing a good picture using his coloring pencils, we need to master our tools to be able to tune the performance of our applications as well.

As we are going to cover performance tuning in Java Enterprise Edition 7, the key to master this art starts from understanding the basic concepts of Java—what are the different capabilities of Java EE until the release of v7, how to use the different performance diagnostic tools available, and finally how we can deal with different performance issues.

The final question is related to how we can program our minds to deal with performance issues, and how we will build our own tactics to address these performance issues. But our solid land here is our knowledge and the more we stand on solid land (that is, knowledge), the more we will be able to handle these performance issues efficiently and master this performance tuning art.

Of course with our continuous dealing with different performance issues, our experience will grow and it will be much easier to draw our picture even with a few set of colors (that is, limited tools). The following diagram shows the basic components of Java EE performance tuning art:

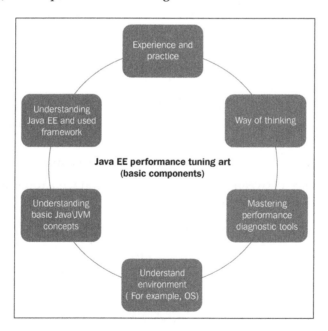

As shown in the previous diagram, we have six basic components to master the performance tuning art in Java EE; four of them are related to our knowledge from bottom to top: **Understand environment** (like OS), **Understand Java/ JVM**, **Understand Java EE** (we should also have some level of knowledge of the framework used in developing the application), and finally **Mastering tools**.

The challenge we face here is in the **Way of thinking** element where we usually need to get trained under an expert on this domain; a possible alternative for this is to read books or tutorials on how we can think when we face performance issues and put it into practice bit by bit.

In this chapter, our focus will be on how we should be thinking and defining our tactics when we deal with performance issues and in the next few chapters, we will apply this thinking strategy so we can master these tactics.

There are other factors that definitely contribute to how we can use our skills and affect our outcome; this includes, for example, the working environment, that is, different constraints and policies.

If we are not able to access the performance test environment to set up the required tools, we would have a high rate of failure, so we need to minimize the impact of such a risk factor by having complete control over such environments.

As an early advice, we as performance experts, should lead the performance-related decisions and remove all existing constraints that can potentially affect our job. We should know that no one will really point to any condition if we failed; they will just blame us for not taking corrective actions for these bad constraints and it will end up destroying our credibility.

> *"Don't ever blame conditions; instead do your best to change them!"*
>
> *-Osama Oransa*

One important thing that should be noted here is that if for any reason we failed to improve the performance of an application or discover the root cause of some performance issues, we will definitely learn something that should contribute to our accumulated knowledge and experience, which is "don't do it that way again!". Remember the following famous quote:

> *"I have not failed. I've just found 10,000 ways that won't work."*
>
> *-Thomas Edison*

When people get overconfident, they are easily susceptible to failure especially when they don't stick to their own troubleshooting process and follow some bad practices; one famous bad practice is jumping to a conclusion early without any real evidence, so the golden advice that we need to stress on here is to always try to stick to our defined process (that is, the way of thinking) even when the issue is really obvious to us, otherwise it will end up being a big failure!

Understanding performance issues

We can define performance tuning issues in general as any issue that causes the application to perform outside the target service-level agreement.

Performance issues can take many forms, for example, increased response time is one of the common forms. Let's list a few forms of application performance issues, as follows:

- Slow transactional response with or without application workload
- Failure to meet the processing rate, for example, 1,000 submitted orders per second
- Failure of the application to serve the required number of concurrent users
- Non-responding application under workload
- Transactional errors during application workload, which could be reported by application users or seen in the application logfiles
- Mismatch between application workload and resource utilization, for example, CPU utilization is 90 percent with a few users or memory utilization is 70 percent even during no user activity
- Abnormal application behavior under certain conditions, for example, the application's response slows down daily at midnight
- All other aspects of application failure to meet functional or nonfunctional requirements under workload

We must differentiate between the application's consistent slow response, and sudden, gradual, or intermittent changes of an application's response to be more sluggish or slower.

Having a design issue is the most common reason behind consistent slow behaviour, which is usually associated with missing or bad quality performance tests that didn't discover such issues early on. Dealing with these issues in the production environment is very difficult, especially if they affect a lot of users' transactions.

The other types of sudden or gradual deterioration of the application response time in some transactions can also be design issues but in most cases, it requires a small fix (for example, configuration, database script, or code fix), and usually we can deploy the issue resolution in the production environment once the fix is tested in the test environment.

User transaction here refers to the set of actions/interactions in a single scenario; it could include a wizard or navigation scenario in our application or it could also be a single interaction or a sequence of interactions.

For example, all these are considered to be user transactions: login, add to basket, checkout, update user data, and so on.

Unfortunately, a majority of performance tuning work is executed in a production environment, where the situation becomes more critical and the environment becomes more sensitive to major changes. When we deal with performance tuning of such applications, we should push the transformation to the correct software engineering model so we can have the performance testing stage in place to catch most of the performance issues early on in the application development cycle.

Classifying performance issues by the discovery phase

If we classify performance issues according to their discovery time in the typical waterfall development process, we can see the following main categories:

- Requirement issues, mainly related to a missing or unrealistic service-level agreement
- Design issues, where the design is the root cause of these issues
- Development issues, such as not following best coding practices, or bad coding quality
- Testing issues, such as missing or bad quality performance testing
- Operational issues, which are mainly related to production environment-specific issues, such as the database size or newly introduced system, and so on

Requirement phase and design-time issues

The best location to discover any potential performance issue is at the design stage where the designer can reduce the cost by discovering and fixing such issues in later steps of the design stage.

The identification of performance issues here means highlighting and taking into consideration some critical **Service-Level Agreements (SLAs)** and also finding possible alternatives for any technology/vendor restrictions.

 An **SLA** is part of a service contract where a service is formally defined; it describes the agreement between the customer and the service provider(s). SLAs are commonly used for nonfunctional requirements like performance measurement, disaster recovery, bug fixing, backup, availability, and so on.

Let's consider the following example.

Let's assume that we have the following SLA (nonfunctional requirements) in our requirement document:

Under the workload of 1,000 concurrent users, the maximum response time allowed should be less than 0.1 second per web service call.

The preceding SLA seems hard to achieve under workload so the designer should be doing the following things:

- Seeking some clarifications on what is meant by "workload" here
- Trying to work around the SLA by adding, for example, a cache to such web services
- Trying to develop a quick **Proof Of Concept (POC)** to get early figures in such a situation

 A **POC** is simply a realization of a certain idea to assess its feasibility, usually small and not completed. In our situation, we need to assess the performance of using such a technology and predict if an SLA can be achieved or not.

We cannot say these are actual performance issues, but they are potential performance issues that will violate the SLAs; the conclusion here is that the designer must pay attention to such requirements and find the best design approach for similar requirements, which should be reflected in all the application layers. Such requirements, if not taken into consideration earlier, should still be caught later in the performance testing phase, but it will be too late for big code changes or architecture/design decisions.

We can consider this as a proactive measure rather than a real reactive measure. It is clearly important in an agile development methodology, where the designer is already familiar with the current system behavior and restrictions, so spotting such issues early on would be easy.

We will discuss the different design decisions and potential performance impact in more details in *Chapter 10*, *Designing High-performance Enterprise Applications*.

Development-time issues

This is where lucky teams discover performance issues! This is almost the last stage where such issues could be fixed by some sort of major design changes, but unfortunately it is not common to really discover any performance-related issues during the development stage, mainly due to the following reasons:

- The nature of the development environment with its limited capabilities, low resources profile (for example, small memory size), logging enablement, and using few concurrent users, where most of the performance issues usually appear under workload.

- Development of the database is usually a small subset of the application's production database, so no valid comparison to the actual performance in the production database.

- Most of the external dependencies are handled through stubbing, which prevents the real system performance examination.

> **Stubbing** means simulating the behavior of the components. It can be done in the following two ways:
>
> - Using a simulator for receiving the request and sending a response back
> - Reading the response from an I/O resource with optionally configured wait time to simulate the system's average response time

- Slow response time nature of the development environment, so the developers neglect any noticeable slow response in the application.
- Continuous changes in the development environment, so that application developers usually adapt to dealing with unstable environments. Hence, they wouldn't actually report any performance issues.
- The stressful development stage where no one would open the door for additional stress.

Testing-time issues

In a typical software engineering process, there should be performance testing in the testing stage of the application development cycle to ensure that the application complies with the nonfunctional requirements and specified SLAs like stability, scalability, response time, and others.

Unfortunately, some projects do not give any importance to this critical stage for different reasons such as budget issues or neglecting small deviations from the SLA, but the cost of such wrong decisions would definitely be very high if a single performance issue is discovered in the production environment especially if the system is dealing with sensitive user data that restricts access to some environment boxes.

Production-time issues

From the previous performance issue types, we now understand that this type is the nightmare type; it is the most critical and costly one, and unfortunately it is the most common type that we will deal with!

We can summarize the main reasons behind discovering performance issues in the production environment as follows:

- Missing or non-efficient performance testing (process and quality issue)
- Under estimation of the expected number of application users with no proper capacity planning (quality issue)
- Non-scalable architecture/design (quality issue)
- No database cleanup, so it keeps growing, especially in large enterprise applications (operational issue)
- No environment optimization for the application from the operating system, application server, database, or Java Virtual Machine (operational issue)
- Sudden changes to the production environment without proper testing of the impact on the performance (operational and process issue)
- Other reasons like using stubs in the testing environment instead of actual integrated test systems, unpredictable issues, and so on

All the issues discussed previously can be summarized in the following diagram:

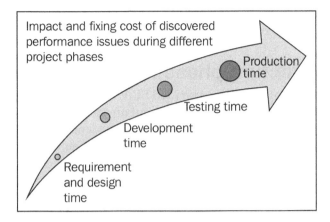

It is important to note that, in the production environment, we should only handle performance issues; no optimization or tuning is to be implemented in the production environment without an actual reported and confirmed issue. Optimization without a real issue can be conducted in the performance testing environment or during development only; otherwise, we are putting the whole application into high-functionality risk, which is much more crucial than reducing the response time a little. So, the production environment is only for fixing critical performance issues that would impact the business and not a place for tuning or improving the performance.

"Things which matter most must never be at the mercy of things which matter least."

-Johann Wolfgang von Goethe

Classifying performance issues by the root phase

In our previous classification, we focused on issue identification time, but if we classified these issues according to the possible root cause from the software engineering perspective, we can have the following types of performance issues:

- Requirement phase issues
- Design/architecture phase issues
- Development phase issues
- Testing phase issues
- Operational and environmental-specific issues

Requirement phase issues

Here, no clear (or sometimes unrealistic) SLAs are present, which do not match the actual production expectations.

Design/architecture phase issues

Here, the design does not fulfill the provided SLA, or is built on certain assumptions retrieved from the vendor specifications without any proof of concept to confirm these assumptions. Also, sometimes the design takes some architecture decisions that do not fulfill the actual customer performance requirements.

The design and architecture phases are very critical as the impact here is not easily fixable later without major changes and high costs that always make such decisions very difficult and risky as well.

 We will discuss performance issues related to design in *Chapter 10, Designing High-performance Enterprise Applications*.

Development phase issues

Bad coding quality, not following performance-oriented coding practices, and missing essential code review (either automated or manual) are the main reasons for this phase.

Following best coding practices should always be forced by the project leaders to avoid any potential issues related to applications that do not perform well; they are not difficult to follow, especially if automated code review tools are used early on during the development phase.

 We will discuss some of the development performance issues in *Chapter 11, Performance Tuning Tips*.

Testing phase issues

This phase's issues occur mainly due to missing or bad quality performance testing including test scripts, test scenarios, number of test users, environment selection, and so on.

We should know that testing responsibilities are the biggest here as developers usually claim they did their job well, but testing should either confirm or nullify this claim.

 We will discuss performance testing in detail in *Chapter 3, Getting Familiar with Performance Testing*.

Operational and environmental-specific issues

A lot of operational issues could impact the application performance, for example, missing frequent housekeeping activities, failure to monitor the application, not taking early correction steps, and implementing improperly-tested changes to the environment (or any of the integrated systems).

Sometimes, specific environment issues like the size of application database, unexpected customer flow, and so on can lead to bad performance in the production environment that we can't catch earlier in the performance test environment.

 We will discuss different application monitoring tools in *Chapter 4, Monitoring Java Applications*.

Performance-handling tactics

Dealing with performance issues is a risk management procedure that should be handled with preventive and curative measures, so we need to stick to the following techniques for successful and peaceful management of performance issues:

- Proactive measures (preventive)
- Reactive measures (curative)

Proactive measures (preventive)

Proactive measures aim to reduce and minimize the occurrence of performance issues by following the software engineering processes properly and having efficient performance requirement, early capacity planning, high quality application development, and proper application testing with special focus on performance testing.

Having the required monitoring tools in place and ensuring that the operation team has the required knowledge is an important aspect. We also have to request the output samples of these tools periodically to ensure that the tools are available to help us when we need them.

The proactive tactics only decrease the possibility of performance issues but do not nullify them, so we should still be expecting some performance issues but we will be in a good position to deal with them as everything we need should be ready.

One of the proactive measures is that we should give a "no go" decision for the application. In case the application fails to pass the agreed SLAs in the performance test environment, it is much easier to troubleshoot and fix issues in the performance environment as compared to the sensitive and stressful production environment.

We can summarize the main proactive tactics as follows:

- Having a working process in place for performance tuning, which should typically include reporting of issues, fixing cycles, and testing processes.
- Having a clear performance SLA and good capacity planning.
- Performance-oriented application design (design documents should be performance reviewed).
- Following best coding practices along with automated and manual code reviews; most of the automated code review tools catch a lot of fine tuning issues. Also, strictly following best application logging practices that can help analyze the issues and prevent performance issues related to logging.
- Having a dedicated performance environment that is more or less similar to the production environment specifications.
- Designing and executing good quality performance testing.
- Training and dedicating a team to handle performance issues.
- Having the tools required for performance ready.
- Continuous monitoring of different application layers from trained operational teams.

 In *Chapter 3, Getting Familiar with Performance Testing*, we will discuss performance testing and its related processes in detail that will cover a lot of these points.

Reactive measures (curative)

These are the tactics that we need to follow when we face or discover any performance issues. If the proactive tactics are already followed, then the reactive tactics would be straightforward and smooth.

Understanding the different layers of an enterprise application

Before we discuss the reactive tactics, we need to have a look at the simple Java enterprise application layers; they are illustrated in the following diagram:

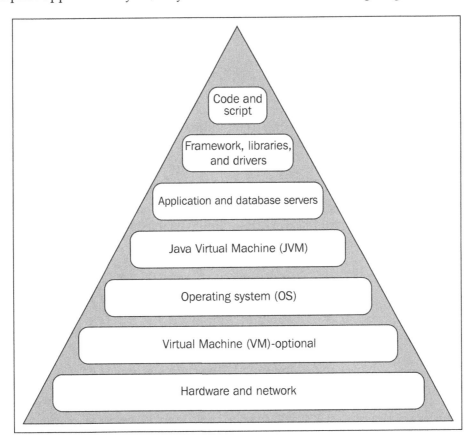

As we can see in the preceding diagram, the application layers represent the code on the top of the pyramid along with some database and configuration scripts.

When we plan to deal with performance issues, we should consider each of these pyramid layers in our investigation. We don't know at which layer we will have the bottleneck, so as an initial conclusion, we need to monitor each of these layers with the suitable monitoring tools: **Operating System (OS)**, **Java Virtual Machine (JVM)**, **Application Server (AS)**, **Database Server (DB)**, **Virtual Machine (VM)** — if it exists, and hardware and networking.

Somehow, the application is usually tightly coupled with the development framework and used libraries, so we can treat them as one layer from the tooling perspective if splitting them is not possible.

One of the common mistakes is to focus on a single layer like the code layer and neglect other layers; this should be avoided. If we have the required monitoring tools for all of these layers, our decision will definitely be much clearer and well guided.

 In *Chapter 4, Monitoring Java Applications*, we will discuss the monitoring tools in detail.

Now, let's have a look at the three important pillars required to enable our performance tuning: process, tools, and team!

The three pillars required for performance tuning

The following three aspects in the vertices of the triangle need to be fulfilled before we start any performance tuning work; they aim to enable us to work efficiently in application performance tuning:

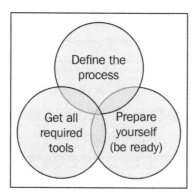

Define the performance process

This is the first and most important task. We need to ensure this process is already in place before we start any work. We should understand the existing performance tuning process, and if the process does not already exist, then we need to create and define one to use.

The process should include many major elements like performance environment, the reporting of performance issues, fixing cycles, acceptable/target performance goals, monitoring tools, team structure (including well-defined roles and responsibilities), and sometimes a performance keyword glossary to clear any possible misunderstanding.

The reporting of performance issues is the important part here to avoid falsely reported issues and wasting unnecessary time on fake issues. The process should handle the confirmation of reported issues and should cover all necessary steps for issue replication and issue evidence, such as log extract, screenshots, recording, and so on.

It is worth adding here that both lesson-learned sessions and performance knowledge-base content should be part of our performance process execution to reduce the occurrence of repeated performance issues in the future.

Getting ready with the required performance tools

Tools are our coloring pencils, as we described them before, and without them we will not be able to draw the picture. As a part of proactive measures, suitable and sufficient monitoring tools should already be installed in both testing and production environments. We should also obtain periodic reports from these tools to ensure that they are working and helpful at the same time; these tools also give us the required application performance baseline, so we can compare any deviations with this baseline.

If the diagnostic tools are not already installed, they should at least be ready for installation. This means that we have at least selected them, checked the compatibility requirements, and secured the essential licenses, if any.

Since most of the monitoring tools are focused on monitoring certain layers of our application, we need to secure at least one tool per layer. The good news is that each layer usually comes with useful monitoring tools that we can use, and we will discuss these tools in more detail in *Chapter 4, Monitoring Java Applications*.

Being ready to deal with performance issues at any time

Now, as a team, it's our turn to be ready even if we haven't faced any performance issues. If we are already facing some performance issues, then we need to be ready to handle our investigation plan.

Leading the performance team and giving them sufficient guidance and recommendations is our job, and it is our call to give decisions and bear the responsibility of any consequences.

> *"It is the set of the sails, not the direction of the wind that determines which way we will go."*

> *-Jim Rohn*

As mentioned before, the first and most essential thing that we need to consider is to confirm that we really are facing a performance issue; this can be done in many ways including replicating the issue, checking a recorded scenario, extracting information from logfiles with the response time recorded, and so on.

Once the issue is confirmed, it's our turn to build the investigation plan. We should focus on the root cause identification rather than fixing the issue. Of course, our goal is to fix the issue and this is what we will get paid for, but we need to fix it with a proper permanent solution and this won't happen unless we discover the correct root cause.

The cycle of learning

The cycle of learning summarizes the process that we need to follow once we have performance issues reported till we fix it. If we take a look at the following diagram that illustrates the cycle of learning, we can see that we must have the following milestones to progress with our learning cycle:

- Knowing where the issues are being *reported*
- *Analysis* and investigation by different tools
- *Thinking* of a way to fix it according to the existing inputs that we have from different tools
- Providing a proper *fix* for the issue

The cycle is repeated from the first step to test and validate the fix. If all the existing issues get resolved, then the cycle is broken; otherwise, we will keep reporting any issues and go through the cycle again.

We need to follow this model and typically try to start the cycle from the reporting step in our model. The following diagram illustrates this model as a whole:

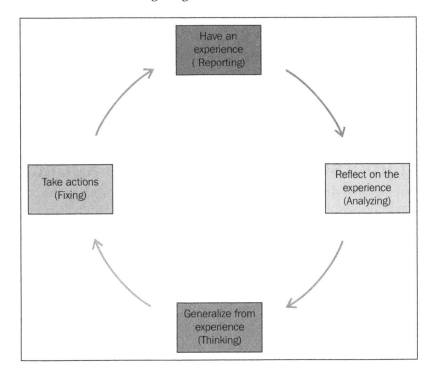

> **Learning cycle** is developed by Peter Honey and Alan Mumford, based on David A. Kolb's ideas about learning styles. The following are the stages of the learning cycle:
> - Doing something, having an experience
> - Reflecting on the experience
> - Concluding from the experience, developing a theory
> - Planning the next steps, to apply or test the theory
>
> Honey and Mumford gave names to the people who prefer to enter the cycle at different stages: activist, reflector, theorist, and pragmatist. While different people prefer to enter at different stages, a cycle must be completed to give a learning that will change behavior.

Let's assume we have an online shopping company that has claimed that their own website's response time deteriorated and a lot of users/customers did not continue their own journeys, and the application logs show frequent timeout and stuck threads (we will explain all these issues later in the book).

The company called a performance tuning expert to lead the investigation in this critical situation, who put in some effort without any progress. The operation team noticed that when they restart the cluster servers one by one, the issues disappeared from the site and they asked if this could be recommended as a solution!

Now, if the performance expert followed this recommendation, the issues will only be masked; the company will be deceived and the issue will explode again at any moment. So, don't think of the solution or the fix but focus on how to identify the reason or the root cause behind this issue. Once discovered, the correct solution will follow.

Tuning yourself before tuning the application

We need to remember the following points each time we are leading the investigation to resolve any performance issues. They are all related to our behavior and attitude when we are working on performance tuning.

Be a true leader

Working on an enterprise application's performance tuning as a performance specialist, we would usually have a team to work with and we should lead and guide this team efficiently.

Here are some of a leader's traits that we need to show the team: support, help, guide, inspire, motivate, advice, listen, and have patience while dealing with their mistakes.

Having a good attitude and behavior towards the team will relieve the pressure from the team and motivate them to work.

Use your power

A successful leader effectively uses some of his/her own powers to influence the team. A lot of different individual powers are available but we should be much more oriented towards using either knowledge/expertise or charismatic powers. These power types have a stronger impact on the team.

Be responsible

A leader shouldn't be self-defending and blame the team for failure, instead the leader should be responsible for the team. Throwing the issues under team responsibility will impact the team's progression to resolve the issue; instead we need to protect our team and give them full support and guidance and bear the consequences of our own decisions.

Trust your team

The team will be much more efficient when we show them our complete trust and support; the more we guide them in a clearly-organized process, the more successful a team we will have.

Keep it simple

If we can't explain the plan in a simple and clear way to our team, then we don't really understand what we are planning to do and we should consider redesigning our investigation plan.

 Stick to the golden **Keep It Simple Stupid** (**KISS**) rule whenever you are leading a team in your investigation.

Respect roles and responsibilities

Everyone should do what is required from them according to their own roles as agreed in the performance process. This will give us the best outcome when everyone is focusing on their own job.

We shouldn't volunteer to do what is beyond our scope, or we will be wasting our time in unnecessary tasks that make us lose our focus. The only exception here is that if there is no one in our team who can do this task and it is really important and relevant to our work, then we can take it up.

Understand the application domain and context

As we are targeting Java enterprise applications performance tuning, a variety of enterprise application technologies exist and applications are built using different frameworks. Before we deal with such applications, we need to understand the framework capabilities and framework-related monitoring tools very well.

A good example here is Oracle ATG e-commerce; this framework supports configuration of the application in layers so we can turn on/off different properties in each application layer or package. Without understanding this simple concept, we won't be able to progress in our troubleshooting to achieve even simple tasks such as enabling the application logging in a certain component. Also, the framework has its own performance monitoring tools that are disabled by default in ATG live configurations. Without knowing this basic information, we won't progress well.

Art Technology Group (ATG) was an independent Internet technology company specializing in e-commerce software and on-demand optimization applications until its acquisition by Oracle on January 5, 2011.

Protect your reputation

No one can harm our reputation more than us; this is a fact, unfortunately. So, for instance, we need to avoid the following things that could destroy our reputation:

- **Don't ever try to shoot in the dark**: If we do not have a solid input from different performance monitoring and analysis tools, then we shouldn't ever try to guess where the issue is. This means our main objective is to have the required tools in place to provide us with the essential inputs.

- **Don't use trial and error**: Trial and error is a good approach for juniors and developers and for learning purposes, but not for performance experts. Also, it is okay to have some trials but don't expand using this approach as it will give a bad impression of insufficient knowledge. It should be mainly used to confirm our thoughts, not to resolve the issue.

- **Quantify your expectations**: Always have a doubt in what is being reported, so don't accept vague words like "the server is okay" or "memory utilization is good". Instead, we should check the results ourselves and ask for solid figures and numbers.

- **Don't jump to conclusions early**: Most of the early conclusions made are not true, so try to be more conservative. Jumping to a conclusion early will convert the current investigation into trials to prove that conclusion!

    One famous example here is the "same values and different interpretations" issue where the single value doesn't mean the same in all domains. So, let's assume we have an application with low CPU utilization; this doesn't necessary mean the application is fine! Instead, it could point to inefficient CPU utilization and is potentially caused by threading or concurrency issues.

- **If it is dark, step back to see some light**: If the current investigation does not reveal any indicators about the issue's root cause and we keep looping without any progress, then try to step back and look from a wider angle to see the missing parts of the picture. Involving other people from outside the current team could help give us some insight.

- **Don't talk too much**: In other words, we need to *talk a little and think a lot*. Don't give what you are thinking of to others, even if you have some early indicators. Keep them for now until we have the required evidence, or even better to keep these thoughts till the issues get resolved. The only exception here is talking to the team to educate them and guide them into the correct direction, or talking during brainstorming sessions.

Standalone applications versus web applications

We are going to discuss the different application tier models here so that we understand the behavior of each application type and the expected tuning effort for each type. While we are working with Java application tuning, we will mainly face the following three different types of application:

- **One-tier application**: In this application everything is installed on one machine only; a standalone application without any remote/external connections.

- **Multi-tier application**: This application is installed on different tiers; two different client types according to the client role, either a thick (fat) client or thin client.

- **Smart/rich client application**: These are the applications where the client can work offline and interact with a remote application online through some interfaces like web services. From a performance tuning perspective, we will deal with this type, which is similar to dealing with a thick client.

The standalone application

This application has the following main characteristics:

- Runs on a single machine (personal computer, tablet, phone, and so on)

- Connects to a local database, if any

- It is designed mostly for a single concurrent user per installed application

- Performs any required processing locally

Performance issues can be easily monitored and diagnosed and are usually related to the data that is being processed. So, sometimes it might be required to get a copy of the data that causes the performance issue so we can replicate the performance issue in our environment.

Thick client application – client-server model

This application has the following main characteristics:

- Thick client is an application that is running on a user machine (personal computer, tablet, phone, and so on), and is connected to a remote machine/server

- It is responsible for GUI and some local processing; it is connected to remote servers mostly for data synchronization (retrieval and persistence)

- It could be an application, applet, Web Start application, or even a widget application

- The server side could be a web application

- Examples of this type of applications are e-mail client, chat application, and so on

- It is usually designed for one user at a time per single device

Performance issues are distributed and investigation could involve both the client and server, and the more functionality the client has, the more value we gain from client application profiling.

Thin client application – web-based model

These applications has the following main characteristics:

- The client does not consume much of the local device hardware and is not installed on the user's machine; users mostly access these applications using browsers on different devices (PC, tablet, phone, and so on)

- The application itself is running on remote servers and these servers are responsible for most of the application functionality

- Processing is done on the servers and only some part of processing can be done on the client side for the presentation layer (like JavaScript code)

- Examples of this type are any browser-based applications, such as e-mail, website, search engine, online tools, and so on

- It is designed typically for multiple concurrent users

Performance issues mostly exist on the server side and are less common on the client side, for example, JavaScript code.

The following diagram illustrates the difference between one-tier and simple multi-tier application models:

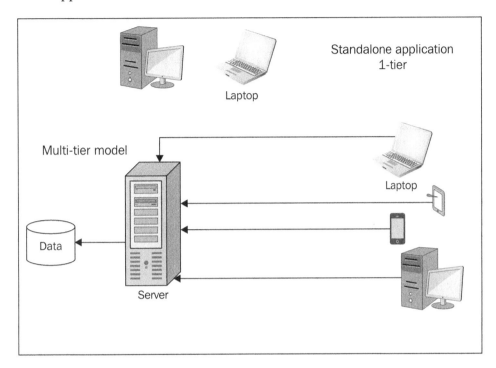

Some web applications are deployed locally and used as standalone applications. This concept differs somehow from the general concept that we have discussed here, where web applications are typically hosted on remote servers and clients access those servers using different browsers.

Dealing with web applications' performance tuning

As we are targeting the performance tuning of Java Enterprise Edition 7, the kind of applications that can be developed by Java EE 7 can fit into either web applications or the server side of the client-server model; both will be handled in nearly the same way from the performance tuning perspective.

If the client is our browser, then some additional tools to analyze the traffic and JavaScript code are required. If it is a standalone application, then almost the same tools that we will use on the server side can be used on the client side as well.

The two dimensions of web applications' performance tuning

When we deal with such applications, we need to think in two dimensions: vertical and horizontal. So, we start with the horizontal dimension to spot the issue's location, then we go vertically through all the layers in this location to point out the root cause.

Horizontal dimension (node-to-node)

From the client to the backend servers, we need to examine each node/component in the flow to spot the root cause of the issue.

Having each node's performance reports or access logs can help us in isolating the bottleneck node in our application.

Vertical dimension (intranode)

In every machine/node in the application, we should check the node from the top to the bottom, passing through all the possible layers.

We definitely do not need to go through this systematic approach in all cases, but we need to understand the complete approach in handling performance issues. After gaining more experience, we will bypass certain components according to the nature of the issue that we are working on.

> *"Bottlenecks occur in surprising places, so don't try to second guess and put in a speed hack until you have proven that's where the bottleneck is."*

> *-Rob Pike*

In the following diagram, we have explained the horizontal nodes and some of the possible vertical dimensions in each node:

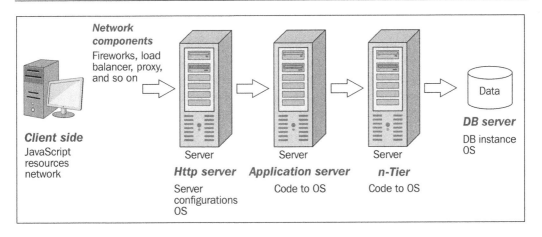

Exploring vertical dimension nodes in horizontal dimension nodes

Now, let's go through the vertical dimensions in some of the application nodes in brief to explain what we need to look into and the possible tools for that.

Client side

On the client side, we have to mainly focus on JavaScript code and the loading time of different resources in our client; rarely do we need to consider **Cascading Style Sheets (CSS)**.

The good news is that all modern browsers have integrated tools to use for this troubleshooting and they are usually named **developer tools**. Also, they have additional useful plugins that can be used for the same purpose.

We can also use external tools that have plugins for different browsers like DynaTrace or Fiddler.

Network components

Checking the performance of network components is an essential part of any performance investigation. Monitoring and checking the traffic through these nodes and their security configurations are important as they could be potentially the root cause of slow application response. The most important network elements include router, firewall, load balancer, and proxy.

HTTP servers (web servers)

Most enterprise deployments tend to have dedicated HTTP servers (like Apache HTTP server) to serve the static enterprise content and assets (help pages, different images, CSS, and JavaScript files). Being a part of the enterprise application architecture, we need to consider checking the server status, server logs, and machine's overall performance during our performance troubleshooting.

It is not common to see issues in HTTP servers, so it might be considered a routine checkup before excluding them from our troubleshooting plan. All HTTP servers have instructions to tune them for the best performance optimization. The operation/deployment team needs to apply these recommendations for the best performance outcome. Most of the performance tuning aspects in these servers are simply configuration parameters that need to be adjusted according to our application type and performance needs.

One example for non-configuration tuning elements is the memory size, which is very critical to HTTP server performance. We need to ensure that sufficient memory is allocated because memory swapping increases the latency of a server's response to user requests.

Application servers

As we clarified earlier in the enterprise application layers diagram, an application has many layers; starting from code up to the operating system. Most common issues are in the application code layer, but we need to ensure that all the other layers are performing as expected; all these layers have supported guidelines and best practices to tune and optimize them, for example, JVM.

We need to have monitoring tools in place including operating system monitoring tools, application server monitoring tools, JVM tools, sometimes framework tools, and virtual machine tools if the deployment has to be done over a virtual machine.

Database servers

Monitoring database servers and getting different database reports or logs such as the Oracle AWR report are essential in the identification of the performance issues' root cause. Let's assume we have a query that retrieves data from a big database table where there is no index used in that table. Checking the database report will show this query listed at the top of slow executing queries in that report.

We can then get an execution plan for that query to identify the root cause of its slow execution and prepare a potential fix.

Checking the status of database servers (operating system), data files, and the underlying hardware is an essential step in our investigations.

Automatic Workload Repository (**AWR**) is a built-in repository (in the SYSAUX tablespace) that exists in the Oracle database.

At regular intervals, the Oracle database takes a snapshot of all of its vital statistics and workload information and stores them in the AWR; it is first introduced in Oracle 10g.

Middleware integration servers

All big enterprise applications are just part of bigger architectures in which different applications are plugged into the integration component, that is, a middleware application or service bus to facilitate the exchange of different messages or data between these integrated systems.

Continuously monitoring the performance of this critical layer is a core performance tuning activity. Of course, we always have a scope to work in, but the integration layer should be neutral during our work; this means all integrated communication shouldn't impact our application's performance.

Also, we should be able to get performance results for different integrated components.

Some applications do not have the integration layer in the testing environment and they use **stubs** instead to simulate the response. The stubs latency should be updated periodically with the actual live systems results, otherwise the testing environment won't simulate the production's actual response time.

If the middleware layer is not optimized for a good performance, all the integrated systems will suffer from bad performance, and if not well monitored, most of the effort of tuning the integrated applications will be incorrectly directed.

One example of a poorly performing middleware application is overutilizing the hardware by deploying too many JVMs for middleware applications; this is usually unnecessary scaling as middleware applications are already designed to connect to too many applications efficiently.

Another point to consider here is that due to the critical nature of this system component, it needs to have some sort of redundancy and fail over features to avoid taking the performance of the whole enterprise application down.

Operating system and hardware

Hardware could be a root cause of our performance issues especially when the capacity planning is not well considered. Pointing to hardware issues is usually done after excluding all other factors.

We also need to take the utilization pattern into consideration as it could point to possible cron job activity.

 Cron job is a time-based job scheduler that gets executed according to the configured schedule table, for example, cron table in Linux or schtasks in Windows. It can be used to archive, back up, load data, scan viruses, and so on.

Let's take some hardware readings and analyze them.

CPU utilization

Web applications usually consume low CPU power per transaction since during each transaction, the application-user interaction includes thinking for a response, selecting different options, filling application forms, and so on.

If the transactional CPU utilization went high, we can suspect a running cron job, for example, an antivirus that is running (pattern is important here), high traffic load (due to incorrect capacity planning), or a common algorithmic logic issue that needs to be fixed.

With low CPU utilization, we can consider using more asynchronous components to increase the efficiency of utilizing the processing power of the machine.

Network traffic

Network bandwidth utilization is very critical in a production environment and it would be funny to forget that automatic application updates are switched on because it consumes the network traffic in an undetectable manner.

It could also point to architecture issues, missing local caching, backup job, and so on.

Memory usage

After excluding memory issues like application memory leakage, we need to check the JVM memory configuration. Missing memory tuning for our JVM is not expected in a production environment but it is worth considering it as a part of our investigation. Also, check the different components of memory consumption and the total free memory left.

Taking the decision to upgrade machine memory is not the only solution; we can also consider moving some components into different boxes, for example, moving certain services, caching components, or even the database server to another machine.

With low memory usage, we need to consider caching more data to speed up the application by utilizing the available memory.

Storage I/O performance

Storage read/write speed is critical in a production environment as I/O operations are usually the most time-consuming operations in relation to application performance. We need to consider using high-speed storage with a good percentage of free space for the running applications.

The storage performance issue becomes more severe when it affects the database servers.

In *Chapter 9, Tuning an Application's Environment*, we will discuss in detail the different tuning and optimization options for some of these nodes.

Summary

In this chapter, we discussed the art of performance tuning and its different aspects. We defined six basic components of this art in relation to the Java enterprise edition. We discussed the performance issues, and classified them into different types according to their discovery time and the responsible software engineering phase.

We explained at a high level the tactics that we need to follow while dealing with performance tuning including both proactive measures like defining processes and reactive measures like using the diagnostic and monitoring tools in performance troubleshooting.

We also focused on how we need to think when we have to deal with performance issues, from our personal behavior, process-wise, and knowledge-wise.

In the last section of this chapter, we dissected our strategy when dealing with different types of Java applications, and took a detailed approach when dealing with enterprise application performance tuning by using both a horizontal-oriented and vertical-oriented analysis.

In the subsequent chapter, *Chapter 2, Understanding Java Fundamentals*, we will pave our way for Java EE performance tuning by establishing a solid understanding of the fundamental concepts in Java EE 7 including recent changes in the Java Enterprise Edition 7, memory structure, garbage collection policies, and different Java concurrency concepts, all being an important part in our performance tuning routine.

2
Understanding Java Fundamentals

An essential part of our journey in Java EE 7 performance tuning is to briefly go over some of the new features of Java EE 7 to understand the different capabilities of this strong framework in developing Enterprise applications. We will discuss selected features in further detail later in this chapter.

As mandatory knowledge, any Java performance-tuning expert must understand memory management in Java applications; garbage collection policies, including the new G1 garbage collection policy and different application scopes (related to memory consumption); and finally, the Java concurrency concepts, including the recent concurrency features in both Java SE and Java EE.

This book is not intended to cover Java EE features; it simply highlights some essential fundamentals we should be aware of while dealing with Java performance tuning. Most of the content of this chapter adheres to Oracle Java documentations as the source of Java specifications and features.

In this chapter, we are going to cover the following topics:

- New features in Java EE 7
- Memory structure in the **Java Virtual Machine (JVM)**
- Different Java garbage collection policies
- Inspection of the available application scopes
- Concurrency in Java
- New concurrency utilities in Java SE and Java EE
- Important concurrency concepts of Java EE components

If you are already aware of these fundamental topics, you can skip to the next chapter.

Discussing the new Java EE 7 features

This section provides us with a sound orientation of some of the new features in Java EE 7, and thus is essential. When working on performance tuning, we will occasionally recommend solutions for existing performance issues, which have already been solved in a standard way in Java EE 7. One example for this is the concurrency issues, which are resolved in a standardized container-managed way in Java EE 7, as we will explain later in this chapter.

Another example of concurrency issues is the flow scope in the JSF pages (@FlowScoped), where instead of loading the user session with an object that is only required during a certain flow/wizard, we use this scope.

We will briefly describe these new features, but it is not our intention to go into the details of all. If you are already aware of the new features in Java EE 7, you can skip this section.

As a general rule, we could diagnose performance issues without much knowledge of these new features, but we may not be able to recommend the best solution to resolve these issues unless we are fully aware of all the Java EE 7 capabilities.

"When you know better, you do better."

– Maya Angelou

We will go through the new features with a few simple statements about each feature, a pseudo-code example, and a link to the Java specification that governs this feature.

> 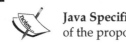 **Java Specification Requests (JSRs)** are the actual descriptions of the proposed and final specifications for the Java platform.

Bean Validation 1.1 (JSR 349)

The Java API for JavaBean Validation provides a facility to validate objects, object members, methods, and constructors. The following points represent some of the features in the Bean Validation APIs:

- Method-level validation (validation of parameters or return values)
- Dependency injection for the different components of Bean Validation
- Integration with **Context and Dependency Injection (CDI)**
- Error message interpolation using the EL expressions

The following code is a sample code for the JavaBeans Validation annotations. The code validates if the name is `NotNull` and its size is between 1 and 12, and the other tag validates if it is a valid e-mail address:

```
@NotNull
@Size(min=1, max=12)
private String name;
@ValidEmail
public String getEmailAddress() {
  return emailAddress;
}
```

Bean Validation's official website is http://beanvalidation.org/.
More details can be found in JSR 349 at http://jcp.org/en/jsr/detail?id=349.

Java API for JSON processing – JSON-P 1.0 (JSR 353)

JSON is a data exchange format widely used in web services and other connected applications. JSR-353 provides an API to parse, transform, and query JSON data using either object or streaming models.

JavaScript Object Notation (JSON) is a text-based open standard designed for human-readable data interchange, and it defines only two data structures: objects and arrays. An object is a set of name-value pairs and an array is a list of values. JSON defines six data types, namely `string`, `number`, `object`, `array`, `true`, `false`, and `null`.

The following code is a sample code for the APIs to read a JSON file to get the `JsonStructure` object:

```
JsonReader reader = Json.createReader(new
  FileReader("my_json_data.txt"));
JsonStructure jsonst = reader.read();
```

For more details, check JSR 353 at http://jcp.org/en/jsr/detail?id=353.

Java API for RESTful web services – JAX-RS 2.0 (JSR 339)

JAX-RS 2.0 (JSR 339) includes a lot of enhanced features to facilitate the development of a RESTful **web service (WS)** as follows:

- Defining standardized client APIs to interact with REST WS
- Using interceptors
- Asynchronous request handling

The following code is a simple example of using new client APIs:

```
Client client = ClientBuilder.newClient();
String name = client.target("http://domain.com/example/name")
  .request(MediaType.TEXT_PLAIN)
  .get(String.class);
```

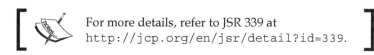

For more details, refer to JSR 339 at http://jcp.org/en/jsr/detail?id=339.

Java Servlet 3.1 (JSR 340)

Both Servlet 3.0 and 3.1 improve the servlet technology providing the following features:

- Providing security improvement (run as, session fixation, and so on)
- Non-blocking IO in an asynchronous servlet and filter
- Deprecating the `SingleThreadModel` interface
- Upgrading support to communication protocol
- Providing annotation support (Servlet 3.0)
- Miscellaneous, such as `ServletResponse.reset` and `sendRedirect` using relative URL and so on

The following code is the sample code to create an asynchronous servlet using annotations:

```
@WebServlet(urlPatterns={"/asyncservlet"}, asyncSupported=true)
public class AsyncServlet extends HttpServlet { ... }
public void doGet(HttpServletRequest req, HttpServletResponse
  resp) {
```

```
    . . .
    AsyncContext acontext = req.startAsync();
    . . .
}
```

We will cover the asynchronous support in Java EE later in this chapter in more detail.

For more details, refer to Servlet 3.1 covered in JSR 340 at `http://jcp.org/en/jsr/detail?id=340`.

Context and Dependency Injection – CDI 1.1 (JSR 346)

In the CDI specifications 1.1, a lot of small changes are included as follows:

- Added global enablement of interceptors
- Added support for the `@AroundConstruct` lifecycle callback for constructors
- Allowed binding interceptors to constructors
- Moved interceptor binding to interceptors spec, allowing for reuse by other specifications
- Added support decorators on built-in beans
- Added `EventMetadata`

The difference between a resource injection and dependency injection is that the former enables us to inject any resource available in the JNDI namespace into any container-managed object, such as a servlet, an Enterprise bean, or a managed bean (at the field or setter method level). On the other hand, the dependency injection enables us to turn regular Java classes into managed objects (using different scopes) and inject them into any other managed object.

The following code is a sample code for the resource and dependency injections:

```
//Resource injection:
@Resource(name="java:comp/DefinedDataSource")
private javax.sql.DataSource myDataSource;
//Dependency injection:
@javax.enterprise.context.RequestScoped
public class MyValidator { ... }
public class MyServlet extends HttpServlet {
  @Inject MyValidator validator;
  ...
}
```

For more details, check JSR 346 at
http://jcp.org/en/jsr/detail?id=346.

Interceptors 1.2 (JSR 318)

Interceptors are used in conjunction with Java EE managed classes to allow developers to invoke the interceptor methods on an associated target class in conjunction with method invocations or lifecycle events.

The common uses of interceptors are logging, auditing, and profiling. Interceptors 1.2 have several new enhancements as follows:

- Rules to specify the interceptor order
- The `@AroundConstruct` interceptors
- The `@Priority` annotation to determine the interceptor order

A sample code to use interceptors is as follows:

```
@Stateless
public class TimerBean {
  @Schedule(minute="*/1", hour="*")
  public void automaticTimerMethod() { ... }
  @AroundTimeout
  public void timeoutMethod(InvocationContext ctx) { .. }
}
```

Interceptors 1.2 specifications are a part of the maintenance release of JSR 318, Enterprise JavaBeans 3.1, which is available at http://jcp.org/en/jsr/detail?id=318.

Enterprise JavaBeans – EJB 3.2 (JSR 345)

EJB 3.2 (JSR 345) includes a lot of minor improvements as follows:

- This includes support for a local asynchronous session bean invocations
- Non-persistent EJB TimerService has been added for the EJB 3.2 Lite set of features
- Restriction on obtaining the current class loader has been removed
- Access to the Java I/O has been altered, replacing **must not** with **should exercise caution**

- The lifecycle callback interceptor methods of the Stateful session bean can now be executed in the transaction context (determined by the lifecycle callback method's transaction attribute)

- It is now possible to completely disable passivation for a specific Stateful session bean

- The `TimerService` API has been extended to query all active timers in the same EJB module

We will discuss the asynchronous method invocation in session beans later in this chapter.

For more details, check JSR 345 at
`http://jcp.org/en/jsr/detail?id=345.`

Java Message Service – JMS 2.0 (JSR 343)

A new JMS Version 2.0 has been introduced, aiming to simplify the messaging interaction. We can list some of these improvements as follows:

- Simplified API consists of three new interfaces: `JMSContext`, `JMSProducer`, `JMSConsumer`, and some new methods

- A default connection factory, which connects to the application server's built-in JMS provider

- Multiple consumers are allowed on the same topic subscription

- Message delivery delay, after which the message is delivered

- Clients have the ability to send messages asynchronously

- `JMSXDeliveryCount` is changed into mandatory

A simple code showing how to use the simplified APIs in JMS 2.0 to send the JMS message using the default connection factory is given as follows:

```
@Resource(lookup="java:comp/DefaultJMSConnectionFactory")
ConnectionFactory connectionFactory
public void sendMessageJMS20(Queue queue, String text) {
  try (JMSContext context = connectionFactory.createContext();){
    context.createProducer().send(queue, text);
  } catch (JMSRuntimeException ex) {
    ..
  }
}
```

We will go through the asynchronous JMS messages in more detail later in this chapter.

For more details about JMS 2.0, check JSR 343 at
`http://jcp.org/en/jsr/detail?id=343`.

Concurrency Utilities 1.0 (JSR 236)

Concurrency Utilities 1.0 (JSR 236) contains the following main components:

- `ManagedExecutorService`: This component is used to execute submitted tasks asynchronously
- `ManagedScheduledExecutorService`: This component is used to execute submitted tasks asynchronously at a specific time
- `ContextService`: This component is used to create dynamic proxy objects that capture the context of a container and enable applications to run within that context at a later time or submit to `ManagedExecutorService`
- `ManagedThreadFactory`: This component is used to create managed threads

We will go through these utilities in further detail later in this chapter.

For more details, check JSR 236 at
`http://jcp.org/en/jsr/detail?id=236`.

Batch Applications 1.0 (JSR 352)

Batch Applications 1.0 (JSR 352) is the specification for batch applications and a runtime to schedule and execute jobs.

The batch framework consists of the following components:

- A job specification language based on XML
- A set of batch annotations and interfaces for application business logic
- A batch container that manages the execution of batch jobs

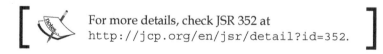

For more details, check JSR 352 at
`http://jcp.org/en/jsr/detail?id=352`.

Java Persistence APIs – JPA 2.1 (JSR 338)

JPA 2.1 includes a lot of changes as follows:

- Support for stored procedures
- Bulk update/delete using the `Criteria` objects
- Predefined and user-defined functions using `FUNCTION`
- Using the `TREAT` and `ON` keywords
- Using CDI for the `Entity` listeners
- Support of unsynchronized persistence context

An example of using the new JPA 2.1 function feature is given as follows:

```
SELECT e FROM Employees e
WHERE FUNCTION('isOldHired', e.joinDate, e.status)
```

The preceding code will select data from the `Employees` table according to the results from the custom-defined function `isOldHired`, which takes two parameters, namely `joinDate` and `status`.

For more details, check JSR 338 at
http://jcp.org/en/jsr/detail?id=338.

JavaServer Faces – JSF 2.2 (JSR 344)

JSF 2.2 includes a lot of new improvement features as follows:

- The Faces Flows feature allows you to create a set of pages for user actions. For example, an online shopping journey. It also has a new defined scope, `@FlowScoped`.
- The Faces Flows feature gives you HTML 5 support using either the pass-through elements or the pass-through attributes.
- The Faces Flows feature gives you resource library contracts.

An example of HTML 5 support in JSF is given as follows:

```
<input type="email" jsf:id="email" name="email"
  value="#{reservationBean.email}" required="required"/>
```

In the preceding example, the `jsf` prefix is placed on the `id` attribute so that the attributes of the HTML 5 input tag are treated as part of the Facelets page (the pass-through elements).

We can use the pass-through attributes as follows:

```
<h:inputText id="month" p:type="number" p:min="1" p:max="12"
  p:required="required" p:title="Enter a number between 1 and 12
    inclusive.">
```

The preceding code will provide the following output:

```
<input id="month" type="number" min="1" max="12"
 required="required" title="Enter a number between 1 and 12 inclusive.">
```

 For more details about JSF 2.2, check JSR 344 at
`http://jcp.org/en/jsr/detail?id=344`.

Expression language 3.0 (JSR 341)

Expression language 3.0 (JSR 341) includes some new enhancements as follows:

- The new operator, `;` ,to separate statements
- The use of a static field and method
- String concatenation operator using `+` or `cat`
- Lambda expression:
  - Lambda expression behaves like a function
  - It can be invoked immediately, such as `((x,y)->x+y)(3,4)` equals to 7

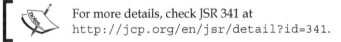 For more details, check JSR 341 at
`http://jcp.org/en/jsr/detail?id=341`.

Java Transaction APIs – JTA 1.2 (JSR 907)

JTA 1.2 includes a few enhancements as follows:

- A new annotation named `javax.transaction.Transactional` and an exception `javax.transaction.TransactionalException`
- A new annotation named `javax.transaction.TransactionScoped`

The following code is an example of using these annotations on the class level and overrides it on the method level:

```
@Transactional(Transactional.TxType.MANDATORY)
public class TransactionBean {
  @Transactional(Transactional.TxType.NEVER)
  public void actionWithoutTransaction() throws Exception

  public void actionWithTransaction() throws Exception
}
```

To get more details, visit JSR 907 at
http://jcp.org/en/jsr/detail?id=907.

Java API for WebSocket 1.0 (JSR 356)

WebSocket API is a new feature in Java EE; it complies with HTML 5 and the WebSocket technology, which is widely adapted by browsers these days.

- It supports the annotated and programmatic patterns
- It uses the ws:// protocol for nonsecure communication and wss:// for secure communication (similar to http:// and https://)
- Each client should connect to one endpoint while a server can connect many clients to a single end point
- Each WebSocket server side is called endpoint; the process to create and deploy a WebSocket endpoint is as follows:
    1. Create an endpoint class.
    2. Implement the lifecycle methods of the endpoint (onOpen, onMessage, onError, and onClose).
    3. Add business logic to the endpoint methods.
    4. Deploy the endpoint method inside a web application.
    5. At the most, we can have three methods annotated with @OnMessage in an endpoint method, one for each message of the text, binary, and pong types.

The following code is a pseudo code to send the confirmation of receiving the message to the connected client:

```
@OnMessage
public void onMessage(Session session, String msg) {
  try {
```

```
        session.getBasicRemote().sendText("The message :"+msg);
    } catch (IOException e) { ... }
}
```

The HTML page will contain a `<td id="message">` element, so we can use it to place the message using the following JavaScript code:

```
<body>
  ...
  <table>
    ...
    <td id="message" name="message">--.--</td>
    ...
```

JavaScript should inject the received message into the message `<td>` as shown in the following code:

```
var wsocket;
function connectMe() {
  wsocket = new
    WebSocket("ws://localhost:8080/app/endPoint");
  wsocket.onmessage = onMessage;
}
function onMessage(evt) {
  document.getElementById("message").innerHTML=evt.data;
}
window.addEventListener("load", connectMe, false);
```

 For more details, check the W3C WebSocket API specification at http://www.w3.org/TR/2011/WD-websockets-20110929/ and JSR 356 at http://jcp.org/en/jsr/detail?id=356.

Understanding memory structure in the JVM

Understanding the memory structure in the JVM is essential to tune the JVM for the better performance of the Java applications, so the essential knowledge to deal with the JVM in general, and in particular, the JVM memory management is required and expected from a performance tuning expert to master.

The JVM is a specification that is released and updated with each new Java release; parts of the specifications are mandatory, while some are left for vendor implementation. This carries additional responsibility to understand the different vendor implementations.

The JVM specifications

The implementation of the Java HotSpot virtual machine is considered as a high-performance virtual machine implementation for the Java platform (another JVM released by Oracle is JRockit).

The Java JDK HotSpot provides the following two different implementations of the JVM:

- **Client virtual machine**: This virtual machine is typically used for client applications. The client virtual machine is tuned to reduce the startup time and memory footprint. It can be invoked by using the `-client` command-line option when launching the application.

- **Server virtual machine**: This virtual machine is designed to maximize program execution speed. It can be invoked by using the `-server` command-line option when launching the application.

We will discuss both types in *Chapter 9*, *Tuning an Application's Environment*.

The memory structure in the JVM specifications in Java SE 7—as illustrated in the following diagram—contains **Heap Area**, **Method Area** (includes runtime constant area), **Java VM Stack**, **Native Method Stack**, and **PC Registers**.

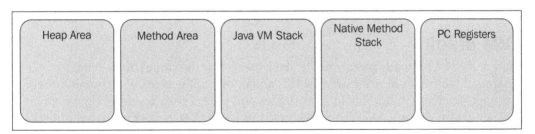

Let's have a quick look at each of these components according to what is mentioned in the JVM specifications.

Heap area

The heap area represents the runtime data area, from which the memory is allocated for all class instances and arrays, and is created during the virtual machine startup.

The heap storage for objects is reclaimed by an automatic storage management system. The heap may be of a fixed or dynamic size, and the memory allocated for the heap area does not need to be contiguous.

Method area and runtime constant pool

The method area is analogous to the storage area for the compiled code of a conventional language or to the `text` segment in an operating system process. It stores per-class structures such as the runtime constant pool; field and method data; the code for methods and constructors, including the special methods used in class, instance, and interface initialization.

The method area is created on the virtual machine startup. Although it is logically a part of the heap, it can or cannot be garbage collected, and it can be of a fixed or dynamic size.

It also contains a runtime constant pool, which is a per-class or per-interface runtime representation of the `constant_pool` table in the class file. It contains several kinds of constants, ranging from numeric literals known at the time of compiling, to method and field references that must be resolved at runtime.

The runtime constant pool serves a function similar to that of a symbol table for a conventional programming language, although it contains a wider range of data than a typical symbol table.

JVM stack

Each of the JVM threads has a private stack created at the same time as that of the thread. The stack stores frames and is analogous to the stack of a conventional language (such as C). It holds local variables and partial results and plays a part in the method invocation and return. Because this stack is never manipulated directly, except to push and pop frames, the frames may be heap allocated. Similar to the heap, the memory for this stack does not need to be contiguous.

This specification permits that stacks can be either of a fixed or dynamic size. If it is of a fixed size, the size of each stack may be chosen independently when that stack is created.

A **frame** is used to store data and partial results and to perform dynamic linking, return values for methods, and dispatch exceptions.

Native method stacks (C stacks)

Native method stacks is called C stacks; it support native methods (methods written in a language other than the Java programming language), typically allocated per each thread when each thread is created.

The size of native method stacks can be either fixed or dynamic.

PC registers

Each of the JVM threads has its own **program counter** (**pc**) register. At any point, each of the JVM threads is executing the code of a single method, namely the current method for that thread.

As the Java applications can contain some native code (for example, using native libraries), we have two different ways for native and nonnative methods. If the method is not native (that is, a Java code), the PC register contains the address of the JVM instruction currently being executed. If the method is native, the value of the JVM's PC register is undefined.

 For more details about JVM specifications, check the Oracle documentation at `http://docs.oracle.com/javase/specs/jvms/se7/html/jvms-2.html`.

Memory structure in the Java HotSpot virtual machine

Now, let's cover the Java HotSpot virtual machine memory structure.

Generational memory structure

When memory is managed using a technique called generational collection, the memory is divided into generations, that is, separate pools holding objects of different ages (object age starts from object creation and memory allocation).

For example, reserve one space for young objects and another one for old objects.

Young generation collections occur relatively frequently and are efficient and fast because the young generation space is usually small and likely to contain a lot of objects that are no longer referenced.

Objects that survive a number of young generation collections are eventually promoted (or tenured) to the old generation.

The Java HotSpot virtual machine generations

If we examine the memory structure in the Java HotSpot virtual machine in more detail, as illustrated in the following diagram, the memory is categorized into three generations—the young generation (the **Eden**, **From**, and **To** survivor spaces), the old generation (tenured space), and the permanent generation.

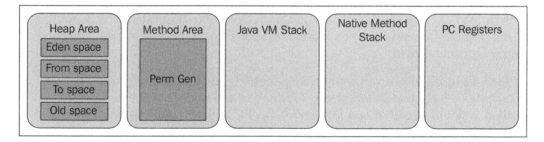

Most objects are initially allocated in the young generation. The old generation contains the objects that have survived a number of young generation collections, as well as some large objects that may be allocated directly in the old generation.

The **permanent generation (Perm Gen)** holds objects describing classes and methods, as well as the classes and methods themselves.

The young generation is further divided into three areas: **Eden space** for initial object allocations and the **From** and **To** survivor spaces, where one of them is used to collect the objects that resist garbage collection in the previous cycle and the other one is empty; they keep exchanging with each garbage collection cycle.

Objects are initially allocated in **Eden space**. As mentioned previously, a few large objects may be allocated directly in the old generation. The survivor spaces hold objects that have survived from at least one young generation garbage collection and have, thus, been given additional chances to die before being considered "old enough" to be promoted to the old generation. At any given time, a survivor space holds such objects, while the other is empty and remains unused until the next collection.

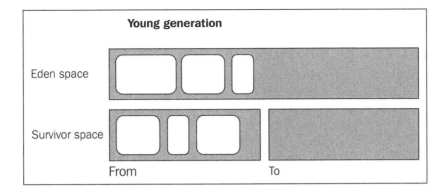

It should be noted that the garbage collector is not only responsible for cleaning the memory but also has three main functions, which are as follows:

- Allocating the needed memory
- Ensuring that any referenced objects remain in memory
- Recovering memory used by objects that are no longer reachable from references in executing the code

In this generational model, the most challenging factor is minimizing the garbage collection **pause times.** For this, a lot of garbage collection policies are proposed, as we will see in the next section.

 The garbage collection pause time is the length of time during which application execution is stopped while garbage collection is occurring.

The main difference between HotSpot and JRockit is that there is no PermGen space for the JRockit virtual machine; instead, it uses the native heap for the data related to the class metadata. We will discuss this in more detail in *Chapter 9, Tuning an Application's Environment.*

Understanding the Java garbage collection policies

Garbage collection is one of the features that characterize the Java language; it went through continuous improvements in the subsequent Java releases. We have the following three main types of garbage collectors:

- **Serial collector**: This collector does the garbage collection in a serial (sequential) manner, followed by compacting the old space to combine the empty space for better object allocations later. This means the application will be stopped during this collection activity.

- **Concurrent mark sweep** (**CMS**): This collector runs in parallel in two different stages—the mark stage to mark the objects that are eligible for garbage collection (three steps) and the sweep stage to remove these objects. However, it doesn't perform any space compacting after garbage collection.

- **Garbage-first** (**G1**): This collector is the latest introduced collection policy, which can be adjusted according to the application needs. It also compacts the space after garbage collection.

It is essential to master the different possible configurations, and the higher the criticality of the application, the more we need to spend time tuning the garbage collector to minimize the application's pause times.

Different GC options

Before we discuss the HotSpot GC strategies, we need to understand some of the available GC options.

Concurrent versus stop-the-world

The stop-the-world garbage collection is simpler since the heap is frozen and the objects do not change during the collection. This type may be undesirable for some applications, such as real-time applications, which can't tolerate this pause time. So it has to use the concurrent collector to minimize the garbage collection's pause time.

The concurrent collector needs extra care, as it operates the objects that might be updated at the same time by the application, so this adds some overhead to the activity and it requires a large heap size as well.

Serial versus parallel collector

In the serial collector, both young and old collections are done serially. In a stop-the-world fashion, an application execution is halted while collection is taking place.

When the parallel collection is used, the task of garbage collection is to split into parts, and those subparts are executed simultaneously on different CPUs. Refer to the following diagram:

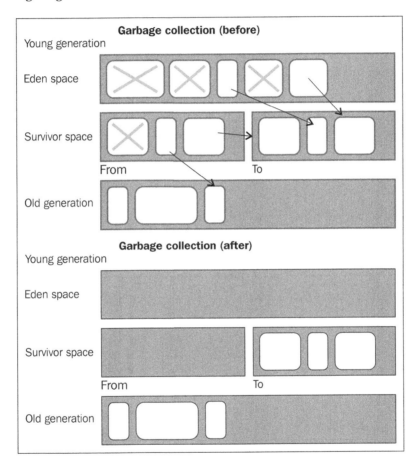

The preceding diagram summarizes the following work done by the serial collector:

- Collecting all live objects (still referenced in the application) from **Eden space** in the empty survivor space (the **To** survivor space in the preceding diagram)
- Collecting all live objects from the nonempty survivor space (the **From** survivor space in preceding diagram) in the other survivor space (the **To** survivor space) and very old objects in the **Old generation** space

- If the **To** survivor space is full, the live objects from **Eden space** or the **From** survivor space that have not been copied to it are tenured, that is, moved to **Old generation** (regardless of how many young generation collection cycles they have survived)

- Any objects remaining in **Eden space** or the **From** survivor space after live objects have been copied are not considered as live objects (objects marked with **X** in the preceding diagram)

- Both Young generation and the **From** survivor spaces will be freed

- Survivor spaces swap rules now; the **From** survivor space now becomes empty and will be the **To** survivor space, and the **To** survivor space becomes full and will be the **From** survivor space in the next cycle

The parallel collector does the same work, but it splits the activity into parts and those subparts are executed simultaneously on different CPUs, as shown in the following figure; this causes reduction in the needed application pause time:

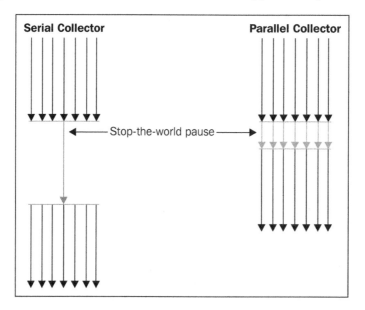

The HotSpot JVM also includes the CMS collector, which is considered a low-latency collector. This collector differs mainly in the way it deals with the old generation space collection. It deals with the young generation in the same way as the parallel collector. It has the following two subsequent steps:

- **Mark step**: This step includes the following three phases:
    - **Initial mark phase**: The collector initially marks all the reachable live objects (the first short pause time)

- ° **Concurrent mark phase**: The concurrent marking of the objects follows perfectly, but because the application is running and updating reference fields while the marking phase is taking place, not all live objects are guaranteed to be marked at the end of this phase

- ° **Final remark phase**: The application stops again for a second pause, and finalizes the marking by revisiting any objects that were modified during the concurrent marking phase

- **Sweep step (concurrent)**: The concurrent sweep phase reclaims all the garbage that has been identified. Refer to the following diagram:

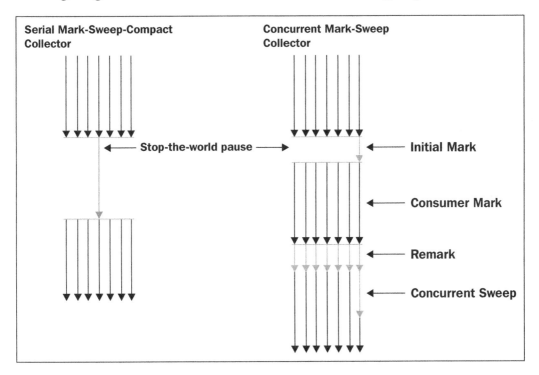

Compacting versus non-compacting

In the compacting type, the old space is compacted by two subsequent steps, the summary phase and compacting phase.

Summary phase

The GC examines the density of the regions, starting with the leftmost one, until it reaches a point where the space that could be recovered from a region, and the density of the region to the right of it is worth the cost of this compacting.

The regions to the right of that point will be compacted by eliminating all the dead spaces.

Compacting phase

Using the summary data, the threads can be independently copied into the regions that need to be filled; this produces a heap that is densely packed on one end, with a single large empty block on the other.

CMS is not a compacting type, but other collectors are compacting collectors. We can see in the following diagram the difference between the noncompacting and compacting garbage collectors:

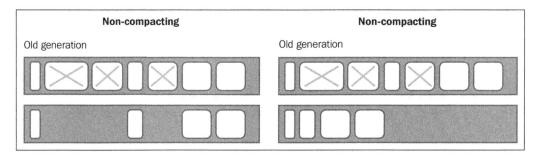

Compacting makes the allocation of a new object easy and fast at the first free location (one pointer is enough to point to the available allocation space).

A noncompacting collector releases the space utilized by the garbage objects in place, so it has the advantage of faster completion, but the drawback is potential heap fragmentation. It needs a number of lists linking together the unallocated regions of memory, and each time an object needs to be allocated, the appropriate list (based on the amount of memory required) must be searched for a region that can hold that object, so allocations in the old generation become more time consuming.

The Garbage-first collector – G1

The G1 collector is a recently introduced garbage collector; it is supported since Oracle JDK 7 update 4. The G1 collector is a server-style garbage collector targeted for multi-processor machines with large memories.

Let's go through how this collector works as follows:

- The heap is partitioned into a set of equal-sized regions, each having a contiguous range of virtual memory.

- G1 performs a concurrent global marking phase to determine the aliveness of objects throughout the heap.

- After the mark phase is complete, G1 knows which regions are mostly empty. It collects the garbage in these regions first, which usually yield a large amount of free space. This is why it is called Garbage-first.

- The regions identified by G1 as ripe for reclamation are garbage collected using evacuation. G1 copies objects from one or more regions of the heap to a single region on the heap, and in the process, it both compacts and frees the memory. This evacuation is performed in parallel on multiprocessors to decrease the pause times and increase throughput.

> **Throughput**: In this context, throughput is the percentage of the total time not spent in garbage collection, considered over long periods of time. It equals the time dedicated for the application to work.

G1 uses a pause prediction model to meet a user-defined pause time target and selects the number of regions to collect the garbage based on the specified pause time target. The following diagram shows an example of G1 heap partitions:

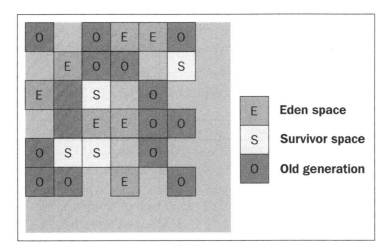

It is important to note that G1 is not a real-time collector. It meets the pause time target with high probability, but not with absolute certainty. Based on the data from the previous collections, G1 does an estimate of how many regions can be collected within the user-specified target time.

G1 is planned as a replacement for the CMS collector. Comparing G1 with CMS, there are differences that make G1 a better solution. One difference is that G1 is a compacting collector (with the advantages of a compacting collector, as mentioned before); it also offers more predictable garbage collection pauses than the CMS collector and allows users to configure the desired pause targets.

 For more details, visit the Oracle Java documentation at `http://docs.oracle.com/javase/7/docs/technotes/guides/vm/G1.html`.

Different application scopes

The application scopes control the lifetime of the objects placed inside. We need to understand the different available scopes in the Java Enterprise application and carefully pick the most suitable scope to use, so we can make the best use of our application memory:

- Global data should be stored in the application scope
- The session scope should be used only for user-specific data that we need throughout the application
- Additional scopes such as conversational or flow should be used whenever suitable

The following table illustrates the different available Java EE 7 application scopes:

Scope	Annotation tag	Usage
Request	`@RequestScoped`	This is a single HTTP interaction.
Session	`@SessionScoped`	This has all user HTTP interactions.
Application	`@ApplicationScoped`	This is shared with all users' interactions per web application server.
Flow	`@FlowScoped`	This is used for Faces Flows (the JSF scope).
View	`@ViewScoped`	Every view has its own unique, non-shared views, and it remains live if the action methods return the user to the same view (the JSF scope).
Flash	`No annotation`	This is used to carry objects to the next view to overcome the page's redirection, which removes the request parameters (the JSF scope).

Scope	Annotation tag	Usage
Dependent	@Dependent	This is the default scope if none is specified; it means that an object exists to serve exactly one client (bean) and has the same lifecycle as that of the client.
Conversation	@ConversationScoped	It shows a user's interaction with a servlet, including the JavaServer Faces applications.

Using the annotation, the CDI is responsible for placing the beans in the specified context and ensures that the objects are created and injected at the correct time, as determined by the scope that is specified for these objects.

A scope gives the object a well-defined lifecycle context. The scoped object can be automatically created when needed and automatically destroyed when the context in which it was created ends; it is shared among any client that executes in the same context.

Also, it should be noted that the static members of classes are globally scoped by nature, so we should be careful when dealing with any static field, and in particular, the static collections, as it will consume the memory without being monitored. A similar issue happens with the instance variables of long-living objects, such as servlets, filters, and listeners.

The most common issue related to using different scopes is abusing the session scope with a lot of unnecessary data. We need to make use of these different scopes for better application memory management and performance.

Understanding concurrency in Java

Concurrency in Java is one of the critical performance issues, particularly in the standalone or desktop applications. For the web applications, it is less critical. We can have a lot of benefits by utilizing the Java concurrency features, especially after the recent modifications to Java EE to add a lot of asynchronous components; we will cover these components in this chapter.

Concurrency is the concept of executing two or more tasks at the same time (in parallel). Tasks may include methods (functions), parts of a program, or even other programs with modern computer architectures; support for multiple cores and multiple processors in a single CPU is very common.

Before Java EE 7, it was not recommended to use concurrency in the Java EE applications as it was not managed by the container. However, standardized ways to utilize the concurrency feature in Enterprise applications have been introduced in Java EE 7.

Process versus thread

Concurrency in Java can be achieved in the following two main ways:

- Using processes:
    - A process corresponds to the operating system's running process; it has its own non-shared runtime resources. For example, each process has its own memory.
    - Our Java application is considered as a standalone process in most of the Java implementations. We can use the `ProcessBuilder` class to create additional processes from inside the application by using following code:

```
Process process= new ProcessBuilder("myCommand",
  "myArguments").start();
```

    - As each process has its own non-shared resource, we need some sort of communication between these processes; for example, most of the operating systems support the **inter-process communication (IPC)** resources, such as pipes and sockets, which are important to distribute the work between different processes. The other alternative is to use a common data store (database or flat files).
    - The following redirect method, for example, can be used to redirect the process output:

```
public ProcessBuilder
  redirectOutput(ProcessBuilder.Redirect destination)
```

    If the destination is set as `Redirect.PIPE`, the standard output of a subprocess can be read using the input stream returned by the `Process.getInputStream()` method. So the parent process can read the output of various subprocesses to follow their execution progress.

- Using threads (a lightweight process):
    - Threads share the process' resources including memory and open files.
    - They exist within a process and every process has at least one thread.

- ° Every thread has a priority and threads with higher priority are executed first. The thread priority is inherited from the parent thread that creates this thread unless explicitly changed.

- ° Threads can be classified into system (daemon) threads and user threads. An example of the system thread is the garbage collector and one of a user thread is the main application thread.

- ° We can create threads by either by implementing the Runnable interface or extending the Thread class, as shown in the following code:

```
public class HelloRunnable implements Runnable {
  public void run() {
    System.out.println("Hello!");
  }
  public static void main(String args[]) {
    (new Thread(new HelloRunnable())).start();
  }
}
```

A concurrency advantage is mainly the efficient utilization of the machine processing power. It is also the value of executing some background activities, which can improve the user's response time by not waiting for these background activities.

It also has some drawbacks such as deadlocks, competition on the shared resources, and potential corruption of the shared data.

Exploring an object monitor

Each object in Java is associated with a monitor, which is considered as the object lock; only one thread at a time may hold a lock of the same object (even multiple times). Holding the lock by a thread means other threads can't access this object.

The monitor is represented inside the JVM as a counter; it represents the number of times the thread holds the lock on this object. The object is unlocked only when the monitor has a count of zero.

Java initially had a single way to obtain this lock, which is implicit locking using the synchronized keyword. Recently, the explicit locking mechanism has been introduced using the Lock interface. Let's learn the implicit locking, and in the next section, we will discuss the explicit locking using the Lock interface in more detail.

First, we need to understand the different `synchronized` keyword usages as follows:

- The `Synchronized` method could be either a static or instance method
- The `Synchronized` block could also be either a static or instance block, for example, `synchronized (object) { }`

When we synchronize around an object, it means that the current thread will try to get the lock or monitor of this object, and once the thread gets the lock, it will start executing this block of code; otherwise, it will wait till it gets that lock.

Using the `synchronized` keyword with methods means one the following situations:

- If the method is an instance method, it locks the monitor associated with the instance for which it was invoked, that is, `this` object
- If the method is static, it locks the monitor associated with the `Class` object that represents the class in which this method is defined (each class in Java has a `Class` attribute that represents this `Class` object).

It is important to understand how to use the different `Thread` class methods to coordinate among concurrently executing threads; for example, if a thread holds the monitor of an object, but needs to perform its task only after other threads do some processing, it can release the object monitor to other threads and go into the wait status by calling its `wait()` method.

When the other threads perform the actions, they need to notify back using the `notify()` or `notifyAll()` method, so the initial thread can be awakened to complete its task.

Using the Java concurrency utilities

The concurrency utilities are important APIs that facilitate the concurrency implementations in the Java applications. We can create the thread pools for execution, use the explicit locking mechanism, use `fork` or `join` to distribute the required task, and utilize the concurrency in context managed in the Java Enterprise applications.

For example, creating a thread pool is simple using `ExecutorService`, where we define the pool size and add all the different threads to that pool; in this way, we can control the execution of all these threads according to the defined pool size.

We need to understand all the available concurrency utilities because one of the performance-improvement techniques is to implement concurrency in certain heavy-processing areas in our application. We will not dissect all these utilities here, instead we will show how to resolve some common tasks using the utilities explained in the next sections.

Creating a thread pool

In Java, we can create a pool of threads using different APIs. One way is to use `ExecutorService`, where we can define the thread pool size and execute these threads according to the required pool size. So if we have 100 threads and we defined a pool size of 10, then, at the most, we will have 10 threads executed at a time. When one thread finishes the execution, a new thread begins execution. This permits us to maximize resource utilization by tuning the thread pool size according to the CPU and hardware profile. We need to be aware of classes such as `ThreadPoolExecutor` and `ScheduledThreadPoolExecutor`.

To get the number of cores/processors in the machine, we can execute the following code:

```
int numberOfCores = Runtime.getRuntime().availableProcessors();
```

Let's have a look at the following sample pseudo code for using a thread pool:

```
ExecutorService execSvc = Executors.newFixedThreadPool( 20);
for( int i = 0; i < 600; i++ ) {
  execSvc.execute( new MyThread() );
}
//check if executor service finished executing threads
while(!execSvc.isTerminated()){
  Thread.sleep(500);
  execSvc.shutdown();
}
class MyThread implements Runnable {
  public void run() {
    ...
  }
}
```

In this code, we created 600 different threads and configured the thread pool to execute only 20 concurrent threads at a time. So the thread pool picks 20 threads initially, and whenever a thread is terminated, it picks another one till no threads are left.

It is important to know that tuning the pool size is an important performance-tuning aspect, because switching between 20 different threads in a processor with 5 or 7 cores will causes a lot of context switchings, which consumes time and will definitely impact the application's performance.

Also, using the thread pool is essential to protect the depletion of application resources. In the previous example, if we create a thread when needed, we will have to create hundreds of threads in a short time and it will end up with `OutOfMemoryError`.

Using explicit locking with the Lock interface

The `Lock` objects work similar to the implicit lock using the `synchronized` keyword, and only one thread can own a `Lock` object at a time. The `Lock` objects also support the `wait` and `notify` mechanisms through their associated `Condition` objects.

The biggest advantage of the `Lock` objects over the implicit lock is their ability to back out of an attempt to acquire a lock. The `tryLock` method backs out if the lock is not available immediately or before a timeout expires (if specified). The `lockInterruptibly` method backs out if another thread sends `interrupt` before the lock is acquired, so we will be able to control the locking, which can prevent deadlocks.

Let's take an example of a famous deadlock situation where two concurrent threads are trying to acquire the same look. In this example, we will have two bank accounts (A and B) and we need to transfer money from account A to account B. At the same time, another thread is trying to transfer from account B to account A. Since these are banking accounts, we need to ensure that each running thread is the only thread currently modifying a single account. (for example, if account A has $1000 and we are trying to withdraw $1000 using two threads concurrently, and if there is no good locking, we could have a situation where the two withdraws happened successfully while the account has only $1000).

```
public void settleTransfers() {
  AccountWithLock firstAccount= new AccountWithLock();
  AccountWithLock secondAccount= new AccountWithLock();
  . . .
  . . .
  TransferLock(1,firstAccount,secondAccount,200);
  TransferLock(2,secondAccount,firstAccount,150);
  Thread t1 = new Thread(transfer1);
  Thread t2 = new Thread(transfer2);
  t1.start();
  t2.start();
}
```

In the preceding code, two threads are trying to execute the transfers at the same time. The following code shows the transfer logic using the synchronized keywords:

```
public void run() {
  int transferAttempts = 3;
  while (transferAttempts > 0) {
    if (fromAccount.transfer(fromAccount, toAccount, amount)) {
      break;
    }
    // sleep for a while to retry
    transferAttempts--;
  }
}
```

The preceding code tries to execute the transfer from the account and sleep for a while to try again. The following code is the actual transfer code:

```
boolean transfer(Account fromAccount, Account toAccount, double
  amount) {
  synchronized(fromAccount) {
    Thread.sleep(50);
    synchronized (toAccount) {
      if(fromAccount.withdraw(amount)) {
        toAccount.deposit(amount);
      }
    ...
}
```

There is an explicit sleep period to ensure both threads are now competing for the required resources (that is, on the two bank accounts), so a deadlock can occur. If we execute the application now, the application will hang because of this deadlock!

Now, let's rewrite the method with the new logic using the new explicit locking as follows:

```
try {
  fromAccount.lock.tryLock(3, TimeUnit.SECONDS);
} catch (InterruptedException ex) {
  ...
}
...
if (!fromAccount.lock.isHeldByCurrentThread()) {
  return false;
}
...
```

```
try {
  toAccount.lock.tryLock(3, TimeUnit.SECONDS);
} catch (InterruptedException ex) {
  ...
}
if(!toAccount.lock.isHeldByCurrentThread()){
  fromAccount.lock.unlock();
  return false;
}
...
if(fromAccount.withdraw(amount)){
  toAccount.deposit(amount);
  fromAccount.lock.unlock();
  toAccount.lock.unlock();
}
...
return true;
```

In the `Account` class, we have added the new `ReentrantLock` attribute as follows:

```
public ReentrantLock lock = new ReentrantLock();
```

This is one implementation technique. Another way is implement the `Lock` interface and override the methods if we need to.

In the following code, we try to get the lock for `fromAccount` using the `tryLock` method and specify the wait time to get the lock for a maximum of 3 seconds:

```
fromAccount.lock.tryLock(3, TimeUnit.SECONDS);
```

Once we get this lock, we try to get the `toAccount` lock. If we succeed in getting it, we can transfer the money as we have the lock of both the objects. We specified three trials to get the lock, so the transfer can occur in subsequent trials rather than a deadlock.

It is worth mentioning that in our modified code, to use the `Lock` interface, we use the new thread safe `ThreadLocalRandom` class as follows:

```
Thread.sleep(ThreadLocalRandom.current().nextInt(500));
```

This new class ensures that the current thread does not share the random object with any other thread. So whenever we need to generate random numbers in multithreaded code, we need to use `ThreadLocalRandom` instead of `Math.random()`. So the random results would be less contention with better performance.

 You can download the code from `http://www.packtpub.com`.

Concurrent resources and utilities

In Java EE 7, the concept of concurrent resources is introduced. Concurrent resources are the managed objects that provide concurrency capabilities to the Java EE applications.

In the application server, we need to configure concurrent resources, and then make them available for use by the application using either the JNDI lookup or resource injection.

The main concurrent resources are explained in the next sections.

The ManagedExecutorService class

A managed executor service is used by the applications to execute submitted tasks asynchronously. It extends the Java SE ExecutorService to provide methods to submit tasks for execution in Java EE.

The executor service accepts both the Runnable task and the Callable task. The main difference between using both is that if we use the Runnable task, no return method is required as the run() method returns void and it can't throw a checked exception. On the other hand, if we use the Callable task, we get the results from the Future object and we can throw the different checked exceptions as well.

A sample code to use this service to submit both the Runnable and Callable tasks should look like the following code:

```java
@Resource
ManagedExecutorService executor;
//or by using JNDI
ManagedExecutorService executor = (ManagedExecutorService)
  context.lookup("java:comp/DefaultManagedExecutorService");
  //then add the Runnable task with no return
  executor.submit(new Runnable() {
  @Override
  public void run() {
    ...
  }
  });
  //or add the Callable task with the result in the Future object
  Future<String> result = executor.submit(new
    Callable<String>() {
  @Override
  public String call() throws Exception {
    ...
    return "Finished";
  }
```

```
});
// get the results using the get() method
// if result.isDone()==true:
out.println("Output: " + result.get());
```

In the preceding code, we submit the `Runnable` task to the executor service to execute it without expecting any result. Then, we submit a `Callable` task to the executor service and wait for the response using the `Future` object callback.

We can also submit a list of the `Callable` objects using the `invokeAll(..)` method and get a list of the `Future<?>` objects so that we can use them to retrieve the results.

The ManagedScheduledExecutorService class

A managed scheduled executor service is used by applications to execute the submitted tasks asynchronously at specific times. The API provides the scheduling functionality that allows users to set a specific date/time for the task execution programmatically in the application.

It is used in the same way as `ManagedExecutorService` but by adding the scheduler configurations. A simple code that schedules the execution of the `Callable` object is shown as follows.

```
@Resource
ManagedScheduledExecutorService executor ;
ScheduledFuture<String> result = executor.schedule(new
  Callable<String>() {
  @Override
  public String call() throws Exception {
    ...
    return "Finished Scheduler work";
  }
}, 60, TimeUnit.SECONDS);
// Get the results using the get() method
// If result.isDone()==true
String output = result.get();
```

In the preceding code, we configured the scheduler task to execute after one minute, and we get the results using the `get()` method from the `ScheduledFuture` object.

The ManagedThreadFactory class

A managed thread factory is used by the applications to create managed threads. The threads are started and managed by the container, which is the standard way to create threads in Java EE instead of the non-recommended way used prior to Java EE 7, which is creating unmanaged threads.

A `ManagedThreadFactory` class extends the Java SE `ThreadFactory` to provide a method to create threads for execution in Java EE. It has a single method, `newThread()`, which is inherited from the `ThreadFactory` class.

Let's see the simple way to create a thread using this managed factory in the following code example:

```
@Resource
ManagedThreadFactory factory;
Thread mThread = factory.newThread(new Runnable() {
  @Override
  public void run() {
    System.out.println("Running ...");
  }
});
mThread.start();
```

In the preceding code, we have added the thread to the managed container by using the `ManagedThreadFactory` class and calling the `newThread(..)` method. Then, we start the thread execution using the `start()` method.

The important Java EE concurrency features

In addition to the concurrent resources and concurrency APIs, Java EE has many concurrency features for asynchronous invocations. We summarize them as follows:

- Servlet/filter asynchronous processing
- Nonblocking I/O APIs for asynchronous servlet/filter
- EJB features, such as singleton EJB, calling asynchronous session bean methods, and sending asynchronous JMS messages

It is important that we recognize all these features so that we can recommend the optimal solutions when faced with performance issues in long processing components.

The SingleThreadModel interface

When `Servlet` implements the `SingleThreadModel` interface. It is guaranteed that the container will let only one thread at a time be executed in a given servlet instance's service method. However, because the container may have a pool of objects for `Servlet`, it is not recommended to use this interface as it could lead to potential synchronization issues. Hence, this interface is deprecated since Servlet API Version 2.4.

If we need to execute certain code areas using just one thread, we can use one of the synchronization methods that we just discussed in the previous section.

Asynchronous servlet and filter

When a servlet or filter component needs to do long processing, they can delegate the work in the asynchronous execution context and get the results once the execution is completed. To enable asynchronous processing on a servlet or a filter, we need to add the parameter `asyncSupported` and set it as `true` on the `@WebServlet` or `@WebFilter` annotation subsequently, as shown in the following code:

```
@WebServlet(urlPatterns={"/asyncservlet"}, asyncSupported=true)
public class MyAsyncServlet extends HttpServlet { ... }
```

To obtain an instance of `AsyncContext`, call the `startAsync()` method on the `HttpServletRequest` object. Then, the execution can run in a separate thread. We can end the execution by calling the `context.complete()` method. The following code is a pseudo-code example illustrating this:

```
AsyncContext context = request.startAsync();
context.start(new Runnable() {...
  public void run(){
    ...
    context.complete();
  }
});
```

We can also add listeners to this kind of asynchronous processing using the method as follows:

```
public void addListener(AsyncListener listener, ServletRequest
  req, ServletResponse res)
```

The preceding code registers the given listener for notifications of the different types: `onTimeout`, `onError`, `onComplete`, or `onStartAsync`.

The new Java EE non-blocking I/O APIs

Java EE introduced the non-blocking I/O support for asynchronous servlets and filters; they are of special importance when processing slow request/response due to slow client network speed.

The following steps summarize how to use the non-blocking I/O APIs to process user requests and write responses inside the servlet service methods:

1. Start servlet asynchronous processing.

2. Get either the input or output stream from the request/response objects in the service method according to what we need to do.

3. Assign a read/write listener to this input/output stream.

4. Process the request/response inside the listener's `callback` methods.

We have two types of listeners, read listener for requests and write listener for responses.

The following methods are the `ReadListener` methods:

*   `void onDataAvailable()`
*   `void onAllDataRead()`
*   `void onError(Throwable t)`

The following methods are the `WriteListener` methods:

*   `void onWritePossible()`
*   `void onError(Throwable t)`

Session beans asynchronous method invocation

Instead of waiting for the session bean method to finish execution before it returns to the caller, we can use asynchronous calls so that the session bean can do the long processing in the background and the client gets the processing status later. This is very useful and similar to the `Servlet` asynchronous processing for the lengthy operations.

Once the method returns a result, the result is an implementation of the `java.util.concurrent.Future<V>` interface, where `V` is the result value type.

This `Future<V>` interface defines the needed methods for the client to check if the method processing is completed (for example, `isDone()` and `isCanceled()`), and then retrieve the results or cancel the invocation.

To use asynchronous invocation, we can simply annotate the session bean business method with `javax.ejb.Asynchronous` or apply `@Asynchronous` at the class level to mark all the methods of this session bean as asynchronous methods.

 The session bean methods that are exposed as web services can't be asynchronous.

The method can return `Future<V>` or `void`, but if it returns `void`, it can't throw an exception. A pseudo code for such a method that does order processing in an asynchronous way will look like the following code:

```
@Asynchronous
public Future<String> processMyOrder(Order order) throws
    BusinessException {
    //process the order
    //..
    String myOrderStatus = order.getStatus();
    return new AsyncResult<String>( myOrderStatus);
}
```

A singleton session bean

A session bean is designed for application scaling by creating a pool of objects that serve the Enterprise application. In some cases, we need the session bean to be created only once; this is known as a singleton session bean. To create a singleton session bean, we only need to add the `@Singleton` annotation.

We can initialize the singleton session bean during the startup of a server by adding the `@Startup` annotation to inform the container about the initialization. What if our session bean depends on other beans? It would potentially fail to get initialized unless these beans are already loaded as well.

In this case, we need to use the `@DependsOn({"classname1", " classname2", "classname3",....})` annotation and list all the required classes to initialize this bean. This will ensure that these classes are loaded before our startup bean.

When creating a singleton session bean, concurrent access to the singleton's business methods can be controlled in two ways, the container-managed concurrency and the bean-managed concurrency. We can use annotations to specify which one we need to use.

For the container-managed concurrency, we can use the following code:

```
@ConcurrencyManagement(ConcurrencyManagementType.CONTAINER)
```

For the bean-managed concurrency, we can use the following code:

```
@ConcurrencyManagement(ConcurrencyManagementType.BEAN)
```

As a lot of concurrent threads can access the bean methods, we need to control this concurrent access by our bean (bean-managed) or by the container (container-managed).

In case we decide to use the bean-managed concurrency, we will have to take care of certain areas in the code that need some sort of locking mechanism to avoid concurrent changes.

If we use the container-managed concurrency, we can control the concurrency using the @Lock annotation. We can specify this on either the class or method level.

Two possible values exist, LockType.READ and LockType.WRITE, where we should specify if the lock is just to read or write as well. We can also control the access timeout of the class or methods by using the annotation @AccessTimeout.

This is an example of how to use all these annotations for a singleton session bean:

```
@ConcurrencyManagement(ConcurrencyManagementType.CONTAINER)
@Singleton
@AccessTimeout(value=20, unit=TimeUnit.SECONDS)
public class ExampleSingletonBean {
  private String state;
  @Lock(LockType.READ)
  public String getState() {
    return state;
  }
  @Lock(LockType.WRITE)
  public void setState(String newState) {
    state = newState;
  }
}
```

Sending asynchronous JMS messages

When dealing with JMS and sending a persistent message, the send method will block the thread execution until the JMS provider confirms that the message was sent successfully. The asynchronous send method here allows the application to send the message without blocking and it can receive the sent notification later.

 This feature is available only for the application clients and the Java SE clients.

As we saw in an asynchronous invocation in the session bean method, we need a callback object with different methods to use. Here, we can use a CompletionListener with an onCompletion method.

The `CompletionListener` interface has two callback methods as follows:

```
void onCompletion(Message message)
void onException(Message message, Exception exception)
```

A pseudo code to use this feature looks like the following code:

```
context.createProducer().setAsync(this).send(destination,
  message);
//"this" is the current class, which implements the
//CompletionListener interface
@Override
public void onCompletion(Message message) {
  System.out.println("Message Sent.");
}
@Override
public void onException(Message message, Exception e) {
  System.out.println("Message sent failed:" + message);
}
```

It worth mentioning here that in our examples in this chapter, we have used a new feature in Java EE, which is the **Default resources**; this new feature requires the platform provider (that is, application servers) to preconfigure a default resource for different elements such as the data source and JMS connection factory.

```
@Resource(lookup = "java:comp/DefaultJMSConnectionFactory")
ConnectionFactory connectionFactory;
```

More information about Java EE 7

A good tutorial of Java EE 7 is available online from Oracle. Navigate inside to understand more about the newly introduced features and how to use them. It includes some useful code samples, and you can also find the different API documentation at `http://docs.oracle.com/javaee/`.

The JVM specification can be found at the following URL:

`http://docs.oracle.com/javase/7/docs/technotes/guides/vm/`

Summary

In this chapter, we have covered some of the essential fundamentals to our performance-tuning book. By end of this chapter, we should have been orientated with the new features of Java EE 7. We have highlighted the essential parts that are related to concurrency. It is really worth it if you spend more time getting more details about some of the covered topics.

We have also covered memory management according to the JVM specification (Java SE 7) with some brief orientation about the memory structure of the HotSpot virtual machine. In addition, we discussed the different garbage collection policies, including the most important three types, the serial collector, concurrent mark sweep collector, and Garbage-one collector, which were recently introduced in Java SE 7. In the next chapters, we will assume that you are already aware of most of the mentioned features and you will see a lot of our sample codes have different annotations described in this chapter. So try not to proceed to the next chapter before being fully aware of all of the mentioned features.

In the next chapter, *Chapter 3, Getting Familiar with Performance Testing*, we will execute the final preparation, which will focus on understanding the performance testing and its tools. The chapter will cover performance testing from different aspects with focus on creating performance test plans. We will learn how to use Apache JMeter to create our test plans and will practice this throughout this book.

3
Getting Familiar with Performance Testing

Performance testing is a cornerstone element to ensure the application quality and reduce the possibility of performance issues in our application. As this is not a testing book, we are going to cover performance testing from the level of detail that would help our investigations. We should be able to read different performance testing results and understand them as well. We should also be able to request special types of performance testing that can help us troubleshoot any issues. We will also discuss performance testing tools as these tools can be used by performance tuning experts to assess the results of performance tuning issues and potential fixes.

In this chapter, we will cover the following topics:

- Explaining performance testing and its different components
- Performance testing terminologies
- Precautions during performance testing in the cloud environment
- Hands-on trials in using **Apache JMeter** to create different types of performance testing

Dissecting performance testing

Performance testing is a special type of application testing where the testing does not mainly aim at testing the application functionality, but instead it aims to measure the performance of the application — this means responsiveness, throughput, reliability, and/or scalability of a system under determined workload.

The following are the main objectives of performance testing:

- Assess the application's performance and compare it to the agreed SLAs
- Assess the application's design and implementation quality
- Assess the application's capacity
- Identify and fix any potential performance issues
- Enhance the performance of the application
- Get performance benchmark or baseline for subsequent releases

As we already highlighted in *Chapter 1, Getting Started with Performance Tuning*, the most important thing in the proactive measures is to have a well-established and agreed upon process that covers all performance elements including performance testing. The process needs to cover all the aspects of performance testing, such as the environment used, fixing cycle, handling performance issues in each project stage/milestones, and defining the rules and responsibilities of team members.

Of course, doing high quality performance testing won't prevent the occurrence of performance issues in the production environment, but at least it will minimize the occurrence of these issues and reduce the potential impact of any undiscovered performance issues.

Exploring performance testing aspects

Let's briefly go through some of the following important aspects of the performance testing process:

- The performance test environment
- Performance in different project milestones
- Rules and responsibilities
- Performance test types
- Testing components
- Testing tools
- Performance benchmarking and baseline
- Isolation testing
- The performance fixing cycle/process
- When to stop performance tuning
- Team rules and responsibilities

"If you don't care about quality, you can meet any other requirement."

-Gerald M. Weinberg

Selecting the performance test environment

All enterprise applications must have a dedicated test environment with almost the same (or nearly the same) architecture of the production environment. A relative capacity should be assessed between both environments. The more the environment is close to the production environment, the more realistic the results we get. The following are some of the aspects we need to consider:

- The same software and operating system versions
- Similar hardware profiles
- Similar network configurations
- Realistic database volumes
- Connect the performance test environment to integrated test systems and limit the usage of stubs as much as possible

If the environment is not exactly the same as the production environment, then we need to initially estimate the proportional gap between both environments and recalculate this proportion with each application release to reflect the difference between the capacities of both environments.

It should be noted here that using the stubbing technique while dealing with external systems in performance environments is not preferred. We should instead connect to the integrated test systems whenever possible. This doesn't mean stubbing does not add useful values to our testing results as it removes the external system dependencies and covers the unusual system responses that can't be covered during normal test scenarios.

If we have to deal with stubbing in the performance test environment, we must ensure that the stub total response time is equal to the average production time. This can be achieved by adding a corresponding latency to the stub response. This latency needs to be updated according to the recent production environment statistics.

It is also important to have a testing client that will run performance testing on a good powerful machine with good connectivity between the machine and testing environment.

Project milestones and performance

Each project has a delivery plan with different milestones and there are a lot of different software development methodologies available, such as waterfall, agile, and others. From the performance perspective, we need to ensure that performance testing is executed with good quality in the project's testing phase, usually before delivering the project to the final acceptance level.

Evaluating the performance at each stage or milestone is essential to prevent any major performance issues, for example, in requirement stages, we need to ensure that all SLAs are checked by the performance team for assessment and get their opinions as early as possible to avoid unrealistic requirements.

In the architecture and design phases, a separate design review for the fulfilment of performance requirements is essential; this could impact the selection of certain products based on each product's performance and capacity limitations.Sometimes a POC is required to assess the feasibility of certain design options to meet the SLA.

After deploying applications into the production environment, performance evaluation should be done using suitable monitoring tools to catch early deviations or deteriorations in the application's performance.

As a part of project planning, all the lessons learned from performance testing and tuning should be shared with the appropriate team to avoid repeating these issues in the future.

Defining different rules and responsibilities

All the assigned resources must be aware of their responsibilities and performance task priorities. Usually, performance troubleshooting needs members from different teams, such as the database administrator, system administrator, development team, testing team, and design team.

A good and sufficient level of understanding of roles and responsibilities ensures smooth cooperation between all the assigned resources and reduces any potential conflicts, especially if each team member understands the priority of the performance tasks. All the involved teams should be capable of dealing with performance tasks, and usually, training them is required in order to avoid misunderstanding of any assigned tasks.

All the teams involved must select the required tools and get them installed in all the possible environments, starting from the development environment. Such tools should cover all the application layers and spread over different application nodes to facilitate performance troubleshooting.

It is recommended to have some sort of knowledge base for all the discovered issues with frequent orientation sessions about performance lessons learned.

Performance testing types

Performance testing refers to different types of testing, such as load testing and stress testing. We will go briefly over each of these types.

Load testing

This type of testing tests the performance of the application under an anticipated workload, by using a specific number of concurrent users with a specific number of transactions.

One of the load testing variants is **Soak/Endurance Testing**. This type of testing tests the performance of the application under a prolonged period of time (12 hours or more) to determine whether the application can withstand the continuous workload or not.

Stress testing

This type of testing tests the performance of the application beyond the anticipated workload. The main objective is to determine the upper limits of the application and its robustness.

One of its variants is to use **spike load** to test the application's response with a sudden increase in workload.

Capacity testing

This type of testing aims to test the maximum capacity of the application while the application can still meet the performance goals (for example, handling the number of concurrent users).

Performance testing components

Understanding different performance testing components can help us in building an efficient performance testing plan. Let's look into these components briefly.

Test data

Test data can be divided into transactional (for example, user orders) and non-transactional data (such as assets, list of values, and master data). Performance testing should have a mix of all types of data with a lot of variations, so do not reuse the same asset data for all user transactions, otherwise we will get false results from cached data. This is one of the most common mistakes in designing performance testing.

Test data is much more driven by the customer's needs and expected live data, for example, if a car selling system is about to launch, then the system should be tested for the most common selected cars similar to the real-life sales of these cars, otherwise the test won't be a real replication of the production environment.

Test users

Test users are specified according to the expected/estimated system capacity. It could be either the actual or forecasted count of concurrent users.

Again mixed types of users should be selected similar to the actual expected user type such as customer, admin, and so on. Users in performance testing are referred to as **Virtual Users (VUsers)**.

We need to understand the difference between concurrent users and simultaneous users. Concurrent users represent the number of users that have an active but possibly idle session with the application, while simultaneous users are those who are actually doing active interaction at a given time.

If the application has 150 concurrent users, we should not assume that 150 requests were being processed all at once because this would mean that 150 user sessions exist where some of the users are actively interacting with the application. But, in reality, many of them could be just reading the page, thinking, or filling in form fields.

While designing the performance test, we should define the number of iterations for each user and decide whether the user session needs to expire after each iteration or not.

Usually, performance testing starts with a **warm-up time (ramp-up)** where the number of users and transactions increases gradually till it reaches a steady number of concurrent users. After the test duration ends, it reaches the final stage, which is **cool-down time (ramp-down)**, where the number of users starts to decrease gradually (logging off).This entire process is illustrated in the following diagram:

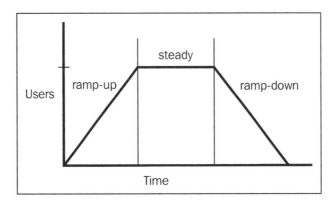

Test scenarios

Test scenarios should target all possible scenarios but in case this is difficult, then the priority is given to the customer's transactions rather than the internal user's transactions (that is, the administrator), also focusing on the most common transactions rather than seldom used transactions. Business priorities should also be considered when building test scenarios and a test scenario should behave like an actual expected normal human being. In another words, the scenario should consider the thinking time of the users on each page and the time taken to fill in different form fields.

 Test scenario is a sequence of steps in the application. It corresponds to a use case scenario, for example, the purchase of products, where the user navigates to the product catalogs, adds products to the basket, checks out, and gets the final confirmation.

Preparing the test environment prior to test execution

Usually, some activities should be executed prior to firing the performance test. The following are the examples of such activities:

- Restoring the environment baseline for different configurations, for example, database size, by restoring the database image for performance testing
- Smoke testing to ensure that everything is in place
- System warm up (if not part of the test) to preheat caches and preload pages
- Configuring the logging level and monitoring tools as required

Smoke testing is a type of software testing that involves testing the non-exhaustive set of tests to ensure that the most important functions are working and the build is stable.

This term came into software testing from a similar type of hardware testing, in which the device passed the test if it did not catch fire (or smoke) the first time it was turned on.

Test automation

Test automation is an important part of performance testing, and it increases the efficiency of the testing and reduces the duration of testing cycles. This is not easy to develop as maintaining the test scripts up to date is not an easy task, especially when the agile development process is implemented by continuously adding new scenarios and modifying old scenarios.

The testing team should get involved early enough to reflect all the new changes in the testing script.

Test quality assurance

Definitely, the better the quality of the test, the less issues related to production performance will need to be reported. So, after discovery of any production issues, assessment of the test script is required as part of the root cause analysis to see why it was not discovered during the performance testing stage, and make any necessary changes to the test script. Also, periodic checks of the testing quality are required to increase the script's quality and skills of the testing team.

Performance testing tools

A lot of performance testing tools can be used, for example, IBM Rational Performance Tester, HP LoadRunner, OpenSTA, Testing Anywhere, Borland Silk Performer, NeoLoad, WebLOAD, SoapUI, LoadUI, Apache JMeter, and a lot of other commercial and open source tools.

In this chapter, we will use Apache JMeter in detail as a good option for doing performance testing.

Performance benchmarking and baseline

Acquiring the application baseline means capturing the performance metrics for different application transactions use it later in evaluating the subsequent changes and determine if the application performance has deteriorated or improved. Without acquiring an application baseline, we won't be able to identify whether the performance issues are old or newly introduced.

The final performance testing results of each of the previous release should be considered as the baseline for the subsequent release. The results should definitely include all types of performance testing and from all the layers of the application, such as database, disk I/O, memory, and CPU utilization.

Benchmarking is the process of comparing the performance results of the application with the industry standard or similar leading applications so that the difference can be distinguished from a performance perspective. It is useful to understand the position of the application in terms of industry performance levels.

Isolation testing

During performance tuning, once we locate the performance issues, we start to isolate them by certain performance testing to narrow the scope and point out the exact location of the issue whenever possible so that it is considered as a customized test according to the performance issues.

Isolation testing is a common troubleshooting strategy. Even if we can't develop specific new test scripts, we can still select parts of our initial scripts to focus on our issue, and exclude unrelated locations.

When we are investigating multiple issues, we must deal with them as separate issues. Even if we have doubts that the issues are related, we must consider them as separate until they are proved to be related to each other. This is done to avoid wasting time in assuming that the issues are related and then later discovering that they are not.

Performance fixing cycle

In *Chapter 1, Getting Started with Performance Tuning*, we discussed the learning cycle that should be followed as our fixing strategy. Here, we are focusing on documenting the process itself and covering all the required activities as a part of our process, which should answer the following questions:

- How to report performance issues? What is the requirement to consider an issue as a performance issue?

- Who should confirm the first line analysis? (Different levels of application support.)

- Who should be responsible for team structure, roles and responsibilities, and priorities for each team member when they are not completely assigned?

- What are the SLAs for fixing the discovered performance issues?

- What is the process to deploy production fixes (that is, path to production)?

- When to consider an issue as fixed or closed?

- What is the required documentation to avoid similar issues in the future?

- Who will define the performance goals?

It is important to follow the golden rule "**One change at a time**", which means implementing and testing one change only, otherwise we won't know which change produces the performance impact, that is, always compare apple to apple.

When to stop tuning?

This is an important question and the answer should be clear to all the involved stakeholders. Definitely, the answer is when the performance issues are resolved, or in other words, when the response time is back within the SLA again (agreed or planned). This is what we call achieving the **performance goals**.

 Performance goals are the criteria that are required to accept the release of the product from performance testing.

In some cases, we need to consider a lot of factors before continuing in endless tuning cycles, such as what are the current performance goal gaps, do we need to do major design changes, is there any possible work-around to reduce the impact of the existing issues, does it depend on third-party products, do we have customer commitments in this release that can't be delayed, what is the business impact if we go live with the current level of performance, and so on.

Performance testing terminologies

Understanding different testing terminologies is essential so that we can be aligned with the testing team. Misinterpretation of testing results could happen if we don't really understand the testing terminologies.

For example, throughput is the number of units of work that can be handled per unit of time, for instance, requests per second, hits per second, and so on. The greater the application throughput value, the better the application's performance.

Now, let's go through the following testing terminologies that we need to be completely aware of to avoid any conflicts or misunderstanding while working with performance tuning:

- **Capacity**: This terminology refers to the total workload that the application can withstand without violating any key performance acceptance criteria.

- **Response time**: This terminology refers to the time taken by the application to respond to a request.

- **Latency**: This terminology refers to the measure of responsiveness that represents the time the application takes to complete the execution of a request.

- **Throughput**: This terminology refers to the number of units of work that can be handled per unit of time, for instance, requests per second, hits per second, and so on.

- **Resource utilization**: This terminology refers to the percentage of time that a resource, such as processor, memory, disk I/O, and network I/O takes up to service user requests. Once these resources are completely utilized, it is known as **saturation**.

- **Iteration**: This terminology refers to the completion of a test case once by a single user (or a virtual user).

- **Scalability**: This terminology refers to the application's ability to handle additional workload without adversely affecting performance. It is of two types: vertical scalability and horizontal scalability.

- **Stability**: This terminology refers to the application's reliability, robustness, functionality, data integrity, availability, and consistency of responsiveness under various conditions.

- **Thinking time**: This terminology refers to the time taken by the users to think or navigate to different pages in the application. It is simulated in test scenarios by pauses. Users will have different thinking times depending on what part of the application they are using. A well-designed load test should be designed to apply a random factor on the configured thinking time to simulate the difference between people's speed when they respond to the application. It can also be dropped during stress testing.

Performance testing in a cloud environment

When we test the performance in a cloud environment, we need to take enough precautions so that we can have accurate performance results. This is because a cloud environment is based on virtualized resources (that is, virtual machines), and environment performance is not guaranteed to be the same for all test execution times.

The main reason behind this is that virtual resources can be markedly affected by other concurrent executions in other virtual resources hosted on the same machine. So, when we propose a performance fix, we need to ensure that the testing results reflect the application performance, not the environment instability results. Therefore, it is better to take one of the following measures to reduce the impact of doing performance testing in a cloud environment:

- Having a dedicated (non-shared) server for our testing
- Executing the test many times and taking out the average
- Calibrating the testing prior to each testing cycle

> **Calibration** is the comparison between two measurements: one known measurement and one unknown measurement.
>
> During our performance testing, we need to use a test with known performance results in the cloud environment, and the percentage of difference with our cloud results should be considered as the difference between the actual results and cloud-based results.

Cloud computing is now considered the first deployment option for many enterprise applications through both private and public clouds. Having a product in the production environment and using cloud gives it the advantages of cloud, which includes elasticity as the biggest advantage where the application can expand or collapse the resources according to the workload on the application.

We can summarize the advantages of deploying the application in a cloud environment as follows:

- Eliminates the need to build and maintain data centers

- Reduces the need to maintain a large IT staff

- Enables organizations to build new systems quickly and easily

- Provides elastic resources that allow applications to scale up and down as needed in response to market demands

- Provides the pay-as-you-go rental model, which allows organizations to defer costs especially during the early project phases

- Increases business continuity by providing inexpensive disaster-recovery options

Cloud computing refers to any deployment model that fulfills the following principals:

- Pooled computing resources available to any subscribing users
- Virtualized computing resources to maximize hardware utilization
- Elastic scaling up or down according to our needs (elasticity)
- Automated creation of new virtual machines or deletion of existing ones
- Resource usage billed only as used (pay-as-you-go model)

From the performance testing perspective, cloud computing will make performance testing harder than usual. This is not because of elasticity as it could be disabled during performance testing (since we are not aiming to test the cloud elasticity but we are testing the application), but because of the unstable nature of the cloud's results in a cloud environment, which is based on virtual machines, we can't guarantee any of the hardware results. One of the most interesting findings we will face when testing in a cloud environment is the I/O operation speed instability, which causes the results to vary.

The best solution is either to have a dedicated non-shared box for performance testing or have multiple executions and take the average of all these tests, or do some sort of calibration prior to each test of the known results and consider the proportion between the calibrated results and the performance results.

Starting with Apache JMeter

Apache JMeter is one of the best open source solutions in doing performance testing. Apache JMeter is an open source desktop application written in Java and is designed to load test functional behavior and measure the performance of an application. Originally, it was designed to test web applications but, it later expanded to perform other test functions.

It can be used to load and performance test many different server/protocol types, as follows:

- Web—HTTP and HTTPS
- SOAP
- FTP
- Database via JDBC
- LDAP
- **Message-Oriented Middleware** (**MOM**) via JMS
- Mail—SMTP(s), POP3(s), and IMAP(s)
- Native commands or shell scripts
- TCP

We need to download and install Apache JMeter to create performance testing test plans in this section.

 To download Apache JMeter, go to `https://jmeter.apache.org/download_jmeter.cgi`.

Using Apache JMeter to build the performance test plan is straightforward. The following simple steps are required to create the test plan:

- Create a thread group, which represents the number of concurrent users with different iterations
- Add test samplers according to our testing component, HTTP component, web service, JDBC script, and so on
- Add the required configurations and testing data
- Add result listeners so that we can get the test results

To test a web application, we use the recording capability in JMeter to capture the scenario in a simple way. This recording can happen by routing the traffic from the browsers into a recording server/proxy that captures the user requests when performing the scenario in the web application; then we use the captured scenarios as performance testing scripts.

Different components of the JMeter test plan

In JMeter, building a test plan is easy once we understand the role of each of the testing components. The following are the main components of JMeter:

- **Thread groups (users)**: This component organizes threads of execution. All the elements that are below this component will be executed according to its configurations. Its configuration elements include the total number of threads (users), the ramp-up period, and the number of test executions. We can have many different thread groups with different configurations according to the needs of our test plan.

- **Request samplers**: This component sends the request to the server and waits for the response. It can send any of the following requests (the list doesn't include all supported types):
    - FTP
    - HTTP
    - JDBC
    - Java object
    - JMS
    - LDAP
    - SOAP/XML-RPC
    - SMTP sampler

    It is obvious from the names that the testing target of each of the preceding samplers, for example, JDBC request, aims to test the database script performance.

- **Logical controllers**: This component controls the flow of the test plan (loops, conditions, ordering, and so on).

- **Listeners (test results)**: This component records, summarizes, and displays request and response data. All the listeners save the same data but they differ in the way they display the results, for example, the following:
  - Simple data writer
  - BeanShell/BSF listener
  - Mail visualizer
  - Results monitor
  - Summary report
  - Aggregate report
  - Aggregate graph
  - Distribution graph

- **Configuration element**: This component includes a lot of configuration elements, such as loading data from a file or configuring default values for different elements.

  In particular, we will deal with the following two types of components, which are of special importance:

  - **CSV dataset config**: This is used to load different test data into variables so that we can customize the test scripts.

Comma-Separated Values (CSV)

These are also called **Character-Separated Values** because the separator character does not have to be a comma. It is a plain text file, which consists of a number of records, separated by line breaks and each record consists of fields, separated by a character or string, most commonly a literal comma or tab. To know more about CSVs, you can go to http://www.ietf.org/rfc/rfc4180.txt.

  - **HTTP cookie manager**: This is used to manage the cookies; we will use it to store the cookies and sessions in a test scenario for each thread/user.

A **cookie manager** should be added to all web tests; otherwise, JMeter will ignore cookies and session tracking by cookies. By adding it at the **Thread Group** level, we ensure that all HTTP requests share the same cookies/session. We will see this component in our web application testing plan example.

- **Test fragments**: This is a special type of controller that exists on the **Test Plan** tree (at the same level as the **Thread Group** element). It is distinguished from a **Thread Group** element in the sense that it is not executed unless it is referenced by either a **Module Controller** or an **Include Controller** element.

- **Test timers**: This introduces delays in the test plan. We will use the **Gaussian Random Timer** element to add random thinking time to each page.

- **Assertion elements**: This asserts facts about responses. For functional testing, it is very useful to ensure that the response is correct. For example, when we need to ensure that our online order is submitted by checking the success message.

- **Preprocessors and postprocessors**: This is used when we need to execute something around (before or after) the execution of any request sampler.

The execution order of components

The elements mentioned in the preceding section are executed in the following order:

- Configuration elements
- Preprocessors
- Timers
- Samplers
- Postprocessors (unless `SampleResult` is null)
- Assertions (unless `SampleResult` is null)
- Listeners (unless `SampleResult` is null)

Testing with JMeter

Now, let's try to use JMeter to execute our performance testing. We will try the following three kinds of performance testing:

- Web services
- Web application
- JDBC

Using JMeter to test web services

In this example, we will have one web service that authenticates users based on their username and password, and returns true/false according to this. It is a stateless session bean.

The following is the code snippet for the ExampleWebService class:

```
@WebService(serviceName = "ExampleWebService")
@Stateless()
public class ExampleWebService {
  @EJB(beanName = "DataHelperSessionBean")
  DataHelperSessionBean dataHelperSessionBean;

  @WebMethod(operationName = "authenticateUser")
  public boolean authenticateUser(@WebParam(name = "username")
    String username,@WebParam(name = "password") String password)
    {
    return dataHelperSessionBean.authenticateUser(username,
      password);
  }
}
```

The following is the code snippet for DataHelperSessionBean that deals with JPA to retrieve any required data from the JPA layer:

```
@PersistenceContext(unitName = "ExampleOnePU")
EntityManager em;
public boolean authenticateUser(String username, String password) {
  Query query = em.createQuery("SELECT a FROM Account a WHERE
    a.username = :username AND a.password = :password AND a.active
    = 0", Account.class);
  query.setParameter("username", username);
  query.setParameter("password", password);
  List<Account> results = query.getResultList();
  try {
    //random wait to have some performance results
    Thread.sleep(ThreadLocalRandom.current().nextInt(500));
  } catch (InterruptedException ex) {
  }
  if (results != null && results.size() > 0) {
    return true;
  }
  return false;
}
```

In the method of the preceding code snippet, we used JPA to query the database to check the existence of the username and password combination. We have defined the `testone` schema in the MySQL database that holds our own test tables: `account` and `user_role`. The following screenshot shows the structure of the `account` table:

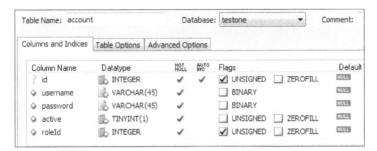

We have added three rows in this table where the username is similar to the password (`osama`, `duke`, and `judy`) so that we can use these users in our test script. The following table shows the populated test data in this table:

id	username	password	active	roleId
1001	osama	osama	0	1
1002	duke	duke	0	2
1003	judy	judy	0	3

The following table shows the test data in the `user_role` table:

Id	role_name
1	customer
2	admin
3	operator
4	superadmin

You need to download the project from `http://www.packtpub.com/`. It includes both the NetBeans project and MySql database schema.

To run the application, you will need to install the required software: Netbeans 7.4 and MySQL 5.5 (and above).

You can also use any other database vendor such as Oracle XE and create the required tables and then create the JPA layer using the NetBeans create JPA wizard.

After starting the application server and successfully deploying the application, right-click on the `ExampleWebService` web services icon and choose **Test Web Service**, as shown in the following screenshot:

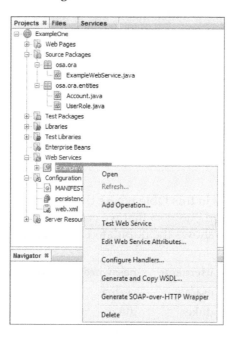

The following URL will open in our browser: `http://localhost:8080/ExampleWebService/ExampleWebService?Tester`.

Here, you can enter the username and password and try the web service operation. Try to enter `osama/osama`. You will get `true` if everything is okay, as shown in the following screenshot:

On the results page, we will see the following response:

```
Method returned
boolean : "true"

SOAP Request

<?xml version="1.0" encoding="UTF-8"?><S:Envelope
   xmlns:S="http://schemas.xmlsoap.org/soap/envelope/" xmlns:SOAP-
   ENV="http://schemas.xmlsoap.org/soap/envelope/"><SOAP-
   ENV:Header/>
   <S:Body>
     <ns2:authenticateUser xmlns:ns2="http://ora.osa/">
       <username>osama</username>
       <password>osama</password>
     </ns2:authenticateUser>
   </S:Body>
</S:Envelope>

SOAP Response

<?xml version="1.0" encoding="UTF-8"?><S:Envelope
   xmlns:S="http://schemas.xmlsoap.org/soap/envelope/" xmlns:SOAP-
   ENV="http://schemas.xmlsoap.org/soap/envelope/"><SOAP-
   ENV:Header/>
   <S:Body>
     <ns2:authenticateUserResponse xmlns:ns2="http://ora.osa/">
       <return>true</return>
     </ns2:authenticateUserResponse>
   </S:Body>
</S:Envelope>
```

We need to capture this SOAP request to use it to test our web service using JMeter.

Now open JMeter (Version 2.10 or later) using the following commands:

```
apache-jmeter-2.10\bin\jmeter.bat (for windows)
Or jmeter.sh (for non-windows)
```

We have discussed the different components that are available in JMeter. We will now use these different components to construct our test plan. Our target test plan will look like the following screenshot:

We will define a parent thread group where we can add the SOAP sampler and different listeners to it in order to show our results in either request/response.

Creating a thread group

While we select **Test Plan**, right-click on it and navigate to **Add | Threads (Users) | Thread Group**.

Now we have created the **Thread Group** element; we can rename it to Load Testing WS and specify the number of users as 100, ramp-up time as 10 seconds, and set the loop/iteration count to 2.

Creating the SOAP sampler

Selecting the thread group we just created, right-click on it and navigate to **Add | Sampler | SOAP/XML-RPC Request**.

We can rename it to Authenticate WS; we now need to add the following details:

- URL (web service endpoint) as http://localhost:8080/ ExampleWebService/ExampleWebService

- SOAP/XML-RPC (SOAP response) as the following:

  ```
  <?xml version="1.0" encoding="UTF-8"?><S:Envelope
    xmlns:S="http://schemas.xmlsoap.org/soap/envelope/"
    xmlns:SOAP-ENV="http://schemas.xmlsoap.org
    /soap/envelope/"><SOAP-ENV:Header/>
    <S:Body>
  ```

```
      <ns2:authenticateUser xmlns:ns2="http://ora.osa/">
        <username>osama</username>
        <password>osama</password>
      </ns2:authenticateUser>
    </S:Body>
  </S:Envelope>
```

This is the SOAP request that we have captured from the test web service page. For now, we can see that the username and password are hardcoded. This means that all the threads will use the same username and password values. We will fix this later.

Creating listeners

Adding a listener is simple as well. Select the **Thread Group** element, right-click on it, and navigate to **Add | Listener | View Result Tree**.

We can name it View Results Tree [authenticate results].

Now, we can execute our created test case by choosing **Run** from the start menu or clicking on the green arrow.

JMeter will show an alert to save the project first; save it to proceed.

If we open the listener during the test execution, we will see that the results are continuously added. If we select one of the results, we can see the request and response data.

If everything is correct, then all the executions will be successfully completed.

Now, try to modify the SOAP request that we have added and change the username or password to an invalid username/password like Kenzy/Kenzy and re-execute the test. What did we discover?

All the execution still shows the successful green results. If we tried to select one of these results to check the response, we will see false as shown in the following code:

```
<?xml version='1.0' encoding='UTF-8'?><S:Envelope
  xmlns:S="http://schemas.xmlsoap.org/soap/envelope
  /"><S:Body><ns2:authenticateUserResponse
  xmlns:ns2="http://ora.osa/"><return>false
  </return></ns2:authenticateUserResponse></S:Body></S:Envelope>
```

This is the correct behavior because we didn't tell JMeter exactly what we are testing, hence the web service is responding successfully, and so JMeter considered this as a successful execution.

Now, let's try to fix this issue by adding an assertion on our response.

Adding an assertion on response

Go back to **Thread Group**, select it, and navigate to **Add | Assertions | Response Assertion**.

We can name it `Assert successful authentication`; we can also add it for more accuracy under the **SOAP sampler** element.

In **Pattern matching rules**, select **contains**, click on the **Add** button, and add the following text:

```
<return>true</return>
```

If we re-execute the test now, all the results will be shown as failed. This is because we have informed JMeter to examine the response if it contains `<return>true</return>`, then consider it as successful, otherwise consider it as unsuccessful.

Now let's fix the remaining issue in this test, which is the hardcoded values in our SOAP request.

Adding the CSV dataset configuration

We need to create a CSV file named, for example, `testusers.csv` with the following content:

```
osama,osama
duke,duke
test,test
judy,judy
kenzy,kenzy
```

This is the file that we will use to get the username and password combinations to use in our SOAP requests. We will perform the following steps to add the CSV dataset configuration:

1. Select the **Thread Group** element, right-click on it, and navigate to **Add | Config Element | CSV Data Set Config**.

2. Name it `CSV Users Data Set Config`.

3. In the `filename` field, enter the full path of the filename such as `c:\testusers.csv`.

4. In the `Variable Names` field, insert `USERNAME, PASSWORD` similar to the order of values in our file.

   We can exclusively use the preceding information for all thread groups or for this thread group only.

5. Now, go to the SOAP sampler and edit the SOAP request to let it use the `USERNAME` and `PASSWORD` variables, as follows:

```
<?xml version="1.0" encoding="UTF-8"?><S:Envelope
  xmlns:S="http://schemas.xmlsoap.org/soap/envelope/"
  xmlns:SOAP-ENV="http://schemas.xmlsoap.org/soap
  /envelope/"><SOAP-ENV:Header/>
  <S:Body>
    <ns2:authenticateUser xmlns:ns2="http://ora.osa/">
      <username>${USERNAME}</username>
      <password>${PASSWORD}</password>
    </ns2:authenticateUser>
  </S:Body>
</S:Envelope>
```

 Any spaces included while defining or using the variables will cause the test to not run successfully.

6. Now re-execute the test and notice the difference in the results. If we check the results in detail, we will see that the HTTP requests uses all the usernames and passwords that are specified in the `c:\testusers.csv` file. We can also see that some of them have succeeded and some of them have failed according to the username/password combinations used.

We now need to add an aggregated result component to our test plan so that we can get the aggregated test results. It is added like other components — select the **Thread Group** element and navigate to **Add** | **Listener** | **Aggregate Report and Aggregate Graph**.

Now, edit the **Thread Group** element and increase the thread count by `300` and loops to `3` loops, save the project, and reset it to clean all the previous results.

Getting the final results

Execute the test plan now so that we can get the final test results. The **Aggregate Report** in our case should be similar to the results shown in the following screenshot (results in milliseconds):

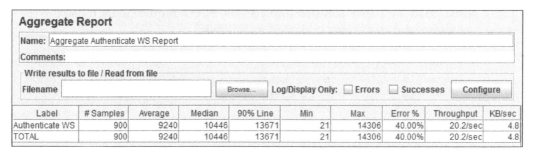

Label	# Samples	Average	Median	90% Line	Min	Max	Error %	Throughput	KB/sec
Authenticate WS	900	9240	10446	13671	21	14306	40.00%	20.2/sec	4.8
TOTAL	900	9240	10446	13671	21	14306	40.00%	20.2/sec	4.8

The total samples are 900 because we have configured our thread group by 300 threads/users in 3 loops/iterations. The report shows the **Min, Max, Average, Median**, and **90% Line** values of the aggregated application response times. The most important value is the **90% Line** or 90th percentile, which represents the response of 90 percent of the sent requests.

The report also shows the percentage of errors. We know errors can either be actual errors/exceptions or our assertion to the returned value (**40%** represents the percentage of invalid users in our excel sheet), so we can consider the test case as passed since the results match our expectations (60 percent success and 40 percent failed).

The final important value here is **Throughput**, which shows the number of processed web service requests per second. In our results, it processes 19.1 requests per second either successfully or unsuccessfully.

We can open the aggregated graph, select what we need to show, and click on **Display Graph** to show the results in a graphical representation. The following graph is a sample of our graphical output showing all the different response time types (**Average, Median, 90% Line, Min**, and **Max**):

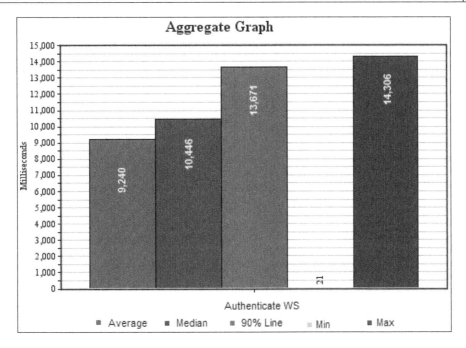

Using JMeter to test a web application

Now, we will use JMeter to test a web application. We will use the same project to log in to our application using login.jsp and give the user the ability to change the user role. If successful, then the confirmation page will show a confirmation message; otherwise, an error page will be displayed. Our simple application flow is illustrated in the following diagram:

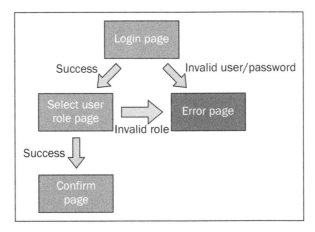

Recording our testing scenarios

Recording our testing scenarios using JMeter is the first and most essential part we need to learn in this section. For this, we can use the recording template by navigating to **File | Templates** and picking up the **Recording Templates**.

Recording depends on configuring the proxy settings in the browser to route the traffic first to JMeter where JMeter picks up the request, routes it back to the server, and the server responds back to JMeter, which in turn picks up the response and routes it back to the browser.

So, we need to change the browser's proxy settings to `localhost` (as we are using JMeter on the same machine) and port to `8888`, and uncheck any selected checkbox to exclude the traffic for `localhost` from passing through this proxy if JMeter is running on the same machine.

The final test plan will look like the following screenshot:

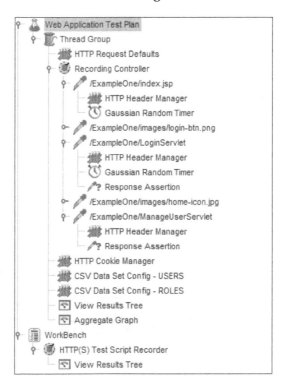

We can see the three pages of our application: `index.jsp`, `loginServlet`, and `ManageUserServlet`, and some new components such as **Gaussian Random Time** (to simulate user thinking time), and also a newly configured user role's CSV file.

Let's perform the following things together to understand what is required to execute web application performance testing.

 If a JAVA_HOME variable is not in your path, you need to add it since JMeter uses a keytool utility in JRE and JDK. So, for example, if you are using Windows, you can either add this to your system variables, or in jmeter.bat, add the following two lines to the beginning of the file:

```
set JAVA_HOME=java path
set PATH=%JAVA_HOME%\bin;%PATH%
```

Creating thread groups

Add it to our test plan similar to what we did earlier.

Creating a configuration element

We will add some configuration items as generic components in our test plan to use them while recording our test plan. For this, navigate to **Add | Config element | HTTP Request Defaults**. This step is required if we have a proxy on our network. We need to configure the proxy IP, port, username, and password in the proxy settings section.

Creating a recording controller

A recording controller is the element in which all the recorded resources will be placed (we will configure it in the coming steps). For this, navigate to **Add | Logic Controller | Recording Controller**. Nothing needs to be changed here, but we can rename it if we want.

Creating a workbench server (HTTP(s) Test Script Recorder)

Select **Workbench** and navigate to **Add | Non-test elements | HTTP(s) Test Script Recorder**.

In **Global Settings**, ensure that the port is 8888. Also, from the target controller dropdown, pick the recording controller that we created in the previous step so that all recorded scenarios are placed under this controller.

We can filter the pages that we need or filter out certain resources but we don't recommend doing this to simulate the correct live scenarios. So if we need to add a value, add .* to **URL Patterns to include**.

Pattern is specified in the following formats:

- . * is used to include all files
- . * \ . png is used to include PNG images

Add a listener to the **HTTP script recorder** element of type **View Result Tree** so that we can watch the request/response of our traffic once it gets captured by this recorder.

Now, before we can click on the **Start** button in **HTTP(s) Test Script Recorder**, save the test plan and update the browser settings (as we will explain in the following section).

Updating browser settings

According to our browser type, we need to change the proxy settings. The following screenshot shows you how to do this in a Firefox browser (portable Firefox v24.0):

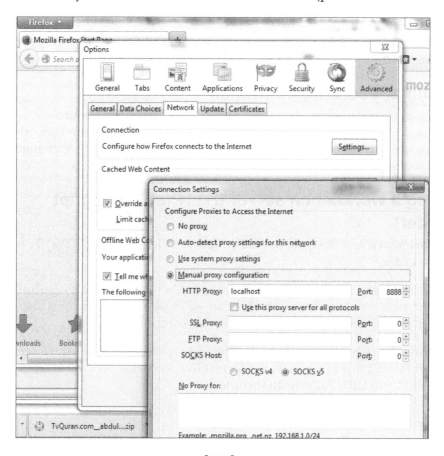

As shown in the preceding screenshot, from the **Advanced** settings, add the proxy we just created on localhost and port 8888, and remove localhost from the **No Proxy for:** box (because we have JMeter on the same machine).

To configure the proxy settings, similar steps can be performed when you are using other browsers, for example, in Internet Explorer, we can configure the settings by navigating to **Settings | Internet Options | Connections | LAN settings**, then setting localhost in **Proxy server**, unchecking the checkbox to bypass the proxy server for local addresses, and clicking on **OK**.

Start recording our journeys/scenarios

Now, go to the index.jsp page of our web application: http://localhost:8080/ ExampleOne/index.jsp.

Enter the username/password as osama/osama. The welcome page with user roles will be displayed; select a new user role and click on **Save**. Now, the confirmation page will be displayed; this ends our recording scenario.

If we go back to JMeter, we will see our requests and responses in **View Results Tree**; click on the **Stop** button to stop the recording.

The work is not finished yet. We now need to go to the recorded scenarios and make further modifications to have a good quality test plan.

Remember to change the proxy settings in your browser back to its original settings.

Adding cookie control

Add an HTTP cookie manager; this is important so that each user (thread) can have its own session during testing. To add this HTTP cookie manager, right-click on the **Thread Group** element and navigate to **Add | Config elements | Http Cookie Manager**.

Select the checkbox **Clear Cookies after each iteration** so that in the next user iteration, a new user session is created for each thread (that is, user) in our test.

Adding a CSV dataset

As we did earlier, we need to configure testusers.csv with the two variables: USERNAME and PASSWORD.

We also need to create `userrole.csv` and configure it with one variable `USER_ROLE`; the content of this file will look like the following code (representing all user role options):

```
1
2
3
4
```

In a CSV dataset, we will configure the filename and variable (that is, `USER_ROLE`) as shown in the following screenshot:

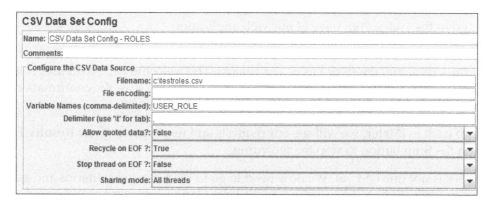

Adding variables to our requests

Now, select the **LoginServlet** option under **Recording Controller** and in the parameters section, change the values from `osama` to `${USERNAME}` for the username and `${PASSWORD}` for the password.

In the **ManageUserServlet** parameters sections, change the value of `user_role` parameter to `${USER_ROLE}`.

All the configured parameters will have the values loaded dynamically from our CSV files now.

Adding suitable thinking time

The next thing we need to do is add some sort of latency where users usually think before they submit the page. This will help the test to behave similar to human traffic, where users fill data in the form fields, such as username and password, or select the values from different options (for example, selects new user role in our application) after spending some time thinking.

While we select `index.jsp`, navigate to **Add | Timer | Gaussian Random Timer** and change the constant delay offset to `1,000`; repeat the same for **LoginServlet**.

Adding response assertions

Now, we need to tell JMeter when to consider the invocation of each page as a failure even if there is a response from the server. We can do this by adding an assertion to **LoginServlet** so that we have a **Welcome** message in response, which means that the user has successfully logged in to the home page.

Also, for **ManageUserServlet**, we need to assert the response to contain `<title>Update confirmation</title>`, which means that the selection of the new roles is successful.

Adding results view

We can add any results view we want to use, such as **View Results Tree**, **Aggregated Graph**, and **Response Time Graph**.

Executing our test plan and getting the results

Set threads as `500`, loops or iterations as `3`, ramp-up time as `10`, and execute the test. The following screenshot shows our execution results in a table representation:

Label	# Samples	Average	Median	90% Li..	Min	Max	Error %	Throughput	KB/sec
/ExampleOne/index.jsp	1500	6807	7152	12408	1	16358	0.00%	20.0/sec	34.1
/ExampleOne/images/login-btn.png	1500	2033	960	5216	0	16198	0.00%	19.9/sec	50.8
/ExampleOne/LoginServlet	1500	6891	6255	12512	29	16598	40.00%	16.7/sec	13.4
/ExampleOne/images/home-icon.jpg	1500	5861	5074	12048	0	16094	0.00%	16.3/sec	32.1
/ExampleOne/ManageUserServlet	1500	2238	1736	3843	1	16269	40.00%	16.2/sec	9.0

We can also get a graphical representation of our performance testing results, as shown in the following graph:

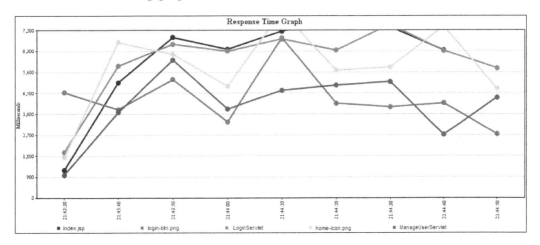

The response times of different transactions/pages in our application can be seen in the preceding graph. As we can see, transactional response time starts with good results during test ramp-up, moves to steady levels, and ends up with lower values during test ramp-down.

Using JMeter to test database scripts

In this section, we will show the steps needed to test database scripts; this is useful to test the performance of the database in response to this script's workload.

> Before we can continue in this section, we need to add a JDBC driver to JMeter's `lib` folder: `apache-jmeter-2.10\lib`.
>
> In our scenario, we are testing the MySQL query so we need the MySQL JDBC driver; we have to place the following JDBC JAR file in the `lib` folder of JMeter:
>
> `mysql-connector-java-5.1.23-bin.jar` (or any newer version)
>
> If you are using any other database, you need to add the corresponding JDBC driver in this `lib` folder before you continue with this section.

As usual, we need to add **Thread Group** to our **Test Plan** element and then continue with the following sections.

Configuring the JDBC connection

We can add it by right-clicking on **Thread Group** and then navigating to **Add | Config Element | JDBC Connection Configuration**.

We then need to fill in the following connection details:

- **Variable Name** as `testone_cp`
- **JDBC URL** as `jdbc:mysql://localhost:3306/testone`
- **JDBC Driver Class** as `com.mysql.jdbc.Driver`
- **Username** as `test`
- **Password** as `test`
- **Validation query** as `select curdate()`

We just performed a connection pooling to the MySQL database.

Adding a JDBC request sampler

A JDBC request sampler can be added by right-clicking on **Thread Group** and then navigating to **Add** | **Sampler** | **JDBC Request**.

We then need to fill in the following details:

- **Variable Name** as `testone_cp` (the exact name we used when defining the connection pool variable name)
- **Query Type** as `Prepared Select Statement`
- **Query** as `SELECT * FROM testone.account a where a.username = ?`
  `and a.password = ?`
- **Parameter Value** as `${USERNAME},${PASSWORD}`
- **Parameter Types** as `VARCHAR,VARCHAR`

We have just configured a prepared statement with two parameters, `username` and `password`, to simulate testing our application's login query.

Adding a CSV dataset configuration

Add a CSV dataset configuration (following the same steps we mentioned earlier) and load the `testusers.csv` file with two variables, `USERNAME` and `PASSWORD`, so that JMeter can send these values as bind parameters for this JDBC query.

Adding listeners to capture test results

Add **View Results Tree** and **Aggregate Graph** to capture the execution results and then execute the test thrice with 100 threads and with five seconds ramp-up. We will get results similar to the following screenshot:

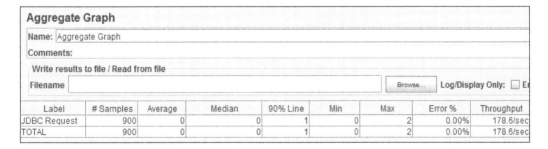

Label	# Samples	Average	Median	90% Line	Min	Max	Error %	Throughput
JDBC Request	900	0	0	1	0	2	0.00%	178.6/sec
TOTAL	900	0	0	1	0	2	0.00%	178.6/sec

As a final comment, we should mention here that JMeter doesn't execute the JavaScript code, so do not assume that you can catch any JavaScript issues using it. Instead, we will show you how to use the different available browser tools for that purpose in *Chapter 5, Recognizing Common Performance Issues*.

> 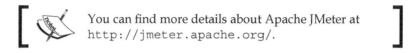 You can find more details about Apache JMeter at
> `http://jmeter.apache.org/`.

Summary

In this chapter, we covered some essential parts related to performance testing — concepts, tools, and some related topics. We didn't dig too much into testing concepts as this is not our intention. We also demonstrated building performance testing scripts using the Apache JMeter tool; we should now be capable of testing the performance of our application. We covered testing web services, web applications, and database scripts as samples of performance testing scripts.

We will use Apache JMeter throughout this book to create different test plans for our book examples, so it is better not to leave this chapter before mastering this useful tool.

In the next chapter, *Chapter 4, Monitoring Java Applications*, we will go through different Java monitoring tools including different Java profiling tools. The chapter will focus on operating system tools, JDK tools such as JConsole and Java Mission Control, IDE tools such as NetBeans and Eclipse, and third-party tools such as JProfiler. We will also cover offline profiling in detail using JProfiler.

Monitoring Java Applications

4

Monitoring tools can be used to monitor different layers in the application. In this chapter, we will go through the different monitoring tools and focus on the JDK tools and different IDE tools, such as NetBeans and Eclipse.

We will also cover JProfiler, which is an advanced third-party tool, with special attention to its offline profiling capability.

In this chapter, we will cover the following topics:

- The different monitoring tools
- The different Java profiling tools
- A brief overview of the JDK tools
- An overview of the NetBeans profiler
- The Eclipse plugin profilers
- An advanced profiler tool, JProfiler
- JProfiler in the offline profiling mode

 Special thanks to EJ Technologies for providing me with the required license of the latest version of JProfiler 8.x, so we could cover the full capabilities of this tool in this book.

Exploring the Java monitoring tools

In this chapter, we will focus on the different profiling/monitoring tools, how to run them, their capabilities, and a brief discussion on how to read the results. Later in this book, we will discuss in further detail the different interpretations of CPU, threading, and memory profiling results in *Chapter 6*, *CPU Time Profiling*, *Chapter 7*, *Thread Profiling*, and *Chapter 8*, *Memory Profiling*.

In the previous chapters, we highlighted the importance of having different monitoring tools in different application layers. We can classify such tools according to the operational level into two main categories, the operating system tools and the Java monitoring tools.

The operating system monitoring tools

The operating system monitoring tools function on the operating system level. They include tools that provide information about the processing power, memory, I/O, and network utilization.

These tools are mainly based on acquiring frequent samples of statistics at all times specified (sometimes configurable).

The Microsoft Windows tools

If we take Microsoft Windows as an example, we can use the Task Manager and retrieve useful data from this tool. The following is a screenshot of the MS Windows 7 Task Manager:

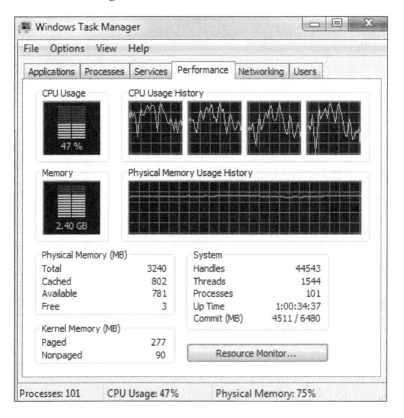

Click on **Resource Monitor...** to launch the **Resource Monitor**. This is used to monitor resources during a specified period and gives more information compared to the Task Manager. We can stop it when we need to take a snapshot of the current monitoring results; it can also be invoked using the following command line:

```
C:\resmon
```

We get the following detailed CPU utilizations, disk speed, network utilization, and memory consumptions by different applications (processes):

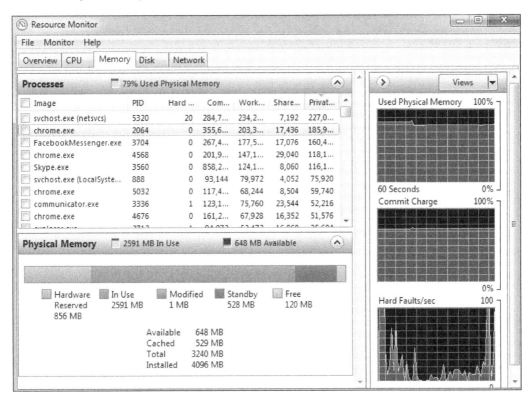

Different command-line tools can also be used to retrieve various machine statistics, for example, execute `netstat` (as shown in the following command) with different options to monitor the network traffic, used ports, and so on:

```
C:\>netstat
```

```
Active Connections
```

Protocol	Local Address	Foreign Address	State
TCP	10.15.112.42:54792	157.55.130.155:40004	ESTABLISHED
TCP	10.15.112.42:54796	db3msgr6011010:https	ESTABLISHED

```
TCP     10.15.112.42:54797      157.55.133.138:12350    ESTABLISHED
TCP     10.15.112.42:54798      owa:https               ESTABLISHED
..
```

Another powerful command-line utility is `Typeperf`, used to get performance counter results. This command-line tool is very useful as it can print the performance output to either the command prompt or a file for better analysis. The general syntax of this command is as follows:

```
Typeperf [Path [path ...]] [-cf FileName] [-f {csv|tsv|bin}] [-si
interval] [-o FileName] [-q [object]] [-qx [object]] [-sc samples]
[-config FileName] [-s computer_name]
```

The parameters in the preceding syntax are explained as follows:

- `-c { Path [ path ... ] | -cf    FileName }`: This parameter specifies the performance counter path to the log. To add multiple counter paths, separate them with spaces.

- `-cf FileName`: This parameter specifies the filename of counter paths we need to monitor (one per line).

- `-f {csv|tsv|bin}`: This parameter specifies the output file format. We can use either `csv` (default), `tsv` (tab delimited), or `bin` (binary).

- `-si interval [ mm: ] ss`: This parameter specifies the time interval between each sample.

- `-o FileName`: This parameter specifies the path of the output file.

- `-q [object]`: This parameter shows all available counters for the specified object. (If there's no name, it will show for all.)

- `-qx [object]`: This parameter shows all the available counters with instances for the specified object. (If there's no name, it will show for all.)

- `-sc samples`: This parameter specifies the number of samples to collect. (By default, it will continue to do so until you press *Ctrl + C*.)

- `-config FileName`: This parameter specifies the path of the settings file that contains the command-line parameters.

- `-s computer_name`: This parameter specifies the system to monitor if no server is specified in the counter path.

For example, to get the memory and process counter details, refer to the following command (the output shows the timestamp, the total available memory in bytes, and the total processing power):

```
C:\>typeperf "\Memory\Available bytes" "\processor(_total)\%processor
time"
"(PDH-CSV 4.0)","\\Computer_name\Memory\Available bytes","\\ Computer_
name\processor(_total)\
% processor time"
"11/07/2013 22:35:49.059","1018003456.000000","4.256353"
"11/07/2013 22:35:50.061","1017634816.000000","15.154014"
"11/07/2013 22:35:51.063","1017683968.000000","4.645563"
"11/07/2013 22:35:52.065","1017683968.000000","5.813161"
The command completed successfully.
```

To get the list of available counters of an object, we can execute the -q option, as shown in the following command:

```
C:\>typeperf -q "\Processor"
\Processor(*)\% Processor Time
\Processor(*)\% User Time
\Processor(*)\% Privileged Time
\Processor(*)\Interrupts/sec
\Processor(*)\% DPC Time
\Processor(*)\% Interrupt Time
\Processor(*)\DPCs Queued/sec
\Processor(*)\DPC Rate
\Processor(*)\% Idle Time
\Processor(*)\% C1 Time
\Processor(*)\% C2 Time
\Processor(*)\C1 Transitions/sec
\Processor(*)\C2 Transitions/sec
The command completed successfully.
```

 Performance counters provide information on how well the operating system, applications, services, or drivers, and so on are performing. The counter data will help to determine the system's bottlenecks and provide guidance on how to fine-tune the system and application performance.

The Unix/Linux tools

A Unix-based operating system has many tools that can be used to get system performance counters as follows:

- `ps/pgrep/pstree`: This command is useful to list the processes and give details about any process

- `top`: This command shows the actual process activities, and by default, it lists the top active processes

- `vmstat`: This command provides information about memory, processes, I/O, and the CPU

- `iostat`: This command shows the average CPU time since the system started and creates a report of the activities, including CPU and disk utilization

- `sar`: This command is used to collect and save system activity information

- `tcpdump`: This command is used to get information about the current network traffic

 To get a detailed description of these tools, use the `man` command to display the comprehensive manual pages for the required command, for example, `man ps`.

An example of high CPU utilization

Let's take an example that consumes the CPU power and checks the reflection on the monitoring tools at the operating system level.

The following code is the Java code of our sample application:

```java
public class HighCPU {
  public static void main(String[] args) {
    ExecutorService execSvc = Executors.newFixedThreadPool(40);
    for (int i = 0; i < 1000; i++) {
      execSvc.execute(new MyThread());
    }
    while (!execSvc.isTerminated()) {
      try {
        Thread.sleep(500);
      } catch (InterruptedException ex) {}
      execSvc.shutdown();
    }
  }
}
```

```
class MyThread implements Runnable {
  @Override
  public void run() {
    int arraySize = 200000;
    int[] bigArray = new int[arraySize];
    for (int i = 0; i < arraySize; i++) {
      bigArray[i] = ThreadLocalRandom.current().nextInt(50000);
    }
    Arrays.sort(bigArray);
    System.out.println("finished!");
  }
}
```

The preceding code creates 1,000 different threads with a maximum of 40 concurrent threads (thread pool size). Each thread creates 200,000 random numbers in an array, and then sorts the array numbers.

When we execute this program, we get the results using **Resource Monitor**. As we can see in the following screenshot, the CPU utilization jumps to 100 percent in all cores with one Java process, which consumes the biggest share of 74 percent in the **Average CPU Utilization** column:

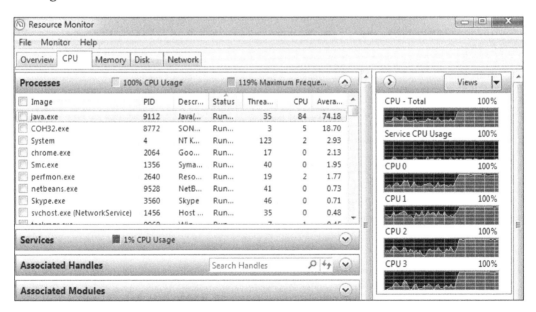

We can use the `typeperf` command to get similar results for the CPU utilization (The results are filtered to show the selected four results. It was 43 percent before the execution of our program, 100 percent in middle of the execution, and 25 percent after the end of the execution CPU utilization). The following command results in the display of each processor utilization and the total utilization in the last column in each timestamp row:

```
C:\>typeperf "\Processor(*)\% Processor Time"
```

```
"(PDH-CSV 4.0)","\\Computer_name\Processor(0)\% Processor Time","\\
COMPUTER_NAME\Processor(1
)\% Processor Time","\\COMPUTER_NAME\Processor(2)\% Processor Time","\\
COMPUTER_NAME\Process
or(3)\% Processor Time","\\COMPUTER_NAME\Processor(_Total)\% Processor
Time"
"11/09/2013 22:12:46.824","54.852592","50.182170","47.068556","23.716448"
,"43.954941"
"11/09/2013 22:12:53.844","98.470666","90.823996","80.118658","81.647992"
,"87.765328"
"11/09/2013 22:12:55.884","100.000000","100.000000","100.000000","100.000
000","100.000000"
"11/09/2013 22:13:10.888","40.723011","54.762298","7.964674","0.165071","
25.903758"
The command completed successfully.
```

To dump such results into a CSV file for better data manipulations, we can use the following command with the -o filename option instead:

```
C:\>typeperf "\Processor(*)\% Processor Time" -o c:\results.csv
```

If we execute the same Java application on Linux (Ubuntu 10.04.3) and the `top` command to monitor the resource utilization, we can get results similar to the following screenshot (our application consumes around 99.4 percent of the CPU power and 5.8 percent of the memory):

```
top - 16:12:58 up  1:42,   3 users,  load average: 26.27, 11.26, 4.30
Tasks: 141 total,   3 running, 138 sleeping,   0 stopped,   0 zombie
Cpu(s): 67.3%us, 31.8%sy,  0.0%ni,  0.0%id,  0.0%wa,  0.6%hi,  0.3%si,  0.0%st
Mem:   1567360k total,  1242496k used,   324864k free,    64868k buffers
Swap:   407544k total,        0k used,   407544k free,   850244k cached

  PID USER      PR  NI  VIRT  RES  SHR S %CPU %MEM    TIME+  COMMAND
 5403 osama     20   0  641m  88m 6356 S 99.4  5.8  0:51.88 java
 5011 osama     20   0  326m  70m  30m S  4.7  4.6  1:01.16 firefox-bin
 1085 root      20   0 48424  24m 9296 S  2.2  1.6  0:34.49 Xorg
 4756 osama     20   0 45276  12m 9908 S  0.9  0.8  0:03.84 gnome-terminal
    6 root      20   0     0    0    0 S  0.3  0.0  0:00.25 events/0
 5477 osama     20   0  2548 1216  924 R  0.3  0.1  0:00.03 top
    1 root      20   0  2804 1640 1200 S  0.0  0.1  0:00.19 init
    2 root      20   0     0    0    0 S  0.0  0.0  0:00.00 kthreadd
    3 root      RT   0     0    0    0 S  0.0  0.0  0:00.00 migration/0
    4 root      20   0     0    0    0 S  0.0  0.0  0:00.03 ksoftirqd/0
    5 root      RT   0     0    0    0 S  0.0  0.0  0:00.00 watchdog/0
    7 root      20   0     0    0    0 S  0.0  0.0  0:00.00 cpuset
    8 root      20   0     0    0    0 S  0.0  0.0  0:00.00 khelper
    9 root      20   0     0    0    0 S  0.0  0.0  0:00.00 async/mgr
   10 root      20   0     0    0    0 S  0.0  0.0  0:00.00 pm
   11 root      20   0     0    0    0 S  0.0  0.0  0:00.00 sync_supers
   12 root      20   0     0    0    0 S  0.0  0.0  0:00.00 bdi-default
```

The aim here is to detect the odd utilization by different tools, and as we clarified before, having high processor utilization doesn't necessary mean wrong findings. But in general, the web applications' processing utilization should be low as per the user transactions because it serves the customers' requests and waits for a reasonable time till the customers invoke subsequent requests. The possible reasons for high processing utilization can be bad logic that consumes unnecessary processing power or inappropriate processor power that is less than the application's needs, incorrect capacity planning, bugs that cause the application to use redundant processing, even excessive useless loops, and so on.

Our target when we tune the performance of Java applications is to maximize the utilization of the high processing power of the servers. The web applications have low processing utilization by nature. One of our strategies is to use asynchronous components that execute some tasks behind the scene instead of blocking the users until finishing such processing tasks.

The Java monitoring tools

The Java monitoring tools are used in JVM monitoring. They show important application details such as memory statistics, time spent by an application method, and different threads status. We can further classify these tools.

The JDK monitoring tools

The JDK monitoring tools include a lot of useful tools such as `jconsole`, `jmap`, `jhat`, `jstat`, `jvisualvm`, and Oracle **Java Mission Control (jmc)**.

We will explore all these tools in the *Understanding different JDK tools* section in details.

The monitoring tools for application servers

Each application server comes with different monitoring capabilities that help monitor the running applications.

For example, if we open the Oracle GlassFish Version 4, we see a lot of monitoring components/resources in the server monitoring, where we can specify the required monitoring level. The following screenshot shows these components (from the GlassFish admin console, select **Monitoring Data** and then **Configure Monitoring**):

Select	Module	Monitoring Level
☐	Web Container	OFF ▾
☐	Thread Pool	OFF ▾
☐	Jersey(RESTful Web Services)	OFF ▾
☐	Jms Service	OFF ▾
☐	Web Services Container	OFF ▾
☐	Java Persistence	OFF ▾
☐	Transaction Service	OFF ▾
☐	Jvm	OFF ▾
☐	Security	OFF ▾
☐	Jdbc Connection Pool	OFF ▾
☐	ORB (Object Request Broker)	OFF ▾
☐	Connector Connection Pool	OFF ▾
☐	Ejb Container	OFF ▾
☐	Deployment	OFF ▾
☐	Connector Service	OFF ▾
☐	Http Service	OFF ▾
		OFF
		LOW
		HIGH

We will cover GlassFish monitoring and tuning in detail in *Chapter 9, Tuning an Application's Environment*.

The IDE monitoring tools

Most of the Java IDEs either include a tool to profile the Java application or support the plugin installation of similar tools. For example, we can download Eclipse plugins, such as the TPTP, JVM monitor, and Memory Analyzer.

Some third-party utilities that run as standalone tools can also integrate with different IDEs. For example, JProfiler can integrate with different versions of NetBeans, JDeveloper, Eclipse, and IntelliJ IDEA.

We will pick up two examples, NetBeans Profiler and Eclipse profiling plugins, and cover them as samples of these tools.

The standalone monitoring tools

The standalone monitoring tools include a lot of third-party utilities. Some examples of these tools are AppDynamics, JBossProfiler, JProbe and JProfiler, and so on.

We will pick JProfiler as an example of this group and discuss it in more detail.

The multifunction monitoring tools

The multifunction monitoring tools are configurable tools that can monitor the environment, application server, different resources, virtual machine, and so on via different available matrices. They also send different alerts, and the best examples for these tools are Intel Foglight, Hyperic HQ, HP SiteScope, and so on.

Understanding the profiling tools

Profilers are the tools that allow us to get dynamic information and monitor our executing program. The main difference between monitoring tools and profilers is the level of detail that can be provided.

Monitoring tools provide high-level information. On the other hand, profilers provide very low-level detail, so it can catch the HotSpot areas more efficiently and point to a single programming statement.

Also, the monitoring tools, as the name suggests, merely inspect the application's performance, while profiling tools are usually much more advanced and can go the extra mile to instrument or probe the application. So it can evaluate each part of the application and point to the underperforming areas, that is, the HotSpot areas.

All tools can be monitoring tools, but not all can be profiler tools.

Profilers modes

Profilers can work on many different strategies, such as event based, instrumental based, and sampling (statistical) as follows:

- **Event based**: In event based, the profiler captures the application's events. The events represent the methods' calls, class loading, thread changes, and so on.

- **Instrumental based**: This method instruments the application with additional instructions to gather more information. This causes the highest impact on the application's execution time compared to the other types.

- **Sampling based (statistical)**: This method probes the target program's counter at regular intervals using operating system interrupts. Sampling profiles are less accurate but give the nearest normal execution time of the target application.

So while working with profilers, if we select the instrumental type, we need to focus on the relativity of the time spent in each method, rather than the actual spent time. But in the sampling mode, we can consider the method execution time, keeping in mind that the results might not be fully accurate as they are statistically based.

JVM TI

Java profilers were initially built using the **Java Virtual Machine Profiler Interface (JVMPI)** and the **Java Virtual Machine Debug Interface (JVMDI)**. Both the interfaces are deprecated and no longer provided since Java JDK 6; both are replaced by **JVM Tool Interface (JVM TI)** in JDK 5.0.

This standard native programming interface enables different tools to inspect the state and control the execution of any application running inside the JVM. It can be used for the tools that monitor, profile, or even debug the Java applications.

Profiler agent

A profiler agent can be developed using any native language that supports C language-calling conventions and C/C++ definitions.

For the agent to start at virtual machine startup, specify the name of the agent library using a command-line option. Implementations might support a mechanism to start agents while the JVM is in the live phase (already running).

The command-line options

We can use one of the two following JVM command-line options to load and run agents and pass any options to the agent in these commands (We will see an example of passing the port number or running mode as parameters later in this chapter.):

```
-agentlib:<agent-lib-name>=<options>
```

```
-agentpath:<path-to-agent>=<options>
```

Agent start-up

The JVM starts each agent by invoking a `start-up()` function that is implemented by the agent. The two possible scenarios are if the agent is started in the loading phase, the JVM will invoke the `Agent_OnLoad()` function; however, if it is started in the live phase, the JVM will invoke the `Agent_OnAttach()` function.

Different profiling patterns

We can classify the profile patterns according to many aspects as follows:

- **Sampling versus instrumental**: This classification is based on how the profiler is used, as described earlier.

- **Attach versus start for profiling**: This classification is based on the time of using the profiling agent either during the JVM startup or by attaching it later.

- **Local versus remote**: This classification considers the location of the profiled application to the profiler tool location if it is in the same machine or other remote machines.

- **Filtered versus non-filtered classes**: This classification is based on whether the profiler will get the results for all classes or it will filter in/out some of these classes.

- **Online versus offline**: This classification is based on whether the profiler is used in an attended or unattended manner. In the offline mode, the profiler results are stored automatically (usually by triggers) in the snapshot files, where they can be used later by the profiler tool for analysis.

- **Web server versus standalone**: This classification is based on whether the application type profiles a web or standalone application. There is no major difference between both, but usually, profiling the web application will need some changes in the server startup scripts to add the profiler instructions.

What we need to know from this section

To summarize what we need to understand from this section, we have different types of profilers methodologies — event based, statistical, and instrumental — and in Java, we have JVM TI to develop profilers. The profiler agents use the JVM parameters to be configured (`-agentpath` or `-agentlib`) and can be used either during the JVM startup or later during runtime (attached); however, some data may not be available in this case. Finally, there are a lot of different patterns to use the profilers.

 For more information about JVM TI, refer to the Oracle documentation at `http://docs.oracle.com/javase/7/docs/platform/jvmti/jvmti.html`.

Understanding the different JDK tools

If we examine the different tools that come with the JDK to monitor Java applications, we see that these tools vary from powerful profiler tools to lightweight specific command-line tools. In this section, we will go through these tools in detail to pick the best-suited tool for whenever we need certain data of our application. As per the Oracle documentation, apart from JConsole utility, all the other tools are experimental in nature, so they should be used keeping this in mind. They may be removed from the JDK in future JDK versions.

These tools can be classified as follows:

- **Monitoring tools**: `jps`, `jstat`, and `jstatd`
- **Troubleshooting tools**: `jinfo`, `jmap`, `jhat`, `jstack`, and `jsadebugd`
- **Profiler tools**: JConsole, JVisualVM, and Oracle Java Mission Control

The monitoring tool for Java virtual machine statistics

The `jstat` tool is used to gather some statistics about the Java virtual machine, mainly memory statistics, different spaces, loaded classes, garbage collections, and so on.

The general syntax of this tool is as follows:

```
jstat [ generalOption | outputOptions vmid [interval[s|ms]
    [count]] ]
```

Each term of the preceding syntax is explained as follows:

- `generalOption`: This parameter is a single general option (`-help` or `-options`)
- `outputOptions`: This parameter is for the output options, such as the `statOption`, `-t`, `-h`, and `-J` options
- `vmid`: This parameter is the virtual machine identifier, which is a unique string representing the JVM as follows:

  ```
  [protocol:][//]lvmid[@hostname[:port]/servername]
  ```

  If using a local JVM, use only the process ID in the preceding parameter

- `interval[s|ms]`: This parameter shows the sampling interval in seconds (`s`) or milliseconds (`ms`)
- `count`: This parameter shows the number of samples to display; otherwise, it will continue displaying the statistics until the JVM is terminated

The following table shows the available `statOption` values:

The statOption values	Description
`class`	Statistics on the behavior of the classloader
`Compiler`	Statistics of the HotSpot Just-in-Time compiler
`Printcompilation`	HotSpot compilation method statistics
`gc`	Statistics of the garbage collected heap
`gcutil`	A summary of the garbage collection statistics
`Gccapacity`	Statistics of the generations' capacities and their corresponding spaces

The statOption values	Description
Gccause	A summary of the garbage collection statistics such as -gcutil with the cause of last and current garbage collection events
gcnew	Statistics of the new generation
Gcnewcapacity	Statistics of the new generations' sizes and its corresponding spaces
gcold	Behavior statistics of the old and permanent generations
Gcoldcapacity	Statistics of the sizes of the old generation
Gcpermcapacity	Statistics of the sizes of the permanent generation

For example, after executing our previous example (it takes the process ID 2452 in my execution), we can then execute the jstat command to get the following results:

```
jstat -gcutil 2452 250 5
  S0     S1     E      O      P      YGC    YGCT    FGC    FGCT    GCT
  0.00   0.00   0.00   37.24  1.85   1220   0.768   67     0.468   1.236
  0.00   0.00   0.00   30.09  1.85   1240   0.779   68     0.475   1.255
  0.00   0.02   0.00   30.09  1.85   1259   0.792   69     0.482   1.274
  0.01   0.00   31.92  37.23  1.85   1280   0.804   70     0.490   1.295
  0.00   0.01   0.00   51.50  1.85   1302   0.817   71     0.496   1.314
```

Let's clarify the preceding result. S0 and S1 are the survivor spaces, E is the Eden space, O stands for the old generation, P for the Perm generation, YGC is the young garbage collection, T stands for the time in YGT, FGC stands for the full garbage collection, T is also time in FGCT, and GCT includes both young and full garbage collection times.

Our application creates large arrays and as we have mentioned in *Chapter 2, Understanding Java Fundamentals*, when we create large objects, they are placed in the old generation space immediately. Thus, we can see that the old generation is growing constantly while the young generation is almost empty (S0 and S1).

To execute the command to get data about the application classes, we can run the following command (process ID `2542`):

```
jstat -class 2542
Loaded  Bytes  Unloaded  Bytes    Time
   434  479.0        0    0.0     0.14
```

The JVM memory map tool

The `jmap` tool is used to display memory information about any running Java process. This can be also used to dump heap memory content. The usage of the tools with the syntax is given as follows:

- The `jmap` tool will print all the shared object mappings. The syntax is as follows:

  ```
  jmap [ option ] pid
  
  <no option>
  ```

- The `-dump` parameter dumps the Java heap content in the `hprof` binary file format. If the `live` suboption is specified, only the current live objects inside the heap are dumped. The syntax is as follows:

  ```
  -dump:[live,]format=b,file=<filename>
  ```

- The `-finalizerinfo` parameter displays information about objects waiting on finalization. The syntax is as follows:

  ```
  -finalizerinfo
  ```

- The `-heap` parameter shows the heap summary. The following is the syntax for an algorithm used for GC, heap configuration, and heap generation usages:

  ```
  -heap
  ```

- The `-histo` parameter prints the heap histogram. For example, for each Java class, the tool will print the number of instances, occupied memory in bytes, and qualified class names. If the `live` suboption is specified, only the current live objects are counted. The syntax is as follows:

  ```
  -histo[:live]
  ```

- The `-permstat` parameter prints the class loader statistics of the heap permanent generation. For example, for each class loader, the tool will print its name, liveness, address, parent class loader, and number and size of classes it has loaded. Also, the number and size of the interned strings are printed. The syntax is as follows:

  ```
  -permstat
  ```

- The `-J` parameter is used to pass different flags to the JVM. The syntax is as follows:

  ```
  -J<flag>
  ```

An example of using the preceding commands on the process ID `2296` to get different memory details is given as follows:

```
jmap -heap 2296
Attaching to process ID 2296, please wait...
Debugger attached successfully.
Client compiler detected.
JVM version is 24.45-b08
using thread-local object allocation.
Mark Sweep Compact GC
Heap Configuration:
   MinHeapFreeRatio = 40
   MaxHeapFreeRatio = 70
   MaxHeapSize      = 268435456 (256.0MB)
   NewSize          = 1048576 (1.0MB)
   MaxNewSize       = 4294901760 (4095.9375MB)
   OldSize          = 4194304 (4.0MB)
   NewRatio         = 2
   SurvivorRatio    = 8
   PermSize         = 12582912 (12.0MB)
   MaxPermSize      = 67108864 (64.0MB)
   G1HeapRegionSize = 0 (0.0MB)
Heap Usage:
New Generation (Eden + 1 Survivor Space):
   capacity = 5308416 (5.0625MB)
   used     = 4262600 (4.065132141113281MB)
   free     = 1045816 (0.9973678588867188MB)
   80.29890649112654% used
Eden Space:
   capacity = 4784128 (4.5625MB)
   used     = 4262552 (4.065086364746094MB)
   free     = 521576 (0.49741363525390625MB)
   89.09778333690069% used
From Space:
   capacity = 524288 (0.5MB)
   used     = 48 (4.57763671875E-5MB)
   free     = 524240 (0.4999542236328125MB)
```

```
   0.0091552734375% used
To Space:
   capacity = 524288 (0.5MB)
   used     = 0 (0.0MB)
   free     = 524288 (0.5MB)
   0.0% used
tenured generation:
   capacity = 11210752 (10.69140625MB)
   used     = 8192464 (7.8129425048828125MB)
   free     = 3018288 (2.8784637451171875MB)
   73.07684622762149% used
Perm Generation:
   capacity = 12582912 (12.0MB)
   used     = 233024 (0.22222900390625MB)
   free     = 12349888 (11.77777099609375MB)
   1.8519083658854167% used
10903 interned Strings occupying 816904 bytes.
```

We can dump the heap content into a file using the preceding command for the process ID 1668 as follows:

```
jmap -dump:format=b,file=mydump 1668
Dumping heap to mydump ...
Heap dump file created
```

We will now navigate through the preceding heap dump file using the jhat command.

The Java heap analysis tool

The jhat tool is used to analyze the heap dumps. The syntax looks like the following code:

```
jhat [ options ] <heap-dump-file>
```

We can open the dump file, which we generated using jmap, as follows:

```
jhat mydump
Reading from mydump...
Dump file created Sun Nov 10 20:44:45 EET 2013
Snapshot read, resolving...
Resolving 46793 objects...
```

```
Chasing references, expect 9 dots
Eliminating duplicate references
Snapshot resolved.
Started HTTP server on port 7000
Server is ready.
```

Now, open the following URL using your browser:

```
http://localhost:7000/
```

We can now see the `dump` file content in the browser, where we can navigate through the heap dump content or even query the heap using the **Object Query Language (OQL)**. Refer to the following screenshot:

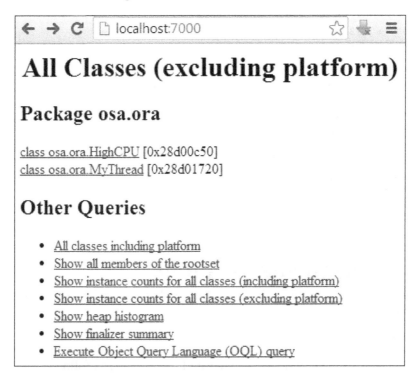

In the following screenshot, we have used OQL to query the heap dump and select our custom thread class `MyThread` by executing `select t from osa.ora. MyThread t`:

To learn more about OQL, the server already contains a helpful documentation in the `jhat` server at `http://localhost:7000/oqlhelp/`.

We will discuss this in more detail in *Chapter 8, Memory Profiling*.

The Java monitoring and management console tool

The `jconsole` tool is a good profiling tool with a graphical user interface that enables us to monitor and manage the Java applications and virtual machines on a local or remote host.

The command syntax looks as follows:

```
jconsole [ options ] [ connection ... ]
```

In the preceding syntax, the `connection` parameter contains one of the following information: `pid`, `host:port`, or `jmxUrl`, explained as follows:

- `pid` – This is the ID of the JVM process (if local)
- `host:port` – This is a host system on which the JVM is running, and depends on the port number as specified by the system property `com.sun.management.jmxremote.port` when the remote JVM was started
- `jmxUrl` – This represents the address of the JMX agent to be connected to

Alternatively, we can run `jconsole` and connect using the GUI connections. The tool GUI displays the following information through different tabs:

- **Overview**: This tab contains information about the JVM and monitored values
- **Memory**: This tab shows the memory details
- **Threads**: This tab shows the threading details
- **Classes**: This tab shows information about loaded classes
- **VM**: This tab shows information about the JVM
- **MBeans**: This tab shows the available MBeans

> **MBeans** or managed beans are JavaBeans that can be managed through defined interfaces. These interfaces follow **Java Management Extension (JMX)** specifications. Five types of interfaces are available, including standard, dynamic, open, model, and MXBean.

Java VisualVM

Java VisualVM provides a visual interface to view detailed information about the Java applications while they are running on a JVM. We can connect to the local or remote running applications. As it is based on the same codebase of the NetBeans profiler; it has almost the same capabilities.

To run Java VisualVM from the command prompt, refer to the following command:

```
jvisualvm
```

To execute our `HighCPU` application, start JVisualVM and attach it to our application (the application will appear in the running Java processes). We can see a graphical representation of the much useful information about our app in the following screenshot:

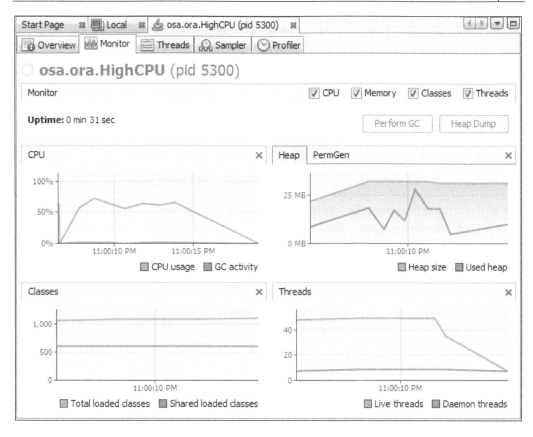

Using the tool, we can check the **CPU**, **Memory**, **Classes**, and **Threads** checkboxes.

We can also perform profiling for the executing application from the **Profiler** tab, where it will calibrate the first time it runs (we will discuss the calibration later in this chapter). Then, we can get useful details about either CPU or memory and determine the HotSpot areas.

JVisualVM supports the plugin installation, which is a good capability to enable its extensibility such as Visual GC. We can install any plugin by performing the following steps:

1. Navigate to the **Tools** menu and select the **Plugins** submenu.
2. Navigate to the **Available Plugins** tab.
3. Select any plugin we need to install from the plugin list and click on **Install**.
4. Click on the **Accept** button to accept the terms and conditions.
5. A restart is sometimes required to execute certain parameters after initial setup.

Oracle Java Mission Control

Java Mission Control is a powerful tool with rich capabilities that allows us to continuously collect low-level and detailed runtime information. **Java Flight Recorder** is a profiling and event collection framework built into the Oracle JDK.

Starting from JDK release 7 (update 40), JMC is bundled with the HotSpot JVM; it was migrated from JRockit and called **JRockit Mission Control (JRMC)**.

The tool can be executed using the following command line:

```
jmc
```

The tool contains two main powerful features: the **MBean server** and **Flight recorder**. The former is considered as the most important feature in `jmc`; it works in the event-based mode, so it doesn't cause noticeable overhead on the profiled application.

The usage of the tool is simple. In the left-hand side window, we can see the current running processes, and can pick our `HighCPU` example and check the amazing graphical representations of the gathered information, as shown in the following screenshot:

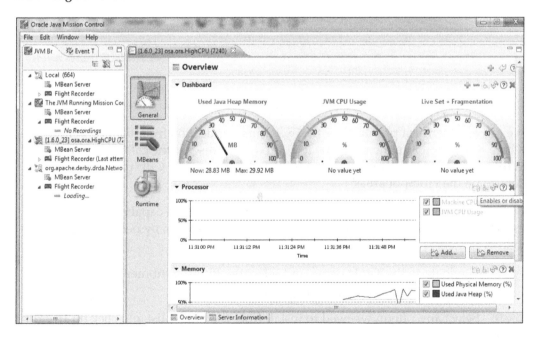

The sidebar contains three different options to display the **General** option for general information, **MBeans** for different attributes and invoke different methods, and **Runtime** for detailed information, as shown in the following screenshot:

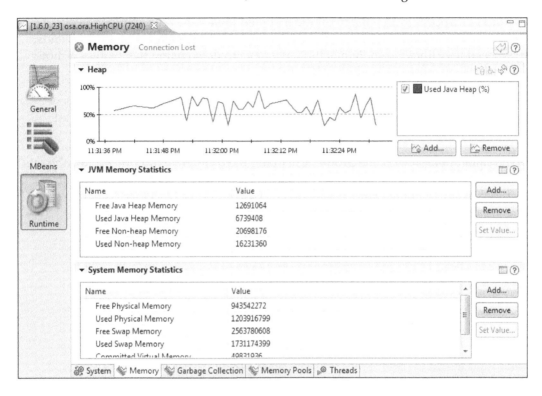

The **Runtime** information includes the **System**, **Memory**, **Garbage Collection**, **Memory Pools**, and **Threads** information tabs.

 We will not dig further into the different information meanings as we will cover all information details when we deal with the different profilers in the next sections.

Starting with the NetBeans profiler

The NetBeans profiler is a useful feature inside NetBeans IDE. It facilitates the identification of performance issues mainly in the development environment; however, it can also be used in other environments.

To start using the NetBeans profiler, perform the essential initial calibration for the used Java platform. This can be done easily from inside NetBeans.

The NetBeans profiler calibration

To run the NetBeans profiler calibration, we need to select the **Profile** menu, select the **Advanced Commands** submenu, and click on the **Run Profiler Calibration**. A pop-up will appear with a list of all the installed Java JDK. We can pick the one we need to calibrate, and it will take few moments before the calibration process ends. If we need to calibrate remote machine, we have to do so using the profiler remote pack for the appropriate remote platform.

Now, let's understand what is meant by calibration. Calibration is the process of measuring the time used to instrument the bytecode; this time causes overhead during profiling the application.

In the calibration process, the profiler calculates the different extra times and subtracts them while profiling the application to reduce this overhead. The calibration data for each JDK is saved in the `.nbprofile` directory in our home directory. The following screenshot is an example of the profiling results:

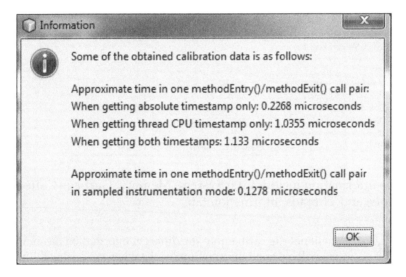

Using the NetBeans profiler

If we open one of our previous NetBeans projects, we can go to the **Profile** menu and click on **Profile Project**. A pop-up screen will appear with three main options; each option has its own suboptions:

- **Monitor**: This option is concerned with threads and different object monitors. It has three options: **Enable threads monitoring**, **Sample threads states**, and **Enable lock contention monitoring**. While selecting the required monitoring level, we see at the bottom the **Overhead** bar that shows the overhead impact by selecting these options on our application execution time.

- **CPU**: This option is concerned with the CPU time, where we can select **Quick (sampled)** or **Advanced (instrumented)**. We have mentioned before the difference between both types. We can select to profile all the classes that are the highest overhead; only the project class; or even define our inclusion/exclusion rules, such as including all the classes within the `org.apache.com.*` package. This useful filtering is required when we need to narrow our investigation scope.

- **Memory**: This option has two modes, **Quick (sampled)** and **Advanced (instrumented)**. If we select **instrumented**, we can further select the **Record full object lifecycle** and **Record stack trace for allocations** options.

If the project is a web-based project, the application server (for example, GlassFish) will start in the profiling mode. The application will be deployed and profiling will record all interactions with the applications. However, if the project is a Java project, the application will be executed directly in the profiling mode.

Let's try now our first NetBeans profiling project using a simple Java application to demonstrate the different capabilities in this profiler.

1. Open the `HighCPU` project.
2. Select the **Profile** menu.
3. Then, select the profile project (`HighCPU`) from the pop-up options, select **Monitor**, and check all available options.

4. Click on **Run**. Refer to the following screenshot:

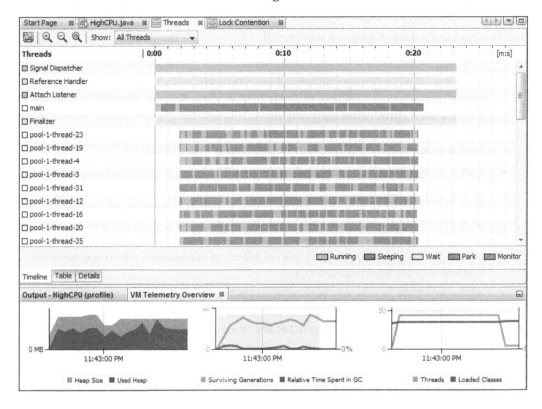

We can see most of the threads are in red for most of the execution time. This means the threads are blocked and are waiting to get the monitors/locks of certain objects. If we open the **Lock Contention** view and expand some threads, we will see that we have a thread locking over `java.io.printStream`, as shown in the following screenshot:

The following are the colors and the statuses they denote for any thread:

- **Monitor** (red): This means the thread is blocked and waiting for the monitor
- **Park** (orange): This indicated the thread is parked and waiting for the permission to continue execution
- **Wait** (yellow): This denotes the thread is waiting in response to the call of the method `object.wait()`
- **Sleeping** (purple): This means the thread is sleeping in response to the call of the method `Thread.sleep()`
- **Running** (green): This implies the thread is running

We get the thread's details by selecting one thread and right-clicking on it. Select the thread's **Details** option. We can see the exact time spent while the thread is in different states, as shown in the following screenshot:

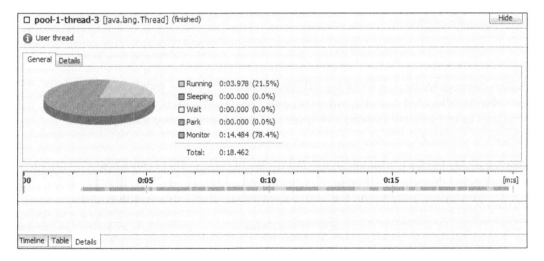

We can re-run the profiler to monitor the memory to get far more details about the application memory usages. The following screenshot is of the memory results when we repeat the profiling for memory consumption (top records):

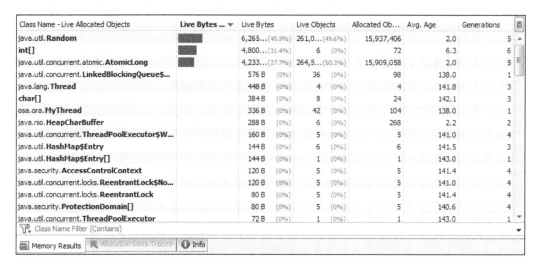

As we can see, we have a lot of useful information about the most created objects, live objects, allocated objects, and so on. We will discuss all the different memory readings in more detail later in a chapter dedicated to memory management: *Chapter 8, Memory Profiling.*

Now, let's see the CPU utilization time in different code parts of our project. Navigate to **Profile** and execute profiling in the **Quick (sampled)** mode. We will get results similar to what's shown in the following screenshot when our execution ends:

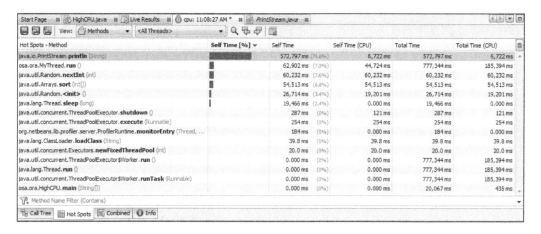

As we can see, most of the execution time (71.8 percent) is spent on the `java.io.PrintStream.println(String)` method. Refer to the following source code of this Java internal method:

```
public void println(String x) {
  synchronized (this) {
    print(x);
    newLine();
  }
}
```

It is now clear that the biggest HotSpot in our code is the `println` statement, where there is a synchronization statement and all the threads are competing with each other to get `PrintStream` object monitor. We will see more details on how to deal with similar issues in subsequent chapters; nevertheless, we have almost covered the NetBeans profiler overview in this section.

The Eclipse tools/plugins

The Eclipse IDE is the most commonly used IDE in the Java development with its different variants. It is a very powerful plugin-based IDE that can be customized according to the different needs.

Several profiling plugins are available for Eclipse, including plugins from famous third-party providers, such as JProfiler and YourKit. Also, some plugins such as **Test and Performance Tools Platform** (**TPTP**) can be used to acquire an application's performance results. We will also cover the **JVM monitor** tool in brief, and in *Chapter 8, Memory Profiling*, we will discuss the Eclipse **Memory Analyzer Tool** (**MAT**).

Using the profilers from inside, IDEs help us produce good and optimized code during the development time.

The JVM monitor

The JVM monitor is a Java profiler integrated with Eclipse to monitor the CPU, threads, and memory usage of the Java applications.

 Download and install the JVM monitor using the instructions at `http://www.jvmmonitor.org/download/index.html`.

Open Eclipse, navigate to the **Window** menu, click on **Show View**, and then select the **JVM Explorer** view. Now, in the JVM explorer, we see all the current running Java processes, where we can select one of the running processes. Right-click on it and click on **Start Monitoring**. A **Properties** window will open with all the process properties, as shown in the following screenshot:

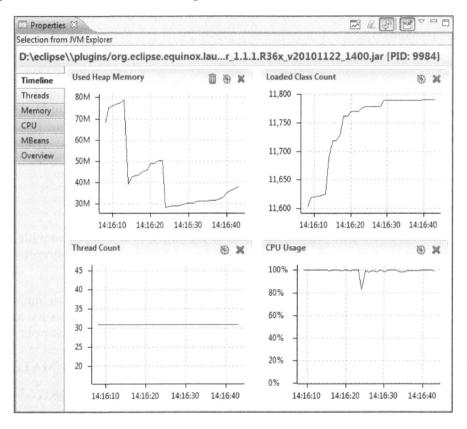

As we can see, the **Properties** window includes a lot of useful information, including **Timeline**, **Threads**, **Memory**, **CPU**, **MBeans**, and **Overview**. We can navigate inside these tabs to see the available process-profiling details.

The Test and Performance Tools Platform

TPTP is one of the Eclipse efficient plugins that can be used in profiling our application.

Download Eclipse with TPTP from http://www.eclipse.org/tptp/ home/downloads/ or download the plugin and install it in your Eclipse.

If we open our Eclipse project `HighCPU` and click on the `Profiling` menu, the usual options to profile the Java applications will appear as shown in the following screenshot:

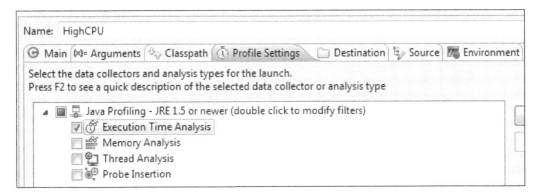

We can select any of the available options, for example, **Execution Time Analysis**. The application will run and we will get results similar to those shown in the following screenshot:

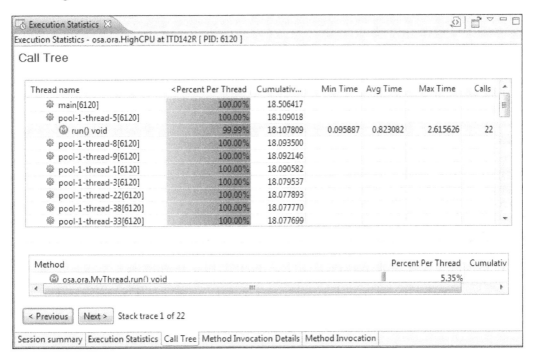

We can expand the method in each thread and see the number of invocations, average time, and minimum and maximum times. We can also right-click on them and get **Method Invocation** or **Method Invocation Details**.

We can repeat this to get the thread profiling by selecting the **Thread Analysis** tab from the **Profile Settings**. The following screenshot shows our application thread analysis results:

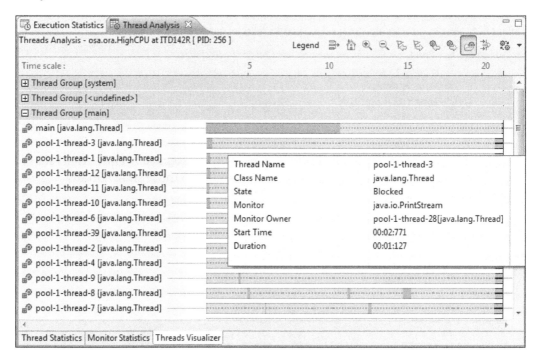

By moving the mouse over the blocked sections, we see the monitor and thread that owns/holds it at each moment along the thread lifetime.

Executing profiling operation from IDE is an easy task for developers and allows them to catch potential performance issues or memory leakages at an early stage. We can download a lot of Eclipse plugins either commercially or for free, and try them to get the best and easiest way to use the IDE-based profilers.

Advanced profiler – JProfiler

JProfiler is a powerful all-in-one tool that enables us to profile local or remote applications. It also integrates with most of the available IDEs (Eclipse, JDeveloper, NetBeans, and so on) and with almost all application servers.

It has a very powerful way to profile the applications offline, where we don't need to connect with GUI to monitor the profiling session. Using this offline mode, we can record the performance information and save the required profiling snapshots either by using the JProfiler trigger system or by calling the JProfiler APIs to control them.

It supports most of the existing operating system platforms, so all these features make JProfiler a very powerful tool.

> Download JProfiler 8.x from `http://www.ej-technologies.com/download/jprofiler/files`.
>
> JProfiler is a commercial product, but the good news is that you can request for the evaluation license to use with this book from `http://www.ej-technologies.com/download/jprofiler/trial`.
>
> They provide a free license for open source projects as well at `http://www.ej-technologies.com/buy/jprofiler/openSource`.

Now, let's start our web application ExampleOne (the example application that we used in *Chapter 3, Getting Familiar with Performance Testing*) on GlassFish application server, so we can start using JProfiler to profile this application.

Once we open JProfiler, we can attach our JProfiler to the running GlassFish. In the start center, navigate to the **New Session** tab and click on **Quick Attach**. We will see all the running Java applications/processes. We need to search for our GlassFish process and select it.

JProfiler will prompt us to select either the **Sampling** or **Instrumentation** mode. We discussed the difference between the both modes earlier.

Let's select the **Sampling** mode. We now need to select the session options; the more we select different options, the more the overhead indicator shows us the current overhead. We always need to keep this to the minimum if possible. Click on **OK** so that we can successfully complete the attachment of the profiler to the running JVM, as shown in the following screenshot:

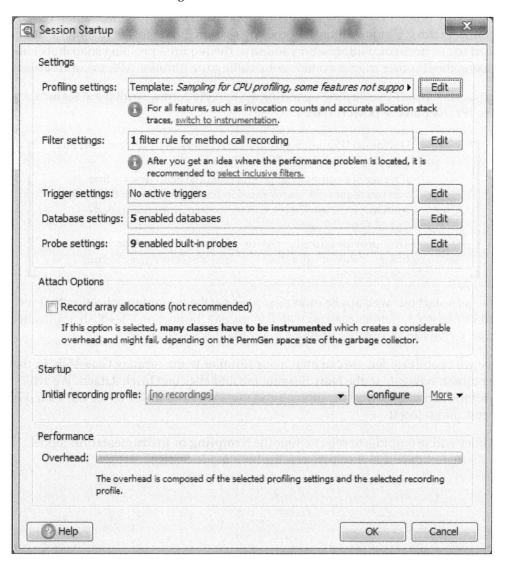

Now, we need to either go to our web application's homepage to invoke our routine scenarios or better execute the JMeter recorded login scenario by many concurrent users. This is to get the location of the HotSpots of our application exactly. We can see a lot of options on the left-hand side of the profiling window related to the different profiling options, such as **Live Memory**, **Heap walker**, **CPU views**, **Threads**, **Monitors & locks**, **Telemetries**, and **Database**.

Navigate to **Database** and click on the record icon that appears in the right-hand side of the window to enable it as our application deals with the database.

Now, start executing the JMeter load test. We already recorded this test scenario in *Chapter 3, Getting Familiar with Performance Testing*.

Once the JMeter execution ends, we can save a snapshot of the profiling results (from the **Session** menu, click on **Save**) and then click on the detach icon to stop profiling our application, as shown in the following screenshot:

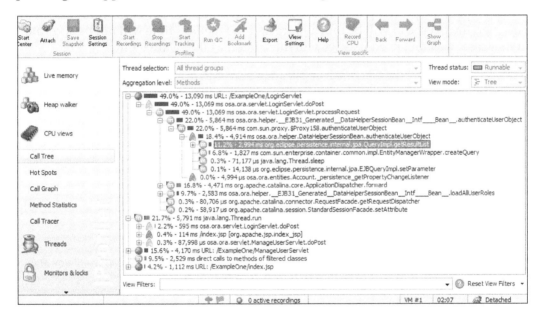

We can see the different invocation's **Call Tree** with the percentage of time spent inside each method. Some of these methods are from our code and some from the used framework or libraries. We can also open the **Hot Spots** tab in the **CPU** view and **Database** to see where most of the time is spent in our application, as shown in the following screenshot.

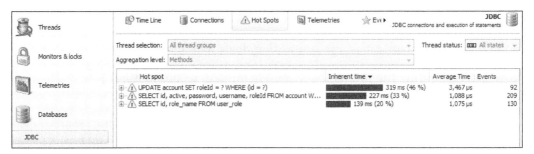

We can repeat the profiling using the **instrumental** mode to get more information; however, the overhead will be much more and the method time will not be accurate. In that case, we don't need it as we will interpret it as the relative time.

Now, let's try to start the GlassFish application server in the profiling mode instead of attaching the profiler in while the server is running. We can use **New Server Integration** from **New Session** in the start center, as shown in the following screenshot (in the **Integration Wizard** dialog box, JProfiler supports the integration with a lot of different application servers):

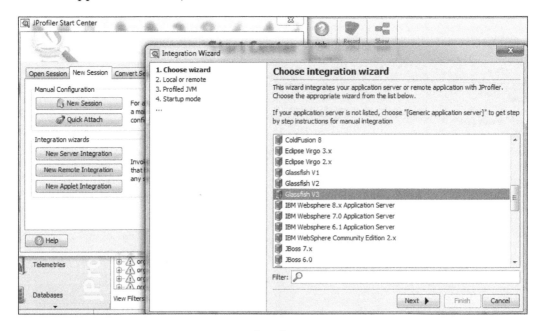

Select **Glassfish V3** (it is similar to V4) from the integration server list. It will prompt for the location of `domain.xml` and `asadmin.bat`. JProfiler will modify the files and create a backup for both. Once all the changes are complete, JProfiler will prompt us if we need to start the GlassFish server now or later. We can select **Start now**. Select any profiling option (for example, database) and run the JMeter load testing again so that we can obtain the required profiling results.

The following code is what JProfiler will modify in `domain.xml` to inject the `agentpath` JVM option:

```
<jvm-options>
-agentpath:D:\ JPROFI~2\bin\windows\jprofilerti.dll=port=8849
</jvm-options>
```

We can see here how to pass an option to the profiling agent, which is `port=8849` in this case.

We can use JProfiler to the profiler Java applets as follows; it works in the same way by injecting the agent information:

```
-agentpath:D:/PROGRA~1/JPROFI~2/bin/windows/jprofilerti.dll=port=8849
```

This information is entered in **Java Control Panel** by setting it on **Java Runtime Environment Settings**, as shown in the following screenshot:

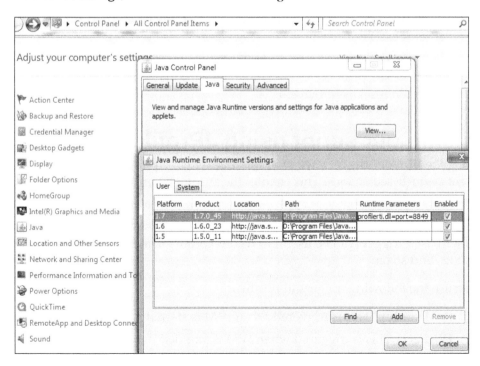

Now, we need to restart the browser and connect to the applet by the profiler to profile it.

 We have the `SimpleApplet` project containing one applet that has the same logic as the `HighCPU` application; you can download the code from `http://packtpub.com/`.

Try to follow the mentioned steps to profile this applet using JProfiler. Once you succeed, try to do the same using the NetBeans profiler.

Using the offline profiling mode

We do not have to connect the JProfiler GUI to our application in order to profile it. By using the JProfiler offline profiling mode, we can use JProfiler's powerful trigger system or even JProfiler APIs to control the profiling agent and save profiling snapshots to the disk. Later, we can open these snapshots using JProfiler for further analysis.

The main advantages and uses of the offline profiling mode (unattended profiling) are as follows:

- No connectivity is required between the remote application server machine and the profiler-installed machine because offline profiling is recorded in the remote server machine
- We can take regular snapshots of the application's performance
- Trigger-based profiling, for example, profiles the application when CPU utilization reaches 80 percent

Building our script using JProfiler triggers

By using the JProfiler triggers, we can build our own scripting scenarios and different event-based actions. This enables the automatic profiling of the application in the offline mode according to these triggers.

For example, a trigger named **JVM startup** can be used to start the recording, while the timer-based triggers can be useful to record certain elements or save periodic snapshots, and so on.

We can use the following triggers in JProfiler:

- **JVM startup**: This is triggered when JVM is started
- **JVM exit**: This is triggered when JVM is stopped

- **Timer**: This is triggered by the configured timer
- **Out of memory exception**: This is triggered in case `OutOfMemoryError` occurs
- **CPU load threshold**: This is triggered when the CPU load exceeds a certain threshold
- **Heap usage threshold**: This is triggered when the used heap exceeds a certain threshold
- **Method invocation**: This is triggered when a certain configured method is invoked

All these triggers can have many actions associated with them. The following screenshot shows the list of all possible actions that can be used as per JProfiler 8.x:

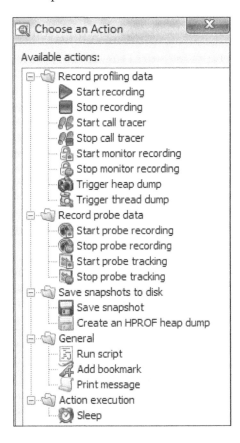

To execute our profiling in the offline mode, the following three additional parameters are required for the profiler agent:

- **Offline**: This parameter informs the agent to perform the profiling in the offline mode.

- **Session ID**: This parameter links to the configured session ID in the JProfiler configuration file.

- **Configuration xml file path**: The configuration file holds the different profiling configurations, such as triggers. If not specified, JProfiler will try to find it on the default location.

    The default location is under the `.jprofiler8` directory in the user's home directory

The complete parameter now looks like the following command:

```
"-agentpath:…../jprofilerti.dll=offline,id=125,config=…../config.xml"
"-Xbootclasspath/a:……\agent.jar"
```

Now, let's create the triggers in our profiling session by performing the following steps:

1. Create a new session and name it `My Profile Session`. We can see the session ID besides the session name. We need this information to pass this value to the profiled JVM.

2. Navigate to the **Triggers Settings** section and add the triggers by clicking on the green plus icon.

3. Add the trigger **JVM startup**, select the action **Start Recording**, and click on **VM Telemetry data**.

4. Add the trigger **Timer** and configure it as **Limited number of times =1, Offset=2 minutes**. Select the action **Start Recording**. Select **CPU data, Thread data**, and **Method statistics**.

5. Add the trigger **Timer** and configure it as **Unlimited, Interval=5 minutes**. Set the action and click on **Save Snapshot** (add the complete file path, such as `c:\snapshot`, and check the checkbox to add unique ID to the snapshot name, so it generates `snapshot.0`, `snapshot.1`, and so on).

6. Click on the **OK** button and close the **Attach** dialog box. If we open **Start Center**, we will find the newly created session with the name we gave to it, `My Profile Session`.

7. Now, we need to use this configuration to profile our application and get the required profiling snapshots. Open `domain.xml` of our **Glassfish V4** (or the corresponding configuration file for the application server) and add the following JVM option:

```
<jvm-options>
  -agentpath:D:/PROGRA~1/JPROFI~2/bin/windows/
    jprofilerti.dll=offline,id=133,config=C:\Users\
      Admin\.jprofiler8\config.xml</jvm-options>
```

 Change the path of JProfiler and configuration file according to your machine and change the ID to that of the created session.

All we need now is to run the application server and the JMeter load testing so that we can have a good offline profiling. We can see the following messages in the GlassFish logs that indicate the saving of profiling snapshots within periodic times according to our configured timer:

```
JProfiler> Saving snapshot c:\snapshot.0.jps ...

JProfiler> Done.

JProfiler> Saving snapshot c:\snapshot.1.jps ...

JProfiler> Done.
```

Once the testing is complete, switch the server off and remove this JVM option, and open the created snapshots using JProfiler.

With the command-line utility `jpenable`, we can start the offline profiling in any running JVM with a Java version of 1.6 or higher without the need to restart it. If we provide the command-line utility arguments, we can automate the process so that it requires no user interaction/input. The usage syntax is as follows:

```
jpenable [options]
```

The offline profiling options are as follows:

- `-d` `--pid=PID`: This is the `pid` option of the JVM that should be profiled
- `-o` `--offline`: This is the JVM that will be profiled in the offline mode
- `-c` `--config=PATH`: This is the path to the `config` file that holds the profiling settings
- `-i` `--id=ID`: This is the session ID in the configuration file

Note that the JVM must run with the same system user as jpenable; otherwise, JProfiler cannot connect to it.

If we execute the jpenable command without any parameter, it will prompt and ask for all the required information to facilitate the configuration. To try this command, let's perform the following steps:

1. Run our application on the GlassFish application server (without any profiling parameters).

2. Run the jpenable command and respond to the questions, as shown in the following command:

```
jpenable
Do you want to search for JVMs running as service?
Yes [y], No [n, Enter]
y
Select a JVM:
<unknown> [7532] [1]
ApacheJMeter.jar [9276] [2]
com.sun.enterprise.glassfish.boots...\glassfish\domains\domain1
[6336] [3]
3
Please select the profiling mode:
GUI mode (attach with JProfiler GUI) [1, Enter]
Offline mode (use config file to set profiling settings) [2]
2
Please enter the path to the JProfiler config file
C:\Users\Administrator\.jprofiler8\config.xml
Please choose the session ID
Animated Bezier Curve Demo [80]
JDBC demo [81]
Offline Profiling [111]
Glassfish V3 on localhost [131]
My Profile Session [133]
133
```

 We will use the same session that we created to profile offline (that is, My Profile Session).

We can then use the `jpcontroller` utility to control our offline session by either starting or stopping the recording, disabling or enabling triggers, heap/thread dumping, saving profiling snapshot, and so on.

Further reading

Refer to the following for more information:

- You can find more details about the different JDK tools at
  `http://docs.oracle.com/javase/7/docs/technotes/tools/index.html`

- You can find more information about the NetBeans profiler at
  `https://netbeans.org/kb/docs/java/profiler-intro.html`

- You can find the online documentation for JProfiler at
  `http://resources.ej-technologies.com/jprofiler/help/doc/`

Summary

In this chapter, we learned different monitoring tools used to monitor our Java application. We selected some tools from each category, including operating system tools (in both Windows and Linux) and Java tools. We should now have a good understanding of different JDK command-line tools, such as `jhat` and `jmap`, and more advanced tools, such as `JConsole`, `JVisualVM`, and Oracle Mission Control.

From the IDE profiler tools, we demonstrated the NetBeans and Eclipse profilers. We also selected JProfiler as an example of the advanced Java profilers with special attention to the offline profiling capability.

In *Chapter 6*, *CPU Time Profiling*, *Chapter 7*, *Thread Profiling*, and *Chapter 8*, *Memory Profiling*, we will go in depth into how to read and interpret the different profiling results and build our strategy to fix any potential performance issues.

In *Chapter 5*, *Recognizing Common Performance Issues*, we will discuss the most common performance issues that we can face. We will categorize them and discuss each one, with special focus on the application's symptoms, giving examples and seeing the different profiling results.

5
Recognizing Common Performance Issues

Before we dig more into the profiling tools and how to interpret the results in the coming chapters, we need to highlight some of the most frequent performance issues that we could face. In this chapter, we will go through different performance issues, classify them into different categories, and then discuss the most common issues briefly.

Here is a list of topics that we will cover in this chapter:

- Slow response time umbrella
- Threading performance issues
- Memory performance issues
- Work as designed performance issues
- Miscellaneous performance issues
- Client-side performance issues

Going through a slow response time umbrella

In general, performance issues mean an impact on the application response time. It could be consistent or intermittent behavior. Sometimes, the performance keeps deteriorating till it impacts the application functionality.

In this chapter, we will try to look at different performance issues in enterprise applications. Understanding the issue is the first step to resolve it; we will use these issues as a template to guide our troubleshooting and investigations. Learning by example is an important type of learning strategy, and it can help us to organize our thoughts as well.

Isolating the issue

Assuming that we have confirmed the existence of the performance issue in our application and we are able to replicate this issue (or at least have some evidence), it is critical that we succeed in isolating the performance issue (that is, determine its location), so we can narrow our investigations and focus all our efforts on the root cause of the issue.

We will summarize what we have learned from the previous chapters. While dealing with performance issues, the role says, "We need to troubleshoot the issues horizontally and vertically". Let's assume that the issue we have is the slow response of a page or transaction in our web application.

With respect to the order, we need to fulfill the following tasks:

- We need to confirm the issue by either replicating it or getting evidence (in case it is not a persistent issue). At this stage, the confirmation might include the customer feedback, replicating the issue, monitoring tools reports, and log extract (for example, access logs). Later, we can involve other tools as profilers in our investigation.
- We need to analyze the issue and draft our investigation plan.
- We need to arrange different team activities according to our plan.

What we will highlight here is the sequence of locating such proved issues whenever we do not have a clear indicator of the issue location. In case we have this indicator, we can shorten our investigation roadmap and focus on the related parts.

Client side

By using the developer tools in different browsers, we can confirm whether the issue is a client- or server-side issue. These tools show the server response time, page size, and resourcing issue (a remote resource that prevents the page from loading), and it can also profile the JavaScript code, as we will see later in this chapter.

HTTP server side (web servers)

In most enterprise applications' deployment, there is an HTTP server up front that works as a proxy and serves the application's static contents, server access logs containing the request timestamp, response status, response size, and response time. This will help in locating the issue either in the network component before the HTTP server (such as a proxy or load balance issue) or in subsequent nodes.

If the response time is correct, we need to check the HTTP server statistics, especially the operating system statistics; otherwise, we will move our investigations to the next node.

 If access logs do not show enough details, we need to reconfigure them to show all the required information that can facilitate the troubleshooting of any issue. We should be careful as excessive logging might affect the performance as well.

Application server issue

We need to do the following activities in parallel while replicating the issue if it's not a persistent issue:

- Check the server statistics from the admin console or from any used monitoring tools (for example, connection pools, thread pools, server logs, and so on)
- Check operating system statistics
- Check cache statistics (if on the same server or a dedicated server)
- Take a heap dump and frequent thread dumps according to the issue type (the frequency of the thread dump should be adjusted according to the response time and it is usually 3 to 5 seconds)
- Examining the application logs

Usually, the production monitoring tools provide a history of different resources' performance that would help us to locate the issue start time, progression, patterns, and so on.

Database server issue

Database server issue is a common reason for enterprise application performance issues. Some of the required activities are as follows:

- Checking the database report and SQL tracing over the period where the performance issue occurred was not persistent, for example, an Oracle AWR report
- Gathering the monitoring tool statistics results, such as the operating system, I/O, memory, and processing speed

Integrated systems

If the impacted transactions are related to interactions with an integrated system through web service, service bus, and so on, we need to gather statistics and get the different available reports for this integration layer to evaluate its performance (including the different available logs).

Networking components

It is important to examine the different networking components, for example, the firewall and different connections.

Code and script analysis

Code and script analysis includes manual inspection of the suspected code, script, and global elements.

 In the global application performance issues, we need to focus more on global elements, such as caching, filters, security, and pooled resources.

Profiling the application

Profiling the application includes profiling the slow response scenario in the test environment (under load). If no issues are observed, profile this in the production environment using the minimal possible profiling overhead. If the issues are not detected, we can increase the level of profiling details till the issue is detected.

Usually in our investigations, we will need at least two snapshots of the data, one as baseline (before the issue) and one during/after the performance issues. The more snapshots available, the better it is for our analysis. Different monitoring tools store valuable historical data that can help us.

These are the samples of gradual isolation strategic steps to locate the performance issue in different application components, such as the operating system, application server, database server, caching components, and integrated system.

Common performance issues

Let's now go through the most common performance issues in enterprise applications that we could face during performance troubleshooting. For each issue, we will define the issue, describe it and its symptoms, and give examples. Let's begin with classifying the most common issues and organizing them into different categories.

Threading performance issues

Threading performance issues are the issues related to concurrency, as follows:

- Lack of threading or excessive threading
- Threads blocking up to starvation (usually from competing on shared resources)
- Deadlock until the complete application hangs (threads waiting for each other)

Memory performance issues

Memory performance issues are the issues that are related to application memory management, as follows:

- **Memory leakage**: This issue is an explicit leakage or implicit leakage as seen in improper hashing
- **Improper caching**: This issue is due to over caching, inadequate size of the object, or missing essential caching
- **Insufficient memory allocation:** This issue is due to missing JVM memory tuning

Algorithmic performance issues

Implementing the application logic requires two important parameters that are related to each other; correctness and optimization. If the logic is not optimized, we have algorithmic issues, as follows:

- Costive algorithmic logic
- Unnecessary logic

Work as designed performance issues

The work as designed performance issue is a group of issues related to the application design. The application behaves exactly as designed but if the design has issues, it will lead to performance issues. Some examples of performance issues are as follows:

- Using synchronous when asynchronous should be used
- Neglecting remoteness, that is, using remote calls as if they are local calls
- Improper loading technique, that is, eager versus lazy loading techniques
- Selection of the size of the object
- Excessive serialization layers
- Web services granularity
- Too much synchronization
- Non-scalable architecture, especially in the integration layer or middleware
- Saturated hardware on a shared infrastructure

Interfacing performance issues

Whenever the application is dealing with resources, we may face the following interfacing issues that could impact our application performance:

- Using an old driver/library
- Missing frequent database housekeeping
- Database issues, such as, missing database indexes
- Low performing JMS or integration service bus
- Logging issues (excessive logging or not following the best practices while logging)
- Network component issues, that is, load balancer, proxy, firewall, and so on

Miscellaneous performance issues

Miscellaneous performance issues include different performance issues, as follows:

- Inconsistent performance of application components, for example, having slow components can cause the whole application to slow down

- Introduced performance issues to delay the processing speed

- Improper configuration tuning of different components, for example, JVM, application server, and so on

- Application-specific performance issues, such as excessive validations, apply many business rules, and so on

Fake performance issues

Fake performance issues could be a temporary issue or not even an issue. The famous examples are as follows:

- Networking temporary issues

- Scheduled running jobs (detected from the associated pattern)

- Software automatic updates (it must be disabled in production)

- Non-reproducible issues

In the following sections, we will go through some of the listed issues, and in subsequent chapters, we will discuss some other issues.

Threading performance issues

Multithreading has the advantage of maximizing the hardware utilization. In particular, it maximizes the processing power by executing multiple tasks concurrently. But it has different side effects, especially if not used wisely inside the application.

For example, in order to distribute tasks among different concurrent threads, there should be no or minimal data dependency, so each thread can complete its task without waiting for other threads to finish. Also, they shouldn't compete over different shared resources or they will be blocked, waiting for each other. We will discuss some of the common threading issues in the next section.

Blocking threads

A common issue where threads are blocked is waiting to obtain the monitor(s) of certain shared resources (objects), that is, holding by other threads. If most of the application server threads are consumed in a certain blocked status, the application becomes gradually unresponsive to user requests.

In the Weblogic application server, if a thread keeps executing for more than a configurable period of time (not idle), it gets promoted to the Stuck thread. The more the threads are in the stuck status, the more the server status becomes critical. Configuring the stuck thread parameters is part of the Weblogic performance tuning, as we will see in *Chapter 9, Tuning an Application's Environment*.

Performance symptoms

The following symptoms are the performance symptoms that usually appear in cases of thread blocking:

- Slow application response (increased single request latency and pending user requests)
- Application server logs might show some stuck threads.
- The server's healthy status becomes critical on monitoring tools (application server console or different monitoring tools)
- Frequent application server restarts either manually or automatically
- Thread dump shows a lot of threads in the blocked status waiting for different resources
- Application profiling shows a lot of thread blocking

An example of thread blocking

To understand the effect of thread blocking on application execution, open the HighCPU project and measure the time it takes for execution by adding the following additional lines:

```
long start= new Date().getTime();
..
..
long duration= new Date().getTime()-start;
System.err.println("total time = "+duration);
```

Now, try to execute the code with a different number of the thread pool size. We can try using the thread pool size as 50 and 5, and compare the results. In our results, the execution of the application with 5 threads is much faster than 50 threads!

Let's now compare the NetBeans profiling results of both the executions to understand the reason behind this unexpected difference.

The following screenshot shows the profiling of 50 threads; we can see a lot of blocking for the monitor in the column and the percentage of **Monitor** to the left waiting around at 75 percent:

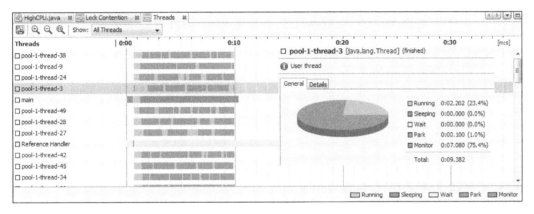

To get the preceding profiling screen, click on the **Profile** menu inside NetBeans, and then click on **Profile Project (HighCPU)**. From the pop-up options, select **Monitor** and check all the available options, and then click on **Run**.

The following screenshot shows the profiling of 5 threads, where there is almost no blocking, that is, less threads compete on these resources:

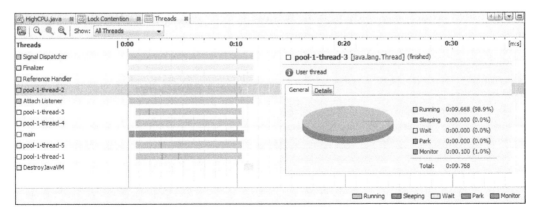

Try to remove the `System.out` statement from inside the `run()` method, re-execute the tests, and compare the results.

Another factor that also affects the selection of the pool size, especially when the thread execution takes long time, is the context switching overhead. This overhead requires the selection of the optimal pool size, usually related to the number of available processors for our application.

 Context switching is the CPU switching from one process (or thread) to another, which requires restoration of the execution data (different CPU registers and program counters). The context switching includes suspension of the current executing process, storing its current data, picking up the next process for execution according to its priority, and restoring its data.

Although it's supported on the hardware level and is faster, most operating systems do this on the level of software context switching to improve the performance. The main reason behind this is the ability of the software context switching to selectively choose the required registers to save.

Thread deadlock

When many threads hold the monitor for objects that they need, this will result in a deadlock unless the implementation uses the new explicit `Lock` interface, which we discussed in the example in *Chapter 2, Understanding Java Fundamentals*. In the example, we had a deadlock caused by two different threads waiting to obtain the monitor that the other thread held.

The thread profiling will show these threads in a continuous blocking status, waiting for the monitors. All threads that go into the deadlock status become out of service for the user's requests, as shown in the following screenshot:

Threads		1:00	1:10	1:20	1:3
☐ Attach Listener					
☐ Finalizer					
☐ Reference Handler					
☐ Signal Dispatcher					
☐ Thread-5					
☐ main					
☐ Thread-6					
☐ DestroyJavaVM					

Usually, this happens if the order of obtaining the locks is not planned. For example, if we need to have a quick and easy fix for a multidirectional thread deadlock, we can always lock the smallest or the largest bank account first, regardless of the transfer direction. This will prevent any deadlock from happening in our simple two-threaded mode. But if we have more threads, we need to have a much more mature way to handle this by using the `Lock` interface or some other technique.

 In *Chapter 7, Thread Profiling*, we will understand the thread dump, different thread profiling interpretations, and our fixing strategy for threading issues.

Memory performance issues

In *Chapter 2, Understanding Java Fundamentals*, we have seen the continuous and tremendous effort to enhance and optimize the JVM garbage collector. In spite of all this great effort put into the allocated and free memory in an optimized way, we still see memory issues in Java Enterprise applications mainly due to the way people are dealing with memory in these applications.

We will discuss mainly three types of memory issues: memory leakage, memory allocation, and application data caching.

Memory leakage

Memory leakage is a common performance issue where the garbage collector is not at fault; it is mainly the design/coding issues where the object is no longer required but it remains referenced in the heap, so the garbage collector can't reclaim its space. If this is repeated with different objects over a long period (according to object size and involved scenarios), it may lead to an out of memory error.

The most common example of memory leakage is adding objects to the static collections (or an instance collection of long living objects, such as a servlet) and forgetting to clean collections totally or partially.

Performance symptoms

The following symptoms are some of the expected performance symptoms during a memory leakage in our application:

- The application uses heap memory increased by time
- The response slows down gradually due to memory congestion

- `OutOfMemoryError` occurs frequently in the logs and sometimes an application server restart is required
- Aggressive execution of garbage collection activities
- Heap dump shows a lot of objects retained (from the leakage types)
- A sudden increase of memory paging as reported by the operating system monitoring tools

An example of memory leakage

We have a sample application `ExampleTwo`; this is a product catalog where users can select products and add them to the basket. The application is written in spaghetti code, so it has a lot of issues, including bad design, improper object scopes, bad caching, and memory leakage. The following screenshot shows the product catalog browser page:

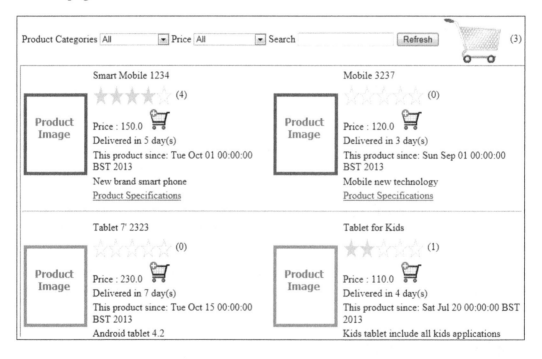

You need to download the project from `http://www.packtpub.com/`. It includes both, the NetBeans project and MySQL database schema. It also includes a simple Apache JMeter test plan, but it's better if you build it yourself.

One of the bad issues is the usage of the servlet instance (or static members), as it causes a lot of issues in multiple threads and has a common location for unnoticed memory leakages.

We have added the following instance variable as a leakage location:

```
private final HashMap<String, HashMap> cachingAllUsersCollection =
   new HashMap();
```

We will add some collections to the preceding code to cause memory leakage. We also used the caching in the session scope, which causes implicit leakage. The session scope leakage is difficult to diagnose, as it follows the session life cycle. Once the session is destroyed, the leakage stops, so we can say it is less severe but more difficult to catch.

Adding global elements, such as a catalog or stock levels, to the session scope has no meaning. The session scope should only be restricted to the user-specific data. Also, forgetting to remove data that is not required from a session makes the memory utilization worse. Refer to the following code:

```
@Stateful
public class CacheSessionBean
```

Instead of using a singleton class here or stateless bean with a static member, we used the `Stateful` bean, so it is instantiated per user session. We used JPA beans in the application layers instead of using `View Objects`. We also used loops over collections instead of querying or retrieving the required object directly, and so on.

It would be good to troubleshoot this application in the coming chapters with different profiling aspects to fix all these issues. All these factors are enough to describe such a project as spaghetti.

We can use our knowledge in Apache JMeter to develop simple testing scenarios. As shown in the following screenshot, the scenario consists of catalog navigations and details of adding some products to the basket:

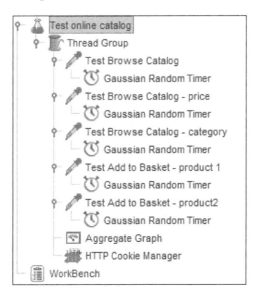

Executing the test plan using many concurrent users over many iterations will show the bad behavior of our application, where the used memory is increased by time. There is no justification as the catalog is the same for all users and there's no specific user data, except for the IDs of the selected products. Actually, it needs to be saved inside the user session, which won't take any remarkable memory space.

In our example, we intend to save a lot of objects in the session, implement a wrong session level, cache, and implement meaningless servlet level caching. All this will contribute to memory leakage. This gradual increase in the memory consumption is what we need to spot in our environment as early as possible (as we can see in the following screenshot, the memory consumption in our application is approaching **200 MB!**):

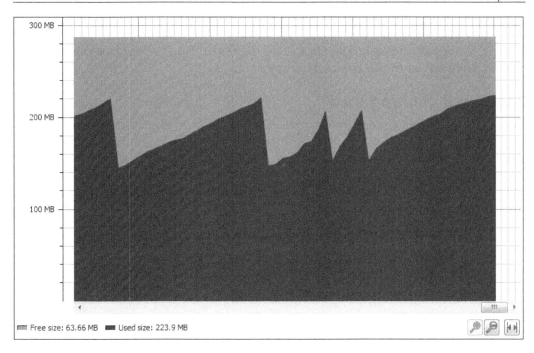

▦ Free size: 63.66 MB   ▮ Used size: 223.9 MB

Improper data caching

Caching is one of the critical components in the enterprise application architecture. It increases the application performance by decreasing the time required to query the object again from its data store, but it also complicates the application design and causes a lot of other secondary issues.

The main concerns in the cache implementation are caching refresh rate, caching invalidation policy, data inconsistency in a distributed environment, locking issues while waiting to obtain the cached object's lock, and so on.

Improper caching issue types

The improper caching issue can take a lot of different variants. We will pick some of them and discuss them in the following sections.

No caching (disabled caching)

Disabled caching will definitely cause a big load over the interfacing resources (for example, database) by hitting it in with almost every interaction. This should be avoided while designing an enterprise application; otherwise; the application won't be usable.

Fortunately, this has less impact than using wrong caching implementation!

Most of the application components such as database, JPA, and application servers already have an out-of-the-box caching support.

Too small caching size

Too small caching size is a common performance issue, where the cache size is initially determined but doesn't get reviewed with the increase of the application data. The cache sizing is affected by many factors such as the memory size. If it allows more caching and the type of the data, lookup data should be cached entirely when possible, while transactional data shouldn't be cached unless required under a very strict locking mechanism.

Also, the cache replacement policy and invalidation play an important role and should be tailored according to the application's needs, for example, `least frequently used`, `least recently used`, `most frequently used`, and so on.

As a general rule, the bigger the cache size, the higher the cache hit rate and the lower the cache miss ratio. Also, the proper replacement policy contributes here; if we are working—as in our example—on an online product catalog, we may use the `least recently used` policy so all the old products will be removed, which makes sense as the users usually look for the new products.

Monitoring of the caching utilization periodically is an essential proactive measure to catch any deviations early and adjust the cache size according to the monitoring results. For example, if the cache saturation is more than 90 percent and the missed cache ratio is high, a cache resizing is required.

Missed cache hits are very costive as they hit the cache first and then the resource itself (for example, database) to get the required object, and then add this loaded object into the cache again by releasing another object (if the cache is 100 percent), according to the used cache replacement policy.

Too big caching size

Too big caching size might cause memory issues. If there is no control over the cache size and it keeps growing, and if it is a Java cache, the garbage collector will consume a lot of time trying to garbage collect that huge memory, aiming to free some memory. This will increase the garbage collection pause time and decrease the cache throughput.

If the cache throughput is decreased, the latency to get objects from the cache will increase causing the cache retrieval cost to be high to the level it might be slower than hitting the actual resources (for example, database).

Using the wrong caching policy

Each application's cache implementation should be tailored according to the application's needs and data types (transactional versus lookup data). If the selection of the caching policy is wrong, the cache will affect the application performance rather than improving it.

Performance symptoms

According to the cache issue type and different cache configurations, we will see the following symptoms:

- Decreased cache hit rate (and increased cache missed ratio)
- Increased cache loading because of the improper size
- Increased cache latency with a huge caching size
- Spiky pattern in the performance testing response time, in case the cache size is not correct, causes continuous invalidation and reloading of the cached objects

An example of improper caching techniques

In our example, `ExampleTwo`, we have demonstrated many caching issues, such as `no policy defined`, `global cache is wrong`, `local cache is improper`, and `no cache invalidation is implemented`. So, we can have stale objects inside the cache.

Cache invalidation is the process of refreshing or updating the existing object inside the cache or simply removing it from the cache. So in the next load, it reflects its recent values. This is to keep the cached objects always updated.

Cache hit rate is the rate or ratio in which cache hits match (finds) the required cached object. It is the main measure for cache effectiveness together with the retrieval cost.

Cache miss rate is the rate or ratio at which the cache hits the required object that is not found in the cache.

Last access time is the timestamp of the last access (successful hit) to the cached objects.

Caching replacement policies or algorithms are algorithms implemented by a cache to replace the existing cached objects with other new objects when there are no rooms available for any additional objects. This follows missed cache hits for these objects. Some examples of these policies are as follows:

- **First-in-first-out (FIFO)**: In this policy, the cached object is aged and the oldest object is removed in favor of the new added ones.

- **Least frequently used (LFU)**: In this policy, the cache picks the less frequently used object to free the memory, which means the cache will record statistics against each cached object.

- **Least recently used (LRU)**: In this policy, the cache replaces the least recently accessed or used items; this means the cache will keep information like the last access time of all cached objects.

- **Most recently used (MRU)**: This policy is the opposite of the previous one; it removes the most recently used items. This policy fits the application where items are no longer needed after the access, such as used exam vouchers.

- **Aging policy**: Every object in the cache will have an age limit, and once it exceeds this limit, it will be removed from the cache in the simple type. In the advanced type, it will also consider the invalidation of the cache according to predefined configuration rules, for example, every three hours, and so on.

It is important for us to understand that caching is not our magic bullet and it has a lot of related issues and drawbacks. Sometimes, it causes overhead if not correctly tailored according to real application needs.

In *Chapter 8, Memory Profiling*, we will dissect heap dump, different memory profiling interpretations, and our fixing strategy for memory issues. In *Chapter 10, Designing High-performance Enterprise Applications*, we will have another detailed discussion about data caching.

Work as designed performance issues

In work as designed performance issues, the application behaves exactly as designed but the design itself has issues that lead to bad performance. Let's go through some examples.

Synchronous where asynchronous is required

The design assumes that some parts of the application can be achieved in sequence without considering the expected time spent in some elements of this flow (or retry logic in certain services). This will lead to a bad performance of the application in these transactions, while in fact it is working as designed.

For example, if the transaction needs to send an e-mail to the customer and the e-mail server is not responding, the request will end up with a timeout after a configurable period, and if there is a retry logic applied, the user will wait until a response is sent back from the application.

Performance symptoms

The identification of the issues usually results from application analysis (for example, code inspection, profiling analysis, and so on), but we can expect the general symptoms when we use synchronous code where we should use the asynchronous one, as follows:

- Slow response time intermittent or consistent in certain application areas
- Customer browser inconsistently gives timeout messages such as
  `408 - Http Request timeout error`

An example of improper synchronous code

A common example of improper synchronous code is how online orders are submitted. As a part of submission of the order, a lot of internal systems communication is usually required. We shouldn't let the customer wait all this time, but instead, we need to show the confirmation page after executing only the essential steps. All other steps that can be executed in the background should be communicated to the customer by the asynchronous communication, that is, Ajax calls or e-mails.

Neglecting remoteness

In the distributed development with different system components, sometimes the developers are not aware that they are actually making remote calls when an abstract layer is used or when they interact with the integration library. So whenever they need to get some information from this interface, they use it without any concerns.

This is a typical development issue. What we mean here by **neglecting remoteness** is that the designer does not respect the remoteness of the system that calls during the design of the application. These remote calls will consume time and could also involve some serialization operations; both will impact the transaction performance.

Performance symptoms

The following symptoms usually appear when we neglect the cost of the remote calls:

- Consistent delay of the application transactions
- Performance tuning cycles do not cause any actual improvements
- Code analysis suggests the response time is almost spent in certain remote calls
- Mismatch between the number of transactions and the number of remote service calls (for example, remote calls double the number of transactions)

An example of using remote calls as local calls

The application displays a lot of the vendor's products. We need to check the product availability and the latest prices prior to displaying it, adding it to the basket, or executing the final checkout.

The operation seems to be simple but it is a remote call. The response time is dependent on the remote system and a sequence of these operations will cause an impact on application response time.

Excessive serialization performance impact

The system design follows the best practices of isolating different application layers and organizing them into loosely coupled layers. One of these layers consists of fine-tuned web services that are orchestrated into larger wrapper web services. This will cause each request to these orchestrated services to go through many serialization layers, from the wrapper web services to the subsequent fine service calls.

Performance symptoms

Excessive serialization can lead to the following performance symptoms:

- Consistent slow performance of the application, in particular, under load
- Low throughput of the application
- Taking thread dump under load will show a lot of threads in serialization logic

An example of excessive serialization

The following two issues represent good examples of the excessive serialization issue.

Object size impact

Determining the object size is essential as it can impact the performance if not optimally designed. For example, small-sized objects can affect the performance if it is in the interfacing layer, and it would require a lot of calls to assemble all the required objects even if only a few attributes are actually needed from each object.

Large objects can also produce useless overhead over network transmission. The same effect takes place from using complex nested object structures. The following diagram represents the impact of selecting the object size during designing, in particular, the interfacing specifications:

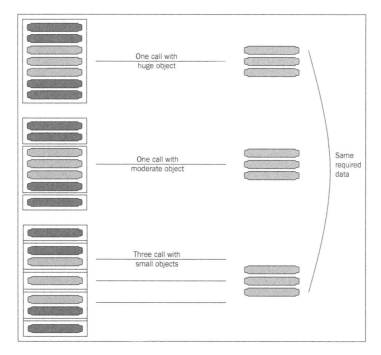

If these calls involve serialization in any form of data, it would produce additional overhead, for example, XML, JSON, and so on.

Another aspect for the object size impact is memory consumption, so if we need to save the User object in the session and if this object holds a lot of unnecessary data, it will be a waste of memory to do that. Instead, we need to add to the session the minimal required information to efficiently utilize the application memory.

Web services granularity impact

Similar to the object size performance concern, web services should be designed to fulfill the requirement in the least number of service calls rather than having multiple calls that produce overhead and decrease the performance of the application.

Let's assume that we have a web service that returns the weather forecast for a given city. We can select one of the following design options:

- If the application wants a week's data, it should call the weather forecast per day option seven times with a different day

- If the application wants a month's data, it should call the weather forecast per week option four to five times to get the complete weather detail of that month, and if it needs just a day detail, it should neglect the extra data

- If the application wants a week or a day's data, it should call the weather forecast per month option and filter out the extra data

- Weather forecast for the required period provides the caller the ability to send the start date and number of days the forecast is required for with a maximum of 30 days of data that will be returned

These options are designed for a decision that should be taken according to application needs, but we can see the fourth option is equivalent to implementing the other three call types. So, it would be better to have a single call of the fourth type rather than having all these call types. At the same time, all the other three call types wouldn't serve all possible scenarios (for example, retrieving the weather forecast for 10 days) without having to make multiple calls or returning extra data that produces performance overhead to retrieve such data from the database and serialize them back to the caller.

In some design decisions to reuse the code, a new web service is created that provides wider user experience by orchestrating many calls to the old web service calls. This will produce performance degradation, especially if these calls are remote calls.

Selected performance issues

In this section, we will pick some performance issues and discuss them in more detail.

Unnecessary application logic

Here, the application developers usually lack a good understanding of the used framework capabilities so they use extra unnecessary logic that either produces extra database hits, memory consumption, or even processing power consumption. Such unwanted code can only be detected if it causes extra hits to resources or external calls, and the best way to detect this is to perform manual code inspection or profiling on the application.

If we open our project, ExampleTwo, we will find a lot of good examples of extra unnecessary logic, such as loading the whole collection to search for an instance inside it, where we can retrieve it directly. Refer to the following code:

```
ProductStock[] stocks = catalogSessionBean.loadAllStocks();
for (ProductStock stock : stocks) {
  if (stock.getProductId().getId()==id) {
    if(catalogSessionBean.updateStock(stock,-1)){
      basketBean.addToBasket(id);
      . . .
    }
    . . .
  }
}
```

Also, we can see that the operation of decreasing the stock once added to the basket is not correct. This should only operate — if required — on the memory level and not actually update the database unless the order is finally submitted. In this case, we won't need the session listener and all this spaghetti unwanted code! Refer to the following code:

```
for (BasketElement basketElement : basketBean.getBasketElements())
{
  ProductStock currentStock = null;
  for (ProductStock stock : stocks) {
    if (stock.getProductId().getId() ==
      basketElement.getProductId()) {
      currentStock = stock;
      break;
    }
  }
```

```
    catalogSessionBean.updateStock(currentStock,
    basketElement.getCount());
}
```

A third example in this project is the bad product catalog filtering logic. It should construct the query according to the parameters rather than having all the possible combinations in such a bad logic that it misses certain scenarios. If the code is not documented, no one will actually be able to catch these issues easily. Refer to the following code:

```
if(criteria.getProductCategory()==0 && criteria.getPrice()>0 &&
    criteria.getSearchKeyword()==null) {
    query = em.createNamedQuery("Product.findByPrice");
    query.setParameter("price", criteria.getPrice());
}else if(criteria.getProductCategory()>0 && criteria.getPrice()==0
    && criteria.getSearchKeyword()==null) {
    query = em.createNamedQuery("Product.findByCategoryId");
    query.setParameter("categoryId", criteria.getProductCategory());
}else if(
...
... // rest of the bad logic code
```

Similar code shouldn't pass through either an automatic or manual code review and we shouldn't allow such code in our enterprise application code. In the production environment, changing such bad logic code is not recommended because of the potential impact unless the impact assessment is clear. Otherwise, it could lead to potential application malfunction, so it is better to address such coding issues early in the development phase by both automated and manual code reviews.

A lot of alternatives are available with better coding quality to solve the previous coding issue. These include using the standard JPA `QueryBuilder` or the dynamic construction of the required query.

Excessive application logging

Logging is very useful in the troubleshooting applications, especially in the production environment, where understanding old user actions or transactions is usually impossible without having meaningful logging.

Logging must strictly follow the best practices guidelines or it will impact our application performance. If we look back at our HighCPU example, we can see that all the threads are blocked, waiting to obtain the lock over the logging System.out object.

Special attention should be paid when logging the XML structures. It will degrade the application performance severely, so it shouldn't be added without the `if(debugEnabled)` condition unless it is not in a common scenario.

It is important to ensure that the logging configurations are correctly deployed in the production environment, as sometimes the performance issue is simply the incorrect enablement of the application debug level.

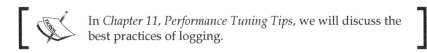

> In *Chapter 11*, *Performance Tuning Tips*, we will discuss the best practices of logging.

Database performance issues

A database is one of the biggest concerns in the enterprise application performance where sometimes the data grows to a huge size and gradually affects the application performance. Different database issues can affect the application performance as follows:

- Using an old database version
- Using an old JDBC driver library
- Missing table indexes in frequently used tables (SQL tuning principals)
- ORM layer tuning (such as JPA caching and index preallocation)
- Missing batch or bulk database operations in massive database manipulations
- Missing regular database housekeeping

Our main concern here is regular database housekeeping, which is essentially required and should be planned while designing the application, not when the performance issues show up! This housekeeping includes the following examples:

- Having frequent backups
- Partitioning the large tables
- Cleaning the different table spaces, for example, temporary and undo table space
- Archiving the old records

When the database size exceeds the handling limit, it will impact the application performance and it will be very difficult to manage all tuning techniques without having a service outage. Database size issue is unique for the production environment and can't be replicated in other environments due to the big difference between the production environment and other environments.

Having database performance issues require the assurance of performing the following steps:

- Checking the database performance report periodically such as the Oracle AWR report
- Tuning the database to suit the application
- Getting low performing queries and identifying issues through the database-specific analysis tools, for example, the SQL execution plan
- Monitoring database server performance and fixing any issues
- Using the latest database drivers
- Performing any necessary housekeeping activities
- Adding a caching layer if it does not already exist
- Changing the application persistent methodology such as using batch or bulk loading techniques for large data insertion instead of separate updates

Bulk database manipulations should be used. Using the database-supporting bulk operations in cases where there are a lot of database operations converts the fine-tuning operations into course-gained operations and can improve the application performance.

Going back to our example application and profile, it uses JProfiler while executing the performance testing (using Apache JMeter). We can see the following database **Hot Spots**:

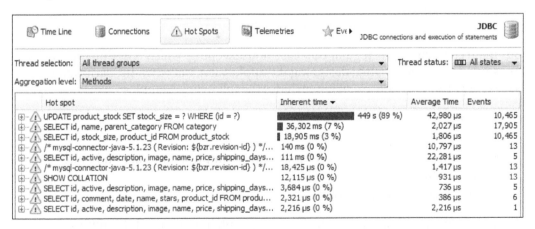

The interesting find in the preceding screenshot is that it informs us that we have a coding issue. We have concluded this because of the number of calls of different queries as it appears in the Events column. If we are hitting the database by thousands of calls for just six product catalogs, we clearly have bad coding issues that need to be fixed first before we continue working on any performance improvement or database tuning.

It is worth mentioning that one of the database-related issues is the data loading policy in either eager or lazy loading techniques. In each application, we need to consider the selection of the proper way to handle each transactional scenario according to the size of data, type of data, frequency of data changes, and whether data caching is used or not.

Missing proactive tuning

In any enterprise system architecture, different application components usually have the performance tuning suggestions that fit each application type. Such a tuning should be done in advance (that is, proactively) and not after facing performance issues.

We can definitely further tune these components in cases of performance issues according to application performance results. But as a baseline, we should be doing the required tuning in advance. An example of such tuning is the operating system tuning, application server tuning, JVM tuning, database tuning, and so on.

 We will discuss different aspects of performance tuning outside our application in *Chapter 9, Tuning an Application's Environment*, and some miscellaneous coding tuning topics in *Chapter 11, Performance Tuning Tips*.

Client-side performance issues

Performance issues on the client side means either a JavaScript coding issue or slow loading of different resources. Rarely do we need to consider **cascading style sheets (CSS)**.

With the advance of web technologies, a lot of developers now rely on the Ajax technology to do a lot of things in the application interface such as loading and submitting contents. Some frameworks come with components that support the Ajax calls, such as JSF and ADF.

The initial set of questions that we need to answer when we face client-side performance issue is as follows:

- Is the issue related to the browser type?

- Is it related to the page size or resources size?

- What happens if we disable JavaScript in the browser?

- Did this issue occur in the performance testing tool?

 Performance testing tools such as Apache JMeter won't execute the JavaScript code, so don't rely on these tools to catch JavaScript issues. Instead, we will use this as an advantage because having performance issues in browsers but not in JMeter suggests that we are facing the most probable JavaScript issue.

A good thing is that all browsers these days have integrated tools that can be used to troubleshoot rendering content. Usually, they are named **Developer tools**. Also, they have additional useful third-party plugins that can be used for the same purpose.

We can also use the external tools (they also have plugins for different browsers), such as DynaTrace or Fiddler.

Chrome developer tools

If you execute the ExampleTwo application in the Chrome browser, press *F12* or select **Developer tools** from the **Tools** menu, and then reload the website again.

 This example is uses Chrome Version 30.0.x m.

Download the latest Chrome browser from
https://www.google.com/intl/en/chrome/browser/.

Network analysis

We can see that a lot of useful information is available and it is organized in different tabs. If we select the **Network** tab, we can see the loading time of different resources, as shown in the following screenshot. This facilitates identifying if a certain resource takes time to load or if it has a large size:

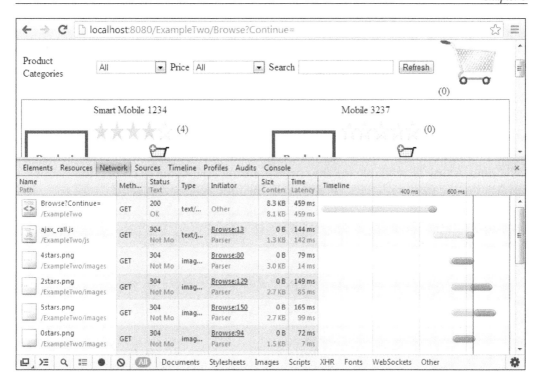

If we move the cursor over any of these **Timeline** figures, we will see more details about the DNS lookup and latency, or we can click on any row to open it for more details. In the following screenshot, we can see one request detail organized in different tabs, including the **Headers**, **Preview**, **Response**, **Cookies**, and **Timing** details:

JavaScript profiling

Open the Chrome browser and navigate to any website, for example, the Packt Publishing website, `http://www.packtpub.com`.

Now, switch to the **Profiles** tab, click on the **Start** button, and refresh the page by pressing *F5*. Once the page is completely loaded, click on the **Stop** button.

Now, we have just profiled the JavaScript code. The profiling data will be under the name **Profile 1** and we will see the JavaScript code performance with every method CPU time. A link is available for the corresponding script source code if this is our application JavaScript method, as shown in the following screenshot:

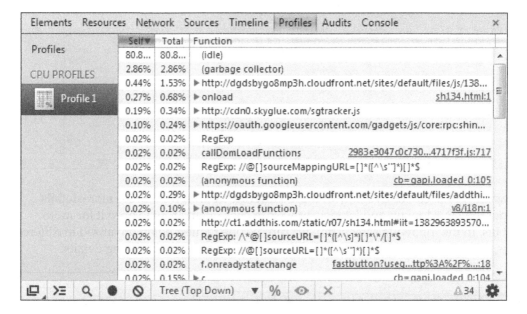

A lot of display features are available, for example, if we click on the toggle button, %, it will show the actual time spent rather than the relative percentage time.

These useful tools will help identify the heaviest JavaScript methods that need some tuning.

Speed Tracer

Speed Tracer is a Chrome plugin tool that helps to identify and fix potential performance issues. It shows different visualized metrics with recommendation hints.

As it instruments the low-level points in the browser, it can help in identifying and locating different issues related to different phases, such as the JavaScript parsing and execution, CSS, DOM event handling, resource loading, and XMLHttpRequest callbacks. Refer to the following screenshot:

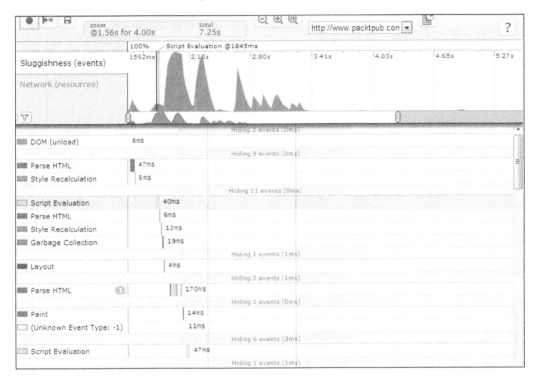

Here is an example of tool recommendation hints. There are all **Info** level hints meaning there are no major issues, as shown in the following screenshot:

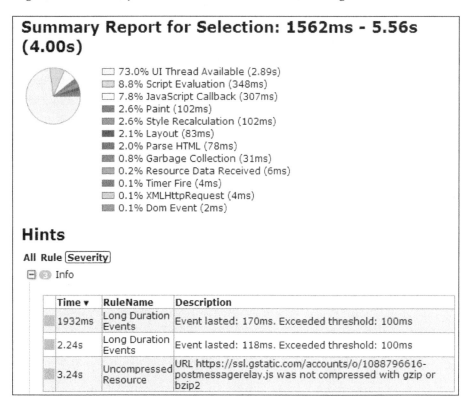

 Speed Tracer can be downloaded from the following URL:
https://developers.google.com/web-toolkit/speedtracer/.

Internet Explorer developer tools

The developer tools are available in Internet Explorer. If we press *F12*, it will open similar developer tools. Select the **Network** tab, click on the **Start capturing** button, and then open the same page, that is, http://www.packtpub.com.

We can see nearly the same tabs that exist in the Chrome developer tools but to the left, and we can start profiling and reloading the page to obtain the JavaScript profiling snapshot. The following screenshot is taken from Internet Explorer Version 11.0.x:

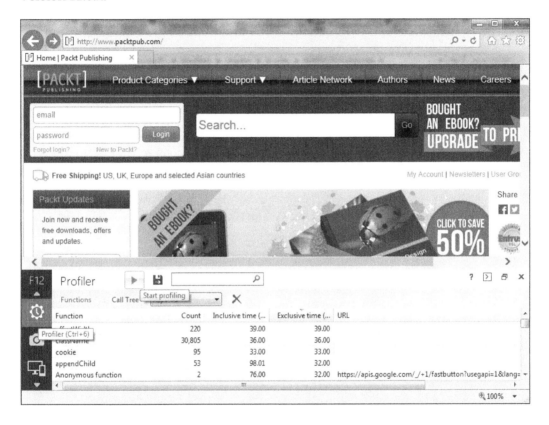

Firefox developer tools

In Firefox, we can select **Toggle Tools** from the **Web Developer** menu option to open the tools. The tools have the same features that exist in IE and Chrome. The following screenshot shows the developer tools in Firefox (the screenshot is taken from Firefox Version 24.0, which is a portable version):

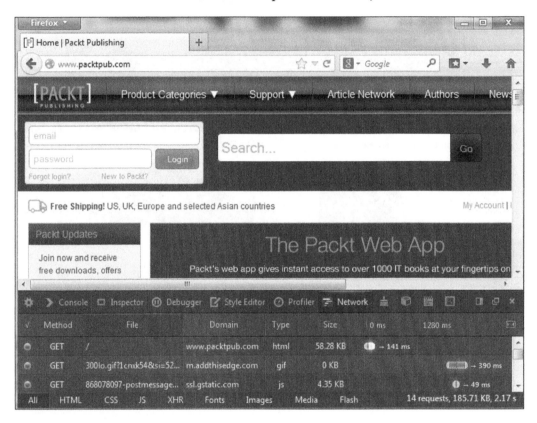

Navigating time specifications

W3C is sponsoring a new specification for an interface for web applications to get different timing information; the specifications define a new interface `PerformanceTiming`, which can be used to get different timings. A sample usage for this interface, once implemented in different browsers (as it is not supported yet), will look like the following code:

```
<head>
<script type="text/javascript">
function onLoad() {
```

```
    var now = new Date().getTime();
    var loadTime = now-performance.timing.navigationStart;
    alert("Page loading time: " + loadTime);
}
</script>
</head>
<body onload="onLoad()">
```

 For more information about these specifications, check the specification documentation at the following URL:

https://dvcs.w3.org/hg/webperf/raw-file/tip/ specs/NavigationTiming/Overview.html

Summary

In this chapter, we learned briefly how to determine performance issue locations and covered some of the common enterprise applications performance issues.

We tried to classify these common issues into different groups, and then we discussed some samples from each group category in more detail. The important point here is to be able to use these issues as models or templates of typical application performance issues, so we can frame any performance issue in these templates.

Finally, we discussed how to diagnose client-side performance issues using existing browser embedded tools.

In subsequent chapters, we will go in-depth on how to read application profiling snapshots and retrieve the required diagnostic information from different profiling aspects, CPU, threading, and memory, so we can diagnose performance issues that we have covered in this chapter.

In the next chapter, *Chapter 6, CPU Time Profiling*, we will start with discussing CPU and time profiling and how to diagnose different application bottlenecks/HotSpots using different profiling tools such as NetBeans, Eclipse, and JProfiler.

6

CPU Time Profiling

In this and the subsequent two chapters, we will detail Java profilers from three main perspectives: CPU time, threading, and memory profiling.

In this chapter, we will cover CPU time profiling to understand and interpret the output of different profilers, its significance, what we need to focus on when reading a profiling session's results, and finally, how to prepare our fix for different readings by defining a fixing strategy.

In this chapter, we will cover the following topics:

- Using different profilers to get the CPU time profiling results
- Reading and interpreting the CPU profiling results
- Analyzing method time versus call frequency
- Identifying potential performance issues
- Learning how to measure and how to fix the performance of an algorithm
- Defining our first performance fixing strategy

When to use CPU profiling

Before we discuss CPU time profiling, we need to understand the underlying objective of CPU profiling. When faced with an application performance issue, the first step is to identify the type of performance issue.

If it is clearly an issue of insufficient memory, we can directly perform the required memory analysis. When the issue is unclear, the best way to identify its nature is CPU profiling.

In CPU time profiling, we must focus on identifying the processes that consume the most execution time so that we can reduce it and improve the application's performance. The issues can be with the code logic, interface (for example, database transaction), blocking (for example, waiting for a remote call or object monitor), threading, and so on.

CPU profiling should also be used during the development stage to ensure that we have a well-performing application before delivering the code; this should be one of our proactive measures in creating a well-performing enterprise application.

In this chapter, we will discuss the various CPU profiling aspects along with how to perform CPU profiling and analyze the profiling results.

Different CPU profiling options

As discussed in *Chapter 4, Monitoring Java Applications*, Java profilers have many different modes and the most commonly used ones are as follows:

- **Event-based**: This is the mode where the profiler captures the application's events such as as method calls, class loading, thread changes, and so on.

- **Instrumental-based**: This is the mode where the profiler instruments the application with additional instructions to gather more information. This causes the highest impact on the application's execution time compared to the other types.

- **Sampling-based (statistical)**: This is the mode where the profiler probes the target program's **program counter** (**PC**) at regular intervals using operating system interrupts. Sampling profiles are less accurate but facilitate a near normal execution time of the target application.

Most of the existing profilers provide support for different profiling modes, in particular, the sampled and instrumented modes.

Before we discuss how to read our application's profiling results, let's look at the different available options to perform CPU time profiling in NetBeans, JMC, and JProfiler as examples of Java profilers.

Using a NetBeans profiler

We already discussed how to use the NetBeans profiler to profile both Java standalone and enterprise applications in *Chapter 4, Monitoring Java Applications*.

The main difference between the two application types is that in the case of web-based applications, the application server (for example, GlassFish) will start in the profiling mode. Next, the application will be deployed and the profiling will record all the interactions with the application server. However, if it is a Java project, then the application will be executed directly in the profiling mode.

We can also attach the NetBeans profiler to any running Java process, a standalone or web application, by using the **Attach Profiler** option in NetBeans' **Profile** menu. Now we will explore how to profile both applications.

 We discussed NetBeans' profiler calibration in *Chapter 4, Monitoring Java Applications*. This calibration should be performed once for each installed JDK, and it should be recalibrated only if certain changes occur in the system's configuration.

Profiling a Java application

First, let's start NetBeans and select our previous project HighCPU. Next, select **Profile Project**. A pop-up will ask us to select a profile option. The three available options are **Monitor**, **CPU**, and **Memory**. Select the **CPU** option to see the different available options in CPU profiling as shown in the following screenshot:

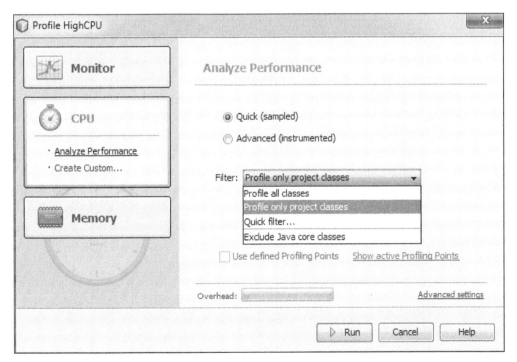

As shown in the preceding screenshot, the two main options are **Quick (sampled)** profiling and **Advanced (instrumented)** profiling, which are available for most of the profiler tools.

Each option has different settings, for example, setting a filter means defining the classes we want to include in the profiling session.

 An example used in *Chapter 4, Monitoring Java Applications*, is `HighCPU`. You can download it from the code bundle of this book available at `http://www.packtpub.com/`.

In both modes, if we click on **Advanced settings**, we see the current profiling settings for each mode. We can see the configuration's name below the **CPU** icon (or **Monitor/Memory** icon) on the left-hand side of the profiling dialog. We can change these predefined configurations by clicking on **Create Custom...**, where we can use existing configurations and modify them as per our usage. Now, click on **Create Custom...**, choose the existing configuration template, and click on **OK**. We can now see the newly created custom configuration available with editable configurations.

Select **Advanced settings** to edit and customize the configuration according to your requirements. For example, you can change the default sampling rate (**10 ms**) as shown in the following screenshot:

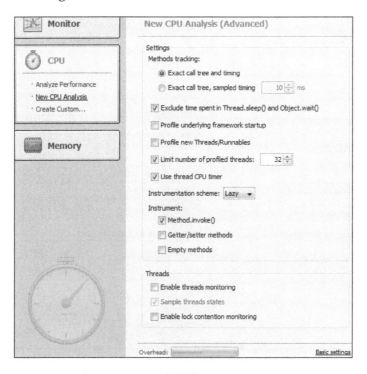

Changing the sampling frequency according to our profiling needs is an important aspect to control the output of a sampled profiling mode.

We can delete this new template by right-clicking on it and clicking on **Delete** from the context menu.

The overhead indicator represents the general overhead from the current settings, which can be monitored when adding or removing different setting options.

We can also set up a filter to profile only certain classes; it can provide us with the following different options:

- **Profile all classes**
- **Profile only project classes**
- **Quick filter...**
- **Exclude Java core classes**

By selecting **Quick filter...**, we can define inclusion or exclusion filters for different classes. This is very useful in the following situations:

- When the scope is limited to certain application areas
- When dealing with a large number of libraries
- When troubleshooting a specific issue (as part of issue isolation)

To add a custom filter, use the simple `osa.ora.*` format, which means that all the classes are present in the `osa.ora` package. Alternatively, we can use the exact class name `osa.ora.HighCPU` to filter the sole class.

Profiling a web application

Following the same steps performed when profiling a Java application, let's open the `ExampleTwo` project in NetBeans as an example of web applications. Select the project, go to the **Profile** menu, and click on **Profile Project**. The same pop-up window will be displayed. From the **CPU** tab, select the **Quick (sampled)** mode and click on the **Run** button.

> The example we used in *Chapter 5, Recognizing Common Performance Issues*, is `ExampleTwo`. You can download it with its database script and JMeter load test script from the code bundle of this book, available at `http://www.packtpub.com/`.

NetBeans will start the GlassFish application server in the profiling mode, and the browser will open with our application's main page. The following two lines will appear in the GlassFish logs, indicating that the server has started in the profiling mode and the profiling agent is connected to NetBeans:

```
Profiler Agent: Waiting for connection on port 5140 (Protocol version:
14)
Profiler Agent: Established connection with the tool
```

On the **Profiler** window, click on the **Live Results** icon to open the **Live Results** tab, and being using the application. With every interaction, we will see that a change occurs in the profiling results. We can also save a snapshot by clicking on the **Take Snapshot** icon (or by pressing *Ctrl + F2*) as shown in the following screenshot:

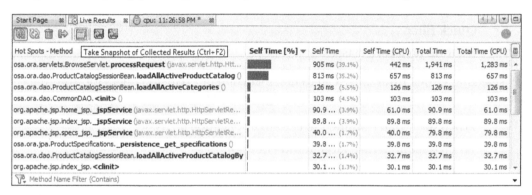

Typically, when profiling web applications, we need to execute load testing to identify the HotSpot areas. Also, it is better to use the sampled mode to reduce the overhead on the application server or the instrumented mode (with the class filter).

 Don't expect to see identical results in your profiling session as the profiling results depend on too many factors, including the hardware profile, a machine's CPU utilization, disk I/O speed, other running applications, and so on.

Open JMeter and execute the `Test online catalog` test plan we have created in *Chapter 5, Recognizing Common Performance Issues*. After the test plan is executed, we will see the HotSpot methods in our application as shown in the following screenshot:

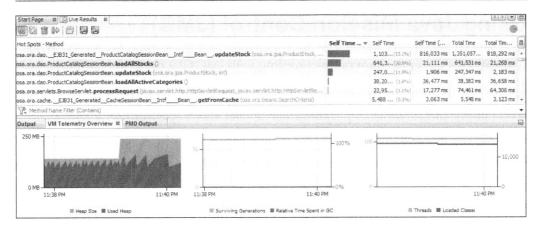

We see that the top HotSpot methods are related to updating the stock and loading the product catalog methods. We will discuss these HotSpots later in this chapter.

Now, save a snapshot of the **Live Results**. It will open a new window. Go to the new window and navigate to the **Combined** tab. The tab will display the application server threads with their corresponding HotSpot areas as shown in the following screenshot:

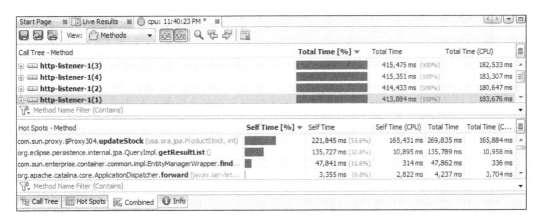

Also note that **VM telemetry** shows the memory consumption and auto resize for the heap memory size because this application has a memory leakage, as discussed in the *Chapter 5, Recognizing Common Performance Issues*.

Using Java Mission Control (JMC)

Now let's try using JMC to retrieve the application's CPU profiling results. We have two options—either perform online profiling with JMC GUI or offline profiling. The main difference is that if the GUI is connected, then we can specify the different recording settings for it. On the other hand, in the case of offline profiling, we will send our profiling settings as parameters. Now, let's try to perform some offline profiling using JMC.

From inside NetBeans, select the `HighCPU` project, right-click on and select **Properties**, go to the **Run** tab, and add the following in **VM options**:

```
-XX:+UnlockCommercialFeatures -XX:+FlightRecorder -XX:StartFlightRecordin
g=duration=30s,filename=d:/recording.jfr
```

The `UnlockCommercialFeatures` parameter allows us to use the flight recorder, which is a commercial feature in Java. In the last parameter, we started the recording and specified the recording duration as 30 seconds, which will be saved in the specified file, `recording.jfr`.

 Commercial features in Java are subjected to license agreements and shouldn't be used in a production environment without a proper license. For more details, refer to the Oracle license documentation at http://www.oracle.com/technetwork/java/javase/terms/license/index.html.

Now, when we run the application, we will see the following lines in the application logs:

```
Started recording 1. The result will be written to:
D:\ recording.jfr
```

Once the application completes the execution, start JMC and open the `recording.jfr` file from the **File** menu. Next, click on **Open file** and select the file. We will see our application's profiling results. Let's check the CPU utilization in this recorded file by selecting **Code** and click on the **Call Tree** tab as shown in the following screenshot:

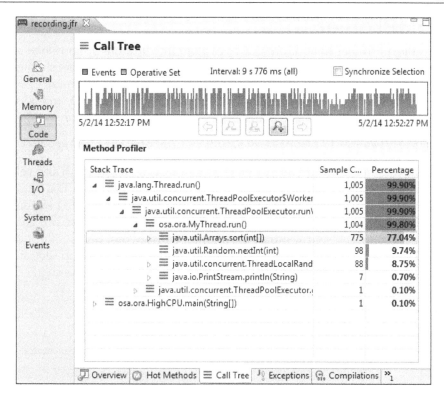

As we can see in the results, JMC CPU profiling points to the `Arrays.sort()` method as the hottest spot in our profiling results, consuming approximately 77 percent of the total execution time.

To profile a web application using JMC, add the same parameters in the application server start script. For example, in the GlassFish application server, add the following parameters in the **VM options** section in the `domain.xml` file to enable the commercial features:

```
<jvm-options>-XX:+UnlockCommercialFeatures</jvm-options>
<jvm-options>-XX:+FlightRecorder</jvm-options>
```

We can also add the same parameters from inside NetBeans by right-clicking on our NetBeans web project and selecting **Properties**. Then go to the **Run** parameters and add the following in **VM Options**:

```
-XX:+UnlockCommercialFeatures  -XX:+FlightRecorder
```

From inside JMC, connect to the GlassFish server by expanding the GlassFish process in JMC's **JVM Browser**, right-clicking on **Flight recorder**, and selecting the **Start Flight Recording** context menu option.

Using JProfiler

Now let's attach JProfiler to both projects to explore the different options available for CPU profiling. Let's first start with the `HighCPU` project (and later in this chapter, we will profile the `ExampleTwo` project). From inside NetBeans, select the `HighCPU` project and right-click on it. Then, select **Project Properties**, go to the **Run** tab, and add the following JVM command line (the path follows the JProfiler installation path):

```
-agentpath:D:/PROGRA~1/JPROFI~2/bin/windows/jprofilerti.dll=port=8849
```

Now open JProfiler and from **Start Center**, go to the **New Session** tab and select **New Session**. Then, select **Attach to profiled JVM** and click on **OK**. The **Session Settings** window will be displayed and will ask for the initial profiling settings, which is the sampled or instrumented mode. Select either because we can change this in the next step. The settings dialog will open with several different options. Select **CPU recording** from the **Initial recording** profile in the **Startup** section. The profiling settings are shown in the following screenshot:

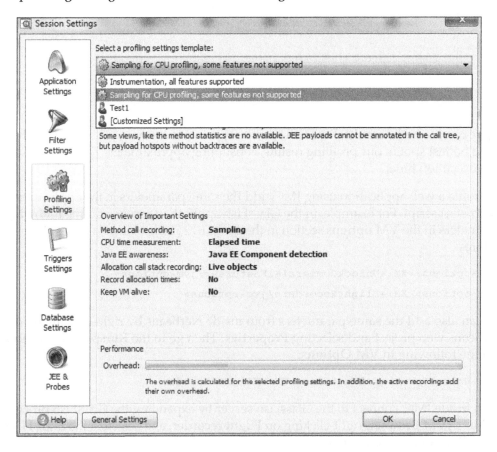

If we check JProfiler profiling options, we can identify the following options with what we saw in the NetBeans profiler:

- Using the sampled or instrumented mode
- Defining a new configuration
- Defining filter criteria similar to those defined in the NetBeans filter

Other options are also available, such as controlling the database profiling options or adding different JEE probes such as Servlet, JNDI, JMS, WebServices, classloader, and so on, as shown in the following screenshot:

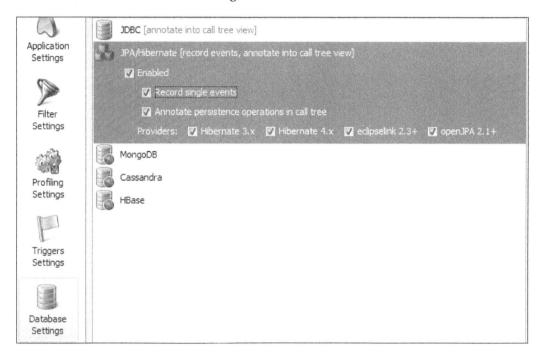

With these abundant options, we can customize our profiling session according to our troubleshooting issues. For example, we can expand the **JEE & Probes** option as shown in the following screenshot:

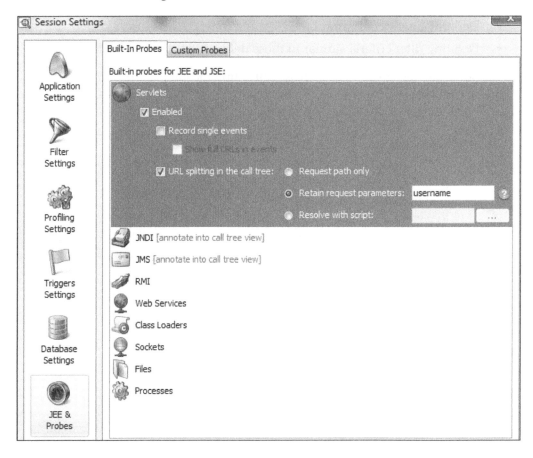

We will see that the result can be split according to the request parameter. So if we face issues with certain request parameters/users, we can identify these issues instead of grouping all the user requests, which might causes the issue to disappear in the accumulated data.

Reading and interpreting CPU profiling results

Now if we execute instrumental (or sampling) profiling, we will see the following basic sections in the snapshot of any profiling result.

The call tree view

This section includes the call stack trace of the invoked methods, which are listed according to the set filter. The level of information will depend on the profiling mode and any other selected options.

The HotSpots view

This section includes the most time-consuming methods, which are listed according to the defined profiler rules. We can change these rules in JProfiler.

The following are the important values that we need to look into:

- Total/inherent method time
- Method invocation count/events
- Average time spent by each method call

Also, it can be useful to arrange them by class or package to isolate the issue in the utilities or libraries used.

The following should be considered before we conclude any thing:

- Method time in the sampled profiling mode
- Relative time (percentage) in the instrumental profiling mode
- Invocation count available only in the instrumental profiling mode

The NetBeans profiling snapshot for our project looks like the following screenshot (The invocation count displayed in the screenshot means that profiling was performed in the instrumented mode.):

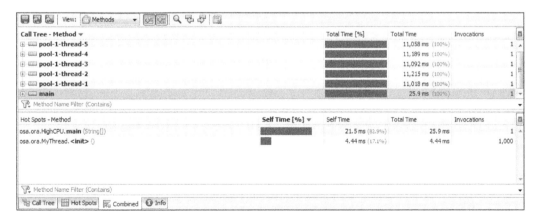

The NetBeans profiling results are displayed in three different view options: **Call Tree**, **Hot Spots**, and **Combined view**. The **Combined view** is a combination of both views (see the previous screenshots).

Using the sampled mode, we see that the following are the top HotSpot methods:

- `Arrays.sort()` consumes around 57 percent of the total time spent in this method alone (38 seconds)

- `Thread.sleep()` takes up around 17 percent

After that, the two HotSpot methods are related to the random integer generation, illustrated in the following screenshot:

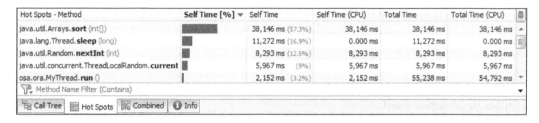

If we tried to do the same in JProfiler, we will see the same results by navigating to **CPU views | Call Tree**, as shown in the following screenshot:

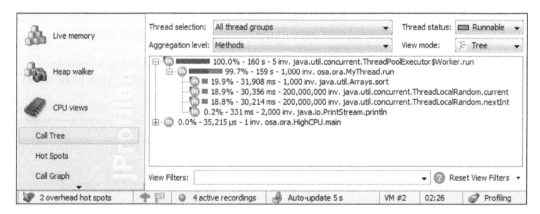

As shown in the preceding screenshot, the **Call Tree** view filters the **Runnable** threads only at the **Methods** level. It also shows the invocations beside the method average time. We can change the current view by selecting different display options such as filtering them according to the thread's status (**Runnable, Waiting, Blocked,** and so on). We can also display them at the **Methods** level or aggregate them at the **Class** or **Package** levels, and so on.

In the previous screenshot, for example, the `Arrays.sort()` method takes around 19.9 percent of the total execution time caused by its invocation in about 1,000 different invocations. The results here are different than the previous ones because the profiling mode and the applied filter show only the **Runnable** threads.

The `Thread.sleep()` method does not appear because the thread is not running and we show only the **Runnable** threads in the previous screenshot.

Another tab shows the **Hot Spots** results. If we open it, we will see the different application HotSpots ordered by the consumed inherent time, and not the average time, as shown in the following screenshot:

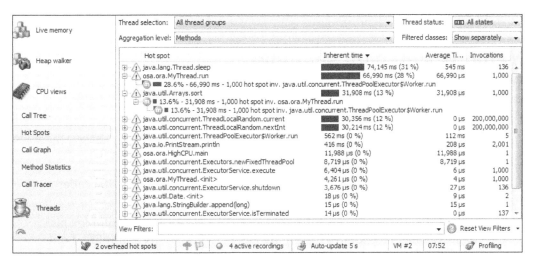

The preceding screenshot shows the **Hot Spots** results for the **All thread groups** status. We can use the drop-down options to change the current view to specify a certain thread status to be displayed, for example, **Runnable**.

Analyzing the method time versus the method invocation count

Now let's analyze the CPU profiling results according to what we have seen in the previous sections. We can pick and discuss some of the following possible combinations of high inherent time, that is, the HotSpot method:

- High self-time
- High invocation events
- High self-time and invocation events

The **self-time** of a method is the time spent by the method itself. Usually, it refers to the average time calculated according to the invocations.

The **inherent time** of a method includes the total time spent in all calls to this method, which is equal to the method's self-time multiplied by the number of invocations or events.

The hot spot method types

We can classify the hot spot methods into the following types according to the root cause of the performance issue.

Methods with high self-time

This is a simple type of hot spot method, where the method itself is the root cause of the issue. So, we need to dig deeper into the method to identify the bottle neck. With this method, we have the following two types of issues:

- If this method is a part of our code, then the issue has mostly to do with the algorithm and logic
- If the method is outside our code, then the usage/logic from the caller is wrong or there is an underperforming library
- If the logic is complex, because the method is performing a complex task, then we must consider revisiting this logic to find a more simplified one

Bad database queries can cause the self-time of the related method to be high. However, fortunately, this can be identified by either profilers or database trace/reports. For example, if we look at JProfiler, we can see a dedicated section for database profiling that supports different frameworks/libraries, such as JPA/Hibernate, HBase, and JDBC, and shows the location for all the calls for each database statement so that we can trace these hot spots (we will see this later in this chapter).

Methods with high invocation events

High invocation events for bad/normal performing code can lead to hot spot areas in an application. A method's self-time can be normal, but the large number of calls/invocations will cause such a hot spot to appear (with high inherent time). This is mostly due to the logic of the method caller.

Methods with high self-time and invocation events

These methods show the lowest performance and and the method itself is invoked too many times, which leads to a hot spot area in our application.

Identifying a hot spot type

The correct identification of the application's hot spot type will point to the correct solution. This will answer two important questions: does the method itself have performance issues? Or, is it the application's logic that's causes the method to be invoked too many times? The first will require the method's logic to be fixed, but the second will require the application logic to be changed to reduce the number of method invocations; sometimes both are required.

If we profile our ExampleTwo application by JProfiler while executing the JMeter load testing, then the hot spots will be visible for our application (in the load testing scenarios covered). This is illustrated in the following screenshot:

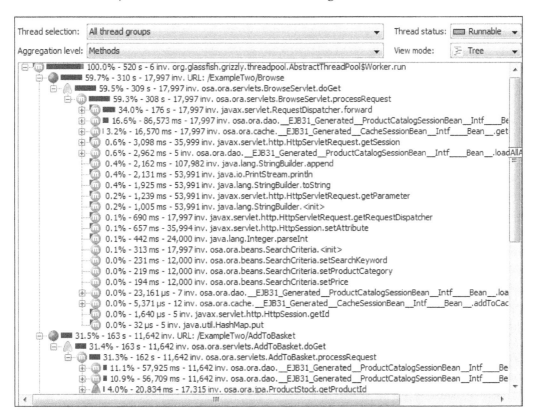

We can expand the hot nodes to see more information or we can switch to the **Hot Spots** tab to see them in a clear view. The useful information about this application's performance can be seen in the database section, where we can get information for both JDBC and JPA. This is illustrated in the following screenshot:

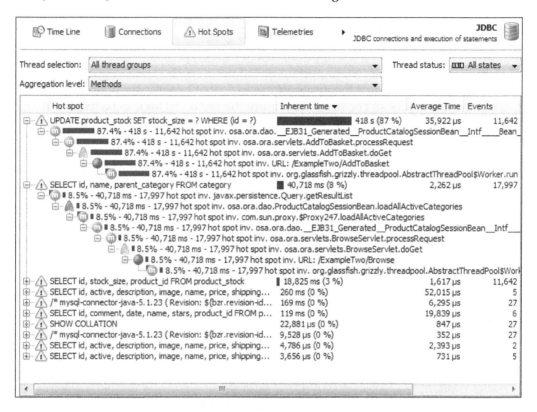

In the database hot spots, we see that the top hot spot statement is UPDATE product_ stock SET stock_size = ? WHERE (id = ?). We have clarified before that this is due to the application's bad logic, which updates the stock when a product is added to the basket, and re-adds it when the user's session has expired.

The second hot spot query is SELECT id, name, parent_category FROM category, which is repeated more than 17,000 times due to the application's bad logic to load the category details of the product with each user request.

We can switch to the JPA section to identify one more hot spot related to updating the product stock, which is similar to our first hot spot. This hot spot points to the two locations (add to basket and session destroy listener) where we used JPA calls to update the stock.

Fixing the application logic will resolve all these hot spots. The following screenshot shows the JPA hot spots:

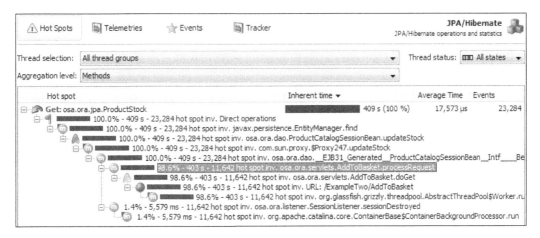

One of the good features in JProfiler is the ability to use Java EE probes, where we can isolate certain component performance issues.

Try to execute `ExampleOne` and run JMeter load testing while JProfiler is attached and the servlet probe is enabled (to enable it, go to **JEE & Probes**, select **Servlets**, and check the **Enabled** checkbox). We will then see the servlets performance figures as shown in the following screenshot (JSPs being translated to servlets are included):

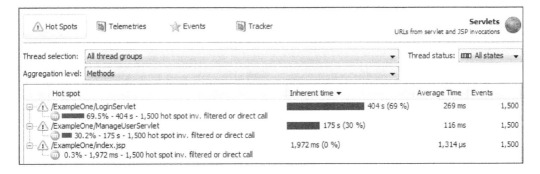

The example we used in *Chapter 3, Getting Familiar with Performance Testing*, is `ExampleOne` is. You can download it from the code bundle of this book available at `http://www.packtpub.com/`.

It shows the **Inherent time**, **Average time**, and the number of **Events**. As we can see in the results, the time taken by `LoginServlet` is the largest. This makes sense because it will hit the database with each request to authenticate the user. But for other servlets, if the user is not already logged in, then the user will be redirected to the error page without executing much logic in these servlets. To confirm this conclusion, take a look at the database hot spots shown in the following screenshot:

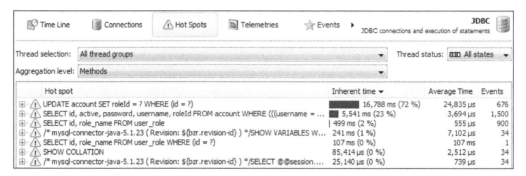

The number of authentication query events that confirm our conclusion is 1,500 times, while the update user role occurs only 676 times (because of the invalid login trials and no update statement being fired if the same user profile is set). The following screenshot shows the hot spots in our application:

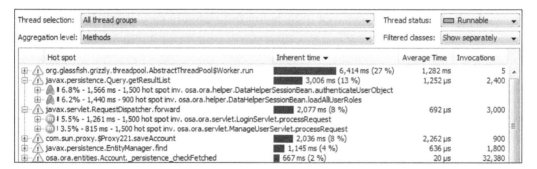

Identifying potential performance issues

In the previous section, we diagnosed different hot spot areas and classified them into different types (either the method's self-time or the invocation count is high, or both). Now let's describe some examples of the potential root causes of these hot spots.

Algorithmic/logic issues

When the application logic is generally the root cause of the performance issue, there can be many variants such as unnecessary loops, underperforming algorithms, repeated calculations, and no caching.

If we look at our online shopping project, ExampleTwo, we see some samples of this ineffective application logic, shown as follows:

```
Product[] allProducts = catalogSessionBean.
  loadAllActiveProductCatalogByCriteria(new SearchCriteria());
for (Product allProduct : allProducts) {
  if(allProduct.getId()==productId){
    outputStream.write(allProduct.getImage());
    outputStream.close();
    return;
  }
}
```

In this logic, instead of getting the product by its ID, we get all the catalog products and then loop the entire list to retrieve our target product, so we can serialize its image!

Another similar example is decreasing the stock by one for the product added to the basket. It continues to looping all the stock elements till it finds the product stock. The optimal way is to get this product stock using the product ID in one step:

```
ProductStock[] stocks = catalogSessionBean.loadAllStocks();
for (ProductStock stock : stocks) {
  if (stock.getProductId().getId()==id) {
    if(catalogSessionBean.updateStock(stock,-1)){
      basketBean.addToBasket(id);
..
..
```

The preceding code is useless and represents a ineffective application logic to do the required task.

There are several examples in this project that are similar to these useless loops, but we need to look at the examples that represent the application's logic errors. One of them is the *add to basket* transaction, which decreases the product stock by one, the other one is the *session destroy listener*, which re-adds this to the stock (because the users didn't buy it).

This is a typical example of an underperforming application logic, where we add a lot of useless code that represents either a business requirement error or a design fault. We see similar issues in faulty application designs (and in few cases, misunderstand the requirements or fail to explain the project's workflow to the business team during the requirements gathering phase).

Regardless of the actual reason we highlighted before, performance issues caused by design faults will require a lot of changes to the project and shouldn't be done as a production performance fix. This is because it needs extensive testing and analysis to avoid a missing scenario (of course, in our project, it is simple fix because it is just a sample application).

Caching issues

Caching is one of the main reasons for poor application performance. Caching is not only for database queries or external calls but also for repeated calculations, in particular, for derived data.

Constructing the product tree/hierarchy in our product catalog is an example. The following diagram shows the recursive relation using a product category tree:

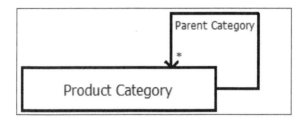

To construct a product tree, add the product category and then loop it till we get its parents tree. For example, if we have a Samsung S5, we can see the following category hierarchy:

Samsung S5 > Samsung Mobiles > Mobiles > Phones > Electronics and Computers

We can construct this and cache the results in our application cache so that there is no need to identify the product's full category tree with each customer request.

Incorrect caching is also a contributing factor in an application's poor performance, where the resource loading time increases (in comparison to no caching) as it requires hitting the cache, loading the resource, and adding it back to the cache.

Resourcing issues

Dealing with networking and different I/O operations usually represents the slowest parts in our application. Communication with any remote system where the response time is not constant can impact our application's performance.

Interfacing with the database storage to load different resources is a major part of our application's tuning effort. This is the main challenge for most present-day enterprise applications, especially in an enterprise application with significantly expanding data.

Threading issues

When the application performs lengthy operations, make use of the hardware processing power to decrease the time taken for such operations.

Profiling the application will point to these areas, that is, where concurrent implementation is required or incorrectly implemented. However, the concurrent processing of the application logic requires a lot of conditions. For example, there should be no dependency on the distributed tasks, otherwise, concurrent threads will wait for each other.

In the *Chapter 7*, *Thread Profiling*, we will navigate through different multithreading issues.

In general, treating an execution as a background activity is also a way to resolve these extensive operations. However, this won't fit every case and needs to be tailored to the required task.

Fixing algorithmic/logic performance

Algorithm complexity (time/space) is the main evaluating factor for any algorithm. Here, time refers to the duration required to execute instructions/steps, while space refers to the space occupied by its data structure. Both are directly related to the performance of an algorithm.

When using an algorithm to resolve a problem in our application, search for the most efficient way to achieve that. This means we have to use an algorithm with minimal possible steps. If we already have an algorithm/logic, and need to optimize its performance, we first need to perform the following steps:

- Understand the logic (its inputs and outputs) and why this logic is required
- Evaluate the logic's performance

- Find the areas that need improvement
- Evaluate different solutions (fix the logic or find other alternatives)
- Resolve poorly performing areas
- Measure the logic's performance after its resolution

We will discuss simplified ways to evaluate an algorithm's performance.

Simple algorithmic evaluation

Before we detail our fixing strategy, let's first understand what we mean by algorithm and logic fixing strategy. We begin with something that can refresh our mind a bit—the famous interview question of the two eggs.

The puzzle is about having two identical eggs and access to a 100-storeyed building. We need to find out the highest possible floor from which the egg will not be broken when dropped out of a window from that floor. The two eggs here represent the two possible trials to identify this floor.

The simplest solution is to start with floor number one and sequentially move up till the egg is broken. This way, we can identify the floor number using just one egg, as shown in the following logic.

```
int thresholdFloor = 0;
for( int i=1;i<101;i++){
   if(egg.drop(i)==true) { //broken at i floor
    thresholdFloor=i;
    break;
  }
}
```

This solution represents what we call a poor application algorithm. In the worst case scenario, if the eggs can only be broken by dropping it from the 100th floor, then we need 100 trials to find the answer!

We can enhance the solution and move up every two floors (or more). If the egg breaks, then we can try with the lower floors (an odd floor) and identify the threshold floor. This way, with 51 trials (that is, in the worst case), if the egg breaks at 99th floor, we can modify the logic shown as follows:

```
int thresholdFloor = 0;
for( int i=2;i<101;i=i+2){
  if(egg.drop(i)==true) { //broken
    if(egg2.drop(i-1)==true) {
```

```
      thresholdFloor=i-1;
      break;
    } else {
      thresholdFloor=i;
     break;


    }
  }
}
```

Similarly, we can use a binary search starting with 50, then either 75 or 25, and so on. Unfortunately, if the egg breaks on the 50th floor (first trial in binary search), we will need to go through 49 floors. This will give us around 50 trials in the worst case scenario, which is not good because this is not a typical binary search problem.

Can we improve this logic a bit more? What if we tried to use 10 steps at a time instead of two? Then if the egg is broken, we can loop at an interval of 10 floors from the bottom to the top. In the worst case, we will have around 19 steps (that is, if the egg breaks at floor 99). The following is the corresponding logic:

```
int thresholdFloor = 0;
for( int i=10;i<101;i=i+10){
  if(egg.drop(i)==true) { //broken
    thresholdFloor=i;
    for(int x=i-9;x<i;x++){
      if(egg2.drop(x)==true) {
        thresholdFloor=x;
        break;
      }
    }
    Break;
  }
}
```

Tuning an application's logic to perform the required task in the shortest possible steps or with minimal impact on different resources is what we call fixing the algorithm. We have seen examples where loading the whole collection and looping them was not required. It is better to load the required resource directly without investing too much cost on the application's performance.

In other words, always search for the worst case scenario while developing the application logic. Sometimes the ideal or common scenario should be considered as well. For example, in our two eggs puzzle, an egg might break on the lower floors. This makes sense and a majority of cases could follow. However, we should always create a good balance between the majority common cases and worst case scenarios and pick what suits our application.

Thus, the best solution in this puzzle using mathematical calculations is to minimize the maximum drops. This allows all the scenarios to have the same number of trials (proving this is out of our scope). The following table shows the detailed solution steps:

Drop	Floor	Action if broken
1	14	Loop 1-13
2	27	Loop 15-26
3	39	Loop 28-38
4	50	Loop 40-49
5	60	Loop 51-59
6	69	Loop 61-68
7	77	Loop 70-76
8	84	Loop 78-83
9	90	Loop 85-89
10	95	Loop 91-94
11	99	Loop 96-98
12	100	No action

The advantage of this solution is that we have reduced the most time-consuming worst case scenario (which was around 19 in a 10-step solution) to 14-15 steps only. Can you think of the solution if we have 1000 floors?

Evaluating an algorithm's complexity

In this section, we will discuss the evaluation of our logic based on an algorithm's complexity and the big O (or big Oh) annotation, but in a simplified way, without any mathematics. An algorithm's evaluation includes three aspect: best case, worst case, and average case scenarios. We can refer to the time as the required steps to achieve a solution.

An algorithm's performance can vary with each of these cases, and usually, we use either the worst case or average case scenario in our evaluation.

To understand the difference between the three cases, let's assume we are searching for an object in an array of size n. The best case scenario is to find this object as the first object in our search, the worst case is to find it at the end of our search, and the average case is to find it in the middle of our search.

The big O notation is widely used to evaluate algorithms using their asymptotic growth (that is, growth rate). It describes the relation between the input size and the processing time and classifies the logic's functions into different orders (levels), hence the name.

To obtain the big O value of our algorithm, we need to follow the ensuing simplified steps/rules:

- Clearly define the input(s) and output(s) of the logic
- Understand the logic well
- Convert our logic into a function $f(n)$, where n is the logic input.
- Remove all the function terms except the one with the highest growth rate
- Remove any constant factors that do not depend on n

Since this is not a book for algorithm complexity, we will map some of these basic steps into a simple piece of code to understand how we can roughly measure the estimated time for a function.

Let's assume we need to measure the big O for the following code:

```
int sum1= 0;
int sum2= 0;
for( int i = 0; i < n; i++) {                   O(n)
   sum1 += i;                                    c1
   System.out.println("total =" + sum1);        c2
}
for( int i = 0; i < n; i++) {                   O(n²)
   for( int j = 0; j < n; j++) {
      if(j%2==0) {                              max(c3,c4)
         sum2+=methodA(j);                       c3
      } else {
         sum2+=methodB(j);                       c4
      }
System.out.println("total =" + sum2);           c5
   }
}
return sum1+sum2;                               c6
```

The input to this algorithm is n and the output is the sum of different calculations related to the value of this number. To calculate the big O for such an algorithm, we need to calculate the following different sections first:

- In the first `for` loop, the iterations are equal to n and the internal executions of the `sum` and `println` statements are constant values for each loop. So, the big O for this section is $O(n*(c1+c2))$, and as both `c1` and `c2` are not dependent on the value of n, according to our rules, we can remove or neglect them. Hence, the outcome is $O(n)$ (that is, linear complexity).

- The second `for` loop contains two nested `for` loops; each one is executed n times. This produces the number of steps equal to n^2. We also have an inner `if` condition that has two alternatives (`methodA` and `methodB`). We need to select the longest time taken by both. This evaluates as `max(c3,c4)`. If we assumed that both `c3` and `c4` are constant, we can drop them as well based on our rules (the same applies to the `println` method). The outcome of all this is $O(n^2)$.

Now the algorithm is evaluated as $O(n)+ O(n^2)+c6$, which can be reduced to $O(n^2)$ (that is, quadratic complexity). As per our rules, keep only the term with the highest growth rate. This is because with the big values of n, the n^2 term will be the dominant factor.

Let's now assume that `methodA` assessment is not constant but evaluated as `O(n)`. This allows the second loop section to result as $O(n^2 * max(n,c))=O(n^2 * n)=O(n^3)$. Thus, the big O will have the value $O(n^3)$ (that is, cubic complexity).

This is a simplified explanation of how to map our logic into different required steps so that we can assess which logic is much better. Let's pick one example from our code as follows:

```
Product[] allProducts =  catalogSessionBean.
   loadAllActiveProductCatalogByCriteria(new SearchCriteria()); //n
for (Product allProduct : allProducts) {                        //n
  if(allProduct.getId()==productId){                            //c1
    outputStream.write(allProduct.getImage());
    outputStream.close();
    return;
  }
}
```

If we assumed that loading all the categories is a function that depends on the product's list size that is evaluated as $O(n)$, in the worst case scenario, the `for` loop will find the product at the end of the list so that the complexity is $O(n)$ as well. The inner loop logic is assumed to be a constant (c_1). So the whole complexity can be expressed as $O(n*n*c_1)$, which will evaluate as $O(n^2)$. Let's now modify the code a bit and reassess the complexity, as follows:

```
Product product = catalogSessionBean.
  findProductById(productId);//n
if(product !=null){            //c1
  outputStream.write(product.getImage());
  outputStream.close();
  return;
}
```

In the preceding modified code, assuming to find the product using the indexed product ID column will take $O(log(n))$, which is the worst case for B-Tree search (used to retrieve the indexed database column).

The `if` condition's logic complexity is constant (c_1), so the overall complexity is $O(log(n)*c_1)$, which will be evaluated as $O(log(n))$. This is definitely more efficient than the old code with $O(n^2)$.

Another aspect here is the memory usage in the first solution that requires the loading of all the products compared to that of selected products in the second solution.

Most of the known algorithms have identified the complexity and we need not waste any time calculating their performance. For example, the selection, insertion, bubble, and quick sorts have their worst case equal to $O(n^2)$, while merge and heap sorts have their worst case as $O(n\ log\ n)$.

If we have our own logic that does not map to an existing algorithm, we need to define exactly what we need to achieve (that is, inputs and outputs) and answer certain questions related to the problem domain so that we can find the best solution for our problem.

The following are example questions:

- Why do we need this? Can we remove all this logic? Can we do this in another way?

- What are the possible alternatives? For example, can we get the list ordered and ready for search? Can we search the database using the indexed columns?

- Can we combine two algorithms (for example, sorting and binary search) to fix the problem more efficiently?

The analysis gives us a simplified way to evaluate different solutions and have the most optimized logic for our problem.

 We have covered here the simplified view of evaluating an application logic. You may further read on algorithm complexity analysis to understand how to deal with different application algorithms.

Our first performance fixing strategy

The correct identification of code hot spots areas is our way of fixing them. We explored different behavior for application bottlenecks or hot spots and grouped them into different root causes. Then, according to the root causes, we can propose our fix.

In the subsequent chapters, we will modify this strategy a little, but for now, because we have learned different CPU time profiling readings, let's draft our fixing strategy.

In the following diagram, we have to answer the first question, which determines our strategy flow: **Is the method performance bad?** or **is it the method invocation count?**:

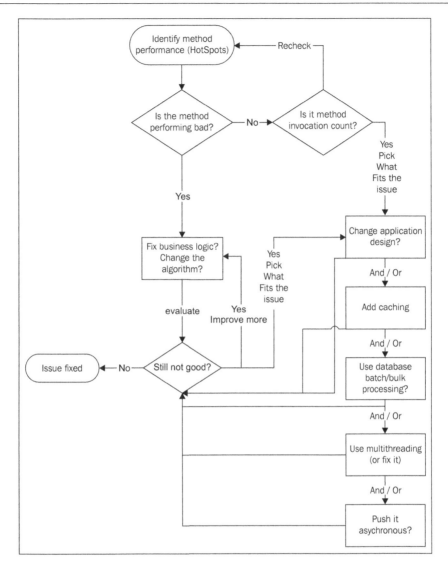

Fixing the application logic/algorithm

This should be our first step, as mentioned before. The issue could have been caused by method logic or an application design fault that causes huge method invocations.

In our examples, instead of loading all the collections to get the required object, we will retrieve what we actually need by using its ID.

Also, instead of adding/removing products to/from a basket, impacting the product stock volume, this should be handled in the cached in-memory product stock in the centralized location and should only be committed to the database if the order has been placed. This is an application design change rather than method tuning.

Poor application logic includes bad programming practices, such as using wrong collections, inefficient string manipulations, and excessive logging (especially for XML logging).

We need to perform the code inspection if the level of detail does not appear in the profiling snapshot.

Adding support for caching

If the hot spot area is due to performing some calculations that can be cached or even done in advance, that is, prior to a customer request, then we can typically cache these calculations. Also if it is involved with loading data from external systems such as database or integrated system, we need to cache this data as well whenever it is possible.

Caching generally can be implemented on two levels: **implicit caching** that comes with the product, for example, database caching, and **explicit application caching,** which we implement and customize according to our application needs and we need to handle all its configurations and policies.

In all these cases, we need to implement the cache appropriately. This means we need to select a suitable caching size, pick the proper invalidation policy that fits our application and data type, select a good replacement policy, monitor the cache, and deploy it correctly.

Caching is one of the magic bullets that improve an application's performance; however, if not implemented correctly, it could worsen the situation. It could even deceive us and disturb the customer's transactions if we cached something that shouldn't be cached.

It is worth mentioning that adding caching support is one of the decisions that needs to be made carefully as it can complicate the application design, mainly because of the invalidation of the cache, object versioning, and locking strategy.

 In *Chapter 10, Designing High-performance Enterprise Applications,* we discuss caching design aspects in more detail.

Optimizing the performance of resources

If the method has no issue but the interfacing resource does, for example, a database query, check the performance of this system/resource and see what can be fixed outside our code to resolve the current performance issue.

The most common example is the need to add a database table column index for the most common-used queries (by guidance of a query execution plan).

We can also change the database interactions, for example, using batch inserts/updates instead of single database statements. Also, in cases of huge data manipulations, we can try to use the bulk upload feature available in most of the existing database engines.

Implementing concurrency or multithreading

This is a good option to consider to improve the performance by introducing concurrent processing into our low-performing code, if not already in place. We shouldn't jump to this solution, except after performing the maximum possible tuning of the code first. This should be done carefully, taking into our consideration that not all the application logic can run concurrently, especially if data dependency exists.

We need to follow the ensuing steps to implement multithreading in our application:

1. Identify the code areas that need parallel execution
2. Understand data dependency
3. Distribute the tasks among different threads with minimal data dependency
4. Collect the results of all the tasks

The implementation should use one of the managed concurrency features in Java EE 7, discussed in *Chapter 2, Understanding Java Fundamentals*.

Using asynchronous methods

One of the possible ways to resolve the performance issue is to push the logic from the bottleneck method to an asynchronous method (that is, move some of the logic to run behind the scene and respond to the customer without waiting for the execution) so that the performance is improved from the customer's perspective.

Definitely not all application scenarios will fit this approach. This also shouldn't be done unless all other ways to resolve the issue don't produce any performance gain. This is because pushing poor performing tasks behind the scene will consume the application's resources and subsequently, impact the application's performance.

In some cases, we need to put this request in a queue for later processing so that it doesn't get lost. Most common scenarios for this is dealing with external systems such as e-mail, JMS, and WebServices. These systems' response time remains undetermined and can affect our application's response time to the customers. So adding the request to a local queue, implementing a retry mechanism, and later notifying the customer with the progress can resolve these cases.

 As a general optimization rule, we need to configure and tune different timeout settings for all application interfacing layers, for example, database connection timeout, transaction timeout, and so on.

In JEE 7, many application components support out-of-the-box asynchronous invocations, such as Servlets and EJBs. We discussed this in detail in *Chapter 2*, *Understanding Java Fundamentals*.

Summary

In this chapter, we covered CPU time analysis using profilers. We used NetBeans, JMC, and JProfiler. We started with how to read and interpret CPU profiling results, then we covered the application's hot spots due to method self-time and/or invocation counts.

We also covered some possible root causes for hot spot areas using simple examples and defined the first draft of our performance fixing strategy.

In the subsequent two chapters, we will cover the missing parts related to concurrency and memory profiling so that we can complete our strategy more generically.

In the next chapter, *Chapter 7*, *Thread Profiling*, we will detail thread profiling by covering different tools and how to read and interpret the profiling results. Then, we will pick some common potential threading issues for further discussion and update our draft fixing strategy a bit more.

7
Thread Profiling

In this chapter, we continue what we started in *Chapter 6, CPU Time Profiling*, by analyzing the output of different profiler tools. In the previous chapter, we discussed the CPU and time profiling results, and in this one, we elaborate on thread profiling.

We also cover some related topics such as reading thread dumps and detecting the root cause of why an application hangs.

In this chapter, we cover the following topics:

- How to read and interpret thread profiling results
- Using thread dumps
- Identifying potential threading issues
- Detecting an application's hang location
- Further improvements to our fixing strategy

Determining when to use thread profiling

Thread profiling is mainly concerned with exploring the different states of an application thread during the profiling period. This determines whether our application is healthy.

It helps us determine issues that prevent different application threads from performing the required tasks. So, for example, if threads are blocked most of the time, the application execution power is reduced.

In web applications, each user gets one or more threads in each request to retrieve the required data from the application. These threads are taken from the application server thread pool to serve the user. They are then returned to the pool, where they are idle and ready to serve another user request.

If, for some reason, the thread takes a considerable amount of time to serve a user request, their return to the pool is delayed.

When most of the application threads are engaged in users' requests, the application's ability to respond to new users diminishes. To avoid this situation, we need to optimize our response to the user (that is, the requester) so that the threads can immediately return to the pool to serve new requests.

One of the factors that could lead to this situation is thread competition for different resources. This is another aspect that we look into during thread profiling.

Exploring the different thread profiling options

In the previous chapter, we discussed the CPU and time profiling by discussing the available profiling options. We start this chapter with the different thread profiling options available in NetBeans, JProfiler, and Java Mission Control.

Thread monitoring using NetBeans

Start the NetBeans IDE, select our project `HighCPU` and from the **Profile** menu, click on **Profile Project**. A pop-up dialog box will open, displaying the three available options. Select **Monitor** to see the different available options for thread profiling as shown in the following screenshot:

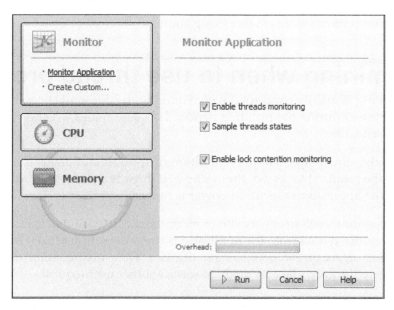

As we can see in the previous screenshot, the three main options available in the NetBeans thread profiling are as follows:

- **Enable threads monitoring**
- **Sample threads states**
- **Enable lock contention monitoring**

We see that the overhead is not affected by selecting the different options available. This is good for our profiling results.

Threads monitoring is used to monitor the threads when an application starts. **Sample threads states** updates the thread states periodically and **Enable lock contention monitoring** shows the threads' lock contention (that is, competition between the threads and the object's monitor).

 The HighCPU project is the example cited in *Chapter 4, Monitoring Java Applications*. You can download it from the Packt website.

Select all the options and execute the application. We get a snapshot of our profiling results to understand the different profiling options. Let's start by using only five threads as the thread pool size in the HighCPU project, as shown in the following code, so that we can trace all our application threads easily:

```
public class HighCPU {
...
    ExecutorService execSvc = Executors.newFixedThreadPool(5);
...
}
```

The profiling results will look similar to what is shown in the following screenshot (thread color reflects its status):

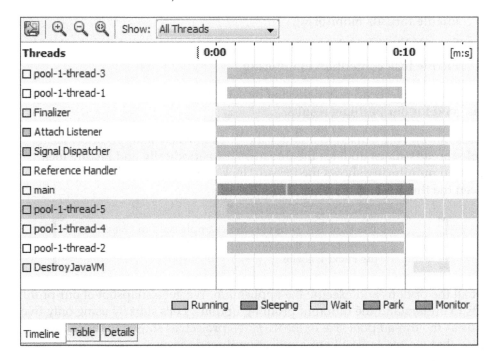

As is shown, the profiling results show the five threads of our thread pool with thread IDs: from **pool-1-thread-1** to **pool-1-thread-5**. If we look back at the remaining application threads in the preceding screenshot, we identify the following threads:

- **main**: This thread is the main application thread
- **Finalizer**: This thread is responsible for the object's finalization, pulls objects that are waiting for finalization, and calls the `finalize()` method of these objects
- **Reference Handler**: This is a memory management thread that is responsible for handling different object references
- **DestroyJavaVM**: This thread is responsible for the JVM termination
- **Attach Listener**: This thread listens for the client's agent and attaches the request to the JVM for the purpose of profiling and debugging
- **Signal Dispatcher**: This thread is responsible for routing fired events (the OS signals) to their own components

All these threads are the system's or JVM threads (that is, the daemon threads) that control the application's behavior or perform background activities such as memory management. The remaining threads are the application threads (that is, user threads), including the parent thread for all the user threads.

Daemon thread versus user thread

In Java, we have two types of threads: the daemon threads, which perform background activities such as garbage collection, and the user threads, which are created from the parent thread (it is also a user thread).

As the main thread is a user thread, by default, all the threads created from inside it are user threads. To create a daemon thread, a call to setDaemon(true) must be invoked before starting the thread execution; otherwise, IllegalThreadStateException will be thrown.

The main difference between both types, other than the function, is that JVM does not wait for the termination of the daemon threads, that is, it terminates once the last user thread ends the execution.

We also see the different available thread states as follows:

- **Running** (green): This denotes that the thread is running
- **Sleeping** (purple): This shows that the thread is sleeping in response to the call of the Thread.sleep() method
- **Wait** (yellow): This indicates that the thread is waiting in response to the call of the object.wait() method
- **Park** (orange): This implies that the thread is parking and waiting for permission to continue with the execution
- **Monitor** (red): This means the thread is blocked and waiting for an object monitor

If we look back at our thread profiling results, we identify that our application was a healthy one and most of the execution time is spent in the thread running status. From the thread profiling perspective, this is our primary target in performance tuning.

We move to the next tab, **Table**, where thread details are displayed with the percent of time spent on each thread status. In the details section, this information is graphically represented.

Let's now set the thread pool size back to `200` using the following code:

```
ExecutorService execSvc = Executors.newFixedThreadPool(200);
```

Profile the application again (select **Enable lock contention monitoring**). We see the blocked or monitor status dominating the thread results in the **Lock Contention** results as shown in the following screenshot:

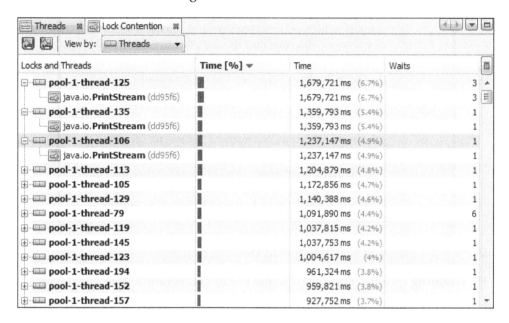

In the **Lock Contention** view, if we expand each thread, it will point to the monitor object, which causes these waits to get its lock/monitor; in our case, `java.io.PrintStream`.

From this exercise, we conclude that increasing the thread pool size invokes competition over the `PrintStream` object. This reduced the application's speed, as most of the thread execution time was spent in waiting to obtain this object monitor. So we always need to set a proper size for our thread pool, as we will see later in this chapter.

Thread monitoring using JProfiler

Let's now attach JProfiler to this project to explore the different options available for thread profiling. From inside NetBeans, select `HighCPU` from the **Project Explorer** view, open the **Project properties** window, and add the following **VM Option** for the JProfiler agent in the **Run** section (this will vary according to your installation path):

```
-agentpath:D:/PROGRA~1/JPROFI~2/bin/windows/jprofilerti.dll=port=8849
```

If we execute the project now, we see the following messages in the **Output** window, which means the project is waiting for the JProfiler connection to resume its execution:

```
JProfiler> Protocol version 38
JProfiler> Using JVMTI
...
JProfiler> Waiting for a connection from the JProfiler GUI ...
```

Now open JProfiler and from **Start Center**, navigate to the **New Session** tab and select **New Session**. Then, select **Attach to profiled JVM** and click on **OK**. The **Session settings** window will show up and ask for the initial profiling settings to be either in the **sampled** or **instrumental** mode.

Select any mode and proceed to the next settings dialog box. Click on **OK** to start profiling the application. Now, click on the **Threads** tab (Thread History). We see JProfiler's thread profiling results as is shown in following screenshot:

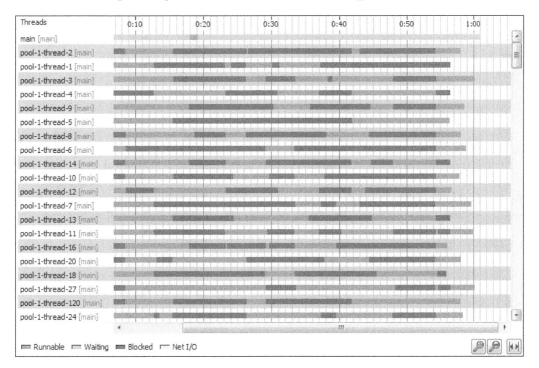

If we switch to the **Monitors & Locks** tab and click on **Current Monitors**, we see a lot of threads in the blocking status waiting to obtain the monitor. The table shows details for **Owning Thread** and **Waiting Thread** with their own stack trace as shown in the following screenshot:

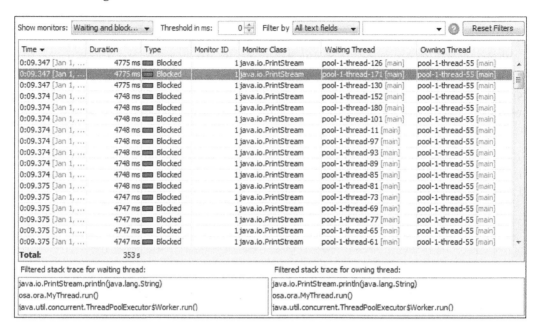

In the preceding screenshot, we can easily locate the monitor lock issue because the stack trace views suggest the blocking section in the `run()` method, which is in the `java.io.PrintStream.println(java.lang.String)` method. If we open the source code of this Java SE method, we see a synchronized statement inside the `println` method in the `java.io.PrintStream` object. Refer to the following code:

```java
public void println(String x) {
    synchronized (this) {
        print(x);
        newLine();
    }
}
```

Another graphical representation of the blocked monitor objects is available. Click on **Current Locking Graph**. The following screenshot shows one monitor object `java.io.PrintStream` with all threads connected to it:

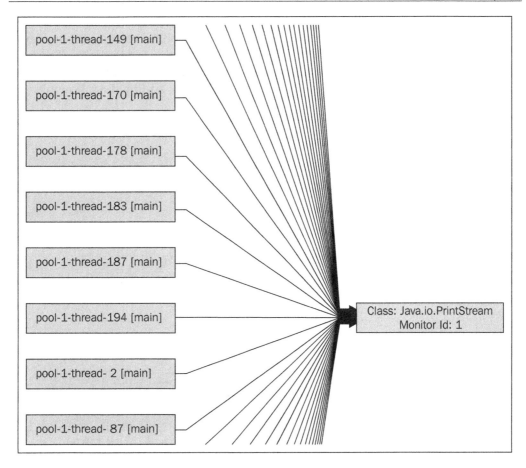

Thread monitoring using Java Mission Control

Similar to the other profiler tools, we perform profiling in **Java Mission Control** (**jmc**) by attaching it to any running Java process. However, we need to add the following JVM parameter to enable the commercial flight recorder feature in the running JVM:

```
-XX:+UnlockCommercialFeatures  -XX:+FlightRecorder
```

If we are profiling web application, the application server must be configured with these parameters so that we can use the JMC with this application server's JVM.

We then use one of the two available options: **Flight Recorder** or **MBean Server**. The JMC **Flight Recorder** option has several effective graphical representation views, covering most of the areas in our Java application. One of these views is the **Thread** tab, where we see a lot of different features available. The next screenshot is obtained using the offline flight recording of our HighCPU project by adding the following third parameter:

```
-XX:StartFlightRecording=duration=30s,filename=d:/recording.jfr
```

Refer to the following screenshot:

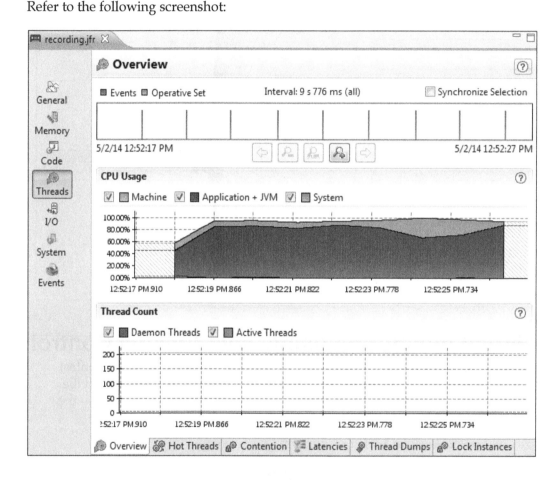

As shown in the previous screenshot, we have several different options for thread data, including **Overview**, **Hot Threads**, **Contention**, **Latencies**, **Thread Dumps**, and **Lock Instances**.

These features are similar to those discussed in the previous tools. For example, if we open the **Latencies** tab, we see that during the recoding period, the application thread latencies are mostly in the blocked status and some are waiting for the monitor as shown in the following screenshot:

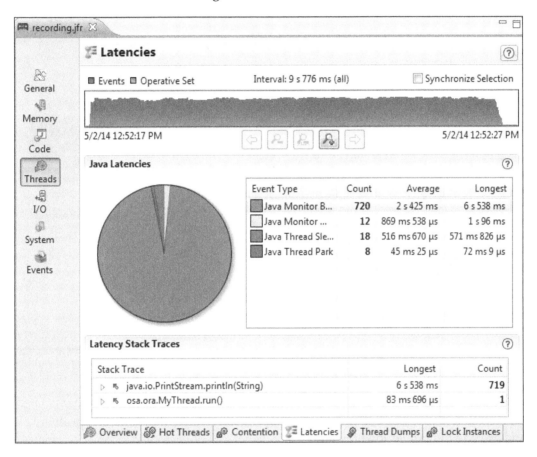

If we switch to the **Lock Instances** tab, we see almost all the threads are waiting for the `java.io.PrintStream` object as shown in the following screenshot:

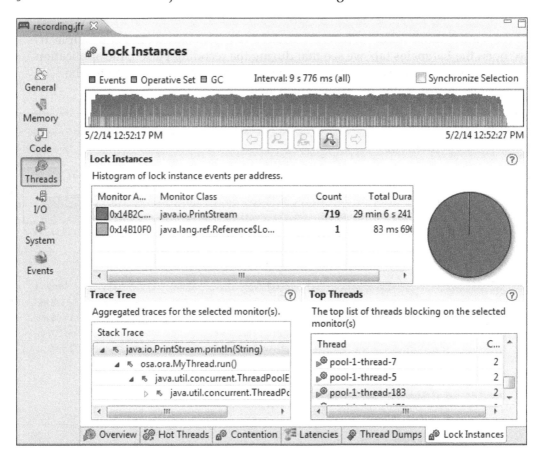

Reading the thread profiling results

Now let's open the ExampleTwo application, profile it using the NetBeans profiler, and execute the JMeter load testing.

 The ExampleTwo application is the example we used in *Chapter 5, Recognizing Common Performance Issues*. You can download the application with its load test plan from the Packt website.

Once we finish executing the performance test, we pick one of the `http-listener` threads to check the thread status. As is shown in the following screenshot, the thread is parked and waiting for the requests. Also, during the performance testing, the thread was healthy, ranging from the running and waiting status. Finally, the thread is back to the parking state and waiting for the next user requests (as in the thread lifetime graph at the bottom of the screenshot):

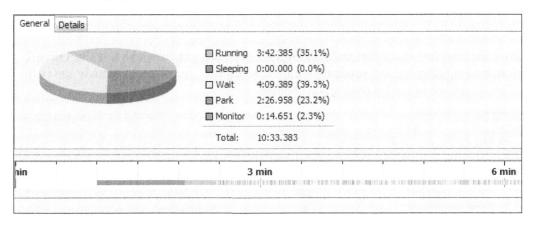

Let's now modify our project a bit. In the `ProductCatalogSessionBean` class, add the following static variable:

```
private static Object MY_LOCK=new Object();
```

Modify the logic in the `updateStock()` method to synchronize this new object and add the `sleep` thread for 2 seconds to simulate a long processing logic (Note that the method's `synchronized` statement is useless here; you be asking, why?):

```
public synchronized boolean updateStock(ProductStock stock,int
  delta) {
  synchronized(MY_LOCK) {
    try {
      Thread.sleep(2000);
    } catch (InterruptedException ex) {}
    ...
    ...
  }
}
```

Now, profile the project again in the monitor mode by clicking on **Enable lock contention monitoring**, and re-execute the load test so that we can have the new profiling results.

During the load test execution, execute the following command twice to thrice (change the filename each time):

```
jstack PID > thread_dump_1.txt
```

In the preceding command, PID is the GlassFish server process ID, so we can get the thread dumps of our application during the load test. (We explain the thread dump in further detail later in this chapter. The JDK tool jstack is available in the JDK bin folder.)

Once the load test execution ends, open the **Lock Contention** view and the **Threads** view by dragging it into a separate window so that we can simultaneously see both views as shown in the following screenshot:

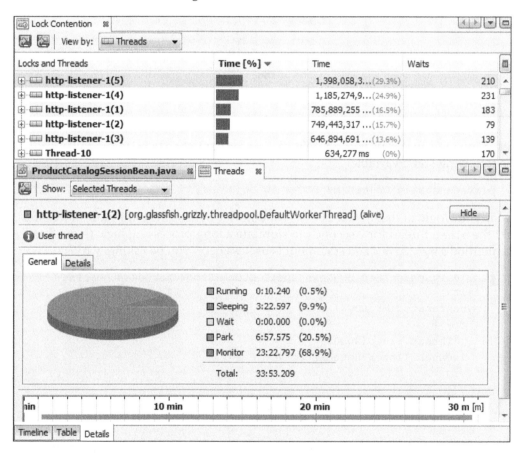

In the **Lock Contention** view, the http-listener threads (these serve the user's requests) are listed in the **Lock Contention** list. If we expand any of them, we see that the lock is around the Object class (that is, the MY_LOCK object).

In the **Threads** view, we see the `http-listener-1(2)` thread as an example. The thread is blocked during most of its execution time and waiting for a monitor. If we look at the timeline of this thread, we see that the thread starts with the **Park** status, waiting to serve the user's requests, and then is mostly blocked during the load test. It then goes back to the **Park** status when the load test execution is finished.

In spite of the large value that the thread profiling has, as shown in this analysis, the quickest way to deal with the thread profiling of enterprise applications is to use frequent thread dumps and analyze them. Let's examine the thread dumps we get during the execution of the load test. We see the following highlighted thread dump extract:

```
"http-listener-1(5)" daemon prio=6 tid=0x063e3400 nid=0x26f4
  waiting for monitor entry [0x0772e000]
  java.lang.Thread.State: BLOCKED (on object monitor)
  at osa.ora.dao.ProductCatalogSessionBean.updateStock
    (ProductCatalogSessionBean.java:123)
  - waiting to lock <0x1e4ba5b8> (a java.lang.Object)
  - locked <0x1f0cddd8> (a osa.ora.dao.ProductCatalogSessionBean)
"http-listener-1(4)" daemon prio=6 tid=0x063e2c00 nid=0x1324
  waiting on condition [0x0756e000]
  java.lang.Thread.State: TIMED_WAITING (sleeping)
  at java.lang.Thread.sleep(Native Method)
  at osa.ora.dao.ProductCatalogSessionBean.updateStock
    (ProductCatalogSessionBean.java:123)
  - locked <0x1e4ba5b8> (a java.lang.Object)
  - locked <0x1f1018c8> (a osa.ora.dao.ProductCatalogSessionBean)
```

We select two threads from the thread dumps as an example. One thread is BLOCKED and the other is TIMID_WAITING (sleeping). The thread dumps give us an idea about the current status of our application threads. In the next section, we see how to get thread dumps and analyze them in detail.

Dealing with thread dumps

A thread dump is a snapshot of the current executing threads with their stack trace. It gives us an overview of the current threads being executed, and by taking subsequent snapshots, we get an idea about the different activities that consume these threads.

There are many ways to get thread dumps, including the use of an application server admin console, command lines, different tools, and MBeans.

Regardless of how we obtain thread dumps, reading them is almost the same even with some differences between each of the JVM implementations. Let's try to explore the different available options to get a thread dump and then describe its content.

Taking a thread dump using the operating system commands

We can use some options from the operating system to produce a thread dump for the executing Java process. In this section, we discuss the different ways to do so in Windows and Linux.

Using the keyboard shortcut Ctrl + Pause Break

This combination produces the thread dump of the current executing application in the standard output stdout in case the application starts with the following command line:

```
java -jar HighCPU.jar
```

Press *Ctrl + Pause Break* and refer to the following output:

```
Full thread dump Java HotSpot(TM) Client VM (24.45-b08 mixed mode,
sharing):
"pool-1-thread-40" prio=6 tid=0x041cc400 nid=0x134c runnable [0x04fee000]
   java.lang.Thread.State: RUNNABLE
  at java.util.DualPivotQuicksort.sort(Unknown Source)
  at java.util.Arrays.sort(Unknown Source)
  at osa.ora.MyThread.run(HighCPU.java:46)
  at java.util.concurrent.ThreadPoolExecutor.runWorker(Unknown Source)
  at java.util.concurrent.ThreadPoolExecutor$Worker.run(Unknown Source)
  at java.lang.Thread.run(Unknown Source)
"pool-1-thread-39" prio=6 tid=0x041cc000 nid=0xbd0 runnable [0x04ecf000]
   java.lang.Thread.State: RUNNABLE
  at osa.ora.MyThread.run(HighCPU.java:44)
  at java.util.concurrent.ThreadPoolExecutor.runWorker(Unknown Source)
...
...
"main" prio=6 tid=0x00b2b800 nid=0x259c waiting on condition [0x002ff000]
   java.lang.Thread.State: TIMED_WAITING (sleeping)
  at java.lang.Thread.sleep(Native Method)
  at osa.ora.HighCPU.main(HighCPU.java:25)
"VM Thread" prio=10 tid=0x009ebc00 nid=0x1d84 runnable
"VM Periodic Task Thread" prio=10 tid=0x00a79c00 nid=0x215c waiting on
condition
Heap
...
...
```

As is shown, when we execute this command, the results include an overview of the heap memory states at the end.

Instead of having this printed out in `stdout` (for example, the console or file in case the application output is directed to a file), we use another way to redirect only the JVM output to a separate file using the following JVM parameter:

```
java -XX:+UnlockDiagnosticVMOptions -XX:+LogVMOutput -XX:LogFile=jvm.log
-jar HighCPU.jar
```

The previous configurations will direct all the JVM output logs to the `jvm.log` file.

We also inform the JVM to print the concurrent locks owned by each thread using the JVM command, `-XX:+PrintConcurrentLocks`. The output will look as follows:

```
"pool-1-thread-6" prio=6 tid=0x01936c00 nid=0x2188 waiting for monitor
entry [0x

03eaf000]

    java.lang.Thread.State: BLOCKED (on object monitor)

        at java.io.PrintStream.println(PrintStream.java:755)

        - waiting to lock <0x28e700f0> (a java.io.PrintStream)

        at osa.ora.MyThread.run(HighCPU.java:47)

        at java.util.concurrent.ThreadPoolExecutor$Worker.
runTask(ThreadPoolExec

utor.java:886)

        at java.util.concurrent.ThreadPoolExecutor$Worker.
run(ThreadPoolExecutor

.java:908)

        at java.lang.Thread.run(Thread.java:662)

    Locked ownable synchronizers:

        - <0x28e75318> (a java.util.concurrent.locks.
ReentrantLock$NonfairSync)
```

Note that the algorithm for thread deadlock detection is executed when we use a thread dump in the Java HotSpot VM. The deadlock detail will be printed at the end of the thread dump in the following format:

```
Found one Java-level deadlock:

=============================

"Thread-1":

  waiting to lock monitor 0x178c766c (object 0x0390e5f8, a osa.ora.beans.
Account),

  which is held by "Thread-0"
```

```
"Thread-0":
  waiting to lock monitor 0x178c694c (object 0x0390e610, a osa.ora.beans.
Account),
  which is held by "Thread-1"
Java stack information for the threads listed above:
====================================================
"Thread-1":
  at osa.ora.beans.Account.transfer(Account.java:56)
  - waiting to lock <0x0390e5f8> (a osa.ora.beans.Account)
  - locked <0x0390e610> (a osa.ora.beans.Account)
  at osa.ora.beans.Transfer.run(Transfer.java:39)
  at java.lang.Thread.run(Thread.java:744)
"Thread-0":
  at osa.ora.beans.Account.transfer(Account.java:56)
  - waiting to lock <0x0390e610> (a osa.ora.beans.Account)
  - locked <0x0390e5f8> (a osa.ora.beans.Account)
  at osa.ora.beans.Transfer.run(Transfer.java:39)
  at java.lang.Thread.run(Thread.java:744)
Found 1 deadlock.
```

We get the preceding result by executing our DeadLockApp project and the BankOperation class from the command line, which will produce deadlock and cause the application to hang; then press *Control + Pause Break* to use the thread dump.

 DeadLockApp is the example we used in *Chapter 2, Understanding Java Fundamentals*. You can download it from the Packt website.

The same lock detection algorithm is available in the JRockit virtual machine thread dump. It detects circular locks (that is, deadlock) as well as blocked and open lock chains.

Sending SIGQUIT to the Java process

In the Linux OS, we send a SIGQUIT signal to a Java process as follows:

```
$ kill -3 PID
```

In the preceding command, PID is the Java process ID. This will printed out the thread dump in stdout.

Taking a thread dump using the JDK tools

The JDK contains many tools that can be used to produce thread dumps, including `jstack`, Java VisualVM, and Java Mission Control.

Thread dump using jstack

The JDK has a tool to generate the thread dump, `jstack`, whose simple application can get the thread dump of any executing Java process using the following format:

```
jstack [-l] PID
```

In the preceding command, `PID` is the Java process ID and the `-l` parameter displays additional information about the locks. We also direct the output into a text file using the directive operator, `>`. For example, refer to the following command:

```
jstack 1000 > thread_dump.txt
```

Thread dump using the Java VisualVM

We use `jvisualvm` to capture thread dumps by right-clicking on the Java process (application) and selecting **Thread Dump** from the context menu as shown in the following screenshot:

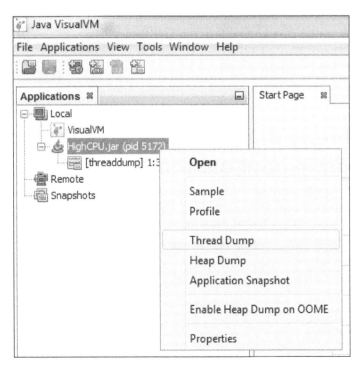

This will produce a thread dump. The context menu also has the options to generate the heap dump and application snapshot. The following screenshot shows the thread dump content:

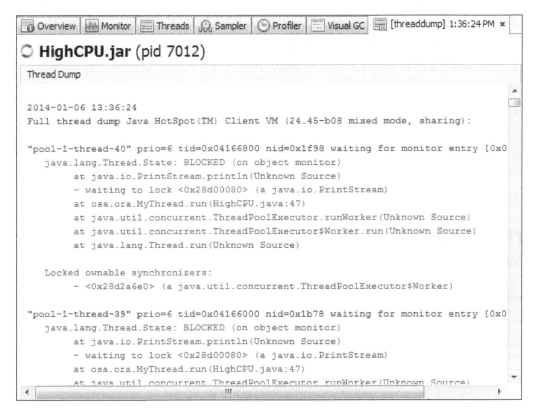

Taking thread dumps using an application's server admin console/tools

We use either an application server's admin console or its packaged tools to get the required thread dumps. For example, if we use the WebLogic application server, there are many ways to get the thread dumps.

Some of the available ways are as follows:

- **Thread dumps using the administration console**: Navigate to **Server** and select the server name. Then navigate to the **Monitoring** tab and select the **Dump** threads stack. A thread dump will show up in the current browser window.

 The only drawback of this method is that it sometimes leads to a truncated or incomplete thread dump, as it shows the thread dump in the browser window and we need to copy it into a text file for analysis.

- **Thread dumps using the JRockit command**: We can get the thread dump by executing the `jrcmd` command and passing `print_threads` as a parameter as shown in the following command:

```
jrcmd PID print_threads
```

- **Thread dumps using the WebLogic service command**: The WebLogic service command tool, `wlsve`, is introduced in the WebLogic Version 10.3.6. It can be used in the following format to produce the required thread dump:

```
wlsve -dump -svcname:<service_name>
```

In the preceding command, `service_name` refers to the WebLogic service name.

Taking a thread dump using profiler tools

Almost all the profiler tools have the ability to take thread dumps. We show how you can do this using both JProfiler and JMC as follows:

- **Thread dump using JProfiler**: In the **Threads** section, there is a tab named **Thread Dump**, where we can click on the icon to generate the thread dump. It will display all existing threads with their stack traces.

- **Thread dump using Java Mission Control**: Using JMC, we generate thread dumps by navigating to the **Threads** section and clicking on the **Thread Dump** tab similar to what's shown in the following screenshot:

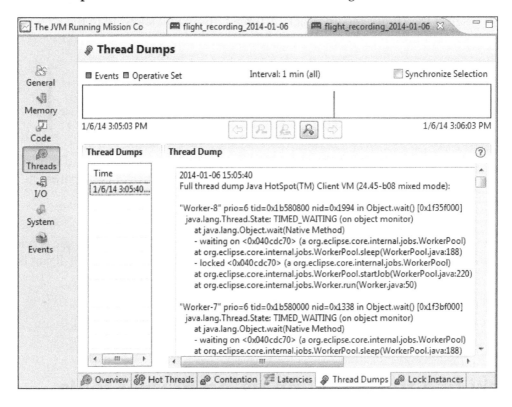

Reading and analyzing the thread dumps

Usually, during performance troubleshooting in enterprise applications, we take frequent thread dumps for analysis. If there is no useful information, we can perform complete thread monitoring (that is, profiling) as part of our application profiling.

The main reason we start with thread dumps is because obtaining thread dumps is easier and does not require any agent to be attached to the application server.

Understanding the thread dump structure

If we understand the thread dump structure well, we are able to make the best use of it. The following is the basic structure of the standard JVM thread dump:

- A header line for each thread
- Stack trace for each thread following the header
- A blank line separating each thread from the following thread

The header comprises the following parts:

Header	Example
Thread name	`"pool-2-thread-1"`
Is it a thread daemon?	`daemon`
Thread priority (prio)	`prio=6`
Thread ID (tid)	`tid=0x1b57d400`
Native thread ID (nid)	`nid=0x1ecc`
Thread status	`waiting on condition`
Address range of the thread stack	`[0x1e8df000]`

The following list is a short description of these different fields:

- **Thread name**: This field is for the the thread's name
- **Daemon flag**: This field indicates whether a thread is a daemon thread or not, if there is a value "daemon" that's means it is a daemon thread, otherwise user thread.
- **Thread priority**: This field contains a numeric value that shows the thread priority
- **Thread ID**: This field is the address of a thread structure in the memory
- **ID of the native thread (nid)**: This field is the thread ID in the operating system and maps to the process ID in the Linux OS and to the Windows thread in the Windows OS
- **Thread state**: This field shows the current state of the thread during the thread dump extraction
- **Address range**: This field is an estimate of the valid stack region of the thread

The available thread states that can be printed in the thread dumps are summarized in the following table:

Status	Description
RUNNABLE	This means the thread is currently being executed
BLOCKED (on object monitor)	This indicates if the thread is blocked and waiting for an object monitor, for example, a synchronized block
WAITING (on object monitor, on condition)	This denotes that the thread is waiting for another thread to perform an action, namely the Object.wait() method on an object
TIMED_WAITING (sleeping, parking)	This shows that the thread is waiting for another thread to perform an action for a specified waiting time, namely the Thread.sleep() or LockSupport.park() method
NEW	This indicates that thread hasn't started yet, so it does not appear in the thread dump (in most of the implementations)
TERMINATED	This means the thread has exited; it does not usually appears in the thread dump

Analyzing the thread dumps

To use thread dumps in our analysis, we take subsequent thread dumps and analyze different thread states. Optimally, we take thread dumps when replicating the performance issues or during load testing.

The frequency of thread dumps should be tailored to the performance issue. So, if a transaction takes 12 seconds, thread dumps must be scheduled every 5 seconds during issue replication. So we can determine what the threads are doing across different thread dumps.

Locating where threads are consuming more execution time that required will help identify the areas to be fixed. For example, if some threads are performing XML processing across different subsequent snapshots, we have a performance issue related to the XML processing or invalid code that performs extra XML processing.

The advantage of using thread dumps in performance tuning can be summarized as follows:

- It is easy to obtain the thread dump using many different methods
- It does not cause any impact or overhead on the application's execution
- It does not require attaching an agent to the application's server
- It can be taken from production servers without security concerns
- It can be analyzed without much understanding of the application
- Good analysis can be performed using some of the available tools

The main goals we need to focus on while performing the thread dump analysis are as follows:

- Detecting deadlocks where threads are waiting for the locks that are held by each other, that is, circular locks. This can be simply detected by identifying what different threads are blocked for. An example of this is the `DeadLockApp` project.
- Rough detection of HotSpot areas by taking consecutive thread dumps. This will be detected by seeing the same threads in the same areas or waiting for certain objects (that is, long running threads performing the same action or waiting for the same locks). An example of this is the `ExampleTwo` project after adding the static lock object.
- A quick overview of the application status, where we can identify the available threads, the thread locks, and so on.

Using Thread Dump Analyzer

One of the advantages of using the thread dumps is that we can use some tools that perform advanced analysis of taken thread dumps; one example for these tools is **Thread Dump Analyzer (TDA)**.

 TDA can be downloaded from the following URL:
`https://java.net/projects/tda`

The advantage of using such tools is that it makes the thread dump readable and we can quickly conclude the results. The following screenshot shows the TDA analysis of three files obtained during the execution of the load testing in the `ExampleTwo` project:

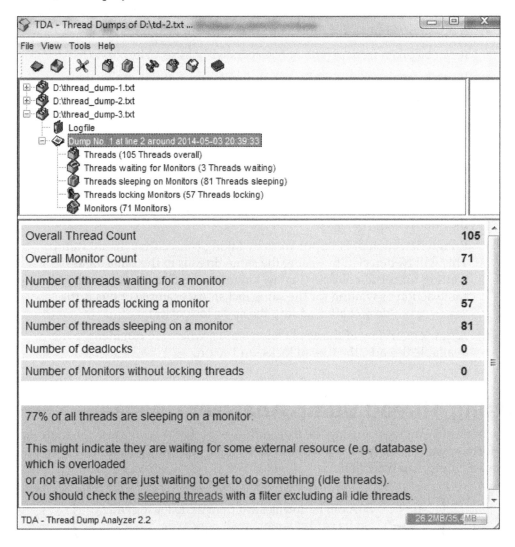

The tool can also detect the long running threads for us, which can help in identifying the HotSpot areas in our application, especially if we use thread dumps with a suitable frequency to the tracked issues.

In fact, this thread dump is just a way to detect applications' performance issues, but we won't depend on thread dumps to identify the HotSpot areas in our application, as we have already seen other accurate ways, such as CPU profiling and HotSpot detections.

Exploring potential threading issues

Threading issues are not common in Java Enterprise applications in comparison to the standalone applications; a web application is a multithreaded application by nature and each user request is served by a separate thread. This means threading issues in web applications are mostly related to thread safety or concurrency-related issues.

Generally, we classify threading issues into performance issues (thread blocking) and functional issues (data corruption). Both these issues are related to each other. In the next section, we will discuss threading performance issues.

Threading performance issues

Threading performance issues affect the application's performance. The next section will cover the examples of these issues.

Threading deadlock

If we have threads' circular dependency on acquiring the monitor of different objects, we can have a deadlock. Deadlocks can be resolved in many ways such as using the explicit Lock interface. In some cases, it will require changes to the underlying application's design or algorithm to resolve them.

Deadlocks are easily identified using the deadlock detection algorithm for a thread dump using thread analyzing tools or even by inspecting thread dumps manually. We can also use the profiler tools to diagnose thread deadlocks.

Blocked/starving/stuck threads

If we have some threads holding up the monitoring of objects for a long time, and other threads are waiting to be monitored, we can have the blocked threads. It can be extended up to starvation; this occurs commonly when dealing with external resources.

We can identify the blocked threads by performing the thread profiling, as seen previously, or by taking subsequent thread dumps.

The WebLogic application server can stop the execution of threads that exceed certain configured time and log them as stuck threads with their full stack trace. We can analyze them and identify why such threads take this long (the default Weblogic stuck thread value is 600 seconds).

Low/over threading

Certain parts of our application can require extensive processing that can be ideally distributed among many threads. To fasten this processing, the distributed tasks/ data must be independent to utilize the benefits of this concurrent execution.

At the same time, creating too many threads (in particular, the standalone application) can harm the application's performance more than we can expect. In our example, HighCPU, we concluded the same (using five threads is faster than using 200 threads in our experiment) mainly because of thread blocking over common resources (such as java.io.PrintStream).

In fact, this is not a big concern in web applications. However, as a high-level rule, for any Java application to best utilize the CPU power and reduce the context switching overhead, concurrent executing threads should ideally match the number of cores in our CPU, that is, Runtime.getRuntime().availableProcessors()±1. The more the threads, the more context switching.

If threads are not competing over resources (as in web applications), we can increase the thread size, maybe to double or triple the number of cores or even more. The limiting factor in web applications is usually the available memory size. This is because each thread requires allocated memory for its stack plus the memory related to runtime object allocation (heap memory).

We will discuss this in more detail in *Chapter 8, Memory Profiling*. While dealing with memory profiling, we must be cautious when creating too many threads in our application, as this can push the application toward instability, especially if unmanaged threads are used. (We will discuss this later in this chapter.)

Threading memory issues

One of the potential issues in multithreading is memory errors. Threads use two main aspects of memory: the thread stack and heap. Each thread has its own stack size, which is configured by the -Xss JVM parameter. The default value is 1 MB; the value is usually tuned according to the application needs.

At the same time, threads share the heap for all runtime variables, so creating too many threads can cause a memory issue. We will discuss the different reasons for OutOfMemoryError in *Chapter 8, Memory Profiling*.

> To identify any JVM flag value, we can use one of the following ways:
>
> * `java -XX:+PrintFlagsFinal` during the JVM startup
> * `jinfo <option> <pid>` to connect to any running JVM (from the JDK tools)
>
> The `<option>` parameter is one of the following values:
>
> * `-flag <name>`: This value is used to print the named VM flag value
> * `-flag [+|-]<name>`: This value is used to enable or disable the named VM flag
> * `-flag <name>=<value>`: This value is used to set the named VM flag to a given value
>
> Refer to the following example:
>
> **`jinfo -flag ThreadStackSize 7880`**
>
> If the output of the tool is `-XX:ThreadStackSize=0`, it means the default JVM stack size for this operating system.

Using unmanaged threads

Unmanaged threads is a traditional web application issue. Invoking an unmanaged thread is prohibited by different Java specifications. People used to use an application server's custom libraries to avoid using threads directly.

In Java EE 7, this issue has been resolved by introducing the managed threads concept in the Java EE specifications. Unmanaged threads have a lot of issues, including thread safe variables, locks, security vulnerabilities, and so on.

Also, unmanaged threads contribute to performance overhead because of the cost associated with creating these threads, while in the managed thread pool, the container recycles these threads.

An additional benefit of using the managed threads is that it lets the container manage the available resources efficiently by having a managed thread pool. Thus, we do not encounter out-of-memory errors easily.

Detecting the root cause of a hung application

An application can hang for various reasons, including over-utilization of the CPU (100 percent), memory utilization, thread deadlocks, and so on.

To identify the CPU utilization issue, we can get the CPU states using a command-line tool, such as the `typeperf` or `top` command (as clarified in *Chapter 4, Monitoring Java Applications*), or by using CPU and time profiling results (as seen in *Chapter 6, CPU Time Profiling*).

For memory issues, we can use a heap memory dump, profile application memory, or the different utility commands, as we will see in *Chapter 8, Memory Profiling*.

Finally, for deadlocks or unknown reasons, we can use one of the following methods to determine the location of the hang.

Detecting the hang location using thread dumps

As we discussed earlier, thread dump can point to the deadlocks at the end of the thread dump using the deadlock detection algorithm, or we can do this analysis manually or by using a tool, such as TDA.

Detecting the hang location using profilers

When the application hangs, the hung method's time will keep increasing in the profilers, so we can determine the hang location (not in all profilers).

Let's try to execute our `DeadLockApp` in the profiling mode using JProfiler. Select the instrumental mode. We can see that the method time is increasing for the application that has hung. In the following screenshot, two subsequent shots with the increasing method time is shown, suggesting the root cause method of the hung application:

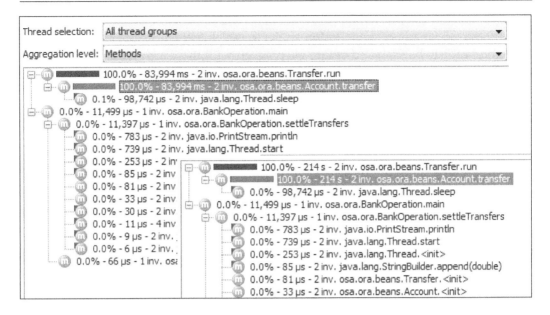

Also, if we switch to the **Monitor and Locks** tab, and click on **Current Locking Graph**, we will see the following typical deadlock graphical representation that can help us in diagnosing our locking root cause:

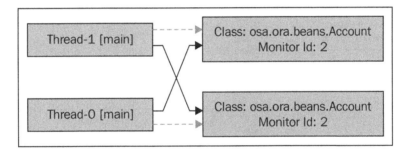

Enhancing our fixing strategy

Let's modify our draft fixing strategy, which we introduced in previous chapter, to reflect our understanding of the threading issues. Some parts related to threading already existed in the strategy, such as **Use multithreading** or **Push it asynchronous**.

We will only add the resolving thread blocking/deadlock and give it a higher priority over the method logic/design analysis, which is the possible root cause for both and needs to be excluded before we proceed with these aspects, as shown in the following modified diagram:

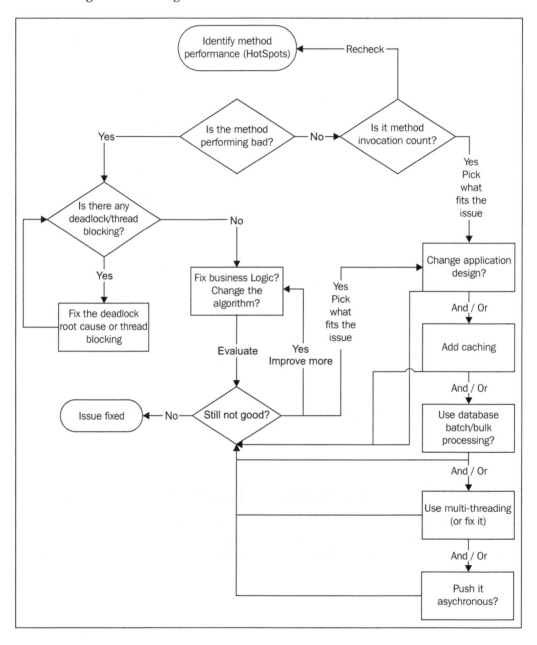

Fixing thread deadlocks and thread blocking

When diagnosing the thread deadlock or blocking, we should focus on resolving the following aspects before we highlight a HotSpot method:

- Fixing thread blocking by modifying the number of threads, changing shared resources, pooling the resources, redesigning the threading data distribution and dependencies, and so on.

- Deadlocks can be resolved by using the explicit locking instead of the implicit locking or any other ways of synchronization. Also, we need to check whether we really need this locking.

We now have a much more mature draft strategy that will be completed in the next chapter after discussing the memory issues and different ways to diagnose and resolve them.

Summary

In this chapter, we covered thread analysis using different profilers. We used the NetBeans profiler, JMC, and JProfiler. We learned how to read and interpret thread profiling.

We also covered how to take thread dumps using different methods (JDK tools, application server, and so on) and how to read and analyze thread dumps manually or using an analyzer tool (TDA).

We also discussed some threading issues and the ways to identify and resolve these issues. Finally, we updated our draft strategy.

In *Chapter 8*, *Memory Profiling*, we will discuss memory profiling, how to read and interpret the profiling results, deal with the memory heap dump, and use **Object Query Language** (**OQL**). We will also discuss some memory issues, including out-of-memory errors.

8
Memory Profiling

This is the third chapter in the series of chapters that explain the different profiling aspects. We covered CPU time profiling in *Chapter 6, CPU Time Profiling*, and thread profiling in *Chapter 7, Thread Profiling*.

In this chapter, we will cover memory profiling; this will include essential topics such as garbage collection, heap dumps, and **Object Query Language** (OQL).

At the end of this chapter, we will have our mature performance fixing strategy for Java enterprise applications.

The following topics will be covered in this chapter:

- Reading and interpreting memory profiling results from different profiling tools
- Dealing with heap dumps
- Using OQL to query heap dumps
- Understanding garbage collection logs and using visualizing tools
- Identifying potential memory issues
- Exploring different reasons for `OutOfMemoryError` scenarios
- Updating our performance fixing strategy

When to use memory profiling?

Memory profiling is important in the enterprise application performance assessment, in particular, to detect any potential memory leaks. This inefficient memory utilization can have a direct impact on the application's performance.

We mentioned when discussing different performance testing aspects in *Chapter 3, Getting Familiar with Performance Testing*, that during performance testing of our application, memory and CPU utilization should be monitored, and if there are any abnormal findings identified, investigations should be done to prevent any performance issues in the production environment.

The following three aspects need to be considered regarding memory performance monitoring:

- Memory profiling
- Taking heap dump for analysis
- Garbage collection activities inspection

We will see the importance of each of these three factors in our performance tuning during our discussion.

Different memory profiling options

In *Chapter 2, Understanding Java Fundamentals*, we discussed memory structure in JVM and identified the roles of many parts in the memory, typically in Java HotSpot VM memory.

In this chapter, we will discuss memory profiling and will mainly look into the following topics:

- Memory utilization (free versus available space)
- Allocated objects (size and locations)
- Garbage collection activities (and GC pauses)
- Memory snapshots and leaks (using heap dumps)

We will go through the preceding topics in this chapter, but let's first start with the different available profiling options in different profilers, as we did in the previous two chapters.

Memory profiling using NetBeans

After we start NetBeans IDE and select our `HighCPU` project, select **Profile Project**. A pop-up dialog will open asking you to select one of the three available options. Let's select the **Memory** option to see the different available memory profiling options in NetBeans; this is illustrated in the following screenshot:

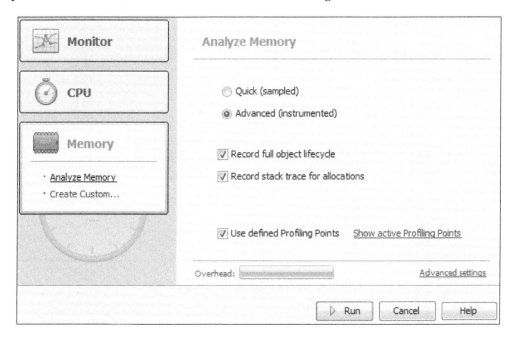

As we can see in the previous screenshot, the options we need to select for CPU profiling are either **Quick (sampled)** or **Advanced (instrumented)**. In the sampled mode, we won't be able to trace an object's full life cycle or stack trace for allocations. Both modes enable us to trace memory leaks and determine the exact location for this leakage.

The overhead is markedly affected by selecting the instrumented mode and checking **Record full object lifecycle** and **Record stack trace for allocations**.

 HighCPU is the example we used in *Chapter 4, Monitoring Java Applications*. You can download it from the code bundle of this book, which is available at `http://www.packtpub.com/`.

Let's take a snapshot of our profiling results so that we can understand different profiling options:

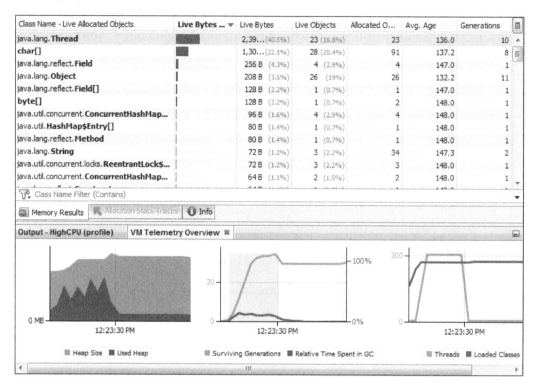

As we can see in the profiling snapshot, if we look into the VM telemetry overview graph (on the left side), we can see that the size of the used heaps keeps growing and then decreases in accordance with the garbage collection activity (saw-tooth appearance) till the application starts to terminate and the used heaps go down.

If we look at the third graph, we will see that the count of threads grows till it reaches the maximum limit, which is the pool size (200), then it terminates with the end of application execution.

In the middle graph, we can see the surviving generation size and the relative time spent on garbage collection.

In the **Live Allocated Objects** column, we can see the `Thread` class on the top, since this small application is just doing thread pooling and some array manipulations. The **Live Bytes** column represents the size occupied by this object in the memory, while the **Live Objects** column represents the current number of instances of this class in the memory.

Now, let's open our `MemoryIssues` project, which contains some classes that produce different `OutOfMemoryError` scenarios, so that we can trace the associated extreme symptoms during memory profiling.

 The `MemoryIssues` project can be downloaded from the code bundle of this book, which is available at `http://www.packtpub.com/`.

If we examine the main class in the `MemoryIssues.java` project, we can see the following code that determines which `OutOfMemoryError` scenario to invoke based on the input arguments; we can also execute any of these classes directly as each of them already has a main method:

```
switch (args[0]) {
  case "0":
    new ManyObjects().addObject();
    break;
  case "1":
    new BigArrays().createArrays();
    break;
  case "2":
    new StackOverflow().callIt(10, 10);
    break;
  case "3":
    new TooManyThreads().createThreads();
    break;
}
```

Let's perform memory profiling for the project after setting the run argument as 0 (or by profiling the `ManyObjects.java` class directly).

 To set the runtime argument in a Java project in NetBeans, go to **Project Properties**, select **Run**, and add the required arguments to the **Arguments** field.

We can see the following memory consumption snapshot:

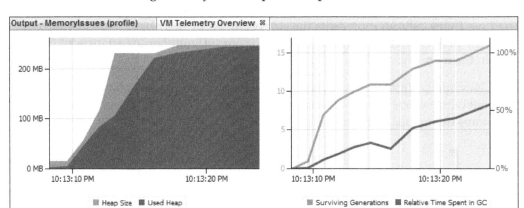

In the preceding screenshot, we can see that the used heap keeps growing until it hits a good percentage of the heap size and then the heap expands. This is repeated four times (each jump in the heap size graph represents resizing of the heap to a new larger size) till no further scaling is allowed (that is, the maximum heap size is reached) and an out of memory error is thrown, as shown in the following output messages:

```
Exception in thread "main" java.lang.OutOfMemoryError: Java heap
   space
   at java.util.Arrays.copyOf(Arrays.java:2245)
   at java.util.Arrays.copyOf(Arrays.java:2219)
```

The heap settings have some parameters that control this auto-resizing including -Xms and -Xmx. They represent the initial heap size and the maximum allowed heap size, respectively. We will discuss this in the next chapter.

The effect of memory consumption can be reflected in the relative time spent on garbage collection as seen in the graph on the right (in the previous screenshot). The garbage collection activities increase to do their best in order to free the heap memory for the application.

Let's now check the garbage collection activities in details. In **Project Properties**, in the **Run** tab, add the -verbose:gc parameter to **VM Options**. Then, execute the application again so that we can see the following garbage collection log messages in the output console:

```
[GC 4416K->3047K(15872K), 0.0070249 secs]
[GC 7463K->4704K(15872K), 0.0111856 secs]
[GC 9067K->8448K(15872K), 0.0163446 secs]
[GC 12864K->11821K(16256K), 0.0118403 secs]
[Full GC 11821K->10773K(16256K), 0.0404765 secs]
```

```
    . . .
    . . .
[Full GC 253439K->253439K(253440K), 0.8030233 secs]
[Full GC 253439K->253356K(253440K), 0.9967519 secs]
[Full GC 253439K->253439K(253440K), 0.9940063 secs]
java.lang.OutOfMemoryError: Java heap space
Dumping heap to java_pid3944.hprof ...
```

We will discuss how to read garbage collection logs in a separate section later in this chapter. But for now, we will briefly explain the garbage collector logs. The collector started by running the minor collections (represented by GC in the logs), which means that the garbage collector collected garbage for the young generations only, but when the heap size started to get depleted, it invoked the full garbage collection activities (that is, Full GC in the logs) hoping to free more memory space till the application is terminated with OutOfMemoryError.

We need to compare the preceding screenshot with another profiling screenshot, which is a result of executing another memory example. From the **Projects** explorer window of NetBeans, select the MemoryIssues project, expand it, and select the TooManyThreads.Java Java class, then right-click on it and select **Profile File**.

In this class, we are trying to create too many threads, and as we mentioned in *Chapter 7, Thread Profiling*, each Java thread needs a stack allocated for it in the memory.

As this class is trying to create too many threads, the area allocated for the thread's native stack will be depleted and OutOfMemoryError will be thrown, as shown in the following output messages:

```
Exception in thread "main" java.lang.OutOfMemoryError: unable to
create new native thread
  at java.lang.Thread.start0(Native Method)
  at java.lang.Thread.start(Thread.java:713)
```

If we examine the high-level memory graph, we can see the following screenshot:

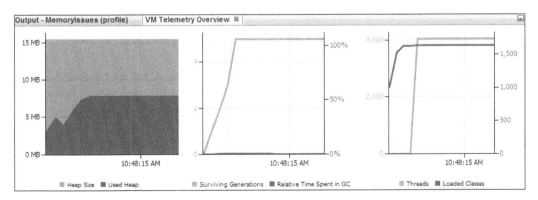

You can see that the used heap consumption is very small (less than 10 MB), which is the same for the surviving generation consumption. So, apparently, there is no memory issue. However, if we look at the third graph, we can see that the number of threads is hitting 4000, which consumes the memory area allocated for thread stacks.

Now let's do a quick exercise in order to understand the concept of stack. Go to **Project Properties** and add the following code to **VM Options**:

```
-XX:ThreadStackSize=50
```

This will change the size of the stack allocated for each thread from the default value (1 MB) to only 50 KB, which will allow us to generate many more threads before the memory gets consumed (with this limited stack size, out of stack space errors can be frequently thrown).

When we profile the application to see the impact of this change, the thread count hits more than 20,000 threads before the OutOfMemoryError gets thrown, as we can see in the following screenshot of **Telemetry Overview**:

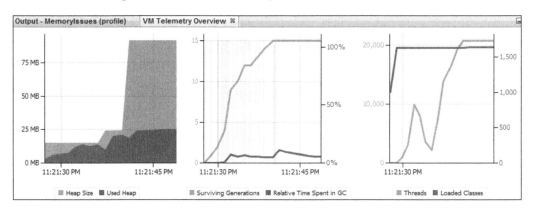

We can also specify the stack size of the thread when we create the thread from the code using the following constructor:

```
public Thread(ThreadGroup group, Runnable target, String name,long
    stackSize)
```

It is important to understand here that the specified stack size is not mandatory for JVM and it has the freedom to take this only as a suggestion (as per the Java documentation). This is especially the case if we specified an unreasonably low value for the platform. Instead, the virtual machine may use some platform-specific minimum value. The same is the case for unreasonably high values; it can use a platform-specific maximum value.

Also, it's worth mentioning here that the stack memory size is not the only deterministic factor for the number of threads, as the maximum threads that can be created per process is an operating system configuration that need to be properly configured in the operating system if our application needs to create a huge number of threads. We won't discuss this as it is not common in enterprise applications and is not recommended either.

Memory profiling using JProfiler

To attach the `MemoryIssues` project to JProfiler, we need to add the required JVM parameter for the JProfiler agent. From the **Projects explorer** view, open **Project Properties**, and under the **Run** section, add the following in **VM Options** for the JProfiler agent (the path of this agent will vary according to your installation path):

```
-agentpath:D:/PROGRA~1/JPROFI~2/bin/windows/
   jprofilerti.dll=port=8849
```

If we execute the project now, we can see the following (or similar) messages in the **Output** window, which means that the project is waiting for the JProfiler connection to resume execution:

```
JProfiler> Protocol version 38
...
JProfiler> Waiting for a connection from the JProfiler GUI ...
```

Now, open JProfiler and from **Start Center**, go to the **New Session** tab and select **New Session**. Then, select **Attach to profiled JVM**, and click on **Ok**. The **Session settings** window will be displayed asking for the initial profiling settings, that is, either the **sampled** or **instrumental** mode.

Select the **sampled** mode, proceed to the next setting dialog box, and click on the **OK** button to start profiling the application.

We have three tabs in JProfiler for memory profiling details: **Live Memory**, **Heap Walker**, and **Telemetries**. We will discuss heap walker in the next section of this chapter while we are discussing heap dumps.

Open the **Live Memory** view to see the different memory elements that consume the heap, as shown in the following screenshot:

Aggregation level: Classes			
Name	Instance count ▼		Size
java.lang.String		4,785,652	114 MB
char[]	6,629		401 kB
short[]	1,542		87,568 bytes
java.lang.Object[]	1,422		41,082 kB
byte[]	1,361		211 kB
java.lang.Class	1,213		455 kB
java.util.TreeMap$Entry	1,059		33,888 bytes
java.lang.Class[]	989		16,584 bytes
java.util.Hashtable$Entry	895		21,480 bytes
Total:	4,815,013		159 MB

In the previous screenshot, we can see the **Instance count** of the objects of `java.lang.String` that we keep adding to a list of arrays. The following is the code for this method:

```java
public void addObject() {
    ArrayList list = new ArrayList();
    while (true) {
        list.add(new String("Osama Oransa"));
    }
}
```

This can be spotted by switching to **Allocation Call Tree**.

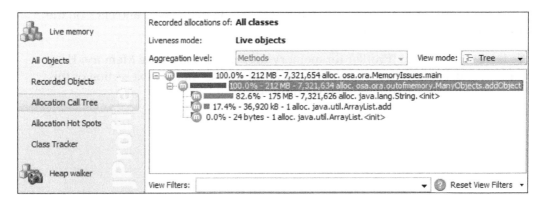

As we can see, the `addObject()` method is responsible for allocating more than 7 million objects, which consumes a memory size of 212 MB.

If we switch to the **Telemetries** tab and select **Memory**, we can see a detailed graph of memory utilization, as shown in the following screenshot. We can also select required memory space in our JVM to explore.

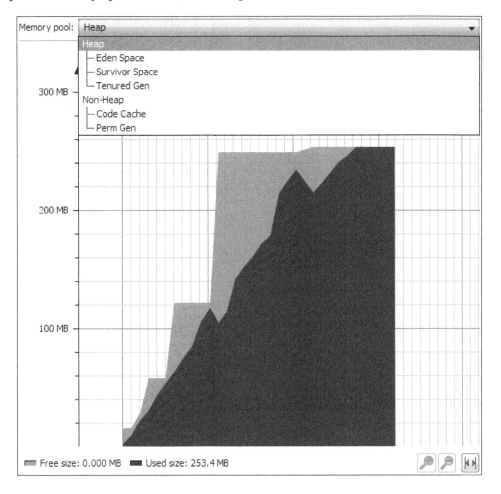

The preceding graph shows the gradual consumption of heap space (used heap keeps growing) and the auto-sizing of the heap size (each jump in heap size represents heap resizing) until it reaches the maximum heap size configured for our application (this is configured by the -Xmx JVM parameter).

If we select the **Recorded throughput** tab, we can see the recorded objects per unit time (seconds), as shown in the following screenshot, without any freed objects activity at all. This potentially means we have a memory leak where created objects are not freed.

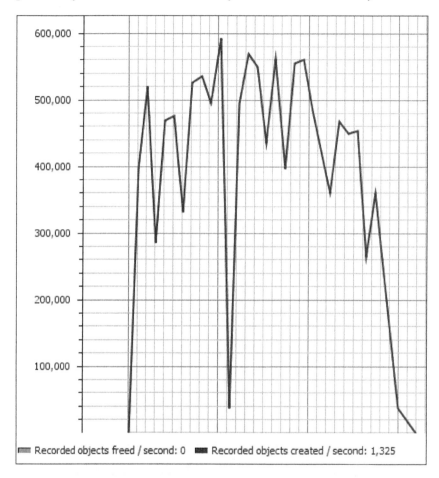

This usually happens when we still have a reference to this object or wrong override of the finalize() method in the leaked object class.

Another interesting view is the **GC activity**, where the garbage activity is visualized in a nice graph. This helps us to understand what the garbage collector was trying to do, as we can see it nearly hits 100 percent just before the application throws the OutOfMemoryError exception.

Garbage collection activity roughly reflects the level of memory consumption, as shown in the following screenshot:

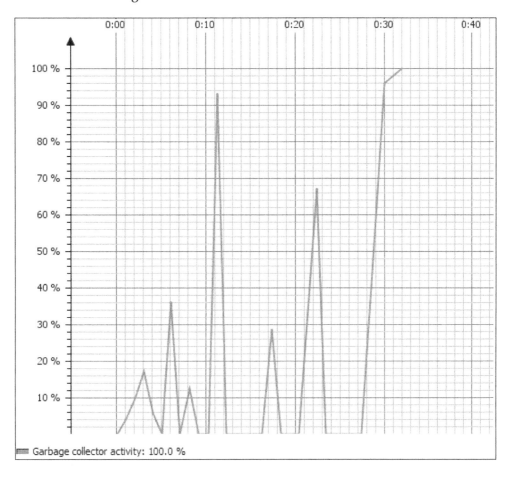

Analyzing memory profiling results

Memory profiling analysis, mainly contains the following four aspects:

- Memory spaces analysis as seen in the telemetric graphs in NetBeans and JProfiler
- Detailed object statistics, as we saw in the live memory allocation tables
- Garbage collection logs or visualized logs
- Heap dump analysis

We will discuss heap dump analysis in a separate section in this chapter. Now let's go through the other three aspects one by one.

Analyzing memory space graphs

Memory profiling graphs are useful to identify memory consumption by the application, as we can see in the following screenshot of the telemetry graph:

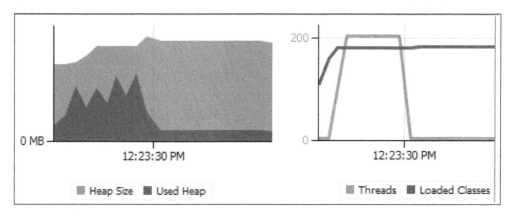

The graph displays the total heap versus the used heap; it also reflects the application's heap memory utilization.

Monitoring the used application memory over a long period is depicted by the saw-tooth appearance shown in the previous graph. This is because with each increase in the memory utilization, it activates the garbage collector to free more memory.

The more the garbage collector activity, the more the application's pause time, which is something we don't want to have.

If the heap memory keeps growing without the saw-tooth appearance, then it usually means that the garbage collector is unable to free memory, and potential memory leakage exists. Sometimes, this can happen with a sudden increase in the application traffic (that is, peak time) where most of the objects are live and referenced objects.

If the heap memory auto-resizing (up and down scaling) is not efficient, we need to revisit the JVM tuning parameters. We will see this in the next chapter where we will discuss JVM tuning.

Finally, thread graphs are important, as we saw during the `MemoryIssues` application profiling, where the number of threads exceeds the memory space allocated for thread stacks. This requires the following things:

- Revisiting the application logic that fires this huge number of threads
- Adjusting the application memory requirements (that is, capacity planning)
- Tuning the JVM thread stack size

Analyzing detailed object statistics

We have two important aspects here—class instance count versus occupied size. Let's start by highlighting the following few points:

- **Number of live objects**: This represents the total count of live objects that belongs to this class
- **Number of live bytes**: This represents the total number of bytes that belong to the object of this class
- **Total allocations**: This represents the number of times a new object is allocated from this class

The most important aspect here is the total live objects, which represent the current objects that are still referenced in the memory. If, for certain objects, this number is high or unexplained, then this could potentially mean that it is a memory leaked object.

The object size is another important factor; along with the objects count, we can calculate the average size of a single non-primitive object. This should match our expectations or there could be potential issues within the object itself (that is, internal object leakage).

For more analysis, we need to look at the allocation call tree to determine the leak locations in the code. JProfiler also provides a view to show the allocation HotSpots and determine the number of allocations and the size of the allocation, as we saw earlier.

Using heap dumps is useful to analyze the memory leakage, as we will see later in this chapter.

Analyzing garbage collection activity logs (HotSpot JVM)

We have the following three different ways to analyze garbage collection activity:

- Examining the memory utilization graphs to roughly understand the GC efforts (we already covered this point earlier)
- Reading garbage collection activity logs
- Monitoring the visualized GC activities (we saw this in JProfiler and we will discuss here how to use `jvisualvm` to do the same)

Now, we will cover how to read garbage collection activity logs and how to visualize this activity.

Reading garbage collection activity logs (HotSpot VM)

When we executed the `MemoryIssues` application with `-verbose:gc` earlier in this chapter, we got the following results in the console log (this is for HotSpot JVM):

```
[GC 163972K->163916K(237748K), 0.1814933 secs]
[Full GC 229516K->214339K(237748K), 0.8321936 secs]
```

Let's explore the different sections in these log statements by defining the general log structure, as follows:

```
Occupied space before -> occupied space after (total committed
    space size), time taken in space activity
```

The first line is for a minor garbage collection activity (that is, young generation only) and the second line is for a full garbage collection activity (that is, including the old generation as well). The following diagram describes how to read these details:

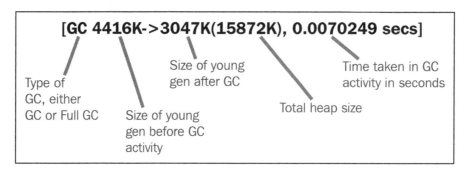

The total heap size represents the **committed memory** size without including even one of the survivor spaces (as only one is usable at a time) and the permanent gen space.

Before we continue here, we need to explain the difference between **virtual** and **committed** size. Committed size is the current size of the memory where this space can be used for/by Java objects without requesting additional memory from the operating system. Virtual memory is the maximum configured memory that may not be completely allocated to JVM yet.

This is controlled by the -Xms (initial heap size) and -Xmx (maximum heap size) parameters plus the memory sizing policy parameters, MinHeapFreeRatio and MaxHeapFreeRatio, where the memory expands or contracts according to the defined heap free ratio with the default values as 40 percent and 70 percent for both parameters.

So, if we are using the default values and the utilization of the memory is between 40 percent and 70 percent, then no heap memory resizing should be expected. The same is the case if we set both the initial and the max size with the same value (this is an important memory performance tuning tip).

We can get more information printed on the console by using the additional JVM parameter -XX:+PrintGCDetails.

The following is an example of two log lines after we execute our application using the -XX:+PrintGCDetails parameter:

```
[GC[DefNew: 73279K->73279K(73280K), 0.0000160 secs][Tenured:
    154677K->137075K(162760K), 0.3357701 secs] 227957K-
    >187895K(236040K), [Perm : 120K->120K(12288K)], 0.3359294 secs]
    [Times: user=0.33 sys=0.00, real=0.34 secs]
[Full GC[Tenured: 173880K->173880K(174784K), 0.4236182 secs]
    252536K->252535K(253440K), [Perm : 120K->120K(12288K)],
    0.4236572 secs] [Times: user=0.41 sys=0.00, real=0.42 secs]
```

Now, we can see that the additional information about different memory spaces is added to the log. In the first line, it starts with the young generation, tenured space, and then permanent generation. In the second line, because it is a full garbage collection, it starts with the tenured space, moves to total heap, and then permanent generation, as shown in the following diagram:

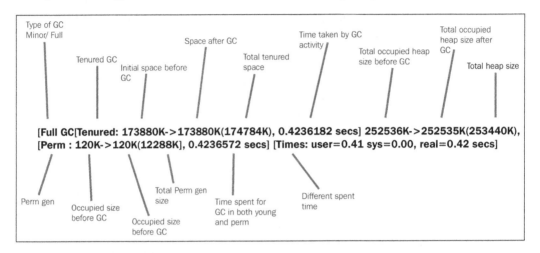

The difference between user time, sys time, and real time represents the following:

- **User time**: This is the time spent in garbage collection while executing user-mode code (non-system calls)
- **Sys time**: This is the time spent in garbage collection during system calls
- **Real time**: This is the total time spent from the start of GC till the end, including the time spent in other process during the execution of this garbage collection activity

The real time in the serial collector should be equal to sys+user as long as the system's performance is healthy from both the CPU and memory aspects, while in concurrent collectors it should be typically less than sys+user with the same healthy conditions.

If the real time is very high compared to the sys+user value; this could mean that the machine's memory is not enough for the application, so a lot of time is spent on virtual memory paging. This is common when we over-utilize the machine by many applications and services.

We can also go one step further and add the following JVM parameter to log more garbage collection information: `-XX:+PrintGCApplicationConcurrentTime` and `-XX:+PrintGCApplicationStoppedTime`. These will print the following additional messages in the log:

```
Total time for which application threads were stopped: 0.4265617
seconds
Application time: 0.6008938 seconds
```

This means that the application is stopped at only 0.42 seconds, while the application was running for 0.6 seconds.

The importance of all these log messages is that we can use them as guidance to our memory tuning effort including machine memory, JVM memory tuning, and garbage collection tuning.

We will discuss different JVM tuning aspects in the next chapter, *Chapter 9*, *Tuning an Application's Environment*.

Visualizing the garbage collection activity

Java VisualVM is a powerful and simple tool to use. We can use it to get memory profiling results similar to what we get from other profiler tools, but the most characteristic feature of this tool is the availability to add useful plugins that can further help us understand our application behavior.

One of these plugins is *Visual GC*. We already described how to install plugins in Java VisualVM in *Chapter 4*, *Monitoring Java Applications*.

The amazing thing in this plugin is visualizing garbage collection in a way that lets anyone watch it for a few minutes to master the garbage collection activity inside JVM. One can see many activities such as the *Eden space* that grows with time, then garbage is collected, one of the *survivor* spaces becomes empty, all survivor objects moves into the other survivor space, and so on.

We can also align the garbage activity and time spent on these changes and see the effect of garbage collection on the *Eden space* in particular. The following screenshot shows an illustration of this useful plugin:

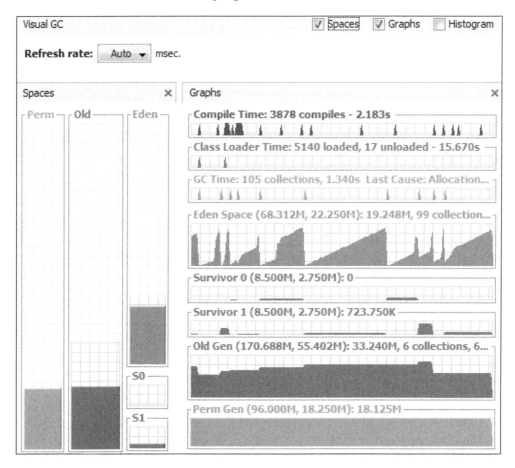

In the preceding screenshot, the same pattern we described earlier as saw-tooth also exists here (but it can be seen if we imagine **Old space**, **Eden space**, and **S0/S1** as one space).

The graphical representation is much more efficient in explaining the garbage collection activities but usually the availability of the logs are much easier. This is why you need to master reading the GC logs.

Other tools that provide GC activity visualization include the following:

- IBM GCMV, which can be found at `https://www.ibm.com/developerworks/java/jdk/tools/gcmv/`.
- HP JMeter, which can be found at `https://h20392.www2.hp.com/portal/swdepot/displayProductInfo.do?productNumber=HPJMETER`.

Dealing with memory heap dumps

As we explained earlier, heap memory is a part of the memory that is used for allocation of runtime objects, and it is shared among all application threads. This heap is classified into old and young generations, where the young generation is further divided into Eden space and two survivor spaces.

A heap dump is a snapshot of the current heap memory content, which is saved in a file. It helps us to identify memory leaks and reasons behind memory consumption. Different tools allow us to navigate and search inside the heap dump using **OQL**, that is, the language that can be used to query objects.

The heap dump file uses the **hprof** binary file format, so it usually ends with either `.hprof` or `.bin`.

Because heap dump is dumping all heap content into a file, it should be handled carefully and with high security precautions as it may contain a user's confidential data, such as personal information and credit card details.

There are many different ways to get heap dumps. We will show some of these ways here including the command-line tools and profiling tools.

Taking heap dumps on the occurrence of JVM OutOfMemoryError

This is a JVM feature that can generate heap dumps once `OutOfMemoryError` is thrown. The required configuration is the following JVM parameters:

-XX:+HeapDumpOnOutOfMemoryError to inform the JVM to dump the heap in case of out of memory.

-XX:HeapDumpPath=filename to inform the JVM with the exact location to place the heap dump file.

The following is an example of OutOfMemoryError:

```
java -XX:+HeapDumpOnOutOfMemoryError   -XX:HeapDumpPath=./dump.hprof -jar
MemoryIssues.jar 0
java.lang.OutOfMemoryError: Java heap space
Dumping heap to ./dump.hprof ...
Heap dump file created [277552186 bytes in 3.689 secs]
Exception in thread "main" java.lang.OutOfMemoryError: Java heap space
    at osa.ora.outofmemory.ManyObjects.addObject(ManyObjects.java:28)
    at osa.ora.MemoryIssues.main(MemoryIssues.java:26)
```

Because we have informed JVM to dump the heap in the dump.hprof file with the occurrence of OutOfMemoryError, it dumps the heap memory into this file when an out of memory error is thrown.

Taking heap dumps using the JDK tools

JDK contains many tools that can be used to produce heap dumps. These are either command-line tools or profiling tools, for example, we can use jmap, Java VisualVM, and Java Mission Control.

Taking heap dump using jmap

We can dump the heap content into a file using the jmap command, which uses the following syntax (PID is a Java process ID):

```
jmap -dump:[live,]format=b,file=filename PID
```

If we use the live optional parameter, it will generate the dump file for live objects in the heap (that is, objects that are still referenced by the application).

 To get the Java process ID, we can use **task manager** in Windows OS or the ps command in UNIX OS. We can also use the JDK command-line utility named jps, which can produce a list of the currently running Java processes with the name beside the process ID, as follows:

```
>jps
13944 jar
14044 Jps
```

We can use the `jhat` JDK tool to read the heap dump file using the following syntax:

```
jhat [ options ] <heap-dump-file>
```

We discussed the usage of this tool to navigate inside the heap dump earlier in *Chapter 4, Monitoring Java Applications*.

Taking heap dumps using Java VisualVM

Using `jvisualvm` is a straightforward and simple way to capture the heap dumps by right-clicking on the Java process (our application) and selecting **Heap Dump** from the context menu as shown in the following screenshot:

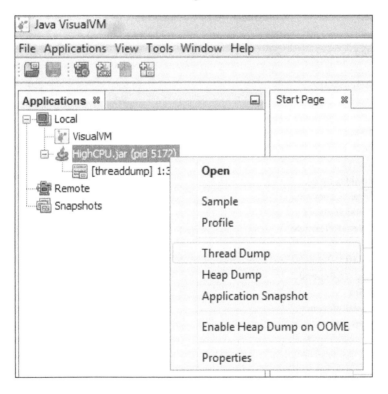

This produces a heap dump that is loaded in the jvisualvm GUI. The following screenshot shows the different instances of classes in the heap and the occupied size; clicking on any class will open the details of the instances of that particular class in the **Instances** tab:

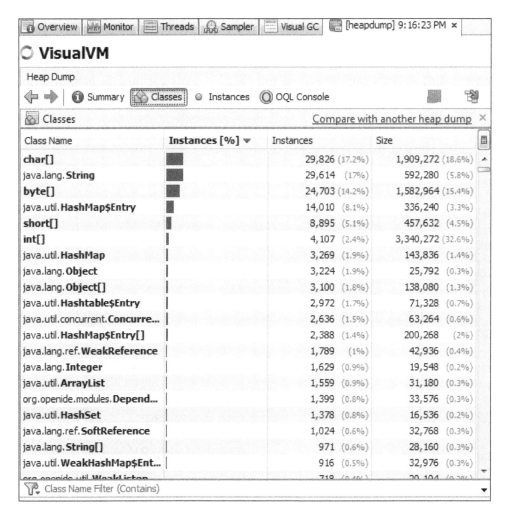

We can also use jvisualvm to configure the currently running process (that is, JVM) and dump the heap on **OutOfMemoryError (OOME)** by using the context menu, as we can see in the previous screenshot (we can also disable this by using the same context menu).

Taking heap dumps using the JRockit command utility

Using the JRockit command (`jrcmd`) to get heap dumps in a Java application that is running on JRockit VM can be done by using the following format:

```
jrcmd processId hprofdump filename=dumpFileName
```

```
e.g. jrcmd  1001  hprofdump filename= file.hprof
```

 This will throw `IOException` if the target process is not running on JRockit VM.

Taking heap dumps using the profiler tools

Similar to thread dump, all profiler tools have the ability to take heap dumps. We will show how we can do this using NetBeans, Eclipse, and JProfiler.

Taking heap dumps using the NetBeans profiler

Using the NetBeans profiler, we can generate heap dumps during profiling of any Java application by clicking on the **Dump Heap** icon. The heap dump is saved and heap dump navigator opens (it is similar to JVisualVM GUI), as seen in following screenshot:

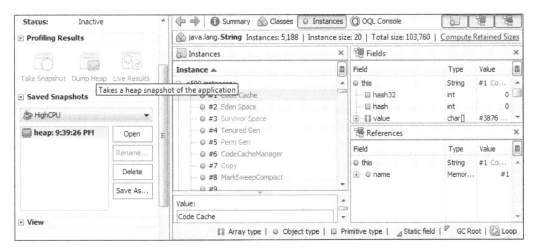

Taking heap dumps using Eclipse Memory Analyzer Tool (MAT)

This Eclipse-based memory analyzer can be used as a standalone tool or as a plugin inside Eclipse. The tool can be used to take heap dumps by navigating to **File | Acquire heap dump** and selecting any running Java process. We can also open a heap dump that is created by other tools by navigating to **File | Open heap dump**.

MAT contains a good feature known as *analysis report*, where the tool analyzes the heap dump and provides a list of issues that exist in the heap dump.

If we execute this report against our `MemoryIssues` heap dump (by clicking on **Leak Suspect**), we can get a report that points to the creation of our `String` object in the `ManyObjects.addObject()` method, as shown in the following screenshot:

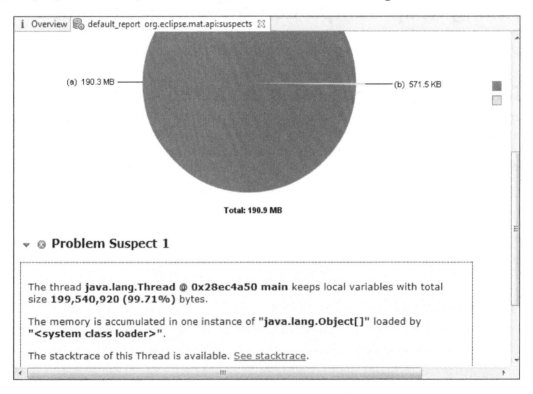

If we follow the **See stacktrace** link, it will point to the stack trace of the memory leakage, as shown in the following code:

```
main
  at java.lang.Thread.sleep(J)V (Native Method)
```

```
at java.lang.Thread.sleep(JI)V (Thread.java:340)
at osa.ora.outofmemory.ManyObjects.addObject()V
   (ManyObjects.java:32)
at osa.ora.outofmemory.ManyObjects.main([Ljava/lang/String;)V
   (ManyObjects.java:20)
```

The tool also supports running OQL and it has an OQL editor for that. It also supports exporting content into different formats such as HTML, CSV, or text. So in general, it is a powerful tool to deal with memory heap dump files.

> To download Eclipse MAT, you can download the plugin from inside your Eclipse by using **Update Manager** and providing the following URL (for Version 1.3.1):
>
> `http://download.eclipse.org/mat/1.3.1/update-site/`
>
> Alternatively, you can download the standalone analyzer from
> `http://www.eclipse.org/mat/downloads.php`.

Taking heap dumps using JProfiler

There is an icon to take heap dumps from the **Heap walker** tab. Once we click on the icon, a pop up will appear asking for some additional options; click on **OK**. Then, the heap dump will be generated and open in the same heap walker window so that we can navigate inside it, as shown in the following screenshot:

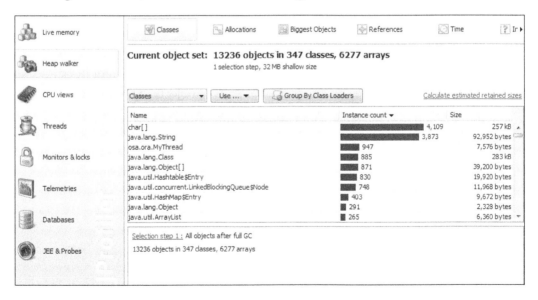

One of the good features of JProfiler is that it can keep JVM alive, so we can navigate inside the heap walker view. This can be configured by navigating to **Customize Profile Settings | Miscellaneous** and checking the **Keep VM alive** checkbox.

In the next section, we will learn how to read heap dumps, how to build different OQL queries, and how to use them to query the dump content.

Analyzing the heap dump

Let's start analyzing the heap dump by understanding how the heap dump file is displayed in most of the heap walker tools.

Navigating inside a heap dump using visual tools

If we look back to the previous screenshots of heap walkers, we can see that the content of the heap is organized by displaying the class of objects that have instances in the heap with a sum of the total instances plus the size occupied by these instances.

Note that arrays in Java are considered as objects. If we select one of these classes, we can navigate inside the different class instances and see the different available information including the different instance attribute values and so on.

When we use the JProfiler **Heap walker**, we can see a lot of useful information such as allocation of these objects in particular when the instrumental profiling mode is selected. So, let's profile the MemoryIssues project using JProfiler with the **Run** parameter set to 0 so that we can create a lot of String objects in the heap.

Remember to configure the **Keep JVM alive** option so that JVM does not terminate when OutOfMemoryError is thrown.

Once the profiling starts, click on the **Take heap snapshot** icon in the **Heap walker** tab; it will take a few seconds before it shows the current content in the heap. We will see `java.lang.String` at the top of the classes as we are creating a lot of objects from it. We can select it and go to the **Allocations** tab to see where these objects are being created, as shown in the following screenshot:

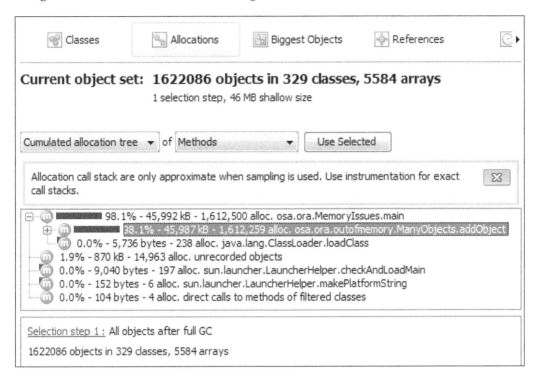

As we can see in the JProfiler alert, to get more accurate information, we need to use the instrumented mode.

We can also navigate to the different instances and see different attributes by selecting the **References** tab. Again, this is a security concern while using the heap dump and we should be careful when dealing with and distributing production heap dumps, as shown in the following screenshot:

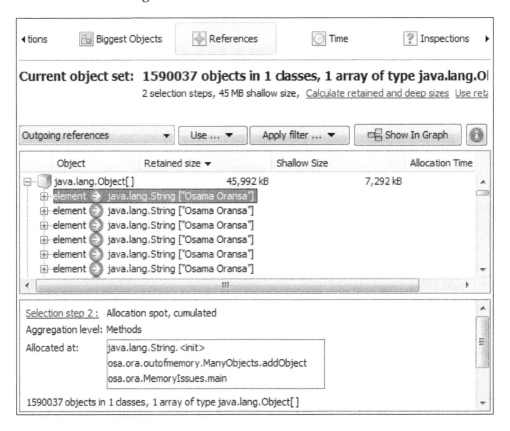

Query heap dumps using OQL

Now, we need to understand OQL and how we can use it to perform a search inside the heap dump. This is useful when the issues are not as clear as the example we used.

In *Chapter 4, Monitoring Java Applications*, we showed you how to use OQL in `jhat` to query the heap dump. Now let's try to do the same using JVisualVM, which is more efficient in dealing with heap dumps.

Open `jvisualvm` and among the running Java processes, select one process (for example, the NetBeans process), then right-click on it and select **Heap Dump** from the context menu. The heap dump will open with the same components that we are familiar with so far: **Summary**, **Classes**, **Instances** (of the selected class), and **OQL Console**.

Navigate inside the available classes in the heap dump classes section and pick one class (for example, `java.lang.String`) so that we can use OQL to query this class.

The following is the general syntax of any query in OQL:

```
select <JavaScript expression to select> [ from [instanceof]
  <class name> <identifier> [ where <JavaScript boolean expression
  to filter> ] ]
```

As we can see, only the `select` statement is mandatory while `from` and `where` are optional; the `select` statement uses the `JavaScript` expression for selection.

Using simple OQL queries

Now let's look at the following query examples and expected outcome of executing them in the heap dump:

- `select result from java.lang.String result`: This will select all the `String` instances in the heap dump

- `select result.value from java.lang.String result`: This will select all values of the `String` instances

- `select result.value.length from java.lang.String result`: This will select only the length of the `String` instances

- `select result.value.length from java.lang.String result where result.value.length>33`: This will limit the previous search results to all the String objects with values more than `33` characters

- `select result from [C result where result.length >= 100`: This will return the `char[]` objects with size more or equal to `100` (for `int[]`, we can use `[I` and for `float[]`, we can use `[F`)

Using OQL built-in objects and functions

These functions can help us to query the heap dump and filter what we need to look into in a more efficient way than using the explorer way or generic queries.

Using a built-in heap object

OQL has a built-in object, which is a heap object that refers to the current heap dump. The heap object has some useful functions that we can use and build our queries. The following are some examples of built-in heap objects:

- `select heap.classes()`: This will return all classes in the heap so that we can filter them

- `select heap.objects()`: This will return all objects in the heap

- `select heap.findClass("java.lang.String")`: This can be used as an alternative to find a specific class in the heap, for instance, `java.lang.String`

Other available functions are `findObject`, `forEachClass`, `forEachObject`, and so on.

Using built-in functions on individual objects

The following are some example of these built-in functions:

- `select sizeof(floats) from [F floats`: This will return the size of all the `float` arrays

- `select referrers(string) from java.lang.String string`: This will return all the `String` referrers in the current heap dump

- `select filter(heap.classes(), "/java.io./(it.name)")`: This function filters and displays all the classes in the `java.io` package

A lot of other functions such as `map`, `sort`, and `filter` are available as well.

The following `jvisualvm` screenshot shows how to use OQL to perform a search inside the heap dump of a running NetBeans IDE process:

 For more information on how to use OQL and the complete list of all supported built-in functions, we can check the complete manual of OQL at `http://localhost:7000/oqlhelp/` after executing the following JHat command:

`jhat any_dump_file`

Potential memory performance issues

In the previous sections, we discussed how to get and read different memory profiling results so that we can understand the memory map of our application. So far, we covered the following topics:

- Reading and configuring GC logs
- Reading and querying heap dumps using OQL
- Reading memory profiling results

Now, it is time to see the sequence that we need to follow, what exactly we can get from dealing with each of these memory analysis options, and when to use each of them.

First of all, we need to check the allocated memory for our application and see whether or not it is enough based on the application's requirements, and the current memory utilization.

It is common to see memory issues if the allocated memory is not suitable for the application or the hardware is over-utilized by a lot of applications.

Possibly in the near future, using Java multitenancy could improve the ability to run many Java applications on the same machine with a more efficient memory utilization.

> **Java multitenancy** refers to the ability of JVM to be shared among different applications, which reduces the wasted memory to load the same resources in many JVM(s). The concept is mainly targeting the cloud environment where the shared resources concept is widely applied.
>
> IBM is releasing this in its SDK for Java 8. To read more about this concept, go to http://www.ibm.com/developerworks/library/j-multitenant-java/index.html.

Basically, using GC logs is useful in all situations as it gives us a good understanding of our application memory utilization and guides our tuning efforts at the same time.

We can change the required level of detail according to our needs; the good thing is that it will not affect the application's performance compared to attaching a profiling tool to the application.

The other advantage of using GC logs over operating system memory analysis is that it gives a good breakdown of different JVM spaces.

If we either find an issue with using the operating system tools, application server admin console, monitoring tools, garbage collection logs, or we already have a memory issue that causes the application to be unstable, then it is the right time to perform memory profiling to understand the low-level details of the application memory.

If we can't attach a profiler or the server is frequently throwing an OutOfMemoryError exception, then we should typically use the heap dump in our investigations as it fits these types of memory issues, that is, OutOfMemoryError or memory leakage.

Application memory leakage (session leakage versus global leakage)

When we have memory leakage in our application, the impact might be variable according to the leakage scope. So, if we have a leakage located in the session scope, then this impact is usually limited to the number of sessions that we are active on.

But the leakage is not severe as the session will timeout and all the scoped objects will be garbage collected. The only exception to this is when the leakage is huge to such a degree that it can impact the application memory.

The most critical application memory leakage is global memory leakage where the situation gets worse with time as the leakage has no controlling factor to reduce its impact (as the session times out).

Global memory leakage can happen potentially in the following locations:

- Static class members
- Instance variables in long living components, for example, Servlet
- Singleton objects
- Application/context scope

When we perform memory profiling, we can see that the leakage objects are retained more than the expected volume/count.

We need to identify the exact location that allocates these objects so that we can determine where exactly this leakage happened. We can also use heap dumps for this purpose.

Sometimes the leakage is not consistent (that is, related to certain values or conditions). In that case, exploring the values in the leaked objects or other objects can help us in determining the exact scenario that caused this leakage.

Improper caching implementation

Caching, as we discussed earlier in *Chapter 5*, *Recognizing Common Performance Issues*, is an important element in enterprise application performance but if it is not implemented and customized (tailored) as per the application needs, then it can impact the application's performance rather than improving it.

Detailed caching statistics are required to help us diagnose different caching issues. Also, profiling the application might show too many or too few caching objects compared to what is actually expected.

Too many or few hits/calls to the caching methods in CPU profiling will point to improper caching (if we are using remote caching, then the caching methods are our interfacing methods with that remote cache).

In *Chapter 10, Designing High-performance Enterprise Applications*, we will discuss design considerations related to the application caching implementation.

Memory issues of objects that contain the finalize() method

When classes implement the `finalize()` method, potential memory issues can happen if the speed of the `finalizer` thread cannot cope with the created objects (for example, during peak times).

The main reason for this is objects that contain the `finalize()` method are not claimed by the garbage collector; instead they are queued for the `finalizer` thread (daemon thread), which pulls them one by one and call their `finalize()` method.

We shouldn't override the `Class finalize()` method except when there is a strong justification and there is no other way to achieve what is required.

If we have to do that, it is essential to write an optimized code in the `finalize()` method and not revive the object again by storing a reference to the `this` object, otherwise the garbage collector won't be able to claim the object during subsequent execution as object's `finalize()` method is called only once.

Invalid contract for the equals() and hashCode() methods

In Java, if any two objects are equal, then their hash code values mush be equal as well. If we override the `hashCode()` method, we must override the `equals()` method as well.

The `hashCode()` method returns an integer-unique representation of the object and this method must return the same value for the object with each subsequent call.

When dealing with collections such as `HashMap` or `HashSet`, if we examine the `HashMap` internal `getEntry(Object key)` method source code, we can see that the following logic is used to return the required entry by the key:

```
if (e.hash == hash && ((k = e.key) == key || (key != null &&
  key.equals(k))))
    return e;
```

The method first checks whether the hash code matches or not. If it does, then it calls the `equals()` method to verify that. This means we must implement the `equals()` method if we need to override the `hashCode()` method. Otherwise, the objects added to such collection types won't be retrievable. Hence, we will keep adding the same objects multiple times to the collection and the object will not be identified as the same object, which will lead to memory leakage.

Different reasons for OOME

Since memory is divided into different areas in our JVM (that is, HotSpot JVM), any generation/area that can't accommodate its content will throw `OutOfMemoryError`. So we can list the following reasons for this error:

- JVM stack
- Native method stack
- Heap (different areas)
- Method area
- Runtime constant pool area
- Operating system memory (when the requested memory can't be obtained)

One additional reason for `OutOfMemoryError` is that if the garbage collector (parallel) spends too much time (more than 98 percent) in performing the garbage collection and it only recovers less than 2 percent, then the JVM will throw `OutOfMemoryError`; this feature can be disabled by using the following JVM parameter:

```
XX:-UseGCOverheadLimit
```

We have added some examples for `OutOfMemoryError` in our application `MemoryIssues`. So, you can try to execute them to see the different reasons why these errors are thrown and the reflection on memory profiling, heap dumps, and GC logs.

Adding memory performance issues to our fixing strategy

To add memory performance issues to our investigation and fixing strategy, we have to inject it from two different aspects: one is related to OutOfMemoryError and another one is related to memory leakage and improper caching.

Fortunately, improper caching is reflected in CPU profiling and we already added it in our draft strategy. So, we do not need to mention it here again (as it impacts the method invocations count).

We have added OutOfMemoryError in a separate path, so we can investigate and fix a plan different from the other normal issues that are related to code logic/flow.

We have also added a few modifications to our previous version including driver/native code issues, tuning the application, and so on.

It is still a simple strategy to go through and can be considered as the high-level guide to troubleshoot our performance issues. We won't complicate this strategy any more as it contains the high-level milestones that we need to cover here.

All the application tuning effort, such as JVM memory and garbage collection tuning, will be discussed in the next chapter.

The following diagram represents the final structure of our performance fixing strategy:

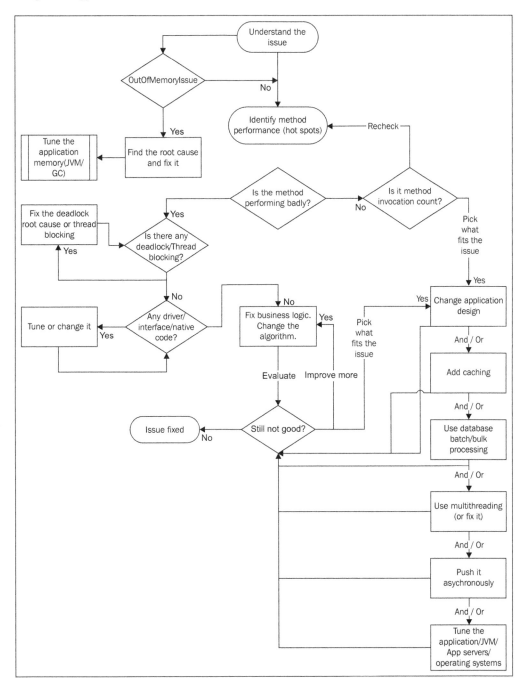

Fixing memory leakage issues

It is clear that we always need to fix the root cause in our performance issues. Yet, in all other types of performance issues, we can find a temporary work-around for the issue by doing some tuning or scaling of our application. In memory issues, in particular, we can't use this temporary fix as it will fail at a certain point.

Fortunately, the diagnosis of this nightmare is straightforward — by taking heap dumps or performing memory profiling. In some cases, if the heap dump is huge and we are not even able to open it by different heap walker applications, then we can try to take the heap dump early before the heap gets expanded, but if this is not useful to catch the actual leakage root cause, then we can simply decrease our application maximum heap size (the -Xms JVM parameter) so that we can have a smaller heap dumps.

By completing this chapter, we have now covered all application profiling aspects using different tools, how to interpret the results, how to think in possible fixes, and so on.

We have also covered the general investigation road map in web applications using both horizontal and vertical dimensions and we have defined a small fixing strategy for the code part of the application. This should be enough to troubleshoot any enterprise application performance issues.

We must now start to practice what we have learned by profiling different applications that we have and trying to get some results and optimization recommendations.

Practicing this high-level strategy (or even your own modified strategy) is essential at this point in the book to master the application performance tuning. One must not only practice but also focus on the important information and neglect other irrelevant information, as we did when we discussed reading and interpreting different profiling results.

> *"Without strategy, execution is aimless. Without execution, strategy is useless."*

> *-Morris Chang*

In the next chapter of this book, *Chapter 9, Tuning an Application's Environment*, we will round off our Java EE performance tuning knowledge by discussing how to tune different application components from outside the application such as JVM, application server, and operating system. In *Chapter 10, Designing High-performance Enterprise Applications*, we will discuss design considerations for high-performing enterprise applications. In *Chapter 11, Performance Tuning Tips*, we will learn about some fine-tuning performance tips. Then, finally, we will go through an example application to troubleshoot its performance in *Chapter 12, Tuning a Sample Application*.

Summary

In this chapter, we covered different aspects of memory analysis using different profiler tools, such as NetBeans profiler, `jvisualvm`, JProfiler, Eclipse MAT, `jhat`, and `jmap`.

We covered the most important aspects in memory profiling: how to use the profiling tools, how to read and interpret the results, and how to propose the fix.

We also covered how to take and use heap dumps, how to query heap dumps using OQL, and how to read garbage collection logs.

We completed our fixing strategy from all the important aspects, so we can use it as a high-level plan for our Java applications and enterprise applications performance troubleshooting.

In the next chapter, *Chapter 9, Tuning an Application's Environment*, we will cover how to tune the application environment; this environment should be tailored to suit our application. We will discuss the tuning of JVM, application server, and operating system. All these components can markedly affect our application performance if not taken early into our consideration during performance tuning.

9
Tuning an Application's Environment

In this chapter, we will discuss the performance tuning around the application, and in the next two chapters, we will discuss the performance tuning inside the application from both the design and coding perspectives.

In this chapter, we will focus on the application's environment, including the JVM, application server, and operating system. In each of these areas, we will pick one or two examples and focus on the improvement areas.

We will cover the following topics in this chapter:

- The JVM tuning
- Tuning the HotSpot and JRockit JVM
- Application server's tuning
- GlassFish and Weblogic application server's tuning
- Web server's tuning
- Apache and Oracle web server's tuning
- Operating system and hardware tuning directions

Understanding environment tuning

In *Chapter 1*, *Getting Started with Performance Tuning*, we discussed the different layers that comprise our enterprise application. These layers include the **Code and script** application on top of the pyramid, followed by the used application **Framework, libraries, and drivers**. We also have the **Application and database servers**, **Java Virtual Machine – JVM**, and **Operating System – OS** layer.

The operating system might be installed on **Virtual Machine – VM (optional)**, which adds an additional layer before the system hardware, as shown in the following diagram:

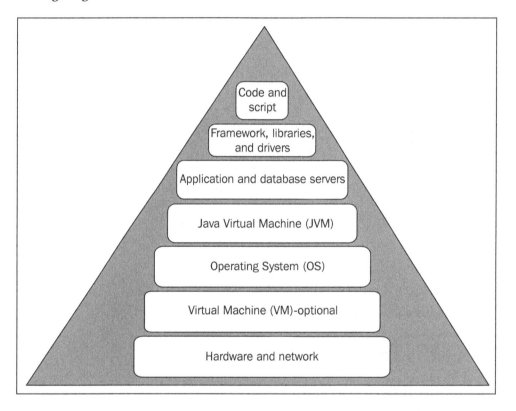

In this chapter, we are going to discuss the tuning efforts for some of the enterprise application layers, which are not part of our code, including the JVM, application server, and operating system.

In this chapter, we will focus on the common and general items and simplify them as much as possible. This will enable us to deal with any other implementations/vendors.

To achieve this goal, we are going to focus on the common things that need to be tuned in most of the similar applications. So, for example, when we discuss application servers, we will pick the Oracle GlassFish server being the Java EE reference implementation server and discuss the common tuning aspects, such as connection pool settings, precompile JSPs, and so on.

These general aspects are required in all the application servers, such as the Weblogic application server, JBoss application server, and IBM Websphere application server.

They will give us a good orientation about the tuning aspects in different application components, but won't replace each product documentation.

Tuning the JVM

The JVM performance keeps improving with subsequent Java releases. One of the big improvements in the JVM is the ability to auto-tune itself according to certain defined ergonomics rules. This reduces the efforts needed from our side to tune it.

This auto-tuning mainly depends on the machine hardware class, yet some efforts still require to ensure the optimal outcome of our JVM.

Having a high performing JVM is critical for our enterprise applications, so let's see the different aspects of the JVM performance tuning, which are as follows:

- Selection of the JVM type (client or server)
- Memory size tuning (heap size and different generational space size)
- Memory management tuning (initial size, maximum size, and auto-scaling)
- Garbage collection tuning (type of collection, collection throughput, and pause time)

We have two main performance metrics, throughput and pause time, to measure the efficiency of our application garbage collector.

Throughput is the percentage of the total application execution time that is not spent on garbage collection activity.

Pause time is the time when the application does not respond since the garbage collection is taking place.

Tuning the Java HotSpot virtual machine

Tuning the JVM represents important aspects in the Java Enterprise application tuning. This tuning should be done in the following three stages:

- The initial tuning of the JVM should be done according to our application by following the tuning guidelines in the application server documentation

- During the performance testing phase, by tuning the JVM and adjusting its configuration according to our application performance results

- After monitoring the application performance and analyzing the different JVM aspects as memory and GC in the production environment

In this section, we will discuss the JVM tuning using the different available JVM parameters.

Understanding the different types of the JVM parameters

The JVM parameters can be classified into the following two main categories:

- **Standard parameters**: These parameters are available in all the JVMs regardless of the implementation vendor; examples of these parameters are `-server`, `-client`, `-classpath`, `-jar`, and so on

- **Non-standard parameters**: These parameters are not guaranteed to be available in all the implementations and they start with –x, for example, `-Xms`, `-Xmx`, `-Xmn`, and so on

We should note that some of the non-standard parameters are subject to change in the subsequent JVM releases, so they are marked with –xx, for example, `-XX:MaxGCPauseMillis=n`, `-XX:ParallelGCThreads=n`, `-XX:+PrintGCDetails`, and so on.

> For more information about the different HotSpot JVM options, refer to the Oracle documentations at `http://www.oracle.com/technetwork/java/javase/tech/vmoptions-jsp-140102.html`.

Selecting the HotSpot JVM type

Java HotSpot provides two different modes for the JVM: one is suitable for servers and the other one for the client machines. Both the modes share the same runtime codebase but the main differences is the compiler type, either the client or server compiler, and some other JVM tuning aspects.

The server mode is optimized for the best application runtime performance, but its starting time is not significant in comparison to the client mode, which runs on the client machines where the start time is important, for example, a Java applet.

Java compilers are built using **Just-In-Time (JIT)** compilers, but different JVMs improve the efficiency of this compiler by performing a global scan, so it detects HotSpots and performs method inlining and dynamic optimizations.

For example, when the method is called the first time it gets compiled, and with subsequent calls if it becomes a HotSpot, some optimization techniques are applied in parallel with the application execution to improve these HotSpots whenever possible. This is done so that the optimization effort is not wasted on rarely used methods.

Another example is method inlining, where the compiler can determine which method needs to be inlined. This has the benefit of removing the method call overhead. Most of the final and short methods are suitable for method inlining but the compiler still determines which method to inline, including the virtual method being smart enough to do this after global code analyzing.

We can summarize the difference between both modes as follows:

- **Client mode**: This mode has small footprints (small memory size) and a faster startup time, hence it is suitable for client applications

- **Server mode**: This mode has a large footprint, (slows the startup time) more advance optimized compilers, and many optimization policies, and is typically designed for server applications

Tuning memory size

The JVM has a lot of parameters that are available to control the memory size and memory behavior. The main parameters that control the memory size are as follows:

- **Initial heap memory size**: -Xms
- **Maximum heap memory size**: -Xmx

As we mentioned earlier, the memory footprints are affected by running machine ergonomics and our configurations (for example, the JVM type). Still, we can override any configuration by supplying our own tuning parameters. The following diagram shows the different HotSpot VM memory structures:

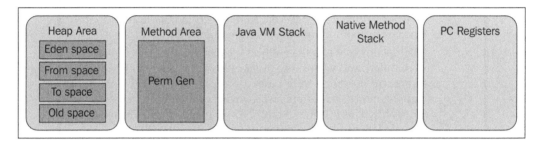

The initial heap size is the memory allocated and ready to be used by our application. This is called the committed heap size. The maximum heap size is the maximum size the memory can be expanded to, which is called the virtual heap size.

In *Chapter 8, Memory Profiling*, we saw how the memory expanded and collapsed according to the current heap utilization, which affected the value of committed heap with each memory resizing.

Sometimes, we need to specify both, the initial and maximum heap size with the same value. This nullifies the expansion/collapse effects (memory auto-sizing); otherwise, the memory will keep resizing according to the following two parameters:

```
-XX:MinHeapFreeRatio=n
-XX:MaxHeapFreeRatio=n
```

These two parameters control when the expansion or collapse occurs and at the same time, to which degree. So, once the heap utilization increases and the minimal heap free ratio is reached (default 40 percent), auto-expansion occurs to keep the current utilization within the minimal and maximum free ratio.

The same occurs for `MaxHeapFreeRatio`. If it exceeds 70 percent (the default value), collapsing of the memory will take place to maintain this ratio, as long as the current committed heap size is more than the initial heap size, and the initial heap size does not equal to the maximum heap size.

We should be aware that the maximum heap size set should be less than the available memory on the machine to avoid performance impact due to page faults and thrashing (by using virtual memory on storage), if we look at the following parameters:

```
-Xmnsize or -XX:NewSize=n
```

```
-XX:MaxNewSize=n
```

The preceding parameters have the same effect as that of auto-sizing but limited to the size of the young generation memory. Also, by setting both parameters to the same value, we will fix the value of the young generation size and remove the auto-sizing feature of the young generation.

The default size of the young generation is calculated as a ratio of the heap using the following parameter:

```
-XX:NewRatio=n
```

We can specify the ratio of the old/young generations (if we set this as 4, this means size of the old generation space is four times the size of the young generation space).

The other available parameters for memory sizing are as follows:

```
-XX:SurvivorRatio=n
-XX:MaxPermSize=n
```

Setting the survivor ratio defines the ratio between Eden and a single survivor space. If we set this to 32 (the default), each survivor space is 1/32 the size of an Eden space.

The `MaxPermSize` parameter sets the size of the permanent generation, which mainly holds the classes and methods metadata.

Thread stack size is an important factor and can be controlled by the following JVM parameter:

```
-XX:ThreadStackSize=n
```

The preceding parameter is an important tuning parameter where we can determine the memory allocated for each thread stack. This parameter controls the application's maximum thread count along with the operating system configurations. We already tested the impact of this parameter in *Chapter 8, Memory Profiling*.

Tuning garbage collection

Tuning garbage collection includes two main activities: using the proper garbage collector policy and defining targets for collector performance metrics.

Using proper garbage collection policy

In *Chapter 2, Understand Java Fundamentals*, we explored the different available collectors in the Java HotSpot VM, including G1 introduced in Java SE 7 (update 4). Here, we will discuss some guidelines to properly select the collector policy.

If there is no issue in the application, let the JVM select the proper collector policy as part of ergonomics. The `-server` mode will pick G1 as the first option.

If the application deals with less data or is running on a single processor and the JVM selected garbage collector is not performing well, then consider switching to a serial collector using the following parameter:

```
-XX:+UseSerialGC
```

If the application deals with a big set of data and is not performing well, try to use G1 if it's not already in use (or upgrade the Java version to use). Consider the concurrent mark sweep if G1 is not supported or not performing as expected. Usually, we use it with the incremental mode for better performance (as it reduces the application pause times) as follows:

```
-XX:+UseG1GC
-XX:+UseConcMarkSweepGC
-XX:+CMSIncrementalMode
```

If switching the collector type doesn't resolve the current issue, try to tune the collector further by setting performance goals/targets for it or try to change its behavior, as we will discuss in the next section.

Setting GC performance targets

Garbage collectors have some sort of targets to achieve. To set the GC pause time, we can use the following parameter:

```
-XX:MaxGCPauseMillis=n
```

The collector will try to meet this specified pause time (it is not mandatory though). Another parameter, which is also useful to specify the ratio between the time spent in the GC to the application execution time is as follows:

```
-XX:GCTimeRatio=n
```

Other parameters available to change or tune the collector behavior are as follows:

- **For G1 collector**: `-XX:G1HeapRegionSize=n`

    This parameter determines the size of the small regions the G1 operates in (it should be between 1 Mb and 32 Mb)

- **For parallel collector and concurrent mark sweep**:
    `-XX:ParallelGCThreads=n` and `-XX:ConcGCThreads=n`

    These parameters are used to determine the number of threads used for GC activities

This is a simplified overview of the different tuning aspects in Java HotSpot VM from both, the memory and garbage collection aspects.

Tuning the JRockit virtual machine

The Oracle JRockit VM is different in comparison to the Oracle HotSpot VM in the following main areas:

- The JRockit VM memory structure supports continuous heap and generational heap while the HotSpot VM only supports generational heap.

- The JRockit VM generational heap is divided into two sections: **Nursery** and **Tenured**. The Nursery area has a small subarea for newly allocated objects just before the garbage collection cycle, **Keep Area**. This means there are no survivor spaces, so moving the old objects inside the heap is reduced by one or more steps.

- JRockit has a TLA to allocate small thread objects; large objects are allocated directly in the heap.

- Classes are considered as objects and allocated in the heap and subjected to garbage collection as well (no perm generation).

- Different garbage collection modes and optimization options.

- JRockit has a real-time version for critical applications named Oracle JRockit Real Time.

The following diagram shows the structure of the JVM for the JRockit generational heap memory:

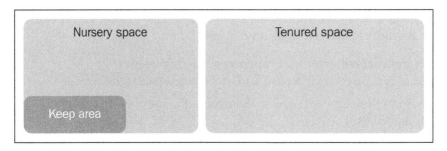

The preceding diagram shows a high-level structure of the generational JRockit heap, where it contains two main sections, one for the old/large objects, which is under **Tenured space**, and another one for object allocations, which is under **Nursery space**. The **Nursery space** contains **Keep area** for just the allocated objects (so it is not considered for garbage collection), and TLAs are reserved for each thread allocation. If TLA is full, the thread area can be expanded into the nursery (TLA is not shown in the diagram).

This means the tuning of the JRockit VM is different than that of the HotSpot VM. We will describe how to tune this JRockit VM in general.

Tuning JRockit memory size

Similar to the HotSpot VM, the same parameters are used to determine the heap size, -Xms and –Xmx.

The recommendation is to keep both parameters with the same value to reduce the auto-sizing overhead. Also, -Xns determines the size of the nursery area.

To increase the thread local areas, use the following parameter:

```
-XXtlaSize:min=size,preferred=size
```

This sets the minimal and preferred size of TLA. The recommendation is to increase it in multithreading applications, allowing larger objects to be allocated for each thread but should be used carefully to avoid memory fragmentation.

Tuning JRockit garbage collection

Garbage collection strategy mostly follows the mark and sweep model for the heap and if the nursery area exists (that is, generational mode), then a generational garbage collection is used.

Another setting is available to set the garbage collection mode among the following modes:

```
-Xgc:throughput
-Xgc:pausetime
-Xgc:deterministic
```

The last mode is only available in JRockit Real Time and it optimizes the garbage collection towards a short and determined pause time.

The other two options optimize the collector towards the required goal, either maximum application throughput or shortest pause time.

To set the target pause time, we can use the following parameter:

```
-XpauseTarget:time
```

As the garbage collector is of the compacting type, this can impact on performance by increasing the pause time. Some options also available to tune this as well, including the following parameter:

```
-XXcompaction:percentage=percentage
-XXcompaction:maxReferences=value
```

The first option to determine the percentage of the heap should be compacted with each old garbage collection. This should be set carefully as it has direct impact to the pause time.

The second option restricts the maximum number of referenced objects in the compacting area. If the number is exceeded, the compacting is cancelled (as it will be moving a large memory area that can increase the pause time as well).

We should also be careful while using this parameter, as setting it to a small value will stop the compacting and will produce memory fragmentation. With more memory fragmentation, the JVM will be forced to compact the whole heap, which would potentially lead to a long pause time.

The last parameter is used to inform JRockit to execute performance optimization as early as possible by running the bottleneck detector in high frequency from the beginning (then decrease the frequency later) and utilize the memory aggressively, as follows:

```
-XXaggressive:memory
```

> For more information about the JRockit VM performance tuning, you can read the Oracle online documentation at http://docs. oracle.com/cd/E15289_01/doc.40/e15060/toc.htm

Tuning application servers

Tuning application servers is an essential step for any enterprise application. There are a lot of areas that must be tuned and tailored according to our application. We will discuss some of these areas here and focus on both, the GlassFish and Weblogic servers.

As we did in the JVM performance tuning, we will focus on the generic and common tuning elements here and try to simplify them so we can understand our tuning strategy when dealing with any application server other than these mentioned servers.

The importance of application server tuning is that it contains the different containers of our application component, for example, web container, EJB container, JMS container (that is, JMS server), and so on.

It also contains and manages the different application resources, for example, JMS, connection pools, thread pools, persistent stores, and so on.

Tuning the Oracle GlassFish application server

The following general items should be configured to improve the performance of our enterprise applications on the GlassFish server. We will go through the configuration as specified in the GlassFish 4 performance tuning guide.

Deployment tuning options

The settings that need to be tuned for the application deployment in the production environment are as follows; the settings can be adjusted during deployment of our application from the application server admin console:

- **Disable auto-deployment**: This option will reduce the impact of interval reload checks. It should normally be disabled on production, as this is not the common way to deploy the application in production.

- **Disable auto-reloading**: This option is useful when we need to change something in the deployed application. In the test and development environment, we can make use of it but in production it is rarely used, so it is better to disable it and remove the check on the resource modification each time.

- **Precompile JSP**: This option will remove the time spent on compiling the pages for the first request (during warm up). The impact will be increased deployment time, but the benefit is a better user experience.

Web container tuning options

We must mainly take care of the following two settings:

- **Set proper session timeout**: The value of the session timeout must fit the application requirements. Too short or too long a timeout has an impact on the application performance (memory utilization and garbage collection). Also, it has a direct impact on the user experience if we set it to a very short period.
- **Disable dynamic JSP reloading**: This setting is not required in the production servers, so it's better to disable it to improve the performance.

EJB container tuning options

A lot of different settings can be tuned. Usually, we won't need to change most of them. Some of these settings are as follows:

- **Optimize EJB pool size**: By setting the minimal pool size, maximum pool size, and pool resize values according to the application needs
- **Optimize EJB pool idle timeout**: This is an important setting as it specifies the maximum time each bean instance is allowed to be idle for in the pool before it gets destroyed and removed (the default is 600 seconds)
- **Optimize EJB cache**: By setting the caching parameters, maximum cache size, resize value, removal timeout, removal policy, cache idle timeout, and refresh period

The following removal policies are supported in the GlassFish EJB container:

- The default value, **Not Recently Used (NRU)**
- **First In, First Out (FIFO)**
- **Least Recently Used (LRU)**

We already discussed these caching policies in *Chapter 5, Recognizing Common Performance Issues.*

Thread pool tuning options

The thread pool can be tuned by setting the `min` and `max` value of the thread pool size. The values of these options depend on the application's average requests and the average time spent on each request.

The recommended value for the maximum size should be between 100 and 500 according to the hardware server profile. Also, setting both, the minimum and maximum options with the same value should be considered unless the application traffic and load varies markedly over the day.

JDBC connection pool tuning options

The aspects mentioned below the following screenshot can be tuned for the JDBC connections:

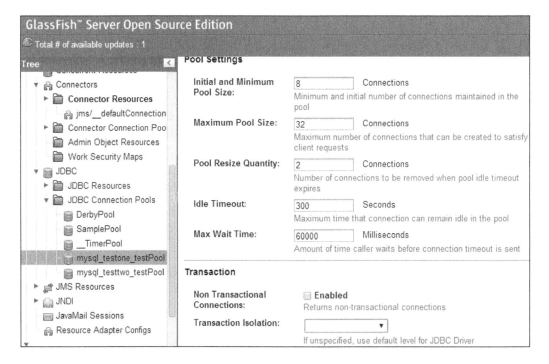

Refer to the following aspects:

- **Optimizing pool size settings**: This aspect sets the minimal, maximum, and resize quantity. These settings should be configured according to the application's nature of dealing with the database and number of supported concurrent users.

- **Optimizing connection timeout**: We need to set the idle timeout (the maximum time the connection remains idle before the connection is closed and removed from the pool) and the maximum wait time (the time the caller should wait for before getting the connection timeout error). Setting this maximum wait time to zero means blocking the caller thread until a connection is available, and this is recommended for better performance.

- **Optimizing connection validation**: If database connectivity is reliable, then disable connection validation; otherwise, the server will validate the connection whenever the pool returns a connection.

- **Optimizing transaction isolation level**: Do not specify the transaction isolation level, if possible, and use the default isolation level in the JDBC driver to avoid any performance overhead in the JDBC driver.

Tuning file cache components

The GlassFish file cache component is used to cache the static files, such as images, CSS, HTML, text files, and so on. The two settings that control the file cache component are `max count` of cached files and `max age`.

The cached `max` file counts need to be tuned by selecting a value between the high value that can consume high memory and the low value that removes the benefit of using this caching service.

The `max age` component should match the frequency of updating the information on our website, that is, the cached files.

Tuning DNS caching

The tuning DNS caching setting should be enabled so that it improves the performance, since it will remove the DNS lookup overhead.

Tuning logging information

Logging can affect the application performance. If it does not, follow the logging best practices. From the application server perspective, we need to consider the following points:

- Tune the log level of GlassFish and the different deployed applications
- Disable access logs if not really required for troubleshooting (or if they can be obtained from another component)
- Change the logfiles location to be in a separate hard drive

This is a simplified overview of some of the GlassFish tuning areas that will be mostly similar to the tuning of other application servers.

 For more details on GlassFish Version 4.0 performance tuning details, check the documentation guide at https://glassfish.java.net/docs/4.0/performance-tuning-guide.pdf.

Tuning the Oracle Weblogic application server

The same settings that we discussed with GlassFish tuning are also available in different forms on the Weblogic server, yet Weblogic has many more advanced settings for the application performance monitoring and tuning.

We will list here a few areas that we didn't deal with in the GlassFish tuning section as an example of the variation between different application servers' performance tuning. Also, they provide additional aspects that we need to consider when dealing with other application servers.

Tuning the internal applications' deployment

Weblogic has many internal applications that get deployed during server startup. They are not required for our application. In this case, we can change the default behavior in our production server from deploying it on startup to on-demand access, in particular when we need to reduce the server memory footprint.

Tuning network components

An example of network tuning is selecting the proper **muxer**. The Java muxer is platform independent but slower than the native muxer, so it is ideal to use the native muxer. But if we have RMI clients, the only way to support this is by using the Java muxer.

 Muxer is a software module in Weblogic that reads incoming server requests and outgoing client responses. Three types of muxer are available to use: Java, native, and non-blocking IO muxer.

Also, memory **chunck** optimization can be done by increasing the memory chunk size, pool size, and partition count that can improve the performance if the application handles a large amount of data per request (the default value is 4 KB with a 2048 pool size in 4 different partitions).

Chunk is the memory unit of the Weblogic network layer reserved memory (client/server side); it is used to read/write data from/to sockets.

Tuning stuck thread configuration

Weblogic has the ability to detect whether a thread is continuously working for a set of time and log it as a stuck thread since this thread is not able to complete its request or serve a new request.

Tuning this is important according to the nature of the application. Also, it is useful when troubleshooting spikes during performance testing to understand where these threads spend time. We do this so we can set the value of the thread that is stuck to something that is less than the spikes' values in order to get them logged to analyze the root cause of the spikes' performance. This is applicable if we are not able to get thread dumps in the exact time of these spikes.

 To read more about the number of options that are available for performance tuning on Weblogic Server 12c, check the Oracle online documentation: http://docs.oracle.com/cd/E24329_01/web.1211/e24390.pdf

Tuning web servers (HTTP servers)

Most of the enterprise applications have a web server placed up front of its application layer. They are used for many reasons, such as serving static site content, load balancing, security reasons, for example, part of the **demilitarized zone (DMZ)**, and so on.

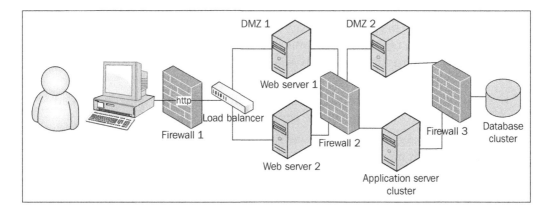

The previous diagram shows a simplified deployment architecture with multiple DMZ zones, up front web servers, and a backend system consisting of the application servers and the database server.

> DMZ is a network architecture where external facing services are on either physical or logical network (or subnetwork). This gives more security since any attack can only get access to these exposed services, and the internal network is protected and can only be accessed from this DMZ zone.

Among the existing web servers, the most commonly used web server is Apache web server. Other vendors also provide different web servers that some of them already use Apache web server in its core (wrapper servers) as Oracle web server.

In this section, we will discuss some points around the Apache web server performance tuning to understand our strategy when we deal with web servers' performance tuning.

Tuning the Apache web server (Apache HTTP server)

Before we start performance tuning of the Apache web server, we must understand the different operating modes. Apache server is a **Multi-process/Multi-thread-based (MPM)** server. Some of the MPMs are platform-specific, for example, mpm_netware, mpmt_os2, and mpm_winnt.

For Unix-based systems, the following MPM modes can be used:

- **Worker MPM**: This mode uses multiple child processes with many threads; each thread handles one connection at a time, and worker fits high-traffic servers because it has a smaller memory footprint.

- **Event MPM**: This mode is threaded as the worker mode but is designed to allow more requests simultaneously by delegating some processing work to the supporting threads and freeing up the main threads to work on new requests.

- **Prefork MPM**: This mode uses multiple child processes with one thread each; each process handles one connection at a time.

  It uses more memory than the worker mode, but since it is not thread-based, it is not recommended to be used. But it has advantages over the worker mode as it can be used with non-thread-safe third-party modules and is easier to be used for debugging on platforms with poor thread debugging support.

We can further tune the selected mode by using the following configurations:

- Removing the unnecessary or unused modules by commenting out the associated `LoadModule` directive; this will help to improve the request processing time

- Switching off dynamically added modules to reduce the associated memory by adding `-DDYNAMIC_MODULE_LIMIT=0` when building our Apache web server

- Allocating as much memory as possible to the server to decrease the latency; we need to avoid memory swap, otherwise the performance will be degraded markedly

- Switch `HostnameLookups` off (this is the default value); if we need to read the log with different IPs, there is a utility that comes with the server named **logresolve**, which can be used to read access logs in a more readable way

 Logresolve is a program that resolves IP addresses in Apache's access log files; it can be downloaded from the following location: `http://httpd.apache.org/docs/2.4/programs/logresolve.html`.

- Disable `AllowOverride` (for the `.htaccess` files) whenever possible and if we need to use `AllowOverride`, we must limit the permit to the required directories only, as shown in the following code:

```
DocumentRoot /www/htdocs
<Directory />
  AllowOverride None
</Directory>
```

- Whenever possible, set `FollowSymLinks` everywhere, and don't try to set `SymLinksIfOwnerMatch`

- Reduce content negotiation if possible, for example, instead of using `DirectoryIndex`, use it with all the possible names allowed as follows:

```
DirectoryIndex index.html index.cgi
```

- Always enable the `send file` and if we have some performance instability, in particular with an NFS-mounted filesystem, disable it only for that directory as follows:

```
EnableSendfile off
```

- Minimize `KeepAliveTimeout` (less than 60 seconds) when `keepAlive` is used, so that the Apache server does not wait too much for subsequent requests (the default is 5 seconds)

An important Apache performance tuning option is the ability to compress the output from the server and decompress the compressed input from the client. This reduces the size of the transmitted data and hence improves the bandwidth of the application and speeds up the communication between the client and the server.

This option is available through the Apache module, `mod_deflate`, which is a filter module that can work as an output filter. In this case, the output data will be compressed and the client browser will decompress it, and if it is added as an input filter, the client can send the compressed body and it will decompress them before processing.

This is configured by ensuring that the module is already loaded in `httpd.conf` using the following parameters:

```
LoadModule deflate_module modules/mod_deflate.so
```

In the `deflate.conf` file, add the required filters for different content types using the following configuration directives:

```
SetOutputFilter\AddOutputFilter DEFLATE (for output filter).
SetInputFilter\AddInputFilter DEFLATE (for input filter).
```

Also, we can specify this by the type of content using another directive:

```
AddOutputFilterByType DEFLATE text/html.
```

Unfortunately, there is critically identified security vulnerability when using this HTTP-level compression with TLS/SSL, which is named as the BREACH attack.

 For more information about the BREACH attack, refer to the following website: `http://breachattack.com/`.

Another important tuning aspect in the Apache server is pushing the browsers to load the different resources from the local cache as long as they are not frequently changeable.

This is done by using the Apache module `mod_expires`, which enables us to override the HTTP headers, `cache-control max-age`, and `expires`, so reduce the load over the server and enable the client to load the resources quickly. We need to ensure this module is loaded using the following parameter in `httpd.conf`:

```
LoadModule expires_module modules/mod_expires.so
```

Now, configure the required changes in the `expire.conf` file using the two directives: `ExpiresDefault` and `ExpiresByType`. The syntax for both the directives is as follows:

```
ExpiresDefault "base [plus num type] [num type] ..."
ExpiresByType type/encoding "base [plus num type] [num type] ..."
Where base is one of access, now (equivalent to 'access') and
modification.
The plus keyword is optional and num should be an integer value.
Type is one of years, months, weeks, days, hours, minutes, and
seconds.
```

An example of how to use these configurations is as follows:

```
ExpiresByType text/html "access plus 20 days"
ExpiresByType image/png "modification plus 48 hours 30 minutes"
```

These are some examples of the Apache web server tuning configurations and mostly apply in other vendors, especially those that use the Apache server in the core.

 For more information about the Apache 2.4 performance tuning, you can read the following Apache online documentation:
`http://httpd.apache.org/docs/2.4/misc/perf-tuning.html`

Tuning the Oracle web server (Oracle HTTP server)

The Oracle web server is based on the Apache server, so most of the configurations are already the same as in the Apache web server.

Similar to the Apache server, Oracle web server supports different modes that should be selected according to the operating system as follows:

- The worker mode uses the MPM made on platforms other than Microsoft Windows (default mode)
- The WinNT mode consists of a parent process and a child process; the parent process is the control process and the child process creates threads to handle requests (this is for Windows only)
- The prefork mode uses processes instead of threads and is considered the least efficient mode

When the sever starts to run, the main process starts to execute, which executes many child processes as specified by the `StartServers` attribute with a maximum number as in `ServerLimit` (this is for non-Windows servers).

After this, each process creates threads using `ThreadsPerChild` with the upper limit as `ThreadLimit`. These threads include multiple worker threads and one listener thread to transfer requests to the workers.

The process then maintains the number of threads by using `MinSpareThreads` (minimum number of idle threads) and `MaxSpareThreads` (maximum number of idle threads).

Let's now explore some of the tuning configurations (most of them exist in the Apache server as well) as follows:

- Setting the maximum number of clients that can connect simultaneously using the `MaxClients` parameter with the default value as `150`, but this can be increased up to 8,000 as long as the resources can support it (note that in the recent Apache releases, the parameter is named `MaxRequestWorkers` but `MaxClients` is still supported). This parameter is only used in non-Windows servers.

- Setting the startup process if we expect always load once the application is up and running. This can be achieved by `StartServers` with the default value as `2`. This is controlled by `ServerLimit`, which specifies the maximum number of clients and has the priority over `StartServers`.

- Setting the number of threads per process by using `ThreadsPerChild`, this is controlled by the maximum thread counts that can be created under each process to serve customer requests using `ThreadLimit`. The default value is `64` except in Windows 1920.

- Control the thread/workers pool by using `MinSpareThreads` and `MaxSpareThreads`.

- Limit the number of enabled modules by removing them out of the `httpd.conf` file, as each request will pass on the different handlers till it finds a suitable handler. Also, static pages will go through all the handlers till they get picked by the default handler.

- Tune the file description limit by tuning the hard limit of the operating system's file descriptor (this is the operating system configuration as we will see later).

 For more information about the Oracle web server tuning 12c, refer to the following Oracle documentation: http://docs.oracle.com/middleware/1212/core/ASPER.pdf.

Tuning the operating system and hardware

If we look back to our application pyramidal model in the early pages of this chapter, we can see that we are now discussing the basement layer of that model, so that this layer performance impact is propagated to all the other layers.

If a virtual machine is used, the impact of the operating system and the virtual machine's own performance is doubled (it is out of the scope of this book to discuss virtual machine performance optimization).

The next section covers the main points that we need to take care of when dealing with the operating system and hardware tuning.

Capacity planning and hardware optimization

A lot of important factors contribute to our decision to scale the application hardware. Among these factors, we can list the following important points:

- Understanding the current hardware capacity
- The existing application utilization
- The application bottleneck areas (that is, CPU, memory, network, and so on)
- The application traffic forecast

The preceding factors can help us understand where the current hardware needs to be scaled in either vertical or horizontal scaling. For example, if the bottleneck is located in a specific component (that is, memory), scaling this component vertically can fix the issue (for example, add more RAM).

Scaling it horizontally might improve it. Also, if the system reaches its full capacity, consider scaling it horizontally to improve its performance. So, the most important factor in the application scaling decision is the application monitoring results. Some of the use cases for hardware scaling are as follows:

- If the CPU utilization is high and bottleneck is on CPU, then changing to multicores or adding more servers should be considered (if no more code tuning is possible). Also, moving some running applications on to different hardware (changing architecture) should be considered.
- If the limitation is for the memory to support more sessions or more concurrent users, add more RAM to the system. Also, avoid using virtual memory, as swapping will severely degrade the performance. It is good to have virtual memory in the legacy systems that does not support large memory RAMs.

- The disk I/O speed must be assessed and if it is not good, replace it with more speed disks. Also, enough disk space should be allocated, and it is preferred if logfiles and non-important files are located in different disk drivers/partitions.

- Network bandwidth should be sufficient not only to serve customer requests but to also synchronize between cluster nodes, for example, session replication, disaster recovery replication, and so on.

- Performance optimization of cluster configurations is always required to improve the application performance so we can get the best outcome from this cluster-like scalability and failover.

The scalability decision in all cases shouldn't be made based on wrong application behavior. So, if we have a memory leak in our application, the solution is not to scale its memory. We should fix all application issues before we decide that a certain component in our system is the limiting factor for our application scalability.

It is worth mentioning here that all the scalability changes must be performance tested and proved to be adding value to the application performance. This is of course for both, end-to-end performance testing and isolated component performance testing. So, performance testing covers two important areas, deciding where to scale and if scaling improves the performance as desired or not. We already covered performance testing in detail in *Chapter 3, Getting Familiar with Performance Testing*.

Operating system configurations optimization

Performance tuning of an operating system must follow the specified tuning guidelines for the JVM, application servers, web servers, and network elements, according to the platform operating system being used.

It is out of our book's scope to discuss operating system and network tuning. A couple of examples for the operating system configuration tuning are as follows:

- **File Descriptor Setting**: By setting this configuration, the maximum number of open files property (in UNIX, by the command `ulimit`)

- **TCP tuning**: By this configuration, adjusting the TCP wait time value, the TCP queue size, connection hash size, and so on if required

Now that we are at the end of this chapter, it is important to completely understand the high-level guidelines and directions that we need to follow when we are targeting to tune our application environment. This will help us while thinking of any enterprise application performance issue. But for detailed steps, you can refer to the specific vendor documentation for more information.

Summary

In this chapter, we briefly covered the tuning aspects in the enterprise application environment, starting from the most important aspect, which is the JVM tuning. We dissected the HotSpot JVM in detail and covered some gaps and differences when we discussed the JRockit JVM performance tuning.

We also discussed the application server tuning and selected the basic server, GlassFish being the reference implementation server as an example for the basic required tuning in the different enterprise application components. We also highlighted some points in the Weblogic server as an example of other areas that we need to look into.

We covered the Apache web server as an example of the HTTP web servers and discussed a few areas for performance tuning. We gave a few hints about the Oracle web server being based on the Apache web server, and then highlighted a few points for the operating system and hardware scaling directions, which must be based on the vendor's recommendations and application monitoring results.

In *Chapter 10, Designing High-performance Enterprise Applications*, we will discuss the importance of the application design from the performance aspect and the different design decisions and their performance impact. We will also discuss data caching on different layers to improve the performance of our applications.

10
Designing High-performance Enterprise Applications

Design is our key to a good performing enterprise application. Some design decisions can cost us a lot in application performance and should be avoided whenever possible.

In this chapter, we will try to cover some of the design areas that we should consider while designing our enterprise applications. We will discuss data caching in more detail, since it is one of the magic pillars for performance improvement.

The following is the list of topics that we will cover in this chapter:

- Design decisions and performance impact
- Performance anti-pattern decisions
- Performance aspects in **Service Oriented Architecture (SOA)**
- Performance of RESTful web services
- Data caching techniques
- Cloud performance considerations

Potential performance impact of different design decisions

Design decisions are always difficult since they are taken under a lot of different considerations and restrictions, including fulfilling both functional and non-functional requirements, project budget, available software license, infrastructure, team skills, product roadmap, previous experience, and so on.

We won't discuss the non-technical constraints such as budget or team skills here, but we will focus on the technical aspects of these decisions.

Before we start discussing the different design decisions, it is important to realize that there is no single point of view in design decisions. When it comes to design, there is nothing absolutely wrong or absolutely right. However, the design direction could be relatively better or worse by evaluating the pros and cons of each design direction in the context of our project. Therefore, in this chapter, we will focus more on the common and general opinions regarding these design decisions and reflect our own experience.

Performance is one of the most important aspects of non-functional requirements. Before we discuss the different design decisions, we need to highlight that the non-functional requirements must be measurable so that the application design can match these requirements.

We shouldn't accept vague or non-measurable goals, such as *the system should be performing well during load time*. This is an example of a general non-measurable requirement statement; instead, the requirement should define exactly what the required performance of the system is (that is, response time) and what is the load time or number of concurrent users? We need to do the same for other non-functional requirements like scalability where we need to have a well-defined scaling measurement.

In this section, we will discuss the high-level considerations in different design decisions from the performance perspective. Then, we will pick some points to discuss in more detail in the next sections of this chapter.

Potential performance impact of the application layer's decisions

The application architecture must consider the required performance of the application while designing the whole application architecture and during the design of each layer in the application. Also, defining the number of application layers should be considered from the performance point of view.

The layered architecture in JEE promotes flexibility mainly due to loose coupling and separation of concerns in application layers, for example, a typical enterprise application could contain the following layers:

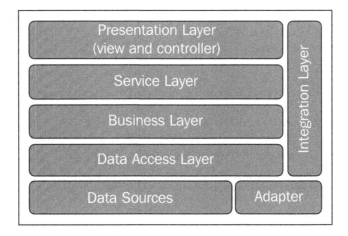

The following are the different components of a typical enterprise application, as shown in the preceding diagram:

- **Presentation layer**: This layer contains the UI elements and presentation logic along with some required validations.

- **Service layer**: This layer contains the services that are exposed either internally or externally. It could be implemented in two ways: tightly coupled with the presentation layer using direct method calls or loosely coupled using EJBs, SOAP/REST web services, JMS, and so on.

- **Business layer**: This layer contains the application's business logic, entities, and workflows, and it is responsible for interacting with the data layer.

- **Data layer**: This layer encapsulates and interacts with the data sources and represents the data that is used by the business layer.

- **Data sources**: This layer consist of different application data sources such as database, different files, external services/systems, and so on.

- **Integration layer**: This layer integrates with other systems that are usually made by using a *middleware* application in the service layer.

- **Adapter**: These are components that might be required when we need to interact with legacy systems or old technologies.

The different components of the application can be distributed into different zones by using the **Demilitarized Zone (DMZ)** concept, which is a basic security architecture consideration. Generally, one or two DMZs are used, but sometimes more.

Each application zone must be redundant with the load balancing feature and the failover technique so that the application can withstand high traffic load and any unexpected production issues.

DMZ is a physical or logical subnetwork that is characterized by exposed services to another less trusted network. The aim of this zone is to add another layer of security to the internal network, as external network attacks can only have direct access to these exposed services in the DMZ but not to the internal network.

DMZ is built using different firewall architectures, and in some enterprise applications, more than one DMZ is used for more security.

One important factor in the application architecture is data replication for both geo-redundancy and disaster-recovery environments. Without having a good performing data replication method between these environments, using these environments during critical situations will be of less value.

We also need to have distributed caching as an essential component to improve the enterprise application performance, yet it should be tailored according to our application's exact needs. The best type of data caching is the lookup and static data.

If transactional data needs to be cached, it needs to be done in a centralized manner as we do not know the actual application instance that will make use of the cached data. This centralized distributed caching is a complex type of caching, and it needs some sort of global locking mechanism, as we will see later in this chapter when we discuss data caching.

Potential performance impact of a component's selection decisions

Selecting different application components requires some deep analysis of the requirements, component capabilities, performance of the components, supporting interfaces, and so on.

The selection of different system components is not an isolated task as it overlaps with other decisions—in particular, the integration strategy.

Each system component must be dedicated to a specific task, limiting the interaction between the system's internal components to exchange the required messages or data (that is, apply the separation of concerns rule).

It is important that when we select system components, we do not focus only on the requirements. We need to think about some of the following additional aspects of these components:

- **Scalability**: This refers to the ability to scale up the component. We can add more servers to scale it horizontally or add more hardware resources (for example, more memory) to scale it vertically. Scalability must be defined in a measurable way and should be taken into consideration from the early architecture stage. Unfortunately, this is commonly missed, which causes us a painful cost in later stages of the project.

- **Expandability**: This refers to the ability of the component to expand and provide support to additional requirements in the future without the need to replace it or do major changes.

- **Flexibility**: If the component can support different interfaces/protocols, then the component is flexible in our architecture and can integrate with other components in many different ways. This promotes loose coupling and allows performance tuning to use the best performing protocol.

- **Customizable**: This is an important feature from the performance perspective. It refers to the ability to switch off certain unnecessary modules/features to improve the performance. We saw this during the tuning of the Apache web server where we can remove some modules from the server to enable more efficient server memory utilization.

Potential performance impact of integration decisions

Integration decisions are directly related to the application performance — in particular, the integration layer of the middleware component. The performance of this layer is the main factor that affects the enterprise application performance.

From the integration point of view, the first question we need to answer is the number of integration layers: how many layers are present in our system? The role of each layer should be well defined by having clear defined inputs and output from each layer/component. This is what we call **separation of concerns**, which aims to reduce the internal communication overhead.

The layers or the components should also be loosely coupled to allow the replacement of any component without impacting other components.

Integration protocols must be standard portable protocols such as XML, JSON, JMS, FTP, JDBC, and HTTP. These standard protocols can allow easy integration, but the performance is not as good compared to native integration, for example, using direct method calls or local EJB calls.

After defining each layer function and integration protocols, we need to keep the interaction granularity in the medium range. For example, using very fine-tuned or very coarse objects on interaction calls can degrade the application performance as it either requires many calls to achieve the task or returns a huge amount of unnecessary data.

The integration mode is an important performance factor, as selecting synchronous interaction is not usually a good decision in all transaction types. Sometimes, asynchronous interaction is required for lengthy or external calls.

The integration layer must be highly available; this is not a luxury for this layer as this layer is considered as the backbone of the application. The performance of this layer must be measured separately from other components to assess the overhead of this layer and improve its performance.

Transaction propagation is one of the important aspects of the integration design: how do we propagate transaction between different components? The aim is to minimize the use of long global transactions (`WS-AtomicTransaction`, that is, two-phase commit) in favor of local or short component transactions whenever this is possible.

Another way to support prolonged transaction is to implement a rollback logic (`WS-BusinessActivity`) whenever the integrated system components fails at a certain level. We can execute the rollback steps from the failure point.

Caching is an essential feature in the integration layer to speed up the application transactions. Most integration service buses provide this feature out of the box to speed up the integration, which is very useful when the data is not changing frequently.

Caching can also be done at the API level by caching the service results. All caching must be implemented correctly to gain better performance. We will discuss caching in detail later in this chapter.

Potential performance impact of security decisions

Security is an essential non-functional requirement, in particular, for enterprise applications that deal with sensitive information such as personal information and health and payment details.

Selection of security measures can affect the application performance. If we take access controls checks as an example, they might require additional checks with each user transaction or request. Typically, generating access tokens for users and caching these tokens can speed up such interactions.

The *SSL* protocol should be used when the user wants to log in to our application, and we don't need to secure the connection in most of the cases before the login step.

Some applications restrict the access to certain whitelisted IP addresses. This adds additional checks on each user request and should be limited to administrative transactions rather than customer transactions (it doesn't add much to the application security).

Data encryption is essential for some sensitive data such as passwords, payment details, and health information. Other data of less value might be optionally encrypted or just encoded. Encryption is a slow process so selection of both the data that needs to be encrypted and the encryption algorithm should be carefully done.

Some database engines already provide a transparent, secure wallet solution for such classified confidential data.

Splitting the user's data from transactional data is another recommended security measure where data is split over many different database schemas. So, having access to any of these schemas reveals data that is anonymous or depersonalized. This can affect the application performance by retrieving data from different data sources without the ability to join queries over these data sources.

Caching of data plus an efficient well-structured data split are the best ways to minimize the performance impact (that is, correct selection of the split tables to minimize any required query joins).

Using a parameterized prepared statement to guard against *SQL injection* can speed up the execution in most of the cases because the statement is compiled. Also, caching against the parameters of the statement becomes much easier rather than caching against the whole query.

The SQL injection security flaw can happen when a user's input is used without any processing to construct SQL queries, for example, `select userId from users_ table where username='"+usernameStr+"' and password='"+passwordStr+"'";`.

If the user enters any value in the username field and enters `' or 1=1` in the password field, the query will return the entire table data based on the `1=1` condition. This will result in (usually) authentication of the user with the first returned user from the query results.

To avoid such security vulnerability, we should either use a bind variable or escape the user's input (the `'` character in the previous example).

We should always use a prepared statement with bind variables, and such programming practice should be prohibited completely to avoid both performance and security impact.

Cross-site Scripting (**XSS**) and **Cross-site Request Forgery** (**CRRF**) are important security vulnerabilities. Measures to protect the users from these attacks can affect the performance depending on the nature of these measures. For example, generating dynamic parameter names for each response and only accepting requests with these can have minor overhead on the application performance to check if the user's request matches the generated parameter names.

Auditing is an important security concept where we store the information required to identify *who made what, when, and why*. If we could push this feature to be asynchronous, it could improve the application's response time.

So as a general comment regarding security, we have to pay some performance overhead as a side effect and we should not permit any violation to the security principles to improve the application performance. What we are recommending here is to just do it in the right way — classify the application data according to its sensitivity and implement the required security measures according to this classification. The customer's security is the first priority in all enterprise applications.

> *"Things which matter most must never be at the mercy of things which matter least."*
>
> *–Johann Wolfgang von Goethe*

Potential performance impact of framework and UI decisions

Java enterprise applications can be developed using many standard set of existing frameworks such as JSF, Servlet and JSP, EJB, and JPA. Various readymade frameworks such as as Spring, Struts 2, and Portal can also be used.

The selection of the used Java frameworks is mainly taken according to the framework capabilities, performance, learning curve, and supportability, so we need to assess and evaluate all these aspects before selecting which application framework to use.

User interface decisions also have some impact according to what is required. For example, using UI technology such as Flex, Flash, and JavaFX as the user interface is not the same as using HTML 5. Each technology has its pros and cons and performance is one of the aspects that needs to be assessed before taking such a decision.

Another UI option that develops a single interface for all client devices can be a valid option with the current improvement of the browser capabilities of smartphones. However, another approach is to create application content that is optimized for display on different client device's configurations, which is better from both performance and user experience point of view.

Potential performance impact of application interaction decisions

Here, interactions refer to either synchronous or asynchronous transaction types. The design should identify the transactions that take time to be asynchronous operations mostly by using some sort of messaging solutions or callback methods.

We can also use Ajax calls for client interactions (Web 2.0) or complete page navigation approach (traditional web). The advantage of using Ajax is that we can retrieve a small set of data from the server instead of a whole web page with each request, which reduces the network traffic and server load in addition to the better user experience of having a desktop-like behavior in our web applications.

Potential performance impact of regulatory decisions

We can describe these decisions as restrictive decisions, for example, some regulation requires the retention of data for various periods due to different reasons like product insurance or customer rights. For enterprise applications, this requires not only enough storage capacity but the more the data we keep, the more is the performance impact on our SQL queries.

The best way to handle such restriction is to have a separate data replica other than the current operational data store and keep the operational data as minimal as possible so that the performance of the enterprise application is not affected by this huge data retention.

Other requirements such as fraud detection and customer credit authorization should be designed in an asynchronous way if they have potential impact on the application performance.

Potential performance impact of some miscellaneous decisions

Some miscellaneous design decisions can affect the application performance in the following ways:

- **Backward compatibility**: In applications that provide services to the customers, background compatibility with previous versions of the application services is usually required to support customers' existing applications. In that case, we might create separate versions of these services and focus on improving the performance of the newly introduced versions to motivate the customers to move to these new versions, which facilitates the deprecations of the old services in the future.

- **Elasticity**: With the introduction of cloud concepts'. the term elasticity has become an important target for enterprise applications in which the application can expand to support users during load times and collapse during low traffic times. Deploying the application in a cloud environment provides this feature out of the box without much effort, but the application should be designed to fit the cloud environment to make use of the cloud benefits including elasticity.

- **Architecture bottlenecks**: A good performing architecture with one or two bottlenecks means all the architecture is useless. This is one of the performance killers when we have good performing components with one or more areas of low performance. If these low performing areas are critical or in the heart of the application (such as integration bus), the whole application performance will be affected.

- **KISS (Keep it simple, stupid) rule**: One of the important rules in software design is to keep everything simple and straightforward (not stupid literally!). Complicating the application design usually results in low performance and difficult troubleshooting of performance issues.

All these are samples of different design decisions and the potential performance impact on our application, and we need to consider them when building our application architecture and designing it.

Avoiding performance anti-patterns

Anti-patterns are patterns that are similar to design patterns in the aspect that they document best solutions to common issues in specific context, but they differ in the aspect that their use or misuse produces negative consequences to the application.

As we are discussing performance anti-patterns, this means the use of these patterns will mostly degrade the application performance or at least will not produce the expected performance results.

Anti-patterns can be classified into the following two major types:

- Software process anti-patterns such as missing proactive performance management or inefficient performance testing

- Technical anti-patterns, including patterns in different software cycle stages such as design, implementation, and testing

Let's see some examples of these technical anti-patterns and briefly discuss them.

Because design patterns represent design solutions that resolve common design issues whenever we have the opportunity to apply these patterns, it would be better for the application performance instead of wasting the time on thinking of solutions or fixes for these issues.

Not following the common design patterns and best practices is performance anti-pattern. Of course, this is a general rule that has many exceptions as sometimes the designed solution has a better performance.

To read more about Java EE design patterns, you can refer to *Core J2EE Patterns Best Practices and Design Strategies* by Dan Malks, Deepak Alur, and John Crupi, and *Patterns of Enterprise Application Architecture* by Martin Fowler.

If design and coding best practices are not followed, it will result in potential performance anti-patterns. One example here is having the user's input validation in both client (using JavaScript) and server sides; when we neglect doing this validations of user inputs or delay it to a later step in the transaction flow, then this causes unnecessary processing that consumes server resources before we might reject the processing (or throw exception to the user) because of some validation errors.

The same is the case in the integration layer; we need to validate the messages before we start processing them to avoid wasting the time processing any invalid messages.

In *Chapter 5, Recognizing Common Performance Issues*, we have listed some common performance issues. These issues are typically performance anti-patterns and some of them are as follows:

- Improper memory management such as memory leakage or missing garbage collection tuning.
- Improper caching technique that is not suitable for the application data.
- Incorrect database manipulations.
- Using synchronous transaction in places that require asynchronous transaction (for example, long operations).
- Using a linear algorithm, which causes the application to perform well with low load, but degrade with high loads. This should be avoided and our algorithms shouldn't degrade with application load by selecting algorithms that scale efficiently.

Missing tuning of different application environment components, is described in the previous chapter, *Chapter 9, Tuning an Application's Environment*. Tuning of different components such as JVM and the application server should be considered as part of our application deployment performance improvement. If we missed this step, then it is a performance anti-pattern.

Coding issues including spaghetti-like code and using large Java classes are critical performance anti-patterns where we won't be able to reuse or optimize such code without spending big efforts and in some cases, it is just easier to rewrite this spaghetti code again in a more efficient way than try to fix it!

In the next chapter, *Chapter 11, Performance Tuning Tips*, we will discuss some performance tuning tips and coding best practices.

Missing application documentations, including inline code comments and Java-docs, are also considered as performance anti-patterns as fixing performance issues that we can face in production environments requires understanding what the code is doing well to fix it in safe way. So, even if this is a documentation issue and is not causing a direct performance issue, it will restrict the ability to provide a safe solution to performance issues without wasting time trying to analyze the code.

These are a few examples of performance anti-patterns that need to be considered. Avoid falling in these patterns to protect our application from undesired performance issues.

Performance aspects of Service Oriented Architecture (SOA)

SOA is the most commonly used architecture in the enterprise applications these days. The architecture is composed of three main different components: service provider, service consumer, and service broker (service registry). The interaction between these three components results in what is called SOA.

The following are the main advantages of this architecture:

- Loose coupling between both service provider and consumer
- Reusability of services and easy orchestration of different services
- Easy migration/upgrade/replacement of services
- Standardization of contract, transaction, and security

The following diagram depicts the basic explanation of SOA and can be found in any book or article discussing SOA:

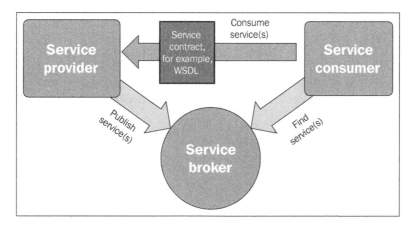

The broker role varies according to the application nature. It can provide all the information about the available services and their contracts to the client, or it can provide just the dynamic or static routing services.

The service itself could be any application service. Most common services are the XML- or SOAP-based web service. The service registry is usually implemented by either a service repository (UDDI) or a service bus that has its own service registry (service repository).

The main concerns of SOA are performance, scalability, and availability. The following are the reasons behind these concerns:

- Using XML interfaces in communication produces overhead for marshalling/unmarshalling the objects (that is, converting to/from XML) as compared to native communications.

- The aggregation of services and orchestration increases the final accumulated response time of web services.

- System availability is the product of all the service availabilities. So, if we need the system to be 98 percent available and we have two web independent services and each has its own availability as 98 percent, then the system's overall availability will be around 96 percent and we will not achieve the required system availability.

In this section, we will highlight some points regarding the performance of SOA applications from different areas with a short description of the performance impact.

Let's start with service dynamic call creation, which is fully supported in Java. Using this complete dynamic invocation is not recommended and not practical to use as well. The best way is to have a well-defined service contract that is shared between both the service provider and consumer, or to delegate this to a service bus layer that performs the required level of abstraction and does the required transformations. Otherwise, a lot of extensive operations will be required on the consumer side to parse a dynamic web service output and analyze its relations.

Implementing service caching is a good performance feature that can be supported at different levels. Two levels of service caching can be supported for better service performance: service data caching and service response/result caching. They are explained as follows:

- **Service data caching**: In this type, we cache the service internal data that is used for processing the coming user's requests. Consider, for example, a weather forecast service — the data of the weather forecast for the coming month in Cairo. We can cache this data and whenever a user requests the weather forecast for a specific day, the service does not have to hit the database to retrieve this information but instead return it from the cache. This will in turn improve the service response time.

- **Service response caching**: In this type, the service caller caches the service response. For example, retrieving the weather forecast of a city in a defined period does not require the processing of another similar call to the web service within a short period as the answer will be the same. By using service response caching, the average service response time becomes much better, and the best place to add this caching is in the routing service bus.

Using service dynamic binding is usually achieved by the application backbone service bus, which is responsible for binding the service calls to the current running services and avoids the invoking of down services or slow-responding services. This improves the application performance.

Service dynamic balancing, which is done by using a load balancer or typically by a service bus that routes service calls to different services, can improve the performance by dynamically distributing the calls over different services so that we can get the best performance out of each service.

Service granularity is an important factor that we have already discussed earlier in *Chapter 5, Recognizing Common Performance Issues*. When we design our web services, we need to design the services with moderate-sized data objects for both the service inputs and outputs so that we can reduce the overhead that is required if we used small or very large objects.

For example, having fine-tuned services (small service output objects) requires massive calls in each transaction to retrieve the full required data, while having coarse-gained services forces us to pay unnecessary overhead to retrieve information that we might not need/use. This important design concept should be followed to have a stable application performance.

A flexible service contract is an important aspect of web service performance. With a dynamic contract for each service invocation, we can customize the response data according to the required subset of data. This flexibility can be achieved mainly using one of the following ways:

- Optional directive in service input/output parameter's internal fields and the caller should send some parameter to the service indicating the required level of data. For elements, we use `minOccurs="0"` as shown in the following example:

```
<xsd:element name="feature" type="xsd:string" minOccurs="0"
  />
```

  ○ For attributes, we use the `use="optional"` directive as shown in the following example:

```
<xsd:attribute name="number" type="xsd:integer"
  use="optional"/>
```

- An output map for all optional values in the service response. This map is filled with the required data according to the input parameters.

- Using data objects, the standard implementation for data objects is **Service Data Object (SDO)** and **Java data object (JDO)**. Both are used to abstract the service data by providing simple APIs to manipulate the data from different data sources.

An SOA service is stateless in nature; stateless services are much better at scalability compared to stateful services, which consume the resources and increase the service implementation complexity to persist the client status and exchange some sort of session identifier (or token) with the client so that all subsequent requests go to the same user service session.

It is not recommended to use the stateful services from a performance perspective as they limit the ability to dynamically route the client calls to different services according to the service load (unless they store user data in a shared location, such as cache, memory, or database).

Invoking the services using concurrent requests is an efficient way to decrease the transactional time required to retrieve data using the same web service. However, without having an upper limit to the concurrent calls from different users or clients, the service can go out of service with few number of users invoking a huge number of concurrent calls. In that case, we need to add some restrictions to the total number of calls the client can invoke per time unit, which we refer to as **service throttling**.

Close monitoring of different services is required to diagnose any services that do not meet the SLA response. If the service bus is intelligent enough, it can route the calls to another better performing service. One of the advantage of SOA is that we can optimize the performance and deploy a new version of the web service and switch the system to use it without interrupting the current application execution.

Performance aspects of Resource Oriented Architecture (ROA)

ROA is the architecture that is based on the concept of resources. These resources must comply with RESTful features, which can be summarized as for each resource, the resource should have a resource identifier that is mapped to a unique URI; this URI is used to communicate with this resource. We can get different representations of that resource according to our application requirements.

> The **REST** term comes from the expression **REpresentational State Transfer**, which represents an architectural style that was first introduced by Roy Fielding in his doctoral dissertation.

RESTful web services are web services that implement the RESTful concept with the following six basic aspects that define their own RESTful communication:

- It is built on the concept of mapping application entities into resources

- Each resource is identified by a unique URI

- Interactions with these resources are done by using a standard set of methods, for instance, HTTP methods (that is, POST, GET, PUT, and DELETE) that map to the **Create, Retrieve, Update and Delete (CRUD)** operations of the resource

- Resource can take many representations according to the required format in both request and response (JSON, XML, image, text, and so on)

- Response contains URIs of resources linked to this resource

- The communication is stateless in nature

> **Uniform Resource Identifier** (**URI**) is any string of characters used to identify a name or a resource. URI can be classified into a locator (URL) and name (URN), or both.

The following diagram shows the six different features of this RESTful communication:

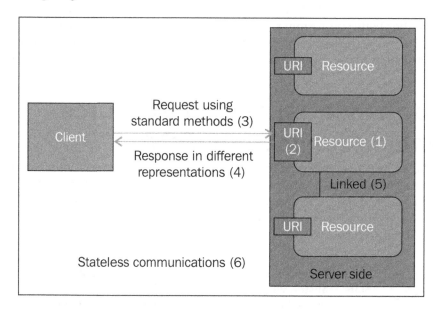

A RESTful web service is described by a standard format named WADL, which is an XML structure that works as a service contract similar to WSDL role in SOAP services.

Web Application Description Language (WADL) contains the description of the following items:

- Set of available resources
- Relationships between resources
- Methods that can be applied to each resource
- The HTTP methods that can be applied to each resource
- The expected inputs and outputs
- The supported formats and resource representation formats of the inputs and outputs
- The supported MIME types and data schemas in use

For more details, refer to the W3C WADL documentation at `http://www.w3.org/Submission/wadl/`.

The advantages of RESTful web services from the client's perspective are that they can be bookmarkable, they are easy to experiment in a browser and are language independent, and have a choice of data representation according to the client requirements. From the server's perspective, the benefits are reduced coupling, easy horizontal scaling, and easy implementation of caching, which can contribute to improve the performance of a RESTful web service.

A RESTful web service can be consumed as a service in SOA or can be used to build an ROA where architecture is built on the concept of resources throughout the application.

The RESTful concept has now become a hot topic in the world of **Internet of Things (IoT)** where each resource in our life can be connected to the Internet and either share information (collected by its sensors) or execute an action (change its state), or do both.

The common representation forms for RESTful web services are JSON and XML.

> **JavaScript Object Notation (JSON)** is a lightweight, text-based, and human-readable computer data interchange format. It is filed by *RFC 4627*.
>
> The content-type used for this type is `application/json`, and filename extension is `.json`. The main usage of this format is for serialization and transmitting structured data over a network connection commonly in Ajax calls. For more information, refer to the online documentation of JSON at `http://json.org`.

From performance comparison, many people believe that ROA (RESTful web services) is faster than SOA (SOAP-based web services) due to the following reasons:

* The ease of scaling in ROA services

* Claims that JSON serialization is faster and more efficient than XML serialization (ROA can also use XML as the representation form)

* Direct binding to the HTTP protocol without the need of an additional layer, such as a SOAP envelope

The second point in particular is vague as it depends on many factors such as data size, which makes this claim false. The performance of XML serialization is also dependent on the implementation and parser type, for example, SAX parsers are efficient and reduces the overhead of XML processing.

Also, in spite of the advantage of both (such as loose coupling and language implementation independency between service provider and consumer, for example, Java and .NET), we can't claim that XML processing is faster than JSON. Also, we can't compare both with the performance of direct method calls or local EJB calls.

Recently, some initiatives were proposed to improve the XML processing speed. One of these initiatives is **Efficient XML Interchange** (**EXI**), which is a W3C initiative that aims to change the XML encoding into an internationally recognized standard for an efficient interchange of XML.

The motivation is to decrease the overhead of XML manipulation (for example, generating, parsing, transmitting, storing, and accessing XML-based data) by introducing another non-textual XML encoding. This might improve the XML performance.

 To read more about encoding and its details, refer to the W3C documentation at http://www.w3.org/XML/EXI/.

We should deal with SOAP and REST not as competitors but as complementary technologies and alternative solutions that we can use and mix for the best outcome of our application. A lot of people support one technique over the other, which is not wrong, but we need to think in a different way.

REST is simple, easy to implement, and efficient to use for integration with different client types (for example, smartphones) without much effort. SOA is much more mature, standardized, and has more options for security, reliability, and distributed transaction handling.

SOAP is more capable of handling workflow and service orchestration compared to REST, which fits more in point-to-point communication (yet it can also be used in workflow). So, mixing both in our architecture will get the benefits of both the technologies.

The performance is generally better in REST (mainly because of scalability) but it actually depends on many things, including the used technology for serialization and the transmitted data volume.

We can use REST services in areas where performance matters and scalability is our main concern, as scaling in REST is much easier and more efficient.

Also, REST has the advantage that it can return the related objects as embedded links so that the caller has the option to decide when to load them (in SOAP, we can achieve this using optional fields). We can use SOAP services where security matters and more service reliability and transactional handling is required.

Let's now do an interesting performance comparison between two simple examples of SOAP and REST web services returning the same set of data. (Note that the results are specific to our application and we can't generalize the results without extensive testing using different data volumes and different serialization implementations.)

Open our `ExampleThree` project in NetBeans after installing the required database schema and execute it on the application server, for example, the Glassfish application server.

To get the `ExampleThree` project, you can download it from `http://www.packtpub.com/`, along with its database schema and Apache JMeter test plan.

To test if the application is correctly running and ensure that all web services are ready to use, we can use the browser and try the following URL to test the RESTful web service (port 8080 can be different according to your application server used port):

`http://localhost:8080/ExampleThree/webresources/osa.ora.beans.`
`empolyee/1001`

Then, use the following URL to test the SOAP web service (this URL is for Glassfish):

`http://localhost:8080/SOAPWebService/SOAPWebService?Tester`

Now open Apache JMeter and load `REST-SOAP test plan.jmx`. This test plan is simple and is composed of a configuration element to load different user IDs, test the RESTful web service, to test the SOAP web service, and finally test result elements.

The test plan is shown in the following screenshot:

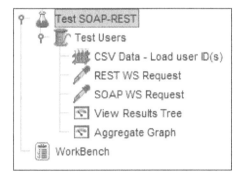

Before we execute our load test, let's have a quick look at the code of both web services. The following is the code of our RESTful web service method for the HTTP GET method:

```
@GET
@Path("{id}")
@Produces({"application/json"})
public Empolyee find(@PathParam("id") Integer id) {
    System.out.println("id="+id);
    return super.find(id);
}
```

In the preceding code, we configured the response of the GET method to be in JSON format only and the method takes the id parameter as a path input parameter and returns the Employee object that corresponds to that ID.

In the SOAP web service, the code is simple. It gets the Employee object that corresponds to the input parameter id (no validation or exception handling in the code of both SOAP and REST web services). The following is the code for the SOAP web service:

```
@WebMethod(operationName = "getEmplyeeData")
public Empolyee getEmployeeData(@WebParam(name = "id") int id) {
    System.out.println("id="+id);
    return em.find(Empolyee.class,id);
}
```

Now, let's execute our load testing to get the performance comparison between both the service types.

As we can see in the following screenshot, the performance of both the services is almost the same:

Label	# Samples	Average	Median	90% Line	Min	Max	Error %	Throughput	KB/sec
REST WS Request	300	4	3	4	2	157	0.00%	59.3/sec	27.3
SOAP WS Request	300	3	3	4	1	50	0.00%	60.9/sec	30.0
TOTAL	600	4	3	4	1	157	0.00%	118.5/sec	56.4

Using this small piece of data, we can analyze that SOAP is slightly better in our results. This means that performance measurement is the best way to decide which one to use from a performance perspective.

We can repeat the load test after modifying the RESTful service to use XML as the representation form instead of using JSON. The code is as follows:

```
@GET
@Path("{id}")
@Produces({"application/xml"})
public Empolyee find(@PathParam("id") Integer id) {
    System.out.println("id="+id);
    return super.find(id);
}
```

Now, execute the test and compare the results with the previous results.

We can conclude from this test that other requirements such as security, transaction handling, reliability, and scalability are much more important factors to decide which type of web service we need to use in our application.

Dissecting performance aspects of data caching

Data caching is an important performance improvement element in any enterprise application. We have discussed data caching issues in *Chapter 5*, *Recognizing Common Performance Issues*. In this section, we will continue our discussion about data caching.

Data caching versus no caching

This is the first question that we need to answer; the answer is not difficult and is mostly related to the nature of the data. In most cases, we can do caching for every type of data. However, in real-time data or data that has a short lifespan (rapidly changeable), caching seems to be a wrong decision as it allows the access of a stale version of the data or it slows down the application performance because it increases the required hits. For example, instead of hitting the data source once, we start by hitting the cache to get the object that is already invalidated, and then we load it from the data source and finally we store it back in the cache. Because the objects are invalidated very quickly, we do not get any benefits from that cache, so we should minimize the use of the cache for this data type. If the data has a reasonably long life span without changes, then it is typically eligible for caching.

Also, when a lot of calculations are involved in preparing the objects, it is better to cache such data to avoid doing the calculations again in subsequent calls.

Caching concurrency and performance

Access to shared/distributed cached data using multiple application instances will need some sort of locking mechanism especially for transactional data, which has frequent changes during user's activities. We have two different ways to obtain the lock over the cached data that we need to change:

- **Optimistic locking**: The application instance updates the data and cached data version as long as it has the data version that is similar to the cached data version. This fits more with the application data that does not frequently change.

- **Pessimistic locking**: The application instance starts by obtaining the lock over the data it needs to change. If it obtains the lock successfully, then it can change the data and the version and release the lock. If it can't obtain the data lock, it will wait till it can get that lock. This affects the application performance and is suitable in case the data frequently changes.

Versioning of the application data is a way to ensure that the application data version matches the same version in the cache, and we should increase the data version with each update so that if any instance has an old version, it can't update the cache (or persistent store) with new changes unless it obtains the following:

- The latest object version
- The object lock by either optimistic or pessimistic lock

Different levels of application data caching

Caching can have multiple levels according to the requirement and data type; one level is the component caching, which could be built-in out of the box caching such as the database query caching. We do not need any effort to get this type of caching, so repeating the same query against the database in subsequent times will be faster being returned from the cache (usually local in-memory caching).

If we are talking about a component that retrieves data from a database, we can implement component data caching to avoid performance impact from using the JDBC connection to hit the database (already supported in ORM libraries, such as JPA).

Another layer of caching can be implemented outside the component processing logic in a separate layer such as the service bus. It can improve the performance of the application under the assumption that if the service inputs are the same, the output will be the same. This will improve the performance by removing the time wasted on networking, processing, and database/component cache interaction.

Caching can also be on the client side using the client browser or client application (desktop or smart phone application). To use the browser in caching our application data, we need to specify the caching parameters in the HTTP headers: `cache-control max-age` and `expires` parameters. This usually fits the static data elements such as images, JavaScript files, CSS, and so on that do not change as frequently as application resources.

Caching can be local, remote, and distributed. The distributed type of caching is the most complex one and it enables the application to cache more data by scaling across many servers.

Nowadays, with the high speed of network cards, the networking latency is almost nullified, which makes the distributed caching the best caching option for enterprise applications especially when we need to reduce the local caching impact in our application server's memory.

The good thing about distributed caching is that we can still deal with it as a single remote cache, and all cache distribution are transparent to our cache access code and most of the cache implementations allow auto-scaling of the cache without affecting the cache retrieval time.

The following diagram summarize a database interaction flow, showing the different caching options in our application from the backend to the frontend, starting from data source caching to service caching, service bus caching, network caching (can be placed on different locations), and finally client/browser caching:

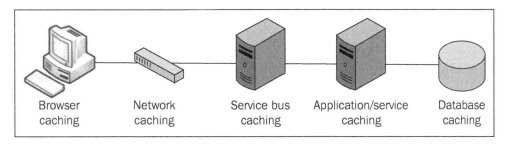

Caching an invalidation/expiration algorithm

The cache invalidation algorithm determines how the objects in the cache are removed even if the cache is not full yet.

Usually it is a time-based policy where we specify the maximum time allowed for objects to remain inside the cache. The following are the three common expiration policies used by defining either absolute or relative expiration time:

- Defining the maximum age since the object is added to the cache
- Defining the maximum age since the object is not used (idle time)
- Defining a certain time for cache expiration (for example, cache invalidation daily at 3 A.M where less traffic over the application is expected)

The idea behind selecting the proper expiration policy is mainly dependent on the nature of the cached data. As a general rule, if the data is session-based, then the best way is to use the idle time so that the data is removed after the session is invalidated and the data is no longer required. However, if the data is global data, then using a maximum cache age is a better option.

To avoid having stale objects in the cache, the expiration time needs to be accurately configured according to data change expectations.

One issue related to cache expiration that might affect the application performance is when the configured expiration time is the same for all objects and our application loads the objects in bulk operations (or loads them nearly at the same time). In that case, the objects will be invalidated from the cache in the same time, which causes the application performance to be spiky during that period.

A workaround is proposed to overcome this issue; one way is to configure the expiration at a specific time characterized by having a low application load (for example, midnight) and reload the cache content again after that (cache refresh).

Another way is to use random expiration delta values for each cached object, which changes the cache expiration to be random so that it does not affect the application performance.

One concern in data caching is the relation between objects; do we need to invalidate the cache if related cached objects are invalidated or not? For example, if the customer object is invalidated, does it make any sense to keep its related orders data?

Two cache models exist. The relational model, which keeps the relation between the different objects, and the independent model, which only stores each object independent of other related objects. Most of the caching implementations are done by using key-value pairs (that is, the independent model), since it is easier and reduces the caching complexity. Therefore, the caching performance becomes better.

Caching data store interaction

Cache component can encapsulate the data source from the application by using **read-through** and **write-through** techniques, where the cache component is placed inline between the application and its data source. This reduces the application complexity since the application only has to handle a single communication with the cache as its data source. All updated data goes to the cache as well which in turn updates the data store with the new changes. This improves the application performance by removing the database bottlenecks.

Read-through means the application reads from the data store through the cache.

Write-through means the application writes to the store by writing into the cache.

Write-behind is a variant of **write-through** where the cache updates the data store asynchronously so that the application does not need to wait this update operation.

The issue of using this pattern is that hitting the cache to load an object for the first time will be a slow operation if the object does not exist in the cache as the cache will need to hit the data store to retrieve this object. Subsequent calls can get benefits from this first overhead as long as the object remains in the cache.

To remove this initial overhead, we can use the preload technique to load the data from the data store into the cache in a periodic way so that the objects can be retrieved directly from the cache without the need to hit the data store with each application request. This will improve the application performance.

The issue with this preload approach is that we can't predict which objects we need to preload in the cache, so we might need to either guess that (using, for example, the last creation or modification time as an indicator for the most recently used data) or load all data.

Hiding the data store or data source from the application restricts the application's ability to execute custom or complex queries against this data source. This means the application will still need to hit the database in certain cases to do these complex queries.

The performance recommendation here for that scenario is to execute these queries to retrieve the object's keys and fetch the objects from the cache.

If the application cache is using the write-through technique, then our application will wait the update for both the cache and the database. This will give a slower response compared to the traditional direct access to the database.

Since cache components support the concept of write-behind (which is a good alternative), using that technique, the caching component updates the data in the cache and handles the data store/database updates asynchronously. This makes the cached object's updates available to the application immediately, without the need to waste time waiting for the database updates. This produces better application performance.

Nothing is absolutely perfect as this technique has the risk of application inconsistency if the object updates failed during synchronization back to the database.

The following diagram summarizes the three different caching models (strategies) that we can use in our application:

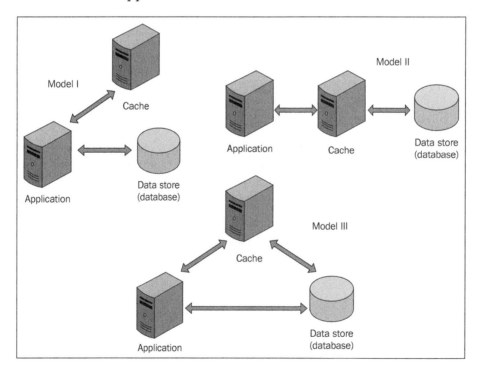

We can describe these models as follows:

- **Model I**: This is a *side-cache* (or *cache-aside*) model, where the application has the full control and it communicates with the data store to retrieve and update data, and the application communicates with the cache to retrieve and store objects.

- **Model II**: This is an *inline cache* model where the application uses the read/write-through techniques, and also delegates the data store manipulation to the cache component. The cache can optionally use the write-behind strategy to speed up the application performance.

- **Model III**: This is a *hybrid cache* model of the first and second model, where both application and cache can retrieve and update data from the data store.

The selection of the application caching model depends on the application performance requirement, application deployment, size, and type of the data.

Model I is the most commonly used model, but Model II is usually better in terms of performance, especially if the data can be preloaded (maybe through warm-up) and write-behind is enabled.

Caching replacement policies

Cache replacement policy is the policy that handles the replacement of cached objects in the cache with new objects when there are no more rooms in the cache.

Usually the cache (as in **Memcached**) will first try to see if executing the expiration policy will release any space for the new object(s) or not. If still enough space is not there, it executes the replacement policy to find an object in the cache that is eligible for replacement with the new coming object. This is called **cache evictions**.

 Memcached is a free open source distributed memory caching system. An in-memory key-value store can be downloaded from http://memcached.org/.

Defining which replacement policy to use varies according to our application nature. If the policy is not properly selected, it might reduce the benefits of using the cache. We will discuss here some of the following commonly used policies:

- **First-in-first-out** (FIFO): When a new object needs to be stored in full cache, the oldest object is removed in favor to this new object. This means only recent objects are kept inside the cache.

This policy is not fair enough to all cache cases as it doesn't consider if the removed object is active and is being accessed or not, but it fits the situation like claimed vouchers where removal of the oldest (that is, used) voucher make sense.

- **Least-frequently used (LFU)**: In this type, the cache picks the least-used object and replaces it. This policy requires storing the count of access times for each object in the cache, so it can determine which objects are least used and replaces them with the new object.

  The drawback of this method is that it doesn't consider if the removed object is still being accessed or not.

- **Least-recently used (LRU)**: This policy picks the object that is less used during a defined recent period and replaces it with the new objects, so the cache will keep information such as the last access time of all cached objects. This is the most commonly used technique.

- **Most-recently used (MRU)**: This is the opposite of the previous LRU policy. It removes the most recently used; this fits the application where items are no longer needed after the access, such as used exam or promotion vouchers.

 Evictions number refers to the total number of objects that are removed from the cache to free up some memory for the new items to the cache because the cache has reached its maximum size.

Data caching performance evaluation

Assessment of caching performance should be a part of our performance tuning. Using the cache statistics is very critical to understand the cache performance. The following are the most important key indicators for cache performance:

- **Cache utilization**: This is a good indicator for cache efficiency but not the most important item as it depends on the time we access the cache statistics as some cache elements might get expired before we access the cache.

- **Cache hit rate**: This represents the ratio in which the cache hits match (find) the required cached object. It is the main measure for cache effectiveness together with the retrieval cost.

- **Cache miss rate**: This is the ratio in which the cache hits do not find the required object in the cache.

Other parameters could also be used as **cache access time** and **cache throughput** are useful as well, and sometimes it is useful to assess the cache statistics regarding the memory consumption, CPU utilization, and any other useful information.

Tuning of the cache includes all the topics that we already covered like which expiration and replacement policies to use, which cache model to use, whether to use local or distributed caching, whether to add additional layer of caching, cache locking, whether to disable caching, cache component specific tuning, and so on.

This covers the cache-related performance concerns that we need to consider when we are designing and implementing a cache in our enterprise applications.

Performance considerations in cloud deployment

Cloud computing is a common deployment model these days especially in medium-sized enterprise applications. Some large enterprises also moved their applications into the cloud, while the majority still prefer to keep their own deployment infrastructure for many different reasons such as data security and to have the full control over the application's infrastructure.

Cloud computing has many advantages from the performance perspective. However, before we can discuss the application performance in the cloud, let's list here the following main advantages of deploying our enterprise application into the cloud:

- It utilizes a large number of pooled computing resources
- It maximizes the hardware utilization by having virtualized computing resources
- It provides elastic scaling up or down according to the application load and needs (Elasticity)
- It allows automatic creation or removal of application virtual machines (no manual work)
- The pay-as-you-go payment model of the used resources

The main advantage of using a cloud for the cloud provider is to utilize the pooled virtualized resources, while the main benefits to the deployed application owner are automatic elasticity and pay-as-you-go payment model. This is of great value, especially in emerging services that lack expectation of user's traffic. So, instead of getting small-scale resources, which can affect the user's experience (in case a large number of users are interested in this service), or buying a large-scale infrastructure (that costs a lot while the users might not be interesting in this service), we can have the application deployed using this elastic cloud deployment model.

The cloud provides the option to go with a few resources that are elastic and expand with the user's load and shrink when they are no longer needed. This makes the idea (that is, the new service) cost effective and reduces the associated risks.

Looking at these points from the performance perspective, we can see elasticity as the main performance-adding value, but we shouldn't forget that we are in a cloud environment where application performance can be affected by the shared virtualized resource's performance.

Now, let's discuss some performance considerations that are required when deploying our applications into a cloud environment. A cloud application must be designed for the cloud, which means that the decision to deploy an application to the cloud is not that easy and should involve changes to the application to fit the cloud environment. After the expansion of the cloud technologies, it is better now to design the application for the cloud from the beginning; follow cloud design patterns and utilize the available cloud services.

The most important factor to consider during designing any enterprise application for the cloud is the ability to scale without any issue. As some people have a lot of concerns about the *public cloud* security, the concept of *hybrid* and *private clouds* have emerged where either the whole cloud architecture is created in the private premises, or only the part of the cloud that contains sensitive information is created in hybrid cloud.

Another type is **Virtual Private Cloud** (**VPC**) where the public cloud gives a secure, isolated cloud pooled resources connected to enterprise private network by VPN so that the enterprise application can expand into these resources.

The link between public and private resources in either hybrid or VPC should have good bandwidth. Otherwise, this can produce a performance bottleneck that reduces the benefits of using these deployment models.

Another point to consider here is the virtual machine type and the operating system used, which can contribute to the cloud performance. Three main virtualization models exist: **full-virtualization**, **para-virtualization**, and **hardware virtualization**. As in the Intel VT and AMD-V processors, hardware virtualization provides the most efficient way to virtualize the host machines.

Machine type has an important role in cloud performance. This includes the machine CPU power, memory size, and driver I/O speed. All these factors are not guaranteed when the hardware is shared among different virtual machines, yet some cloud providers provide some ways to increase the portion of the processing power given to the application based on the application needs.

Some providers have the ability to upgrade the machine type as well according to the application needs, which is usually determined by understanding the application behavior (for example, CPU utilization) using cloud performance monitoring tools.

In the cloud environment, we can use different database types. We have the option to use either **NoSQL** database (actually non-relational database) or use traditional **RDBMS** (relational database).

The decision is not easy to answer as NoSQL, being in-memory database, has many advantages such as good performance, easy scalability, simplicity (it avoids table joins as in rational database), and flexibility (changes are easy and no predesigned schema is required). RDBMS is much more mature in transactional handling, data model mapping, and supporting of complex queries.

The comparison has a lot of other parameters that we need to consider, but the most important factors are the application data nature and database scaling ability in the cloud, which is more efficient in NoSQL database.

Some companies now provide solutions to use a hybrid SQL-NoSQL model where we can use SQL as frontend queries for NoSQL database (this can facilitate the application migration to the cloud).

Data caching is usually provided as a service in the cloud (**caching as-a-service**) that we need to consider to improve our application performance. We have already discussed the different caching techniques in this chapter. The only valid recommendation here is to use centralized caching and not local caching so that we don't have many versions of cached objects in different application instances, which makes the application inconsistent, and we don't need to implement cache synchronization mechanism, which utilizes unnecessary CPU power.

Summary

In this chapter, we briefly covered the different design and architecture considerations that are required when we make different design decisions. We have classified these decisions into architecture layers, integration, component selection, interaction, security, regulatory, and miscellaneous decisions.

We also explored in more detail the SOA performance consideration for the SOA services in particular and compared it with the ROA services. Then, we gave a quick performance measurement for a simple application that uses both SOAP and RESTful web services.

We also discussed data caching in more detail, since it is an important performance improvement factor in our enterprise application. Finally, we discussed some of the performance design aspects of the cloud environment.

In the next chapter, *Chapter 11*, *Performance Tuning Tips*, we will move from the design discussion to different development techniques and performance considerations, such as agile and **Test-Driven Development** (TDD).

We will also discuss some development performance tips such as tuning tips of Java EE components, database tuning tips, miscellaneous best practices topics (for example, exception handling, logging, and so on), and using the `javap` tool to analyze the compiled Java code.

11
Performance Tuning Tips

In this chapter, we will share some performance tuning tips. This chapter begins by covering the performance considerations in the Agile methodology and **test-driven development (TDD)** as two common development approaches.

We will discuss the performance tuning tips for the different Java EE components and some general Java performance tuning tips, mostly at micro-optimization level, and will explain the correlation between written code and compiled code using the `javap` tool.

The list of topics that we will cover in this chapter is as follows:

- Performance and development processes
- Performance tips for Java EE components
- Java performance tuning, for example, string handling, I/O operations, and Java collections
- Logging and exception handling best practices
- Using the `javap` tool to analyze the compiled code
- Database performance tips
- Client-side optimization

Performance and development processes

In this section, we will provide a brief overview of the performance considerations for the Agile development methodology, the benefits of using TDD, and the importance of code review for our application's performance.

Agile and performance

The Agile development methodology is the preferred development strategy by many software houses. Agile iterations (that is, sprints) are usually short and include the development of a set of prioritized requirements selected from the application requirement **backlog**.

We will briefly discuss a few points related to Agile and the application's performance.

Application performance requirements should be included as part of each feature's requirement (**user story**), so the development team can consider these requirements when designing and implementing these features.

These performance requirements should be submitted to the performance testing team in the early phases of each sprint so that they understand the requirements and how the test scenarios are designed. This also gives them sufficient time to validate the requirements.

Some of the performance requirements are global requirements that are defined at the beginning of the project and other requirements can be tailored to match the sprint features. This is because in Agile sprint, usually we do not implement the whole functionality of the feature; the performance testing of such a feature should be deferred till the feature development is completed.

The advantage of the performance testing in Agile is that the scope of the changes in each sprint is limited to new sprint features. So usually, fixing the performance issues during each of the Agile iterations is straightforward. The performance issues become more complex if the performance testing result is neglected for some iterations, in which case the scope will be wider than it should be.

Performance testing should be a continuous operation during each sprint, particularly when using a **continuous integration** (**CI**) environment, where we can execute regression testing including performance testing (for previous sprints' features).

In this case, we can be confident that nothing is broken in the previous sprints' functionality from a performance perspective. Once the delivery of our new features is complete and their performance scenarios are developed, we can focus more on these new features in our performance testing.

An example of a continuous integration tool is **Jenkins**, which has a performance plugin to capture different reports from both JUnit and Apache JMeter and consolidate the results. For more information, visit the project's website `https://jenkins-ci.org/`.

When performance testing identifies performance issues, it should be fixed before releasing or accepting this sprint. In some cases, if the required changes to fix these issues are not minor, the changes can be submitted to the requirement backlog as a technical requirement with high priority, so it can be picked in one of the coming sprints.

The main idea behind this approach is to avoid losing the sprint timelines and business commitment. If the performance issues need major changes (for example, design changes), which can impact the project delivery plan, this approach gives the development team more time to prepare the optimal fix.

It is essential to track the effects of the changes on the application's performance over different iterations so that we can trace transactions performance trends, identify any deviation at an early stage, and address the deviation by adding these trends to the backlog as investigation tasks.

Performance and test-driven development (TDD)

TDD is a recently used development methodology, where the implementation starts by writing the test cases before having the actual implementation. These tests are written according to the application design and requirements, so it guides the implementation in the right direction.

TDD is flexible, efficient, and less error prone since it is more oriented toward testing the code from the beginning. This helps in producing high-quality code that fulfills the requirements.

Of course, writing the test cases before the actual implementation is difficult and needs a lot of training to organize the development team's thoughts to use this approach.

The most challenging area here is the test cases that cover the non-functional requirements, which do not usually follow the test case patterns of pass or failed. We should be able to convert some of these requirements into actual test methods.

Different proposals to execute performance tests as part of the development test cases (in TDD) include using the following methods:

- Adding code hocks, for example, the StopWatch and MemoryMonitor classes. These hocks measure the required performance data.

- Parsing the logfiles with performance log entries. This requires strict logging formats in all the required methods.

- Using interceptors/aspect programming.

In all these methods, we compare the obtained performance results with our performance requirements (that is, benchmark) for each transaction.

> The MemoryMonitor class is designed to measure the total memory before and after execution. This class indicates the method memory consumption and possible memory leakage.
>
> The StopWatch class is designed to provide mainly the start() and stop() methods to measure the performance of certain parts in our applications. The main idea behind this class is to measure the time in milliseconds at the start and end, and get the delta. An example of this class is available at https://commons.apache. org/proper/commons-lang/javadocs/api-2.6/org/ apache/commons/lang/time/StopWatch.html.

The advantage of using TDD from the performance perspective is the ability to control the application's performance and the early detection of any deviation. Definitely, we won't be able to test all the performance requirements from the code, but the majority of performance transactional requirements can be achieved by using this development strategy, while the remaining will be addressed in the performance testing stage.

Manual and automated code review

Code review using code analyzer tools, such as **FindBugs**, **PMD**, **CheckStyle**, **Dependency Finder**, and **SonarQube,** can help improve the quality of the code, which usually directly impacts the code's performance. Good quality code also allows easier troubleshooting of performance issues in the code, which helps in producing clean and correct performance fixes.

PMD is a source code static analyzer. Refer to `http://pmd.sourceforge.net/`.

FindBugs is a static analyzer to look for bugs in the Java code. Refer to `http://findbugs.sourceforge.net/`.

Checkstyle is a development tool to help programmers write the Java code that adheres to a coding standard. Refer to `http://checkstyle.sourceforge.net/`.

Dependency Finder is a suite of tools to analyze the compiled Java code. Refer to `http://depfind.sourceforge.net/`.

All these plugins can be downloaded for the NetBeans IDE using the **Kenai** project available at `https://kenai.com/projects/sqe/pages/Home`.

SonarQube is an open source code analyzer project. Refer to `http://www.sonarqube.org/`.

Installing the code analysis tools can be part of a continuous integration environment or the development IDE, which is better because all of these tools already have different plugins for different IDEs, including Eclipse, NetBeans, and so on.

In NetBeans, if we click on the **Tools** menu and select **Plugins**, it will open a list of the available NetBeans plugins ready for download and installation. Now, select **PMD** from the list (if it is available) and click on the **Install** button. NetBeans will open **Terms and conditions** for this plugin. Accept the conditions to start installing the PMD plugin. After completing the installation, you might need to restart NetBeans so that the installed plugin is ready for use.

If PMD and other plugins do not exist in NetBeans 7.x, navigate to the **Plugins** menu, and in the **Settings** tab, click on the **Add** button to add `http://deadlock.netbeans.org/hudson/job/sqe/lastStableBuild/artifact/build/full-sqe-updatecenter/updates.xml`. Name it `Hudson tools`. All these plugins will be available in the **Plugins** tab after this step.

To customize the PMD rules, navigate to the **Tools** menu, select **Options**, and then click on the **Miscellaneous** tab and select **PMD**. A pop-up dialog box will show up with the different PMD configurations as shown in the following screenshot:

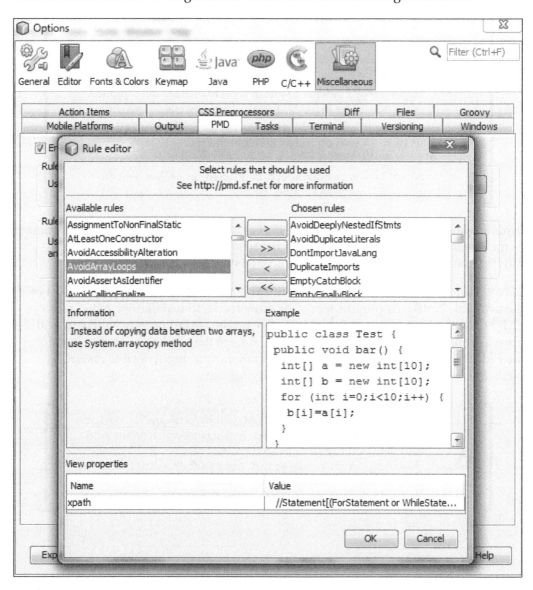

Select the **PMD** rules from the available rules. An example of these rules, as shown in the preceding screenshot, is to use `System.arraycopy()` instead of the loop and copy different array items. This definitely is more efficient and better in performance.

Select any Java code from our previous projects and execute them by navigating to **Tools | PMD** to get the PMD analysis results (or from the **Context** menu, click on **Tools** and select **PMD**).

Using these tools doesn't mean we should neglect a manual code review, which can catch exceptions leading to potential issues that are otherwise not easily detected. As part of project development process, we must allocate suitable time for team peer reviews and technical leader team reviews.

It is also worth mentioning that we need to involve the performance team in performance code review. If the code changes are huge (usually in the waterfall development methodology), we can select certain parts of the code for a performance review, including those parts that have a higher probability of performance issues or which have clear SLA requirements.

Having this in place as part of our development process will help to improve the project's code quality, reduce the required effort during the performance testing stage, and finally, facilitate the fixing of emerging performance issues.

Java EE performance tuning tips

Performance tuning tips are general guidelines to improve performance. Some of these tips get change with each new Java version, so we have to revisit our beliefs with each new Java version.

Most of these tips can be classified as micro-optimization techniques, which might not produce tangible performance improvements in our application.

Modern IDEs already suggest some of these optimization techniques to warn developers regarding required changes when writing the code. Also, automatic code analyzer tools (as we clarified in the previous section) can apply some of these recommendation tips.

Finally, the JIT compiler considerably improves the written code by different optimization techniques, as inlining the final methods, neglecting the dead code, and other methods can vary with each JVM type, for example, HotSpot (client and server) and JRockit.

In the next section, we will discuss a few performance tuning tips for some of the basic components in Java EE as web services, JSP, JPA, EJB, and so on.

Web service (WS) performance tuning tips

We discussed the web service performance recommendations in *Chapter 10, Designing High-performance Enterprise Applications*. We summarize here some of the web service performance tips.

Use medium object data in web services (avoid fine- or coarse-tuned web services) and avoid using complex objects as they will take time during serialization.

Perform the orchestration in the same web service layer, that is, do not orchestrate different web services using another web service layer. Instead, create a new web service that performs this orchestration in the same level using local calls (for example, the local EJB calls) to different web services (in case we are the owner of all the orchestrated services).

Minimize the extended transaction handling and implement WS-BusinessActivity if we need to support transaction across many web services.

Use different levels of web service caching: web service data caching and web service result caching.

Always use service bus dynamic routing and load balancing for a well-distributed load across different web service instances.

It is better to implement the web services as a stateless services and in the case of prolonged processing operations, we can use queue and/or asynchronous callbacks.

Limit the use of **SOAP with Attachments (SwA)**, reduce the number of used web service handlers, and only use the handlers for global actions as security and logging.

The last recommendation is to support different web service flavors, that is, SOAP and REST, so clients can utilize the web services according to their capabilities and needs.

EJB performance tuning tips

EJB is scalable in nature. It is used to design an application that can withstand the load in an efficient and scalable manner, with a pool that can increase and decrease according to the application load.

The new modifications to Enterprise JavaBeans in the recent Java EE release includes the supporting of local asynchronous invocations. So we can use it in a more efficient way in long transactions.

Configuring and tuning enterprise JavaBeans caching can improve the application's performance, and destroying the stateful session beans once they are no longer required is an important performance consideration for memory management.

Use container-managed transactions whenever possible for more efficiency and to avoid improper handling user management transactions in the user management transaction.

Always tune the Enterprise beans performance using application server tuning guidelines as cache configurations. An example of these tuning configurations is the use of pass-by-reference rather than pass-by-value to speed up the lookup of enterprise beans if they are co-located and there is no local interface (EJB versions before 3.0).

Servlets and JSP performance tuning tips

Servlets are the basic web components in our enterprise application (JSPs are compiled to servlets). Here we will discuss some development performance tuning tips.

When we want to redirect the user to a page, it is preferable to use the server-side redirection, `RequestDispatcher.forward()`, rather than using the client-side redirection, `HttpServletResponse.sendRedirect()`, which goes to the client browser and hits the server back.

Set a proper buffer size in JSP, which fits the volume of the transmitted data. Note that setting the `autoflush` directive as `false` will throw an exception once the buffer is full:

```
<%@page buffer="8kb" autoflush="true" %>
```

Use the proper application scope while storing different application objects. If we need the object throughout the application's lifespan, we can use the application scope. If we want it to be available only during a user session, we can use the session scope.

We also have a page scope for using the object across the same page, and request scope where the object exists only in the scope of request object. For more details on the different application scopes, refer to *Chapter 2, Understanding Java Fundamentals*.

If the JSP page does not use the session object, we can ask the context not to inject the session object for the current JSP using the session directive as follows:

```
<%@page session="false"%>
```

Configure the session timeout to a reasonable time according to our application's nature and try to reduce it to the smallest possible value; the timeout can be later tailored based on a user's average time spent on the application.

Cache global calculations to avoid repeating the calculations. For static content, preferably, cache on the client side using the HTML header caching directives.

Reduce the complexity of the application data model and try to stick to a uniform method of accessing them inside the JSPs, that is, either use JSTL (which is recommended) or use the `scriptlet` code; however, do not mix both in the same JSP page. Ideally, it should be consistent across all the application pages as well.

When using a database-specific resource bundle, implementing data caching is essential if not provided out of the box as in JPA.

Avoid using a single threaded servlet, which is deprecated in Java EE 7 (servlet that implements the `SingleThreadModel` interface), as it can lead to synchronization issues.

From the application server configurations, always enable pre-compile JSP and disable JSP autoloading as no changes to the JSP files are expected in the production environment.

It is also essential to follow all the best practices for Java coding, including what has already been mentioned in this book (such as using managed thread pools) or what we will discuss in the next section.

JSF performance tuning tips

JSF provides a lot of object scopes. We need to use the proper scope with each object. Usually, use the scope only where the object is required. New scopes are added in latest JSF version, for example, `FlowScope`, which can be used in pages such as the wizard page.

Decreasing the page complexity is another way to improve the JSF performance. Also, from the performance perspective, using `Facelet` (in JSF 2.0 and later) is better than JSP.

The specification also adds support for the stateless views, where the `UIComponent` state for the components is not saved. This can improve the performance if no persistent status is required for such components. This is supported only in the views based on `Facelet`.

Always keep the view getter method as simple as possible; if it requires any logic, then possibly precalculate the logic and keep the `getter` method as simple as possible.

JSF configuration tuning parameters include both common and specific implementation parameters. Refer to the following example:

```
javax.faces.FACELETS_REFRESH_PERIOD or
facelets.REFRESH_PERIOD (for backward compatibility with old
  Facelets tag libraries).
```

The preceding configuration can be used to disable the compiler checks for the `Facelet` pages' modifications (by setting to `-1`). Recompiling the changed `Facelet` pages is useful in the development time but not common in the production environment.

JPA performance tuning tips

Java persistent APIs refer to the standard specifications for an object-relational model. A lot of implementations are available. The performance tuning of this layer includes common items for different implementations and other specific items for specific implementations.

For example, use the proper loading strategy from either lazy loading or eager data loading according to our data size and usage; for small data volume, eager loading always make sense.

The same applies if the data is being used extensively in most of the application transactions. Lazy loading usually fits huge data or user-specific data, where we need to pay the cost on demand basis (that is, on the user's requests).

Query results pagination is also an important JPA feature. The importance of this feature is to avoid memory issues when the returned data is huge.

The JPA provides two methods to control this pagination: `setMaxResults(int maxResult)` and `setFirstResult(int startPosition)` in the `Query` object.

We should also customize that usage according to our application user's behavior. So for example, in the order management system, most of the users will be interested to navigate to the latest submitted orders. In this case, we need to return only a subset of the recent orders (ordered by date), and only a few users will navigate and use the pagination to retrieve more data.

We can also use data chunking to return the required data only from the database side, instead of filtering in the application side using the `IN` keyword and adding the list of IDs to the query.

Increasing the index pre-allocation size can speed up the creation of new objects. Also try to minimize the usage of composite primary keys for different entities.

Enabling entity caching is important to improve the performance, but if we are working in the cluster environment, disable the JPA caching or decrease the caching timeout to avoid the stale objects. The exact value of the timeout depends on the application data nature. Refer to the following code:

```
@Entity
@Cacheable(true)
public class Order
```

As entity caching is working on `primary key/entity id`, we can also enable the query-level caching for better performance. One way to do that is by adding a hint to the named query as follows:

```
hints={@QueryHint(name="eclipselink.query-results-cache",
    value="true")}
```

Yet using the external cache in a clustered environment is preferred to remove the possibilities of stale objects and data inconsistency, as discussed in *Chapter 10, Designing High-performance Enterprise Applications.*

Also, using batch interaction by sending a group of inserts/updates/deletes to the database in a single transaction by setting `"eclipselink.jdbc.batch-writing"="JDBC"` in `persistence.xml`, we can also specify the size of the batch using another property, `"eclipselink.jdbc.batch-writing.size"="2000"`. (We will discuss the JDBC batch processing later in this chapter when discussing the database tuning.)

Use the read-only entities when the entities are not going to be modified, such as entities for lookup data (for example, e-mail templates). This can be done using the `@ReadOnly` annotation on the level of the entity.

Finally, it is preferred to access the JPA from stateless session beans as a façade layer to get benefits from different resource injections and EJB transactional and security handling, and encapsulate all JPA access logic.

 More details on JPA performance tuning can be found at the **EclipseLink** documentation at `http://www.eclipse.org/eclipselink/documentation/2.5/solutions/toc.htm`.

Java performance tuning tips

In this section, we will discuss some general Java performance tuning tips, including string manipulation, dealing with the Java collections, using the synchronized code, and logging and exception handling best practices.

String manipulation performance tuning tips

Different classes and techniques are involved in the string manipulation in the Java application. We will discuss the string creation, string concatenation, and the usage of the `StringBuilder` and `StringBuffer` classes.

String creation tips

String creation can take many forms either by using the direct assignment operator or the `new String()` constructor. The interesting fact is that creating the `String` object using the assignment operator (that is, string literal) is much more faster than using the constructor call. Refer to the following code:

```
String myStr = "";
String myStr = "Osama Oransa";
```

The new `String()` method is slower as it doesn't use the string pool area, where the unique string values are stored (interned strings). So, while creating a literal string, JVM searches in the pool area. If it finds an existing one, it returns a reference to it.

Since a `String` object is an immutable object, modifying this interned object will result in creating a new `String` object rather than changing the existing value, which allows the sharing of the same string values:

```
String myStr = new String("");
String myStr = new String ("Osama Oransa");
```

The interned string concept explains the impact of using `==` to compare the two `String` objects versus using the `equals()` method. If both the `String` objects contain the same value and are interned, using `==` will return `true` (same reference values). Since we do not guarantee that all our `String` objects are interned, we should always use the `equals()` method for the string comparison.

To force the `new String()` method to use the interned string area, we can use the `intern()` method in the `String` object.

String concatenation tips

String concatenation operations are important performance tuning areas, where they include the creation of the new `String` objects. Java supports different ways of string concatenations, which include using the + operator, the `String.concat()` method, `StringBuilder.append()`, and `StringBuffer.append()`.

Let's see some examples and the performance impact of using these types of operations as per Java SE 7.

Many people believe that using the + operator for the string concatenation is a slow operation. This is true, but not in all cases, so consider the following code example:

```
String myStr = "My "+" Name"+" is Osama";
```

This one is really fast as Java will use a single constant to replace all these literal values and replace this constant with a direct assignment operation, which makes this approach definitely faster than using any other way to implement this as `StringBuilder`:

```
int i=3;
String myStr = "My "+" Name"+" is Osama"+ i;
```

This preceding example is replaced during compilation by the `StringBuilder` operation, as `StringBuilder` is created with the full-string literal values and the `append(i)` method is called to append the i variable. This approach is still an efficient way to concatenate the `String` objects.

The following invocation does not have good performance and is considered the worst performance option to concatenate the `String` objects:

```
String myStr = "";
for(int i=0;i<20;i++){
  myStr += i;
}
```

With each loop, a new `StringBuilder` object will be created to implement this concatenation operation. Instead, the best way to implement it is using the following optimized code:

```
StringBuilder strBuilder = new StringBuilder();
for(int i=0;i<20;i++){
    strBuilder.append(i);
}
String myStr = strBuilder.toString();
```

The difference between `StringBuilder` and `StringBuffer` is that `StringBuffer` is thread safe, while `StringBuilder` is not. So, if we are using the object in a local method and no thread safety is concerned, it is better to use `StringBuilder` because it is faster. Whereas if many threads are modifying the object (that is, not a local method object), it is better to use `StringBuffer` to avoid concurrency issues.

Using the `String.concat()` method is an alternative way, but the `concat()` method accepts only the `String` object. In this case, we have to convert the concatenated value into a `String` object first using the `String.valueOf()` method as follows:

```
String myStr="";
for(int i=0;i<20;i++){
  myStr = myStr.concat(String.valueOf(i));
}
```

This is still slower than using `StringBuilder` as it involves the following parameters:

* Constructing a new `String` object created by the `valueOf()` method
* Creating `new Char[]` for the `concat()` method
* Creating a new `String` object with `char[]`
* Returning the new `String` object

The JVM String tuning parameters

The Java HotSpot VM comes with some tuning parameters for string manipulations. Refer to the following example:

-XX:+UseStringCache

The preceding flag enables the caching of the commonly allocated strings. Refer to the following parameter:

-XX:+UseCompressedStrings

The preceding flag allows the usage of `byte[]` for strings (not `char[]`), which can be represented as pure ASCII (added in Java 6 update 21). Refer to the following parameter:

-XX:+OptimizeStringConcat

The preceding flag optimizes the string concatenation operations wherever possible (added in Java 6 update 20). The flag attempts to detect the size of `char[]` to allocate in `StringBuilder` and `StringBuffer` based on the appended string value.

Some of these flags are only available in the server type of the HotSpot VM such as -XX:+OptimizeStringConcat and some of them come with the default value false, such as XX:+UseStringCache. In all cases, firstly, we need to ensure these flags exist in our Java version before we can decide to use them. We can identify this by executing the following command:

```
java -XX:+PrintFlagsFinal
```

The preceding command will print all the existing flags, so we can determine whether the flag we need to use exists.

Java collections and performance

Dealing with the Java collections can affect performance in different aspects. We will discuss some of these aspects as follows:

- Have we selected the required collection?
- Do we need the collection to be thread safe?
- Is the collection performance acceptable? Do we have alternatives?
- Do we have any collection memory leakages?
- What is the collection size expansion policy and performance?

The proper selection of the required collection is not only a functional aspect but also has essential performance considerations. Many people tend to use different collections and change them across the application as per their needs, which adds performance overhead.

Therefore, it is better to understand the requirements and the ways we are going to use this collection across the application. Then, we select the proper collection to use; for example, instead of using Array and converting it into ArrayList and then into HashMap (using the objects keys) in different locations in the applications, it would be much better to use one type of the collection that suits our application.

Another point that is related to the selection of the proper collection type is thread safety, if the collection is used locally (that is, only accessed by a single thread at a time), there's no need to use the synchronized collection. So for instance, using Vector (replaced now with CopyOnWriteArrayList), which is the synchronized collection, shouldn't be a locally used collection. Instead, ArrayList would better suit our needs. Collection synchronization is performance overhead and we should only pay this overhead to gain the benefits of thread safety.

Another factor is understanding the different available options with each Java new release. For example, we should no longer use the `Vector`, `Stack`, and `Hashtable` collections. Instead, we should use for the single-thread access, `ArrayList`, `Deque`, and `HashMap`. For the thread-safe access, we can use `CopyOnWriteArrayList`, `ConcurrentLinkedDeque`, and `ConcurrentHashMap`.

Another noteworthy mention is that we shouldn't permit any memory leakage while dealing with different collections. The application design must ensure that we have a way to remove the added items. So for any `add` method, there should be corresponding `remove` method calls. For example, if we have a collection that stores a user's objects, we must ensure that we remove these items explicitly when the user logs out or when there is a session timeout; otherwise, memory leakage will occur.

Using synchronized blocks

Most of the enterprise applications have certain parts in the code that can't be accessed except by a single thread at a time. In this case, we use the `synchronized` Java key word. In *Chapter 2, Understanding Java Fundamentals*, we saw how to use explicit locking by using the `Lock` interface instead of using implicit locking; this is a good alternative.

If we need to use the synchronized blocks or methods, minimize the synchronized code block using one of the following strategies:

- Use synchronization over a lock object and minimize the lock in a small part of the code that can't be accessed by different threads:

```
synchronized (lockObject) {
  //minimal code that needs synchronization
}
```

  Another advantage of using this limited synchronization model is that it allows us to have many synchronized blocks in the same class without impacting each other (in comparison with `synchronized` over the `this` or `class` objects).

- Extract a small `private` method that contains the small piece of a code that needs to be synchronized and use the `synchronized` keyword to tag this method. This is better than synchronizing over the whole method but not better than the `lockObject` synchronization. It fits more when the class does not have any other synchronization locations.

The I/O operations and performance

The I/O operations are considered as performance killer operations. We can adopt the following guidelines to minimize the performance impact of these operations:

- Use buffered read/write objects (for example, `BufferedInputStream`, `MappedByteBuffer`) and tune the buffer size, if required, according to the average size of the files need to read/write

- Use asynchronous methods to access the files instead of providing the files access in the transaction's critical path

- Cache the file's contents and specify the cache expiration according to the frequency of changes in the file

- Write the file's contents to the memory during transactions and synchronize back to the disk to speed up the transaction time or use the new IO Java capabilities such as `MappedByteBuffer`, which do a similar job

- Move any file structure validation into a separate process (outside the application) or thread (inside the application) so that the application does not spend time during the transaction when performing the required validation of the file

- Use Java SE 7 NIO.2 for better performance

In Java EE 7, a non-blocking I/O support is introduced for servlets and filters when they process a user's requests in the asynchronous mode. So if we implement asynchronous components, we need to use this new feature to make the best use of the user's threads.

> For more information on Java NIO.2, check the online Oracle documentation at http://docs.oracle.com/javase/7/ docs/technotes/guides/io/.

Exception handling and performance

Exception handling is an important feature in Java language. What we need to highlight is some incorrect ways of implementing exception handling that might impact the application's performance.

On the top of this list is using the exception as method return flags, which is not a good way. Consider the following example:

```
public void checkUserExist(String username){
   //login logic here
```

```
    if(user not found) throw new Exception("not exist");
    else if(user is not active) throw new Exception("not active");
    else throw new Exception("not known issue");
}
```

This is bad coding behavior with a negative impact on the application's performance due to the overhead of creating the exceptions and its stack trace. Instead it should be replaced with other flags as returning `boolean` or `int` value flags.

The same issue is usually faced when developers create their own custom exception classes and use them to cluster different exception into different types. Usually, this does not add any value, except that it logs the exception with a different name; for example, `BusinessException` and `TechnicalException`.

So unless we are going to deal with these exceptions differently, and as long as logging is enough in these cases, tagging these exceptions is a waste of time. The only exception to this rule is when we are building a library or communicating this meaningful exception to the application's clients (for example, web service exceptions):

```
logger.error("Business exception: user can't buy 2 orders!",ex);
```

Use the new Java language enhancements in Java 7, such as using multiple exceptions in the catch block:

```
try{
  ...
}catch(IOException | IllegalAccessError ex){
  //handle exception..
}
```

Also, use the new and improved `try` resources syntax as we don't need to pay close attention to the open resources.

These resources should implement the `java.lang.AutoCloseable` interface used with this new `try` resources enhancement:

```
try (BufferedReader bufferReader = new BufferedReader(new
  FileReader(filePath))) {
  //read from the buffer reader ..
}catch(Exception ex){
  //handle exception …
}
//no need for a final block
```

If we are using the old `try/catch/finally` format, make sure to release or close any resources in the `final` block as this can impact the application's performance and cause resources leakages.

Do not throw the exception into too many levels, for example, data layer, business layer, business delegate layer, and so on. This produces a lot of performance overhead. The exception should be handled where it occurs and if this is not possible, then throw it into a higher level.

Propagating the exception away from its source will cause inefficient handling and usually ends up by displaying the error message or repeating the whole transaction.

Logging of the exception should include logging of the exception object itself, so we can troubleshoot issues more efficiently.

Finally, avoid the nightmare, that is, when the developer decides to eat the exception by having an empty catch block, which makes any investigation impossible; therefore, such practice should be forbidden!

Application logging and performance

The best practices of application logging must be strictly followed, otherwise, the logging will impact the application's performance or it will become useless. Here, we will list some of these best practices.

Use logging levels according to the exact scenario, for example, FATAL is used for severe application issues such as an application can't connect to the database and using the ERROR level for unrecoverable errors where the application flow usually stops.

While the WARN level means that something has happened that we need to pay attention to, the application flow can continue; we log it to either take action later or to understand the impact.

The INFO level is used to log important information messages (for example, order submitted), while the DEBUG level is used to log different development messages (for example, the enter or leave method). The TRACE level is used for detailed debugging messages that might impact the application's performance and is only used by the development team for troubleshooting activities.

Java logging uses alternative levels that have the same meaning: SEVERE (the highest value), WARNING, INFO, CONFIG, FINE, FINER, and FINEST (the lowest value).

After understanding the meaning and usage of different logging levels, we must only log messages if the corresponding level is enabled to avoid unnecessary processing; refer to the following example:

```
logger.debug("The total number of records = " +
  calculateRecords(records) );
```

Instead of performing string processing (using `StringBuilder` as we saw before) and invoking the calculate method while the logging debug is not enabled, it is better to follow the best practice by checking whether the logging level is enabled:

```
if(logger.isDebugEnabled()) {
  logger.debug("The total number of records = " +
    calculateRecords(records) );
}
```

It is worth mentioning that some people believe that exporting logging into a separate method will resolve this problem; however, this is not true—it might worsen it even more:

```
debugMyMessages( "The total number of records = " +
  calculateRecords(records) );
...
private void debugMyMessages(String message) {
  if(logger.isDebugEnabled()) {
    logger.debug(message);
  }
}
```

This syntax will result in the same performance overhead of invoking the calculate method, construct the `String` object, push the message into the stack, and call the method that performs the logging-level check! So this approach should be avoided. The motivation behind this code style is when the code analyzer warns about the number of if-conditions inside the method.

Logging messages must be expressive, that is, all useful information should be included, and in particular, the trace level must be able to help us identify any execution anomalies. It is also recommended to log both method input parameters and return values.

An important logging aspect is to keep the logging behavior consistent across the application code so that we can make best use of this logging.

Also, avoid eating the exception and logging other messages that do not help us to understand the exception's root cause. Instead log the exception object so that the full-exception stack trace can identify the root cause of this exception. The following pattern should be completely avoided:

```
try {
...
} catch(Exception ex) {
  logger.error("Error during order submission!");
}
```

Logging must not affect the application's performance or functionality, for example, the logging message shouldn't throw a null pointer exception:

```
If( logger.infoEnabled() ){
    logger.info("order submitted successfully, id:"+order.getId()+
      …+… +",order address 2:"+ order.getAddress2().getDetails());
}
order.submit();
```

In cases where `order Address2` is not mandatory and can be null, the application functionality will be broken and the order will not be submitted by this informative message!

Another impact on the application's performance is that logging extensive data, for example, large XML structures, can cause the application's performance to deteriorate markedly:

```
logger.info("order submitted = " + order.toXML() );
```

We should also tune the logging message information by configuring the level of information that we need, for example, timestamp, class name, method name, and so on. This includes both application's logging and server access logs, and is usually done by configuring the logger appender.

If we can push the logging into asynchronous calls, it can improve the application's performance.

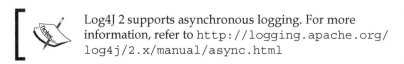

Log4J 2 supports asynchronous logging. For more information, refer to `http://logging.apache.org/log4j/2.x/manual/async.html`

Finally, we need to use a standard way of logging in our application, for example, using **Apache Log4J** (and **Log4J 2**), **Java logging**, **Apache Commons Logging**, or **Simple Logging Facade for Java (SLF4J)**. The advantage of using these standard logging libraries is that they are performance optimized for enterprise application logging, and everyone is aware of how to configure and use these libraries.

Also, some of these libraries provide useful advantages for the application; for example, Log4J 2 can automatically reload its configuration once modified. This allows easy troubleshooting of the application's issues, as we can switch certain logging levels on/off in our troubleshooting area.

Using the javap tool to understand micro-optimizations

The `javap` tool is one of the JDK tools used to disassemble class files. The benefits of using this tool is to understand how the compiler deals with our code in case we have doubts about some of the micro-optimization techniques.

The syntax of the tool is as follows:

```
javap [options]   <classes>
```

We can add many classes and separate them using spaces. The most important options are as follows:

- The method has one flag that specifies that the method access is public (`ACC_PUBLIC`)
- `-l`: This option is to print line and local variable tables
- `-public`: This option is to show only public classes and members
- `-protected`: This option is to show only protected and public classes and members
- `-package`: This option is to show only package, protected, and public classes and members
- `-private/-p`: This option is to show all classes and members
- `-s`: This option is to print internal type signatures
- `-constants`: This option is to show static final constants
- `-c`: This option is to print disassembled code
- `-verbose`: This option is to print stack size, number of locals, and arguments for methods

The bytecode instructions can be found in JVM specifications. We do not need to understand these instructions in detail; a quick overview is enough.

Let's take a look at the simple Java class example to understand the tool output to use it in our own investigations and how a Java compiler deals with and optimizes our written Java code. The following code is simply prints out a `hello` message and concatenates the array elements:

```
package osa.ora;
public class TestClass {
  public static void main(String[] args){
    TestClass test=new TestClass();
    test.hello("Osama");
```

```
        test.concatArray(12);
    }
    public void hello(String name) {
        String s = "Hello ,"+" Your Name is "+ name;
    }
    public void concatArray(int arraySize) {
        String s="";
        for(int i=0;i<arraySize;i++){
            s+=i;
        }
    }
}
```

Compile the following code using the Java compiler, `javac`:

```
javac TestClass.java
```

Now, execute the `javap` command without any parameters:

```
javap TestClass.class

Compiled from "TestClass.java"
public class osa.ora.TestClass {
  public osa.ora.TestClass();
  public static void main(java.lang.String[]);
  public void hello(java.lang.String);
  public void concatArray(int);
}
```

This command is just listing the class outlines. Now let's try to execute the `javap` command with additional options to get more details on the class bytecode as follows:

javap -c -s -v /osa/ora/TestClass.class

This will produce a detailed disassembled output of this class. We will extract one method here to look into to understand how to read this compiled code:

```
    public void hello(java.lang.String);
      flags: ACC_PUBLIC
      Code:
        stack=2, locals=3, args_size=2
            0: new             #7        // class java/lang/StringBuilder
            3: dup
            4: invokespecial #8         // Method java/lang/StringBuilder.
"<init>":()V
```

```
      7: ldc              #9        // String Hello , Your Name is
      9: invokevirtual #10         // Method java/lang/StringBuilder.
append:(Ljava/lang/String;)Ljava/lang/StringBuilder;
     12: aload_1
     13: invokevirtual #10         // Method java/lang/StringBuilder.
append:(Ljava/lang/String;)Ljava/lang/StringBuilder;
     16: invokevirtual #11         // Method java/lang/StringBuilder.
toString:()Ljava/lang/String;
     19: astore_2
     20: return
```

We can simplify the previous class code instructions using the following points:

- The code starts with creating a new object from the `StringBuilder` class (`new #7`)

- Invoke the `StringBuilder.init()` method (`invokevirutal #8`)

- Load the constant string `Hello, Your Name is` (by `ldc #9`) into this class using the `StringBuilder.append()` method (`invokevirutal #10`)

- Load the `name` parameter from the stack (`aload_1`) and concatenate the `name` parameter into this `StringBuilder` instance using the `append()` method (`invokevirutal #10`)

- Finally, convert the `StringBuilder` into the `String` object by calling the `toString()` method (`invokevirutal #11`) and return

Looking at the constant pool table. We can see the following entry #9 referenced by the `ldc` instruction:

```
   #9 = String               #47              //  Hello , Your Name is
```

We can see the `invokevirtual` instruction, which invokes the different methods that are referenced in the constant table, for example, the following `invokevirtual #10`. Refer to the `StringBuilder.append()` method (which is in turn reference method #48 in `StringBuilder class #7`):

```
   #10 = Methodref   #7.#48 //  java/lang/StringBuilder.append:(Lj
   ava/lang/String;)Ljava/lang/StringBuilder;
```

The `StringBuilder` class is referenced by the item number #7 in the same table:

```
   #7 = Class                #46      //  java/lang/StringBuilder
```

So when the code creates the `new` instance, it references this class as #7 (`new #7`).

This gives us a good overview of how to read the compiled code. We need to highlight two points here, which we already discussed in the `String` performance discussion:

- `"Hello ,"+" Your Name is "` is converted into a single literal value `"Hello , Your Name is "`

- Concatenating the name to the static string, that is, the + name is converted to `StringBuilder` using two `append()` method calls; one is to add the literal string values and the other is to add the name variable content

This example gives us an idea of how to make use of `javap` to understand our micro-optimization techniques by isolating the code into a small class for analysis.

The full list of different class instructions can be found in the virtual machine specifications if we want to gain a deeper understanding of the class file format and the different instructions listed.

> For more information about `javap`, refer to Oracle's online documentation:
>
> `http://docs.oracle.com/javase/7/docs/technotes/tools/windows/javap.html`
>
> To get more details about the class file structure and different instructions in Java virtual machine (Java SE 7), refer to Oracle's online documentations:
>
> `http://docs.oracle.com/javase/specs/jvms/se7/html/jvms-4.html#jvms-4.10.1.9`

Database performance tuning tips

Database performance is considered as the most critical factor in our application's performance, and most of a transaction's latency is caused by the database. In this section, we will provide some performance recommendations when dealing with the database from the development perspective.

Always stick to using a server-managed connection pooling when accessing the database and avoid using direct connections to the database.

The connection should be released immediately after finishing our database interaction. Also, it is recommended that you use prepared statements as it gets compiled and hence, is more efficient to use when executing the same query many times with different parameters.

If we are using the **Object-relational mapping (ORM)** library, we need to make use of the different capabilities that exist in the used ORM framework. Each framework has its own best practices and performance recommendations, as we saw while discussing JPA performance tips. In general, we need to stick to these recommendations for better performance.

Database machine optimization is important in the aspects of allocated memory, CPU power, and the number of cores. Also, database tuning effort is required to create essential table indices to speed up different application queries.

Use table row-locking and avoid entire table-locking. Also increase database buffer size for better performance.

Monitoring the database performance on a regular-basis is a basic operational requirement so we can address any issue as it happens.

Database-specific performance tuning recommendations should be followed according to the database provider recommendations.

Making use of the available database functionality, for example, loading data from a remote database in Oracle can be achieved by executing a query against a remote database link. This can be accelerated if we use a materialized view that utilizes this link, which can be refreshed in a frequency that matches the speed of data changes (for example, nightly job). Thus, during runtime, the application will execute the queries against this materialized view, but not from the remote database.

Using Oracle database optimizer hints are useful to force the database optimizer to use a certain index or execute the query in parallel:

```
SELECT /*+ PARALLEL(2) */ id, name FROM users;
```

Also, using a SQL statement execution plan (according to the database engine) to understand our application queries and optimize them accordingly is essential during both development and production time, where the data size can change the execution plan and reveal a different cost of execution.

> A database link is a schema object in one database that enables us to access objects on another database.
>
> A materialized view is a replica of a target master from a single point in time (that is, a snapshot).
>
> Optimizer hints can be used with SQL statements to alter execution plans; for example, `SELECT /*+ INDEX(index_name) */ * FROM table_name;`.
>
> A database statement's execution plan is the sequence of operations performed to run this statement. Each database has its own format to get this execution plan, for example, in Oracle, we can get it by executing `EXPLAIN PLAN`:
>
> **`EXPLAIN PLAN FOR SELECT last_name FROM employees;`**

We can use batch load and bulk load operations to speed up the loading of data into the database, for example, the following Java code inserts a batch with 1,000 rows:

```
private void saveInDBUsingBatch(String name, int count) {
    int batchLimit = 1000;
    Connection con = null;
    try {
        Class.forName(DRIVER);
        con = DriverManager.getConnection(DB_URL,
          USER, PASSWORD);
        con.setAutoCommit( false );
        String sql =
"insert into \"TEST_TABLE\"(id, value) VALUES (?, ?)";
        PreparedStatement  insertStatement =
        con.prepareStatement(sql);
        for(int i=0; i < count; i++){
            insertStatement.setInt(1, i);
            insertStatement.setString(2, name);
            insertStatement.addBatch();
            batchLimit--;
            if ( batchLimit == 0 ) {
                insertStatement.executeBatch();
                insertStatement.clearBatch();
                batchLimit = 1000;
            }
            insertStatement.clearParameters();
        }
        //for the remaining ones
        insertStatement.executeBatch();
        //commit your updates
```

```
        con.commit();
    }catch(Exception ex){
        //handle error
    }finally {
        con.setAutoCommit(true);
        con.close();
    }
}
```

The `saveInDBUsingBatch` method takes a `name` parameter and inserts it in the database table equal to number of times that match the other `count` parameter. The method, instead of hitting the database with each insert statement, creates batch inserts and hits the database once per 1,000 inserts, which can speed up the application's interaction with the database.

The other way to do this is using the bulk load facility provided by most of the database engines. It is usually used for bulk inserting huge data in a short period of time. The data is formatted according to the database table structure in a file format or by streaming directly into the database.

For example, Oracle uses `SQL loader` that require two files: control and data (that can be combined into a single file). Also, the Postgres database supports bulk load using a file or by streaming directly to the database using the `CopyAPI` `copyIn()` method in the following format:

```
((PGConnection) con).getCopyAPI().copyIn(statement, inputStream);
```

In MySQL, we can do the same by using the LOAD DATA INFILE statement:

```
LOAD DATA INFILE 'myData.txt' INTO TABLE my_data_table;
```

For more information about the Oracle bulk load utility, visit
http://docs.oracle.com/cd/E27559_01/dev.1112/e27150/bulkload.htm.

For more information about Postgres CopyManager, refer to the Postgres documentation:
http://jdbc.postgresql.org/documentation/publicapi/org/postgresql/copy/CopyManager.html.

For more information about the LOAD DATA INFILE syntax, refer to MySQL database:
http://dev.mysql.com/doc/refman/5.7/en/load-data.html

This is an overview of database performance tuning tips, which we need to consider during designing and developing database interactions within our applications.

Client-side optimization

We will end this chapter by discussing a few points that we need to consider in our presentation layer that are related to client-side performance tuning tips.

In *Chapter 9, Tuning an Application's Environment*, we discussed static content caching in a user's browser using HTTP caching header directives (for example, cache-control, max_age). Zipping the contents is another valid option to speed up the transfer, and reduce the required network bandwidth that can improve the performance.

Using Ajax also can speed up the interactivity by reducing the required output from the server.

Other recommendations to improve the presentation layer performance include combining the CSS and JavaScript files so that we have the minimal possible number of files. Also, we could move the CSS files to the top of the page whenever possible so that the page does not wait until the files are downloaded to be rendered.

Avoid embedding the CSS and JavaScript code in the page; instead put them into separate files so that they can get cached in the client browser's cache.

PageSpeed Insights is a tool provided by Google to analyze web page performance and provide some suggestions. We can use it to evaluate our pages structure and improve the performance. The following figure shows the page analysis output for my personal blog (both desktop and mobile versions), osama-oransa.blogspot.com:

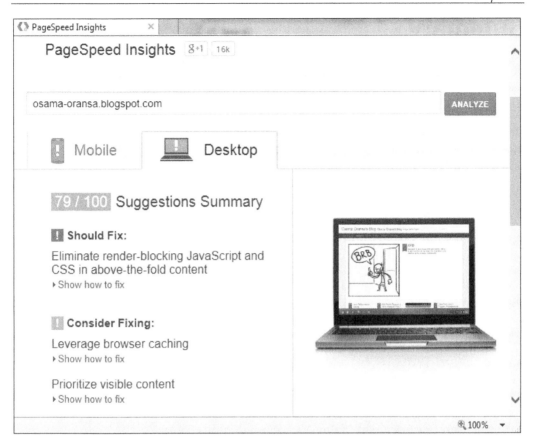

We can expand each of these recommendations to see what exactly is being recommended to improve the page's performance.

Google PageSpeed Insights is available at `http://developers.google.com/speed/pagespeed/insights/`.

Summary

In this chapter, we covered the Agile development methodology and the related performance considerations. We discussed some performance consideration when using test-driven development (TDD) as our development strategy.

We highlighted the importance of performing code reviews either manually or using static code analyzer tools, and went through different performance recommendations in many development areas, including different Java EE components such as JSF, JPA, EJB, and so on.

We also provided fine-tuning tips such as string manipulations, using different Java collections, I/O operations, logging and exception handling best practices.

We covered some tips to improve database transactions and some client-side recommendations to improve our application's presentation layer performance.

As most of these recommendations are almost micro-optimization techniques, we showed the use of the `javap` JDK tool to analyze the compilation results of our Java code to comprehend the outcome and tune it accordingly in combination with other ways, which in turn gives us a good understanding of our application's performance as profiling.

In the next chapter, *Chapter 12, Tuning a Sample Application*, we will proceed to the last station in our book, where we will get a sample application and conduct performance analyses, including performance testing and profiling, and performance improvement, so that we can practice a part of what we learned in this book.

12
Tuning a Sample Application

In this chapter, we are going to demonstrate the performance tuning activities of a small application so that we can practice some of the activities that we have learned in this book. This will include code review, performance testing, profiling the application, identification of some performance issues, and discussion of possible fixes. We will then summarize our conclusion at the end.

The following is a list of topics that we will cover in this chapter:

- Application functionality overview
- Performance testing our application
- Profiling the application and detecting performance issues
- Application performance code review
- Resolving some of the identified issues
- Result and conclusion

Reaching our final destination

As we have reached the final chapter, we need to practice some of the areas that we covered earlier in this book. Practicing performance tuning is essential in order to gain the required experience to work smoothly during performance tuning of an enterprise application.

In this book, we tried to cover the maximum possible topics that we would need when we deal with Java enterprise application performance tuning. We also focused on how to think while dealing with performance issues, how to organize our thoughts to draft our investigation plan, how to utilize the existing monitoring tools, and so on.

The main challenge here is how to practically use this knowledge and turn what we have learned into an actual experience.

We can ideally start by executing the performance testing of any of our old projects. We can first identify the areas of slow transactions, execute isolated performance testing on these transactions while performing some profiling to understand the root causes of performance issues, and finally we can try to fix the root causes of the issues and repeat the cycle. By repeating this activity many times with many different projects, we can gain our own self-experience that we can utilize in troubleshooting more mature enterprise applications.

In this chapter, we will try to perform some parts of this self-learning experience together so that we can continue doing our own experiments using the same approach.

No single book can cover everything about performance tuning, but we did our best in this book to cover the most common areas that enable us to establish our own solid foundations. We can make use of these foundations to go through any new areas that we are going to hit in the future. Of course, tracking the performance recommendation is a continuous process where changes happen from one Java version to another, from one framework version to another, and so on. Fortunately, the changes are not usually in the core part, and at the end, this is the unavoidable cost we need to pay to work in performance tuning. Now, let's start our practice in this chapter.

> *"I cannot teach anybody anything. I can only make them think."*
>
> *–Socrates*

Setting up the ExcellentSurvey application

To set up the ExcellentSurvey application, we need to perform the following steps:

1. Download the application and database scripts.
2. Import the database scripts; this will install the Survey schema in the MySQL database.
3. Create the database user test if it does not already exist in MySQL (the test user's password should be set as test).
4. Grant all database privileges to our database user test over the Survey schema.
5. Open the ExcellentSurvey application in NetBeans 7.x.
6. Build the application and run it.

7. Ensure that the e-mail settings are configured correctly from the `ExcellentSurvey` admin GUI. Log in to the system using `admin` as the username and `admin` as password, select **Configure the System**, and then populate all the required e-mail configurations, as shown in the following screenshot:

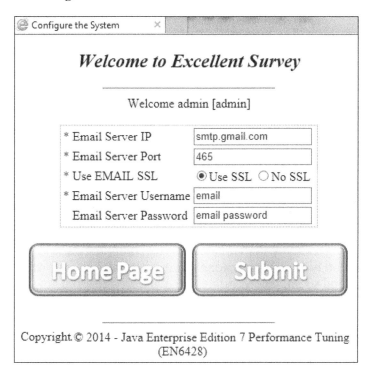

Welcome to Excellent Survey

Welcome admin [admin]

* Email Server IP	smtp.gmail.com
* Email Server Port	465
* Use EMAIL SSL	◉ Use SSL ○ No SSL
* Email Server Username	email
Email Server Password	email password

Home Page   **Submit**

Copyright © 2014 - Java Enterprise Edition 7 Performance Tuning (EN6428)

 If you want to use your Gmail account, you can use the same configurations as in the previous screenshot and insert your Gmail username and password in the appropriate fields.

8. Ensure that the e-mails of all the users point to a valid e-mail address, from `user1` to `user10`, by changing the e-mail address in the `user` database table with the help of the following script:

```
update survey.`user` u set u.email='your.email@mail.com' where
u.name like 'user%';
```

9. Take a backup of the database so that we can use this backup as our baseline database snapshot, which we will import before we start any performance testing.

Once the server starts and the application gets deployed, open the following application link (if the default browser doesn't open it automatically):
`http://localhost:8080/ExcellentSurvey/`

If the application gets deployed successfully, the login/register page will show up in the browser. Try to log in using `admin`/`admin` or `user`/`user` (default populated).

 To get the `ExcellentSurvey` project, you can download its code along with its database schema from the code bundle of this book, which is available at `http://www.packtpub.com/`.

Functional overview of the ExcellentSurvey application

The ExcellentSurvey application is a simple application that creates custom surveys, either public or private, and allows users to share these created surveys with different users to participate in them.

The idea of creating a survey depends mainly on asking the users to provide different evaluation type questions, for example, yes/no, values from 1 to 10, agree/disagree, and so on.

The following screenshot represents one of the surveys created using this application:

Welcome to Excellent Survey
Welcome osama2 [user]
Book user's survey This survey to get the user's feedback about the book; Java Enterprise Edition 7 Performance Tuning Please fill all survey questions: 20 question * 1 : Are you working in performance tuning? Is your current job related to performance tuning ? ◉ Yes ◎ No
* 2 : The book change your view? Regarding performance tuning, does this book changed your view ? ◉ Totally Agree ◎ Agree ◎ Neutral ◎ Disagree ◎ Totally Disagree
* 3 : Do you like the chapter sequence? Do you feel the book chapters are well organized? ◉ True ◎ False
* 4 : Do you like book examples? Is book examples are good? ◉ Yes ◎ No

It is important from a performance perspective to understand the application's capabilities and the used technologies so that we can understand what we are dealing with.

The ExcellentSurvey application has the following main features:

- Log in (GUI functionality)
- Register (GUI only)
- Create a survey (GUI and web service)
- Manage a survey, such as activate survey, close survey, delete survey, and get survey report (GUI and web service)
- Participate in a survey (GUI and web service)
- Configure systems (admin user in the GUI only)

The application uses the following Java EE 7 technologies:

- **JSPs, servlets, and filters**: JSPs are used as our application view layer, servlets are used as the view controller, and a filter class is used as an intercepting filter for security
- **EJBs (stateless session beans):** These are used in the business delegate, business objects, and DAO layer
- **JPA**: This is used as the persistence layer in the application
- **Java mail APIs:** These are used to send e-mails to different application users
- **SOAP web services**: These are used to expose the application services to different clients that can consume the services to provide their own services

The code is well organized in the following different layers:

- **Presentation tier**: This uses JSP as a view and servlet as a controller
- **Business Delegate (BD) layer**: This is an abstraction layer for the business layer (stateless session beans)
- **Web Service (WS) layer**: This uses the business delegate layer to access the business objects (stateless session beans)
- **Business layer**: This uses the business objects (stateless session beans)
- **Data Access layer (DAO)**: This abstracts the data sources from the business layers (stateless session beans); this layer has a helper layer to actually interact with the resources
- **DAO helper**: This layer helps the DAO layer to encapsulate all access to the persistence layer (facade pattern)
- **Persistence layer**: This uses JPA, which abstracts the data source (database access)

The following diagram represents the different layers inside this application starting from **Presentation tier** till the **Persistence layer**:

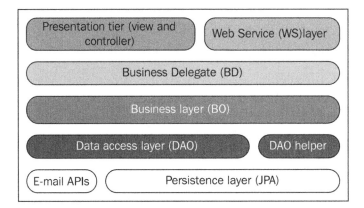

The following is a generic sequence diagram that represents the system's interactions between the internal layers of the application when it receives a user's request:

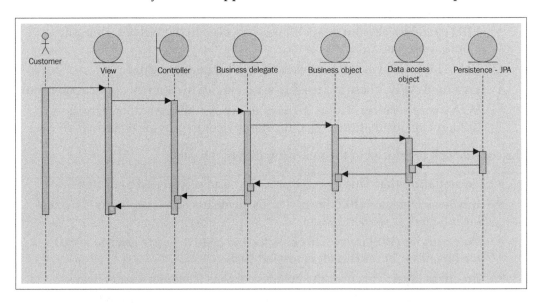

The user interacts with the application view (GUI), which sends the user's action to the controller. The controller is responsible to invoke the business object via the abstraction layer (business delegate layer) and dispatch the user's request to the appropriate view.

System registration ends by sending an e-mail to the registered e-mail address, which contains a link to activate the registration account. Once activated, the user can log in to the application.

Understanding the different application flows is an essential step to build the corresponding performance test plan for the performance testing team. Understanding the internal flow in the application will help to understand the system behavior and profiling results, while understanding the technologies used in the application can help us to provide the optimal performance resolution.

ExcellentSurvey performance assessment

In this section, we will create a performance testing plan for the application, execute it, and get the performance results. We will select the **Create Survey** option for our performance testing as a sample of our application's transactions. The following points give a description of what the flow of this transaction includes:

1. A user login page will be displayed, where the user is asked to log in.
2. If the login is successful, then a home page with different menu options will be displayed; if the login fails, then the user is redirected to the login page again.
3. The user is then asked to select the **Create Survey** menu option.
4. The first step is displayed, which contains the general survey fields such as the title, description, number of questions, whether it is public or restricted, and e-mails of the target audience.
5. The second step is then displayed once we click on the **Continue** button. The user should select the survey questions, description for each question, and question type from among the eight different types.
6. Once we click on the **Submit** button, the confirmation page or error page will be displayed.
7. If the confirmation is successful, an e-mail will be sent to the survey owner (that is, creator).
8. The user goes to the home page by clicking on the **Home Page** button (optional step).
9. The user logs out by clicking on the **Logout** icon on the home page (optional step).

The application has a business rule to prevent the creation of more than 15 surveys for each user, so we will design the performance test script to invoke 17 creation requests with the expectation that 2 of them will be routed to the error page because of this rule.

Let's assume that our application's performance SLA is less than 1 second in the 90th percentile for all application transactions under an application load of 10 concurrent users.

We will also use 10 users who are already registered in the system and 1 user who is not registered (that is, `user11`). So, we expect the transactions associated with this user to be routed to the index page (login page) every time.

We will need to create the following `survey_users.csv` file to use it inside our test script in order to store users' credentials:

```
user1,user1
user2,user2
...
...
user10,user10
user11,user11
```

The test script will look like the following screenshot:

The test plan includes testing the application flow that starts when the user logs in and creates a new survey and ends when the user logs out. It also includes some random timers to slow down the transaction flow as the user will need some time to enter survey-specific data.

To get this test plan, you can record it using what we learned in *Chapter 3, Getting Familiar with Performance Testing*, which we recommend, and once created, you can download our version and compare it to your version (for example, our test plan does not have success assertions).

Alternatively, our test plan can be downloaded from `http://www.packtpub.com/`.

After executing each performance test, we need to restore the environment so that we can compare the results after optimizing the application. The simplest way is to restore the database schema after each execution.

Before we can start the performance test execution, we need to ensure the following:

- Ensure that the filename for usernames and passwords is correctly configured in the CSV load module of the load test in our test plan.
- Make a database backup and name it baseline database so that we can restore the database after each execution. This will ensure that we have the same database baseline with each performance test so we can compare the performance test results.

The following table shows our performance test results (the transaction time is measured in milliseconds):

Label	# Samples	Average	Median	90% Line	Min	Max
/ExcellentSurvey/	187	137	5	12	2	4414
/ExcellentSurvey/images/register.jpg	187	53	4	13	2	2273
/ExcellentSurvey/images/login.gif	187	9	4	8	2	752
/ExcellentSurvey/LoginServlet	374	95	10	81	2	3290
/ExcellentSurvey/images/logout.png	187	6	3	10	1	60
/ExcellentSurvey/images/manage.png	187	27	3	9	1	2211
/ExcellentSurvey/images/take.png	187	38	3	8	1	2218
/ExcellentSurvey/images/create.png	187	15	3	7	1	2228
/ExcellentSurvey/create.jsp	187	89	4	15	2	2546
/ExcellentSurvey/images/home.png	187	5	3	8	2	63
/ExcellentSurvey/images/continue.png	187	28	3	11	1	2213
/ExcellentSurvey/CreateServlet	374	2891	17	9348	2	14479
/ExcellentSurvey/images/submit.png	187	5	3	9	1	50
/ExcellentSurvey/home.jsp	187	56	5	22	2	2267
TOTAL	2992	402	4	58	1	14479

Looking at these results, we can identify that the `CreateServlet` transaction has been performing bad and its 90th percentile response time is around 9 seconds (9348 milliseconds). This represents two different steps, create survey step 1 and create survey step 2, which explains why the total samples for this transaction, which is 374 is double the number of samples for other transactions, which is 187.

The 90th percentile response times for all the other transactions are within the application performance SLA, which is less than 1 second.

Performance investigation plan

After we have identified the transactions that have performed poorly by executing the performance test, we need to make a plan to follow so that we can organize our activities till we identify the root cause of the performance issue.

As we stated before, we need to investigate in both horizontal and vertical dimensions so that we can locate the exact location of our performance issue. As our application is a simple web application that is deployed on our local machine, we have only one node that contains the following tiers:

- Client tier
- Server tier
- Database tier

All these tiers are deployed on the same machine. Now, let's put the vertical dimension in each of these tiers as follows:

- In the client tier, we can use browser developer tools to see if there are any additional issues in the application on the client side, for example, JavaScript code, resource loading time, and so on. Note that JMeter does not execute any JavaScript code, so the already identified performance issues are not related to JavaScript.

- In the server tier, we have the application, JVM, the application server, and the operating system. To investigate these layers, we need to add our monitoring/ profiler tools to identify any potential issues. We can investigate the layers of the server tier with the help of the following points:

  ° For the application, we can profile the application, get the thread dump, get the heap dump (if required), and so on.

  ° For the JVM, we need to get memory and garbage collection statistics.

  ° For the application server, we need to get some monitoring results using either the application server administrative console or external monitoring tools. We also need to get server logs to check if there are any issues in the application (including access logs).

  ° For the operating system, we need to get CPU, memory, and I/O data.

- In the database tier, we need to have either a database monitoring tool or a database performance report. The MySQL administrative console already contains a section for the database server health check where we can see the connection health, memory health, and other useful information.

We do not have any network components here as everything is located on the same machine.

All these things need to be done while executing the application performance testing. We have already covered how to do these things in this book.

Profiling our ExcellentSurvey application

We will now profile our application. As we clarified earlier, we need to first restore the database schema so that we can work on the baseline again. We will then restart our application server, attaching one of the profilers, which we have already learned how to do earlier in *Chapter 4*, *Monitoring Java Applications*, and finally we will execute our performance test to get the profiling results.

Usually, it is recommended to use the sampling mode as it won't affect the application performance, but the instrumental mode can reveal more information. So, it is better to start with sampling, and if the information is not enough, we can perform instrumental profiling to certain selected areas/transactions of our application.

 At this moment, you can try to perform the profiling yourself and then compare your results with our results. Feel free to use any profiling tool as long as you can use it efficiently.

Getting CPU profiling results

Here, we will attach JProfiler in the instrumental mode to get the maximum information for demonstration; the advantage of using JProfiler is that we will have application, JVM, and operating system statistics. So, to complete our investigation plan, we will need to do the following:

- Check the client-side performance using the browser's developer tools
- Check the application server logs
- Add monitoring elements to the GlassFish application server using its admin console
- Check the database health using MySQL administrative tools

Let's start with the CPU profiling results, which are shown in the following screenshot:

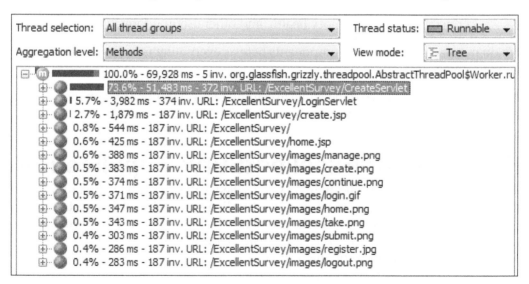

The previous screenshot shows the same performance issue that exists in the create survey transaction. If we expand this a bit more, we can see the following main areas of bad performance:

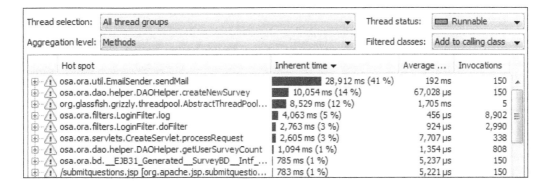

In this expanded view, we can see the two main transactions that cause this slow performance in `CommonDAO.sendMail()` and `DAOHelper.createNewSurvey()` (the arrows point to both, with more than 60 percent of the time spent on both methods).

If we switch to the **Hot spot** tab, we can see the following HotSpot areas in our transactions:

	Hot spot	Inherent time ▾	Average ...	Invocations
⊞ ⚠	osa.ora.util.EmailSender.sendMail	28,912 ms (41 %)	192 ms	150
⊞ ⚠	osa.ora.dao.helper.DAOHelper.createNewSurvey	10,054 ms (14 %)	67,028 μs	150
⊞ ⚠	org.glassfish.grizzly.threadpool.AbstractThreadPool...	8,529 ms (12 %)	1,705 ms	5
⊞ ⚠	osa.ora.filters.LoginFilter.log	4,063 ms (5 %)	456 μs	8,902
⊞ ⚠	osa.ora.filters.LoginFilter.doFilter	2,763 ms (3 %)	924 μs	2,990
⊞ ⚠	osa.ora.servlets.CreateServlet.processRequest	2,605 ms (3 %)	7,707 μs	338
⊞ ⚠	osa.ora.dao.helper.DAOHelper.getUserSurveyCount	1,094 ms (1 %)	1,354 μs	808
⊞ ⚠	osa.ora.bd.__EJB31_Generated__SurveyBD__Intf_...	785 ms (1 %)	5,237 μs	150
⊞ ⚠	/submitquestions.jsp [org.apache.jsp.submitquestio...	783 ms (1 %)	5,221 μs	150

Thread selection: All thread groups | Thread status: Runnable
Aggregation level: Methods | Filtered classes: Add to calling class

In the **Hot spot** tab (filtered by the calling class option), we can see the same list of HotSpot methods (that is, `CommonDAO.sendMail()` and `DAOHelper.createNewSurvey()`). We can also see the `log()` method, `doFilter()` method, and `proccessRequest()` method in `CreateServlet`; other than these methods, all the other methods are not considered as HotSpot areas.

You can download this JProfiler instrumental snapshot from http://www.packtpub.com/.

Getting memory and thread profiling results

If we check the memory usage, garbage collection activities, thread states, and monitor sections, we can see that they all look normal. The following memory telemetry view shows the normal sawtooth appearance of the heap memory used by the application:

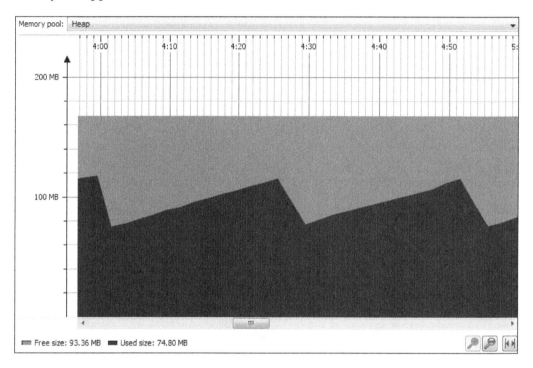

We can also take frequent thread dumps to see that the threads are almost waiting for execution, which means that the application is healthy with respect to thread utilization.

Getting database CPU profiling results

Now, let's move into the database interaction tab to see if there is any HotSpot in the database interface area, as shown in the following screenshot:

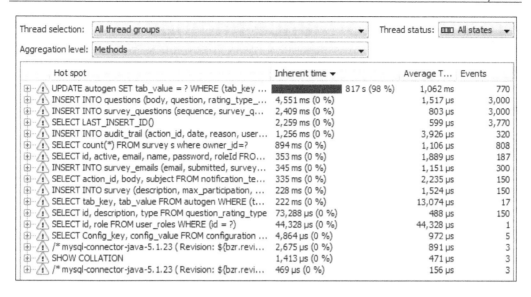

As we can see, one query consumes around 98 percent of the time with around only 700 events; this is the hottest spot in our application so far:

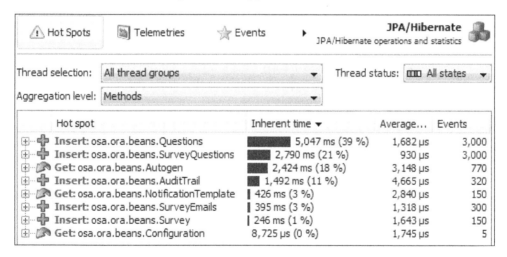

The JPA view looks almost normal. In the top JPA HotSpots, we can see the insert statements for both `Questions` and `SurveyQuestions`. In spite of the average time and total time being good, both the statements are repeated around 3,000 times to insert all survey questions.

We can also see that the `NotificationTemplate` objects are loaded around 150 times, which corresponds to the number of surveys created.

Profiling performance findings

Now, let's summarize our findings while looking at the code to understand the performance issues and plan to resolve them.

Detected HotSpot methods

The following methods will describe the detected HotSpot methods from our profiling results analysis:

- `EmailSender.sendEmail()`: This method contains the code to send e-mails, such as `Session.getInstance(props, auth)` and `Transport.send(msg)`. Both are blocking calls that will wait for the remote system to respond (e-mail server).

- `DAOHelper.createNewSurvey()`: This method contains the following findings:
    - Call to the synchronized method `getUserSurveyCount(userId)`
    - Three calls to the synchronized method `generatedId(String key, int size)`
    - Some debugging messages at the `INFO` level without checking whether the level is enabled or not

- `LoginFilter.log()`: This method is invoked many times to log some messages. Some messages already check if the debug is enabled and others do not, which is not correct; particularly in this critical component, where all users' requests pass through.

Detected HotSpot database statements

The following is the detected HotSpot database SQL statement:

- **SQL Statement that updates the autogen table**: This statement takes more than one second to update the table, which is used to generate different insert entities' keys

Potential wrong logic issues

The following four issues do not impact the application's performance but represent inefficient implementation as concluded from the execution count, and could possibly impact the application in the long run:

- **SQL Statement that do insert in questions and survey questions tables**: Each of these insert statements are repeated around 3,000 times to insert different exam questions. These statements do not cause any performance issue with the current scale of our performance testing.

- **SQL query that retrieves the notification templates**: This query retrieves the same notification template 150 times, which is equal to the number of surveys created. In spite, it returns the same notification template every time.

- **SQL query that retrieves the question rating types**: This query retrieves the question rating type 150 times. This is a static list that needs to be retrieved only once and then cached.

- **SQL query that counts user's surveys**: The `SELECT count(*) FROM survey s where owner_id=?` query gets executed more than 808 times to ensure no one from the 11 test users will exceed the survey creation limit, which is equal to 15 surveys per user. In spite of the fact that the overall performance impact is not noticeable, we still need to look into such issues to avoid potential impact when the data size grows up, and also for educational purposes to understand how to deal with similar situations.

ExcellentSurvey issues and possible resolutions

In this section, we will discuss each of our findings using source code inspection and discuss how to fix the different performance issues identified.

At this moment, you can try to scan the code of the identified performance issues and do your own analysis and possible resolutions, and then compare your results with our results.

You may review our fixing strategy as well from *Chapter 8, Memory Profiling*.

Fixing the EmailSender.sendEmail() HotSpot method

The issue here is clear that the application hangs while waiting for a response from the mail server. What we can do here is push mail sending as an asynchronous operation, so that our application responds back to the user and the mail is sent in a background thread.

This used to be implemented before Java EE 7 by creating a new thread around the method call, but fortunately, in the Java EE specifications, we can do this by using a managed thread factory, which we can use to create managed threads.

The following are the required changes in the CommonDAO class:

```
@Resource
ManagedThreadFactory threadFactory;
```

And inside the commonDAO.sendMail method, we need to wrap the call to the emailSender.sendMail method with the following code:

```
Thread mailThread = threadFactory.newThread(new Runnable() {
  @Override
  public void run() {
    emailSender.sendMail(toUserEmail, subject, body, myImage,
      file, isPicture);
  }
});
mailThread.start();
```

We can also use ManagedExecutotrService to better manage the results of sending e-mails. In other words, if we need to confirm that the e-mail was really sent or not, the code should look like the following (we need to change the emailSender.sendMail() method so that it returns a Boolean value in order to indicate if the mail was successfully sent or not):

```
@Resource
ManagedExecutorService executorService;
Future<Boolean> result = executorService.submit(new
  Callable<Boolean>() {
  @Override
  public Boolean call() throws Exception {
    return emailSender.sendMail(toUserEmail, subject, body,
      myImage, file, isPicture);
  }
});
//and get the status from the Future object.
```

We will use the managed thread factory as we do not need to ensure that the mail has been delivered.

The sendEmail() method has a debug message that needs to have an additional check on the debug level before it logs the message.

Another finding is the non-efficient way of sending mails. Each time, we have to create the mail session object and then use the transport to send the message; instead, we can create the session object once in the initialization section on the `EmailSender` class, as follows:

```
public void init(Configuration[] configs) {
  Authenticator auth = new SMTPAuthenticator();
  session = Session.getInstance(props, auth);
  initialized = true;
}
```

By modifying the code in this way, we create the mail session once and reuse it to send mails. We could also tune it more by defining the transport and connecting it so that we can call send e-mail directly without having to authenticate each time. This has the drawback that the mail server connection will be terminated after a certain period or certain number of e-mails, and we will need to reopen the `transport` connection again. So, before sending any mail, we check if `transport.isConnected()` is connected or not; otherwise, we connect it again.

In case an exception occurs, we set the e-mail initialization back to `false`. So, in subsequent calls, we open a new session and connect the transport again, but this will cause a failure when sending some e-mails. The following is an example for this improvement:

```
session = Session.getInstance(props, auth);
transport = session.getTransport("smtp");
transport.connect();
initialized = true;
```

This issue alerts us that there is no retry mechanism implemented to send e-mails, and the best way to handle both asynchronous communication and the retry mechanism is to implement a queue to place the e-mails that need to be sent. A separate thread/process can pick e-mails from this queue and remove them from the queue once they are successfully sent; this is a design change that needs to be considered in this application.

Fixing the DAOHelper.createNewSurvey() HotSpot method

The `DAOHelper.createNewSurvey()` method initiates by checking the user's survey count. From a business perspective, we won't be able to remove the first check on the user's survey count as the user can open many concurrent sessions. So ideally, we must keep this check, but we can move it to the business layer being a business rule. We will discuss later how to improve this check.

The `createNewSurvey()` method contains another two or three time calls to a synchronized method, `generatedId(String key, int size)`, which represents a lack of knowledge in how JPA handles the auto-incremental keys in the MySQL database.

We need to simply create the object and persist it. Once persisted, we can use its ID in subsequent insert statements. In that case, we won't need the `autogen` table at all, so we won't need to call this synchronized method.

Now, let's amend the following code in the `createNewSurvey` method to improve the method performance:

```
int id = 0;//generatedId("SURVEY", 1);
int questionId = 0;//generatedId("QUESTION",
  surveyVO.getNoOfQuestions());
int emailId = 0;//surveyVO.getSurveyEmails() != null ?
  generatedId("EMAIL", surveyVO.getSurveyEmails().length) : 0;

em.persist(survey);
em.flush();
id=survey.getId();
...
em.persist(newQuestion);
em.flush();
//associate survey to questions
SurveyQuestions surveyMapQuestion = new SurveyQuestions(new
  SurveyQuestionsPK(id, newQuestion.getId()),
  surveyQuestion.getSequence());
```

In the preceding code, we have commented out the call to the `generatedId()` method that gets the ID(s) from the `autogen` table, and if we need to use the IDs in the subsequent insert statements, we get these IDs from the persisted objects.

If these tables (that is, the `Survey` and `Question` tables) were joined using actual database foreign keys, then we can just add question objects on the survey object and the ORM will handle this for us. So, another way to improve this method performance is to let ORM handle this on behalf of us by defining the correct relations on the database level and regenerating the JPA entity beans again.

Fixing the LoginFilter.log() HotSpot method

As we clarified in *Chapter 11*, *Performance Tuning Tips*, we must stick to logging best practices. This means, in our application, we need to surround each logging statement with a check on the level of the logging before we actually waste time constructing the logging messages, which usually concatenate different strings.

Another issue with the existing application logging is that it uses the INFO level in locations where we should use the DEBUG level. Therefore, we have to use a proper logging level; otherwise, the logging will become useless and potentially impact the application's performance.

Fixing the HotSpot autogen table update statement

By fixing the previous CreateSurvey method, this HotSpot method will be removed partially from our list; yet, it will be used in other transactions, for example, to register a user and audit trail.

We need to fix this for the createAuditTrail() method, which is used in the login and create survey transactions. We can fix the following code in the createAuditTrail method:

```
public void createAuditTrail(AuditTrailVO auditVO) {
  AuditTrail newTrail = new AuditTrail();
    int id = 0;//generatedId("AUDIT", 1);
}
```

Now, we need to do the same fix of removing the autogen table to register users (to get the users' IDs) and create a survey report (to get the reports' IDs). So, we can drop this autogen table from our schema.

We will tag the generatedId() method as deprecated as a temporary first step solution till we can assess the code better before removing it completely (conservative approach):

```
@Deprecated
private synchronized int generatedId(String key, int size) {
  ...
}
```

Later, we will need to delete this generatedId() method, drop the autogen table, and delete the Autogen JPA entity bean.

Fixing HotSpot statements to insert questions and survey questions

If the insert statements are causing performance issues, we will have to fix them. But with the current performance test results, the performance is acceptable.

One of the possible ways to fix this potential issue is to use batch inserts instead of an individual insert statement. To do this, we need to perform the following steps:

1. Add the required JPA configurations in the `persistence.xml` file, as follows:

   ```
   "eclipselink.jdbc.batch-writing"="JDBC"
   "eclipselink.jdbc.batch-writing.size"="1000"
   ```

2. We can further tune the batch size according to the performance results.

3. Change the logic in the code to be similar to the following pseudocode:

   ```
   for (QuestionVO surveryQuestion :
   surveyVO.getSurveryQuestions()) {
     Questions newQuestion = new Questions();
     newQuestion.set…// fill its data
     em.persist(newQuestion);
   }
   for (QuestionVO surveryQuestion :
   surveyVO.getSurveryQuestions()) {
     SurveyQuestions surveyQuestion = new SurveyQuestions();
     surveyQuestion.set…// fill its data
     em.persist(surveyQuestion);
   }
   em.flush();
   ```

The current small number of survey questions will gain only a minor improvement from such code changes since batch processing is useful in cases where we have a huge number of insert statements. So, we will skip this item from our fixes.

Fixing HotSpot queries that get the notification templates/question rating types

We need to cache notification template query results so that subsequent calls get the notification template from the cache instead of hitting the database (JPA already supports caching the results).

The same fix needs to be applied to question rating types as rating types are static list that do not change and no need to reload this list with each survey creation. The following actions need to be performed in order to fix the performance of these queries:

- Use the latest JPA version to make use of the latest optimizations.
- Use the `@ReadOnly` annotation with these beans as they shouldn't change in the application (unless we have an administrative module in our application to update both).
- Add the `@Cacheable` or `@Cache` annotation to use the L2 shared cache for these beans in the application. The alternative to this JPA cache is to have an internal/external cache support.

Since both the queries (that is, notification templates and question rating types queries) do not cause an actual impact on the application's performance, we won't fix them at this stage.

Fixing the HotSpot query that counts user surveys

The HotSpot query that counts user surveys gets executed more than 808 times to ensure that no one from the 10 test users exceeds the survey creation limit, which is 15 surveys/users. If we examine the code, we can see that this query is fired from the following four different locations:

- It is fired from `LoginServlet` to load the user's survey count so that we can show/hide the **Create Survey** menu option, as shown in the following code:

```
int surveyCount=surveyBD.getUserSurveyCount(userAccount);
userAccount.setCountOfSurvey(surveyCount);
```

- It is fired from `CreateServlet` to prevent the user from accessing this servlet, as shown in the following code:

```
int surveyCount=surveyBD.getUserSurveyCount(userAccount);
if(surveyCount>=IConstant.MAX_USER_SURVEYS){
  request.getRequestDispatcher("/error.jsp").
    forward(request, response);
  return;
}
userAccount.setCountOfSurvey(surveyCount);
```

- It is fired from `CreateServlet` after the successful creation of the survey. The counter is fixed in the user's object in the session, so we can show/hide the menu option of creating a new survey, as shown in the following code:

```
surveyCount=surveyBD.getUserSurveyCount(userAccount);
userAccount.setCountOfSurvey(surveyCount);
```

- It is fired from `DAOHelper` to check the count of surveys before creating a new survey, as shown in the following code:

```
if(getUserSurveyCount(userId)>=IConstant.MAX_USER_SURVEYS){
   return null;
}
```

The logic makes sense, but the main objection to this logic is that it should be moved into the business layer as this represents a business rule and shouldn't be placed in the controller layer or data access layer. Also, it is better to use a configuration table for such values.

The enhancement can be done by removing the query overhead of scanning the table for user surveys (especially when the amount of data increases), so we can add the number of user-created surveys in a column in the user's table (or an associated table).

The overhead of having synchronization on updating this value with each created survey is worth the removal of potential performance overhead when the data grows in that table. Also, it will remove the required first query as the value can be selected with the login query, but we should take care and decrease the counter when the user deletes any survey.

If we neglect all the previous comments and decide to keep the existing logic, we can still tune this HotSpot by removing the two calls in `CreateServlet`, or one of them at least. For example, the call after a survey creation can be replaced by an incremental statement to the current surveys' count, as shown in the following code:

```
//surveyCount=surveyBD.getUserSurveyCount(userAccount);
userAccount.setCountOfSurvey(surveyCount+1);
```

Performance code review

As an important step, we need to evaluate our code from a performance perspective.

 You may now review the project code and record your code review findings and compare your findings with the list that will follow.

The following are the samples of code review comments that we identified after reviewing the application code:

- Logging best practice is not followed.

- Exception handling is poor except in the web service layer.

- No user input validation, which is not a good practice for the application's performance as it causes unnecessary load over the application. This might turn to be invalid at the end and throw an error to the customer.

  - It is always a good practice to perform this validation in the presentation layer using JavaScript validation plus server-side validation to ensure that the validation is not bypassed

- No split of the CSS and JavaScript code in separate files, so we won't be able to make use of browser caching of these files.

- Resource bundle is not used, which makes it difficult to change the interface text as labels, error messages, and so on. This makes the application code changes difficult because we need to trace the source of each hardcoded message. The best examples are the error messages that are created in the application servlets.

- Mixing JSTL with Scriptlet in some of the application JSP pages, which makes it difficult to understand and fix these pages without errors.

  - The following code snippet is an example of this from the page `submitquestions.jsp`:

    ```
    <c:forEach begin="1" end="<%= survey.getNoOfQuestions() %>"
        var="current">
    ```

- Some values that can be configured are hardcoded in the application as the maximum user's surveys count. This can be placed in the configuration table and loaded and cached during application startup instead of being hardcoded.

- The creation of audit trail records (and sending e-mails) can be pushed asynchronously.

- Poor inline comments, which make any changes in the code difficult and risky.

- Some layers perform actions that do not belong to them, for example, the controller or DAO validate a business rule about the maximum number of user surveys allowed. This confuses the performance fixes and widens the scope of the required changes.

We can also perform some application functional reviews to detect application features that can be added to improve the performance so we can recommend adding them. For example, currently, the application does not have any edit survey functionalities.

Yet, this does not seem to be related to application performance, but if we assumed that the user needs to modify one question without providing this functionality, the user will hit the application to delete the old survey and create a new one. We can avoid this if we provide the edit survey feature.

Testing the application after our fixes

After fixing some of the listed issues (we won't fix all the issues such as logging issues), we need to perform some functional testing to ensure that everything is okay. We can then kick off another performance test to get the new performance results.

 You can download the application after applying our performance fixes from http://www.packtpub.com/.

We need to restore the database schema to its baseline before we kick off the performance test again. The following table represents our performance test results:

Label	# Samples	Average	Median	90% Line	Min	Max	Through...
/ExcellentSurvey/	187	7	5	10	2	61	28.5/min
/ExcellentSurvey/images/register.jpg	187	6	4	9	2	99	28.5/min
/ExcellentSurvey/images/login.gif	187	8	4	9	2	594	28.5/min
/ExcellentSurvey/LoginServlet	374	40	10	101	2	380	55.5/min
/ExcellentSurvey/images/logout.png	187	6	5	9	2	71	28.5/min
/ExcellentSurvey/images/manage.png	187	6	5	9	2	59	28.5/min
/ExcellentSurvey/images/take.png	187	6	4	9	2	47	28.5/min
/ExcellentSurvey/images/create.png	187	14	5	9	2	1621	28.5/min
/ExcellentSurvey/create.jsp	187	7	3	10	2	254	28.3/min
/ExcellentSurvey/images/home.png	187	7	5	10	1	92	28.3/min
/ExcellentSurvey/images/continue.png	187	9	5	10	2	313	28.3/min
/ExcellentSurvey/CreateServlet	374	67	15	146	2	943	55.9/min
/ExcellentSurvey/images/submit.png	187	7	5	10	1	143	28.0/min
/ExcellentSurvey/home.jsp	187	6	4	8	2	93	28.0/min
TOTAL	2992	19	5	49	1	1621	7.4/sec

As we can see in these numbers, the `CreateServlet` 90th percentile response time dropped from 9,348 milliseconds to only 146 milliseconds! This is around a 98.5 percent improvement of this transaction. Is it enough? The answer mainly depends on the transaction SLA, and the main purpose of performance tuning is to reach the response time SLA.

> Try to profile the application again to see the performance improvements of our HotSpot areas after applying different performance fixes.
>
> Also, try to draft your first performance analysis report, which includes most of what we discussed here and cover all the application performance aspects.

Result and conclusion

After improving our application performance in the create survey transaction, we can complete our exercise by covering other application transactions to ensure all application transactions are performed within the acceptable SLA.

We need to perform regression testing before we execute our performance testing to ensure we didn't break any application functionality with our performance fixes. Performance fixes also need to follow the normal application life cycle, which passed through different testing and quality phases.

To summarize what we did in the previous sections, we executed a load test to get low performance transactions. Then, we investigated these transactions using profiler and code inspection. We then identified some performance issues and did some analysis on how to fix them. We finally proposed some fixes and did both functional and performance testing to validate our results.

If the performance fixes are correct and produce the required performance gain (that is, they meet the SLA), we can stop the cycle; otherwise, we can keep performing the optimization till we meet the required SLA, and this is what we have referred to in the first chapter of this book by following the cycle of the learning model.

Now, let's review what we started this book with, which is the art of performance tuning. We defined six basic components composing the art of performance tuning, as shown in the following diagram:

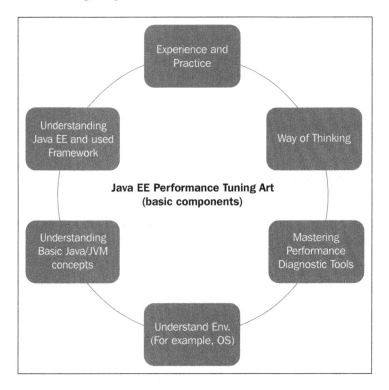

In this book, we have covered all of the following six components:

- **Way of thinking** mainly in *Chapter 1, Getting Started with Performance Tuning; Chapter 5, Recognizing Common Performance Issues; Chapter 9, Tuning an Application's Environment; Chapter 10, Designing High-performance Enterprise Applications;* and *Chapter 11, Performance Tuning Tips*
- **Understanding basic Java/JVM concepts** and **Understanding Java EE and used framework** in *Chapter 2, Understanding Java Fundamentals*
- **Mastering performance diagnostic tools** in *Chapter 3, Getting Familiar with Performance Testing; Chapter 4, Monitoring Java Applications; Chapter 6, CPU Time Profiling; Chapter 7, Thread Profiling;* and *Chapter 8, Memory Profiling*
- **Understanding environment** in *Chapter 9, Tuning an Application's Environment*
- Finally, we did some practice on performance tuning in this chapter and other chapters of this book

As a final statement in this chapter, I'd like to list some of the following personal recommendations to anyone going to work in performance tuning:

- Practice what we have learned in this book

- Always understand the application domain, framework, and technology before you start working on performance tuning

- Understand the difference between each Java framework version and keep yourself updated with latest performance recommendations

- Try to use and master a wide range of application monitoring/profiling tools to have some sort of flexibility

- Don't be afraid of failure; always consider failure as our roadmap to learn, experience, and be successful

- Do not be arrogant with your knowledge as there is a clear difference between arrogance and self-confidence

> *"And you have not been given of knowledge of everything, except a little"*
>
> *–The Noble Qur'an*

Summary

In this chapter, we practiced some application performance tuning. We started the chapter by exploring our sample application functionality and the used technologies as an essential step to understand what we are dealing with.

We selected a few transactions to measure (login/create survey/logout), and developed a limited scope performance testing script. We then executed it to get our performance test results.

We performed an analysis and drafted our investigation plan. We profiled the application, did a code inspection to propose some performance fixes, and finally tested the application to ensure that our fixes resolve the performance issues without impacting the application functionality. So, we explored a simplified end-to-end scenario of how to deal with Java enterprise application performance tuning.

And yes, this is the end of our book, but not the end of our performance tuning journey. It's just the beginning...

Index

Symbols

-cf FileName parameter 120
-config FileName parameter 120
-constants option 391
-c option 391
-c { Path [path ...] | -cf FileName }
    parameter 120
-dump tool
  about 133
  syntax 133
-f {csv | tsv | bin} parameter 120
-finalizerinfo tool
  about 133
  syntax 133
-heap tool
  about 133
  syntax 133
-histo tool
  about 133
  syntax 133
-J tool
  about 134
  syntax 134
-l option 391
-o FileName parameter 120
-package option 391
-permstat tool
  about 133
  syntax 133
-private/-p option 391
-protected option 391
-public option 391
-q [object] parameter 120
-qx [object] parameter 120

@ReadOnly annotation 380
-s computer_name parameter 120
-sc samples parameter 120
-si interval [mm:] ss parameter 120
-s option 391
-verbose option 391
-XX:ConcGCThreads=n parameter 317
-XX:G1HeapRegionSize=n parameter 317

A

adapter component 337
Agent_OnAttach() function 129
Agent_OnLoad() function 129
Agile development methodology
  performance considerations 370, 371
aging policy 180
algorithmic complexity
  evaluating 224-227
algorithmic performance
  algorithm complexity, evaluating 224-228
  fixing 221
  simple evaluation 222-224
algorithmic performance issues
  about 168, 219
  examples 219
anti-patterns 345
Apache Commons Logging 390
Apache JMeter
  about 94
  installing, URL 94
  testing with 97
  used, for building performance test 94, 95
  used, for testing database scripts 114
  used, for testing web application 107

used, for testing web services 98-102
Apache JMeter, database scripts test
  CSV dataset configuration, adding 115
  JDBC connection configuration 114
  JDBC request sampler addition 115
  listeners, adding to capture test results 115
Apache JMeter, testing web services
  listeners creation 103-106
  SOAP sampler creation 102, 103
  thread group creation 102
Apache JMeter test plan components
  configuration element 96, 97
  execution order 97
  listeners (test results) 96
  logical controllers 95
  request samplers 95
  thread groups (users) 95
Apache JMeter, web application test
  scenarios, recording 108, 109
Apache Log4J 390
Apache web server
  tuning 326-329
application
  post fixing, tests 426
  profiling, to locate performance issue 166
application algorithm
  fixing 230
application components
  selecting 338
application data
  versioning 358
application data caching
  multiple levels 358, 359
application layer decision
  performance impact 336
application logging
  and performance 388
application logging levels
  DEBUG 388
  ERROR 388
  FATAL 388
  INFO 388
  TRACE 388
  used, according to scenario 388
  WARN 388
application memory leakage 301
application requirement backlog 370

Application scope 62
application scopes
  about 62, 63
  Application 62
  Conversation 63
  Dependent 63
  Flash 62
  Flow 62
  Request 62
  Session 62
  View 62
application server issue
  confirming 165
application servers (AS)
  about 22
  Oracle GlassFish, tuning 320-324
  Oracle Weblogic, tuning 324, 325
  tuning 320
application's server admin console/tools
  used, for obtaining thread dump 252, 253
application threads
  Attach Listener 236
  DestroyJavaVM 236
  Finalizer 236
  main 236
  Reference Handler 236
  Signal Dispatcher 236
Arrays.sort() method 212, 213
asynchronous JMS message
  sending 77, 78
asynchronous methods
  using 231
asynchronous processing
  performed, on servlet or filter 74
asynchronous servlet
  and filter 74
auditing 342
Automatic Workload Repository (AWR) 35

B

Batch Applications 1.0 (JSR 352)
  features 46
  URL 46
Bean Validation 1.1 (JSR 349)
  features 40
  pseudo-code example 41

URL 41
behavior
  and attitude, while working on
    performance tuning 26-29
blocked threads
  about 259
BLOCKED thread state 256
BREACH attack
  URL 328
Business Delegate layer (BD) 405
Business layer 337, 405

C

cache evictions 363
cache hit rate 180
cache invalidation 180
cache miss rate 180
caching 301, 340
caching issues 220
caching models
  Model I 363
  Model II 363
  Model III 363
caching performance
  assessing 364, 365
  key indicators 364
caching replacement policies
  about 180
  aging policy 180
  FIFO 180
  LFU 180
  LRU 180
  MRU 180
caching support
  addition 230
  explicit application caching 230
  implicit caching 230
call tree view section 211
capacity terminology 91
capacity testing 85
Cascading Style Sheets (CSS) 33, 189
CDI 40
CDI 1.1 (JSR 346)
  features 43
  pseudo-code example 43
  URL 44

Character-Separated Values. *See* **CSVs**
Checkstyle
  about 373
  URL 373
Chrome browser
  URL 190
Chrome developer tools
  about 190
  JavaScript profiling 192
  network analysis 190, 191
  Speed Tracer 193, 194
chunck 325
class value 131
client mode 313
client-side optimization 398, 399
client-side performance issue
  about 189, 190
  confirming 165
  fixing, Chrome developer tools
    used 190-194
  fixing, Firefox developer tools used 196
  fixing, Internet Explorer developer
    tools used 194
  timing specifications, navigation 196, 197
cloud (caching as-a-service) 367
Cloud computing
  about 93, 365
  advantages 365
cloud deployment
  performance 365-367
cloud environment, performance testing
  about 92
  advantages 93
CMS 56
CMS GC steps
  mark step 58, 59
  sweep step (concurrent) 59
code
  and script analysis 166
code analyzer tools
  CheckStyle 372
  Dependency Finder 372
  FindBugs 372
  PMD 372
  SonarQube 372
code review
  about 372

performing 372-375
committed memory size 283
committed size 283
common performance issues
  algorithmic issues 168
  fake issues 169
  interfacing issues 168
  memory performance issues 167
  miscellaneous 169
  threading performance issues 167
  Work as designed performance issue 168
compacting GC
  versus non-compacting GC 59, 60
compacting GC phases
  compacting phase 60
  summary phase 59
Compiler value 131
component selection decisions
  performance impact 338, 339
concurrency
  caching 358
  implementing 231
concurrency, Java
  about 63
  achieving, processes used 64
  achieving, threads used 64, 65
  advantage 65
  disadvantages 65
concurrency utilities
  concurrent resources 71-73
  Lock interface 68-70
  thread pool, creating 67
  using 66
Concurrency Utilities 1.0 (JSR 236)
  ContextService 46
  ManagedExecutorService 46
  ManagedScheduledExecutorService 46
  ManagedThreadFactory 46
  URL 46
Concurrent mark sweep. *See* **CMS**
concurrent resources
  about 71
  ManagedExecutorService class 71
  ManagedScheduledExecutorService
    class 72
  ManagedThreadFactory class 72, 73

configuration elements
  CSV dataset config 96
  HTTP cookie manager 96
configuration xml file path parameter 158
Context and Dependency Injection. *See* **CDI**
context.complete() method 74
context switching 172
continuous integration (CI) 370
Conversation scope 63
cool-down time 86
CopyAPI copyIn() command
  using 397
count parameter 131
CPU option 143
CPU profiling
  underlying objective, determining 199, 200
CPU profiling options
  event based 200
  instrumental based 200
  JMC, using 206, 207
  JProfiler, using 208-210
  NetBeans profiler, using 200-205
  sampling based (statistical) 200
CPU profiling results
  analyzing 213-218
  interpreting 210-213
  reading 210-213
CPU profiling result sections
  call tree view 211
  HotSpots view 211-213
createAuditTrail() method 421
Cross-site Request Forgery (CRRF) 342
Cross-site Scripting (XSS) 342
CSV dataset config 96
CSV dataset configuration
  adding 115
CSVs
  about 96
  URL 96
customizable feature, system
    components 339

D

daemon thread
  versus user thread 237
DAO helper 405

DAOHelper.createNewSurvey()
    HotSpot method
  about 416
  fixing 419, 420
Data Access layer (DAO) 405
database link 396
database performance 394
database performance issues 187-189
database performance tuning
  tips 394-397
Database Server (DB) 22
database server issue
  confirming 166
data caching
  versus no caching 357
data encryption
  about 341
data layer 337
data sources layer 337
data store interaction
  caching 361, 362
DEBUG level
  using 388
Demilitarized Zone (DMZ) 325, 337
Dependency Finder
  about 373
  URL 373
Dependent scope 63
deployment tuning options, Oracle
    GlassFish
  auto-deployment, disabling 320
  auto-reload, disabling 320
  JSP, precompiling 321
design decisions
  about 335
  performance impact 335, 336
detailed object statistics
  analyzing 281
developer tools 33
development processes
  agile 370, 371
  and performance 370
  TDD 371, 372
discovery phase
  performance issues, classifying by 13-17
DNS caching

tuning 323
draft fixing strategy
  enhancing 263, 264
  thread blocking fix 265
  thread deadlocks, fixing 265

E

EclipseLink documentation
  URL 380
Eclipse MAT
  URL, for downloading 293
Eclipse Memory Analyzer Tool. See MAT
Eclipse tools/plugins
  about 147
  JVM monitor 147, 148
  TPTP 148-150
Eden space 54, 285
Efficient XML Interchange (EXI) 354
EJB 3.2 (JSR 345)
  improvements 44, 45
  URL 45
EJB container tuning options
  EJB cache, optimizing 321
  EJB pool idle timeout, optimizing 321
  EJB pool size, optimizing 321
EJB performance tuning tips 376
EmailSender.sendEmail() HotSpot method
  fixing 418
EmailSender.sendEmail() method 416
enterprise application
  adapter component 337
  business layer 337
  data layer 337
  data sources layer 337
  integration layer 337
  presentation layer 337
  service layer 337
enterprise application layers 21, 22
Enterprise JavaBeans. See EJB 3.2 (JSR 345)
environment tuning 310, 311
equals() method 302
ERROR level
  using 388
ExcellentSurvey application
  Business Delegate (BD) layer 405
  Business layer 405

client tier 411
code, organizing 405
CPU profiling results, obtaining 412, 413
DAO helper 405
Data Access layer (DAO) 405
database CPU profiling results,
    obtaining 414, 415
features 405
functional overview 404-407
issues, fixing 417-424
Java EE 7 technologies, using 405
memory results, obtaining 414
performance assessment plan,
    creating 407-409
performance investigation plan,
    creating 410, 411
Persistence layer 405
Presentation tier 405
profiling 411
server tier 411
setting up 402-404
thread profiling, obtaining 414
Web Service (WS) layer 405
ExcellentSurvey application issues
DAOHelper.createNewSurvey() HotSpot
    method 417
exception handling
and performance 386-388
excessive application logging 186
excessive serialization
about 182
examples 183, 184
performance symptoms 183
execution plan, database statement 396
expandability, system components 339
expiration algorithm
caching 360, 361
explicit lock
using, with Lock interface 68-70
Expression language 3.0 (JSR 341)
enhancements 48
URL 48
extra unnecessary logic
about 185
examples 185, 186

F

fake performance issues
about 169
examples 169
FATAL level
using 388
FIFO policy 180, 363
file cache components
tuning 323
finalize() method 302
FindBugs
about 373
URL 373
Firefox developer tools 196
First-in-first-out. *See* **FIFO policy**
fixing strategy
memory performance issues, adding to 304
Flash scope 62
flexibility, system components 339
flexible service contract
about 350
performing 350
Flow scope 62
frame 53
full-virtualization 367

G

G1
about 56, 60
working 60, 61
garbage collection. *See* **GC 56**
garbage collection activity
visualizing 285, 286
garbage collection activity logs
analyzing 282
reading 282-284
garbage collection, HotSpot JVM
performance targets, setting 316, 317
proper collector policy, selecting 316
tuning 316
garbage collection, JRockit VM
tuning 318, 319
garbage collection options
compacting versus non-compacting 59, 60

concurrent versus stop-the-world 56
G1 collector 60-62
serial versus parallel collector 57-59
garbage collectors
CMS 56
G1 56
serial collector 56
Garbage-first. *See* **G1**
Gccapacity value 131
Gccause value 132
GC logs 300
Gcnewcapacity value 132
gcnew value 132
Gcoldcapacity value 132
gcold value 132
Gcpermcapacity value 132
gcutil value 131
gc value 131
generalOption parameter 131
global memory leakage
about 301
versus session memory leakage 301
Google PageSpeed Insights
URL 399

H

hardware scaling
factors 331
use cases 331
hardware tuning
Capacity planning and hardware
optimization 331, 332
OS configurations optimization 332
hardware virtualization 367
hashCode() method 302
heap area 52
heap dump
analyzing 294
navigating, visual tools used 294, 295
querying, OQL used 296, 297
taking, Eclipse Memory Analyzer Tool
(MAT) used 292
taking, Java VisualVM used 289, 290
taking, JDK tools used 288

taking, jmap used 288, 289
taking, JProfiler used 293
taking, JRockit command used 291
taking, NetBeans profiler used 291
taking, on occurrence of JVM
OutOfMemoryError 288
taking, profiler tools used 291
heap memory 287
HotSpot autogen table update statement
fixing 421
HotSpot database statements
Statement that updates the autogen
table 416
HotSpot methods
DAOHelper.createNewSurvey() 416
EmailSender.sendEmail() 416
LoginFilter.log() 416
HotSpot method types
high invocation event methods 214
high self-time and invocation event
methods 215
high self-time methods 214
HotSpot statements
fixing, to insert questions 422
fixing, to survey questions 422
HotSpots view methods
Arrays.sort() 212
Thread.sleep() 212
HotSpots view section
about 211
methods 212
HotSpot type
identifying 215-218
HP JMeter
URL 287
hprof binary file format 287
HTTP cookie manager 96
HTTP server side performance issue
detecting 165
hung application
hang location, detecting with
profilers 262, 263
hang location, detecting with thread
dumps 262
root cause, detecting 262

I

IBM GCMV
  URL 287
IDE monitoring tools 127
improper caching implementation 301
improper caching issue types
  disabled caching 177, 178
  too big caching size 179
  too small caching size 178
  wrong caching policy use 179
improper data caching
  about 177
  example 179, 180
  issue types 177-179
  performance symptoms 179
improper synchronous code
  about 181
  example 181
  performance symptoms 181
INFO level
  using 388
inherent time 214
integrated system issue
  confirming 166
integration decisions
  performance impact 339, 340
integration layer 337
interaction decisions
  performance impact 343
Interceptors 1.2 (JSR 318)
  improvements 44
  pseudo-code example 44
  URL 44
interfacing performance issues 168
internal applications' deployment
  tuning 324
Internet Explorer developer tools 194
Internet of Things (IoT) 353
inter-process communication (IPC) 64
interval[s | ms] parameter 131
invalidation algorithm
  caching 360, 361
I/O operations
  and performance 386
iostat command 122

isolation testing 89
iteration terminology 91

J

Java collections
  and performance 384
Java data object (JDO) 350
Java EE 7 features
  about 40
  Batch Applications 1.0 (JSR 352) 46
  Bean Validation 1.1 (JSR 349) 40, 41
  CDI 1.1 (JSR 346) 43
  Concurrency Utilities 1.0 (JSR 236) 46
  EJB 3.2 (JSR 345) 44, 45
  Expression language 3.0 (JSR 341) 48
  Interceptors 1.2 (JSR 318) 44
  Java Servlet 3.1 (JSR 340) 42, 43
  JAX-RS 2.0 (JSR 339) 42
  JMS 2.0 (JSR 343) 45
  JPA 2.1 (JSR 338) 47
  JSF 2.2 (JSR 344) 47, 48
  JSON-P 1.0 (JSR 353) 41
  JTA 1.2 (JSR 907) 48, 49
  WebSocket 1.0 (JSR 356) 49, 50
Java EE 7 technologies
  EJBs (stateless session beans) 405
  filters 405
  Java mail APIs 405
  JPA 405
  JSPs 405
  servlets 405
  SOAP web services 405
Java EE 7 tutorial
  URL 78
Java EE concurrency features
  about 73
  asynchronous JMS message, sending 77, 78
  asynchronous servlet and filter 74
  non-blocking I/O APIs 74, 75
  session beans asynchronous method
    invocation 75, 76
  SingleThreadModel interface 73, 74
  singleton session bean 76, 77
Java EE performance tuning tips
  about 375

EJB performance tuning tips 376
JPA performance tuning tips 379, 380
JSF performance tuning tips 378
JSP performance tuning tips 377, 378
Servlets performance tuning tips 377, 378
WS performance tuning tips 376
Java Flight Recorder 140
Java framework
performance impact 343
Java heap analysis tool. *See* **jhat tool**
Java HotSpot virtual machine
garbage collection, tuning 316
memory size, tuning 314, 315
tuning 312
type, selecting 313
Java HotSpot virtual machine generations
about 54
permanent generation (Perm Gen) 54
Java HotSpot virtual machine modes
client 313
server 313
Java logging 390
Java Management Extension. *See* **JMX**
Java Message Service. *See* **JMS 2.0 (JSR 343)**
Java Mission Control. *See* **JMC**
Java monitoring and management console tool. *See* **jconsole tool**
Java monitoring tools
about 117
application servers monitoring tools 126
IDE monitoring tools 127
JDK monitoring tools 126
multifunction monitoring tools 127
standalone monitoring tools 127
Java multitenancy 300
Java performance tuning tips
application logging 388-390
exception handling implementation 386-388
I/O operations 386
Java collections, dealing with 384
string manipulation tips 381-383
synchronized blocks, using 385
Java Persistence APIs. *See* **JPA 2.1 (JSR 338)**
javap tool
syntax 391

used, for understanding micro-optimizations 391-394
JavaScript Object Notation. *See* **JSON**
JavaScript Object Notation (JSON) 353
JavaServer Faces. *See* **JSF 2.2 (JSR 344)**
Java Servlet 3.1 (JSR 340)
features 42
pseudo-code example 42
URL 43
Java Specification Requests (JSRs) 40
Java Transaction APIs. *See* **JTA 1.2 (JSR 907)**
Java Virtual Machine Debug Interface (JVMDI) 128
Java Virtual Machine (JVM) 22
Java Virtual Machine Profiler Interface (JVMPI) 128
Java VisualVM
about 138, 285
running 138
used, for generating thread dump 251, 252
used, for taking heap dump 289, 290
using 139
JAX-RS 2.0 (JSR 339)
features 42
pseudo-code example 42
URL 42
jconsole tool
about 137
running 138
syntax 137
JDBC connection
configuring 114
JDBC connection pool tuning options
about 322
connection timeout, optimizing 323
connection validation, optimizing 323
pool size settings, optimizing 322
transaction isolation level, optimizing 323
JDBC request sampler
adding 115
JDK monitoring tools 126
JDK tools
about 130
Java VisualVM 251, 252
jstack 251
monitoring tools 130-132

profiler tools 130, 137-141
troubleshooting tools 130-136
used, for obtaining thread dump 251, 252
used, for taking heap dump 288

JDK tools details
URL 161

Jenkins
about 371
URL 371

jhat tool
about 135
using 135, 136

jmap
used, for taking heap dump 288, 289

jmap tool
about 133
example 134, 135
usage and syntax 133, 134

JMC
about 126
used, for CPU profiling 206, 207
used, for monitoring threads 241-244

JMC Flight Recorder option 242
JMS 2.0 (JSR 343)
improvements 45
pseudo-code example 45
URL 46

JMX 138
JPA 2.1 (JSR 338)
features 47
pseudo-code example 47
URL 47

JPA performance tuning tips
about 379, 380
URL 380

jpenable command-line utility
using 159

JProfiler
about 151
free license, URL 151
used, for CPU profiling 208-210
used, for monitoring threads 238-240
used, for taking heap dump 293
using 151-156
using, for memory profiling 275-278

JProfiler 8.x
URL 151

JProfiler details
URL 161

JProfiler triggers
CPU load threshold 157
creating, steps 158
Heap usage threshold 157
JVM exit 156
JVM startup 156
Method invocation 157
Out of memory exception 157
Timer 157
used, for building script 156

JRockit command
used, for taking heap dump 291

JRockit Mission Control (JRMC) 140
JRockit virtual machine. *See* **JRockit VM**
JRockit VM
garbage collection, tuning 318, 319
memory size, tuning 318
tuning 317, 318

JRockit VM generational heap sections
Nursery area 317, 318
Tenured area 317, 318

JSF 2.2 (JSR 344)
features 47
pseudo-code example 47
URL 48

JSF performance tuning tips 378
JSON-P 1.0 (JSR 353)
pseudo-code example 41
URL 41

JSP performance tuning tips 377, 378
jstack
used, for generating thread dump 251

jstat tool
statOption values 131, 132
syntax 131
used, for monitoring JVM statistics 131, 132

jstat tool syntax parameters
count 131
generalOption 131
interval[s | ms] 131
outputOptions 131
vmid 131

JTA 1.2 (JSR 907)
features 48
pseudo-code example 49

URL 49
Just-In-Time (JIT) compilers 313
JVM
  Java HotSpot virtual machine, tuning 312
  tuning 311
JVM implementations
  client virtual machine 51
  server virtual machine 51
JVM memory map tool. *See* **jmap tool**
JVM monitor
  about 147, 148
  URL 147
JVM parameters classification
  non-standard parameters 312
  standard parameters 312
JVM performance tuning
  aspects 311
JVM specifications
  URL 53
JVM stack 52
JVM string tuning parameters
  using 383
JVM TI 128
JVM Tool Interface. *See* **JVM TI**

K

Keep Area 317, 318
Keep It Simple and Stupid (KISS) 27
Kenai project
  URL 373

L

last access time 180
latency terminology 91
learning cycle 24-26
Least frequently used. *See* **LFU policy**
Least-Frequently Used (LFU) 364
Least recently used. *See* **LRU policy**
Least-recently Used (LRU) 364
LFU policy 180
listeners
  adding, to capture test results 115
  assertion, adding on response 104
  creating 103, 104

CSV dataset configuration, adding 104, 105
  final results, obtaining 106
listeners (test results) 96
load testing 85
Lock interface
  explicit lock, using with 68-70
logic issues, performance findings 417
LoginFilter.log() HotSpot method
  fixing 421
LoginFilter.log() method 416
low threading 260
LRU policy 180

M

managed beans. *See* **MBeans**
ManagedExecutorService class
  about 71
  using, sample code 71
ManagedScheduledExecutorService class
  about 72
  using, sample code 72
ManagedThreadFactory class
  about 72
  using, sample code 73
MAT
  about 147
  used, for taking heat dump 292
materialized view 396
MaxPermSize parameter 315
MBeans 138
MBean server 140
Memcached
  about 363
  URL 363
memory chunk optimization 324
memory heap dumps
  dealing with 287
memory leakage
  about 173
  example 174-176
  performance symptoms 173, 174
memory leakage issues
  fixing 306
MemoryMonitor class 372
Memory option 143

memory performance issues
about 167, 173
adding, to fixing strategy 304
improper caching 167, 177-180
insufficient memory allocation 167
memory leakage 167, 173-176
memory performance monitoring
aspects 268
memory potential performance issues
about 299, 300
application memory leakage 301
improper caching implementation 301
invalid contract, for equals() method 302
invalid contract, for hashCode()
    method 302
memory issues of objects, with
    finalize() method 302
OOME, reasons 303
memory profiling
about 268
detailed object statistics, analyzing 281
garbage collection activity logs,
    analyzing 282
JProfiler used 275-278
memory spaces graphs, analyzing 280
NetBeans used 269-274
options 268
results, analyzing 279
memory profiling analysis
aspects 279
memory size, HotSpot JVM
tuning 314, 315
memory size, JRockit VM
tuning 318
memory spaces graphs
analyzing 280
memory structure
about 50
in Java HotSpot virtual machine 53-55
in JVM specifications 51-53
memory structure, Java HotSpot virtual
    machine
generational collection 53-55
memory structure, JVM specifications
heap area 52

JVM stack 52
method area and runtime constant pool 52
native method stacks (C stacks) 53
pc registers 53
method area
and runtime constant pool 52
method inlining 313
method invocation count
versus method time, analyzing 213-218
method time
inherent time 214
self-time 214
versus method invocation count, analyzing
    213-218
micro-optimizations
understanding, javap tool used 391-393
Microsoft Windows tools
about 118
Resource Monitor 119
Typeperf command-line utility 120, 121
miscellaneous decisions
performance impact 344, 345
miscellaneous performance issues 169
Model I, caching models 363
Model II, caching models 363
Model III, caching models 363
monitoring tools, application
    servers 126, 127
Monitor option 143
Most recently used. *See* **MRU policy**
Most-Recently Used (MRU) 364
MPM modes, Unix-based systems
Event MPM 326
Prefork MPM 326
Worker MPM 326
MPM server 326
MRU policy 180
multifunction monitoring tools 127
Multi-process/Multi-thread-based
    server. *See* **MPM server**
multithreading
implementing 231
muxer
about 324
types 324

N

native method stacks (C stacks) **53**
NetBeans
  using, for memory profiling 269-274
NetBeans profiler
  used, for taking heap dump 291
NetBeans profiler
  about 141
  calibration, running 142
  used, for CPU time profiling 201
  used, for monitoring threads 234-238
  used, for profiling Java application 201-203
  used, for profiling web application 203-205
  using 143-147
NetBeans profiler details
  URL 161
network components
  tuning 324
networking components
  examining 166
NEW thread state **256**
no caching
  versus data caching 357
non-blocking I/O APIs
  about 74
  using 74
non-compacting GC
  versus compacting GC 59, 60
notification template HotSpot query
  fixing 423
Nursery space **318**

O

object monitor
  exploring 65, 66
Object Query Language. *See* OQL
Object-relational mapping (ORM) **395**
offline parameter **158**
offline profiling mode
  advantages and uses 156
  JProfiler triggers, used for building script
    156-161
  using 156
OOME
  about 290

reasons 303
operating system monitoring tools
  about 118
  Microsoft Windows tools 118-121
  Unix/Linux tools 122-125
Operating System (OS) **22**
Optimistic locking **358**
OQL
  about 136, 287
  built-in functions, using on individual
    objects 298
  built-in heap object, using 298
  used, for querying heap dump 296, 297
OQL queries
  using 297
Oracle GlassFish application server
  deployment tuning options 320, 321
  DNS caching, tuning 323
  EJB container tuning options 321
  file cache components, tuning 323
  JDBC connection pool tuning
    options 322, 323
  logging information, tuning 323, 324
  thread pool tuning options 322
  tuning 320
  web container tuning options 321
Oracle Java Mission Control
  about 140
  Flight recorder feature 140
  MBean server feature 140
  using 140, 141
Oracle Weblogic application server
  internal applications' deployment,
    tuning 324
  network components, tuning 324
  stuck thread configuration, tuning 325
  tuning 324
Oracle web server
  tuning 329, 330
OS
  and hardware, tuning 331, 332
OS commands
  SIGQUIT, sending to Java process 250
  used, for obtaining thread dump 248- 250
OS configurations
  optimization 332

OS configuration, tuning examples
  File Descriptor, setting 332
  TCP tuning 332
OutOfMemoryError. *See* **OOME**
  about 287
  heap dump, taking on occurrence of 288
outputOptions parameter 131
over threading 260

P

parallel GC
  versus serial GC 57-59
para-virtualization 367
pc register 53
performance
  and agile 370, 371
  and development processes 370-375
  and TDD 371, 372
  caching 358
  evaluating 84
performance anti-patterns
  performance issues 346
  software process anti-patterns 345
  technical anti-patterns 345
  using 345-347
performance assessment plan
  creating, of ExcellentSurvey
      application 407-410
performance baseline 89
performance benchmarking 89
performance code
  reviewing 425, 426
performance counters 121
performance findings
  HotSpot database statements 416
  HotSpot methods 416
  logic issues 416
performance fixing cycle 90
performance fixing strategy
  about 228
  application logic/algorithm, fixing 229
  asynchronous methods, using 231
  caching support addition 230
  concurrency or multithreading,
      implementing 231
  resource performance, optimizing 231

performance goals 90
performance-handling tactics
  about 19
  proactive measures (preventive) 19, 20
  reactive measures (curative) 21
performance issue isolation
  application profiling 166
  application server issue 165
  client-side 165
  code and script analysis 166
  database server issue 166
  HTTP server side 165
  integrated system 166
  networking components 166
performance issues
  about 12
  classifying, by discovery phase 13-17
  classifying, by root phase 17-19
  cycle of learning 24-26
  handling, tactics 19-24
  isolating 164
  types 12, 13
performance issues classification,
      discovery phase
  design-time issues 14, 15
  development-time issues 15, 16
  production-time issues 16, 17
  requirement phase 14, 15
  testing-time issues 16
performance issues classification, root phase
  design/architecture phase issues 18
  development phase issues 18
  environmental-specific issues 19
  operational issues 19
  requirement phase issues 18
  testing phase issues 18
performance test environment
  selecting 83
performance testing
  dissection 81, 82
  in cloud environment 92
  objectives 82
performance testing aspects
  about 82
  benchmarking and baseline 89
  fix cycle 90
  isolation test 89

performance evaluation 84
performance goals 90
project milestones 84
rules and responsibilities, defining 84
test components 85-88
test environment selection 83
test tools 88
test types 85
performance testing components
test data 86
test scenarios 87
test users 86
performance testing terminologies
about 91
capacity 91
iteration 91
latency 91
resource utilization 91
response time 91
scalability 91
stability 91
thinking time 92
throughput 91
performance testing tools
using 88
performance testing types
capacity testing 85
load testing 85
stress testing 85
performance tuning
about 10-12
components 10, 11
overview 401, 402
recommendations 429
results 427
performance tuning components
Mastering Tools 11
Understand environment 11
Understand Java EE 11
Understand Java/JVM 11
Way of thinking element 11
performance tuning issues. *See*
performance issues
performance tuning pillars
about 22
performance issues, facing 24
performance process, defining 23

performance tools, getting ready 23
Persistence layer 405
Pessimistic locking 358
PMD
about 373
URL 373
PMD rules
customizing 374, 375
potential performance issues
algorithmic/logic issues 219, 220
caching issues 220
identifying 218
resourcing issues 221
threading issues 221
presentation layer 337
Presentation tier 405
Printcompilation value 131
proactive tactics 20
proactive tuning 189
process
used, for achieving concurrency 64
versus thread 64, 65
profile patterns 129, 130
profile patterns classification
attach versus start for profiling 129
filtered versus non-filtered classes 129
local versus remote 129
online versus offline 130
sampling versus instrumental 129
web server versus standalone 130
profiler agent
about 129
running, command-line options used 129
starting, start-up() function used 129
profiler modes
event based 128
instrumental based 128
sampling based (statistical) 128
profilers
about 127
agent 129
JVM TI 128
modes 128
profile patterns 129, 130
profiler tools
used, for obtaining thread dump 253
used, for taking heap dump 291

profiling tools. *See* **profilers**
program counter (PC) 200
program counter register. *See* **pc register**
project milestones 84
Proof Of Concept (POC) 14
ps/pgrep/pstree command 122

Q

question rating types HotSpot query
fixing 422

R

reactive tactics
about 21
enterprise application layers 21, 22
performance tuning pillars 22-24
Read-through
about 361
ReentrantLock attribute 70
regulatory decisions
performance impact 344
remoteness negligence
about 182
example 182
performance symptoms 182
replacement policy
caching 363, 364
First-In-First-Out (FIFO) 363
Least-Frequently Used (LFU) 364
Least-recently Used (LRU) 364
Most-Recently Used (MRU) 364
request samplers 95
Request scope 62
Resource Oriented Architecture. *See* **ROA**
resource performance
optimizing 231
resource utilization terminology 91
resourcing issues 221
response time terminology 91
REST
advantages 354
RESTful web services
about 351, 352
advantages 353
features 351

RESTful WS development
facilitating, JAX-RS 2.0 (JSR 339) used 42
REST services
using 354
ROA
about 351
and SOA, performance comparison 353,
354
performance 351-357
root phase
performance issues, classifying by 17-19
rules
and responsibilities, defining 84
RUNNABLE thread state 256

S

sar command 122
saturation 91
saveInDBUsingBatch method
about 397
count parameter 397
name parameter 397
scalability, system components 339
scalability terminology 91
script
building, JProfiler triggers used 156-161
security decisions
performance impact 341
selected performance issues
absent proactive tuning 189
database issues 187, 189
excessive application logging 186
unnecessary application logic 185, 186
self-time 214
separation of concerns 339
serial collector 56
serial GC
versus parallel GC 57-59
server mode 313
service caching
implementing 348, 349
service data caching 349
service response/result caching 349
service data caching 349
Service Data Object (SDO) 350

service dynamic binding
  using 349
service layer 337
Service-Level Agreements. *See* SLAs
service response/result caching 349
service throttling 350
Servlets performance tuning tips 377, 378
session beans asynchronous method
        invocation
  about 75
  using 75
session ID parameter 158
session memory leakage
  versus global memory leakage 301
session scope 62
simple algorithmic evaluation
  about 222
  performing 222-224
Simple Logging Facade for Java (SLF4J) 390
SingleThreadModel interface 73
singleton session bean
  creating 76
  using 76, 77
SLAs 14
SOA
  about 347
  advantages 347
  and ROA, performance
        comparison 353, 354
  performance 347-350
  using 348
Soak/Endurance Testing 85
SOAP sampler
  creating 102, 103
SOAP with Attachments (SwA) 376
SOA service
  characteristics 350
software process anti-patterns 345
SonarQube
  about 373
  URL 373
Speed Tracer
  URL 194
spike load 85
stability terminology 91
standalone application
  characteristics 29

versus web applications 29-31
standalone monitoring tools 127
start-up() function
  used, for profiler agent start-up 129
starving threads. *See* blocked threads
statOption values
  class 131
  Compiler 131
  gc 131
  Gccapacity 131
  Gccause 132
  gcnew 132
  Gcnewcapacity 132
  gcold 132
  Gcoldcapacity 132
  Gcpermcapacity 132
  gcutil 131
  Printcompilation 131
stop-the-world GC
  versus concurrent GC 56
StopWatch class
  about 372
  example, URL 372
stress testing 85
StringBuffer operation
  versus StringBuilder operation 383
StringBuilder.append() method 393
StringBuilder class 393
StringBuilder.init() method 393
StringBuilder operation
  versus StringBuffer operation 383
String.concat() method
  using 383
string manipulation performance
        tuning tips
  JVM string tuning parameters 383
  string concatenation tips 382, 383
  string creation tips 381
String() method 381
String object 381
String.valueOf() method
  using 383
Stubbing 15
stuck thread configuration
  tuning 325
stuck threads. *See* blocked threads

survivor spaces 285
synchronized code block
  minimizing, strategies 385
  using 385
synchronized keyword
  using 385
system components
  selecting 339
system components, aspects
  customizable feature 339
  expandability 339
  flexibility 339
  scalability 339

T

task manager 288
tcpdump command 122
TDA
  URL 257
  used, for analyzing thread dump 257-259
TDD
  about 369
  advanrage 372
  performance considerations 371, 372
technical anti-patterns 345
Tenured space 318
TERMINATED thread state 256
Test and Performance Tools
      Platform. *See* TPTP
test automation 88
test data 86
test-driven development. *See* TDD
test environment
  preparing, prior to test execution 87, 88
test quality assurance 88
test scenarios 87
test users
  about 86
  VUsers 86
thick client application(client-server model)
  characteristics 30
thin client application(web-based model)
  characteristics 30, 31
thinking time terminology 92
thread blocking
  about 170

example 170-172
fixing 265
performance symptoms 170
thread deadlock 172, 173
thread deadlocks
  fixing 265
thread dump
  about 247
  analyzing 256-259
  obtaining 247
  obtaining, application's server admin
      console/tools used 252, 253
  obtaining, JDK tools used 251, 252
  obtaining, OS commands used 248-250
  obtaining, profiler tools used 253
  reading 254, 255
  using, advantages 257
thread dump analysis
  main goals 257
Thread Dump Analyzer. *See* TDA
thread dump structure
  understanding 255, 256
thread group
  creating 102
thread groups (users) 95
thread header parts
  Address range 255
  Daemon flag 255
  nid 255
  Thread ID 255
  Thread name 255
  Thread priority 255
  Thread state 255
threading deadlock 259
threading issues
  about 221, 259
  hung application, root cause
      detection 262, 263
  performance issues 259-261
threading memory issues 260, 261
threading performance issues
  about 167-169
  blocked/starving/stuck threads 259
  blocking threads 170-172
  deadlocks 259
  low/over threading 260

memory issues 260, 261
thread deadlock 172
unmanaged threads 261
ThreadLocalRandom class 70
thread pool
creating 67
thread pool tuning options 322
thread profiling
about 233
options 234
usage conditions 233, 234
thread profiling options
threads, monitoring with jmc 241-244
threads, monitoring with JProfiler 238- 240
threads, monitoring with NetBeans 234-238
thread profiling results
reading 244-247
threads
used, for achieving concurrency 64, 65
Thread.sleep() method 212, 213
thread states
Monitor (red) 237
Park (orange) 237
Running (green) 237
Sleeping (purple) 237
Wait (yellow) 237
thread states printed in thread dumps
BLOCKED 256
NEW 256
RUNNABLE 256
TERMINATED 256
TIMED_WAITING 256
WAITING 256
throughput terminology 91
TIMED_WAITING thread state 256
timing specifications
navigation 196, 197
top command 122
TPTP
about 148-150
URL 148
TRACE level
using 388
tryLock method 68, 70
Typeperf command-line utility
about 120
syntax 120

syntax parameters 120
Typeperf syntax parameters
-cf FileName 120
-config FileName 120
-c { Path [path ...] | -cf FileName } 120
-f {csv | tsv | bin} 120
-o FileName 120
-q [object] 120
-qx [object] 120
-s computer_name 120
-sc samples 120
-si interval [mm:] ss 120

U

UI decisions
performance impact 343
Uniform Resource Identifier (URI) 351
Unix/Linux tools
about 122
high CPU utilization, example 122-125
iostat command 122
ps/pgrep/pstree 122
sar command 122
tcpdump command 122
top command 122
vmstat command 122
UnlockCommercialFeatures parameter 206
unmanaged threads
using 261
updateStock() method
used, for synchronizing object 245
user survey count HotSpot query
fixing 423, 424
user story 370
user thread
versus daemon thread 237

V

vertical dimension nodes
application servers 34
client side 33
CPU utilization 36
database servers 34, 35
exploring, in horizontal dimension
nodes 33-37

HTTP servers (web servers) 34
  memory usage 37
  middleware integration servers 35
  network components 33
  network traffic 36
  operating system and hardware 36
  storage I/O performance 37
View scope 62
virtualization models
  full-virtualization 367
  hardware virtualization 367
  para-virtualization 367
Virtual Machine (VM) 22
Virtual Private Cloud (VPC) 366
virtual size 283
Virtual Users. *See* VUsers
Visual GC 285
visual tools
  used, for navigating inside heap
    dump 294, 295
vmid parameter 131
vmstat command 122
VUsers 86

W

W3C WADL documentation
  URL 352
WAITING thread state 256
warm-up time 86
**Web Application Description Language
  (WADL) 352**
web applications
  performance tuning 31, 32
**web applications, performance tuning
  dimensions**
  horizontal dimension (node-to-node) 32
  vertical dimension (intranode) 32
web application test scenarios
  browser settings, updating 110, 111
  configuration element, creating 109
  cookie control, adding 111
  CSV dataset, adding 111
  recording 111
  recording controller creation 109
  response assertions, adding 113
  results view, adding 113

suitable thinking time addition 112
  test plan execution 113
  thread groups, creating 109
  variables, adding to requests 112
  workbench server, creating 109
web container tuning options
  disable dynamic JSP reloading 321
  session timeout, setting 321
web servers (HTTP servers)
  Apache, tuning 326-328
  Oracle, tuning 329, 330
  tuning 325, 326
web service performance tuning tips.
    See **WS performance tuning tips**
Web Service (WS) layer 405
WebSocket 1.0 (JSR 356)
  features 49
  pseudo-code example 49
  URL 50
work as designed performance issues
  about 168, 181
  excessive serialization 182-184
  improper synchronous code 181
  remoteness, neglecting 182
Write-behind 361
Write-through 361
WS performance tuning tips 376

X

XX:ParallelGCThreads=n parameter 317

Thank you for buying
Java EE 7 Performance Tuning and Optimization

About Packt Publishing

Packt, pronounced 'packed', published its first book "Mastering phpMyAdmin for Effective MySQL Management" in April 2004 and subsequently continued to specialize in publishing highly focused books on specific technologies and solutions.

Our books and publications share the experiences of your fellow IT professionals in adapting and customizing today's systems, applications, and frameworks. Our solution based books give you the knowledge and power to customize the software and technologies you're using to get the job done. Packt books are more specific and less general than the IT books you have seen in the past. Our unique business model allows us to bring you more focused information, giving you more of what you need to know, and less of what you don't.

Packt is a modern, yet unique publishing company, which focuses on producing quality, cutting-edge books for communities of developers, administrators, and newbies alike. For more information, please visit our website: www.packtpub.com.

About Packt Enterprise

In 2010, Packt launched two new brands, Packt Enterprise and Packt Open Source, in order to continue its focus on specialization. This book is part of the Packt Enterprise brand, home to books published on enterprise software – software created by major vendors, including (but not limited to) IBM, Microsoft and Oracle, often for use in other corporations. Its titles will offer information relevant to a range of users of this software, including administrators, developers, architects, and end users.

Writing for Packt

We welcome all inquiries from people who are interested in authoring. Book proposals should be sent to author@packtpub.com. If your book idea is still at an early stage and you would like to discuss it first before writing a formal book proposal, contact us; one of our commissioning editors will get in touch with you.

We're not just looking for published authors; if you have strong technical skills but no writing experience, our experienced editors can help you develop a writing career, or simply get some additional reward for your expertise.

Java EE 7 First Look

ISBN: 978-1-84969-923-5 Paperback: 188 pages

Discover the new features of Java EE 7 and learn to put them together to build a large-scale application

1. Explore changes brought in by the Java EE 7 platform.

2. Master the new specifications that have been added in Java EE to develop applications without any hassle.

3. Quick guide on the new features introduced in Java EE 7.

Java EE 7 with GlassFish 4 Application Server

ISBN: 978-1-78217-688-6 Paperback: 348 pages

A practical guide to install and configure the GlassFish 4 application server and develop Java EE 7 applications to be deployed to this server

1. Install and configure GlassFish 4.

2. Covers all major Java EE 7 APIs and includes new additions such as JSON Processing.

3. Packed with clear, step-by-step instructions, practical examples, and straightforward explanations.

Please check **www.PacktPub.com** for information on our titles

Java EE Development with Eclipse

ISBN: 978-1-78216-096-0   Paperback: 426 pages

Develop Java EE applications with Eclipse and commonly used technologies and frameworks

1. Each chapter includes an end-to-end sample application.

2. Develop applications with some of the commonly used technologies using the project facets in Eclipse 3.7.

3. Clear explanations enriched with the necessary screenshots.

Java EE 7 Developer Handbook

ISBN: 978-1-84968-794-2   Paperback: 634 pages

Develop professional applications in Java EE 7 with this essential reference guide

1. Learn about local and remote service endpoints, containers, architecture, synchronous and asynchronous invocations, and remote communications in a concise reference.

2. Learn about integration test development on Java EE with Arquillian Framework and the Gradle build system.

3. Learn about containerless builds featuring the GlassFish 4.0 embedded application server.

Please check **www.PacktPub.com** for information on our titles

CPSIA information can be obtained at www.ICGtesting.com
Printed in the USA
LVOW03s2003270614

392082LV00005B/34/P

9 781782 176428